Studies in Finance and Accounting

The 'Studies in Finance and Accounting' series publishes contemporary research findings in the fields of accounting and finance. It embraces a broad range of research methods, with a strong emphasis on empirical work, whether quantitative or qualitative. The series includes theoretically grounded and innovative dissertations that are of interest to both the academic community and business practitioners.

Claudio Schütz

Populism and Financial Markets

A Mixed Methods Analysis on Investors' Reactions and Political Risk Assessment

Springer Gabler

Claudio Schütz
ESCP Business School
Berlin, Germany

Dissertation, ESCP Business School Berlin, 2024, submitted and approved dissertation entitled: Populism and Financial Markets—A Mixed Methods Analysis on Investors' Reactions and Political Risk Assessment.

ISSN 3059-3468 ISSN 3059-3476 (electronic)
Studies in Finance and Accounting
ISBN 978-3-658-46857-6 ISBN 978-3-658-46858-3 (eBook)
https://doi.org/10.1007/978-3-658-46858-3

This Springer Gabler imprint is published by the registered company Springer Fachmedien Wiesbaden GmbH, part of Springer Nature.
The registered company address is: Abraham-Lincoln-Str. 46, 65189 Wiesbaden, Germany

A mio Papà.

Foreword

In an age of rising political uncertainty, political causes and consequences play an increasingly central role, including in the financial world. My interest in these complex consequences beyond the political realm integrating insights from various academic disciplines was sparked during my university studies. The opportunity to delve into the impact of populism on financial markets in a comprehensive dissertation provided me with an enlightening journey that greatly expanded my knowledge and was an intellectual enrichment and challenge on many levels.

The completion of this journey owes much to the generous contributions of many individuals, without whom this dissertation would not have been successfully completed. Throughout its development, I have had the privilege of working alongside a diverse group of scholars, practitioners, and political risk experts whose insights have greatly enriched my understanding and shaped the research outcomes.

First and foremost, I would like to express my deepest gratitude to my doctoral supervisor, Prof. Dr. Ulrich Pape of the ESCP Business School Berlin, for his wide guidance throughout this doctoral research. His trust in my exploration of this interdisciplinary topic, which has fascinated me throughout my academic career, has been invaluable. He has not only provided motivation and critical insights but also shaped the foundational knowledge and encouragement that have been essential to the success of this dissertation. Furthermore, he has been a constant source of strength and inspiration on a personal level, and his mentorship has had a profound impact on my professional development and personal growth.

I would further like to express my sincere gratitude to Prof. Dr. Houdou Basse-Mama from the ESCP Business School Berlin, who served as the co-supervisor for this work and whose constructive, insightful, and enlightening feedback was a great source of expertise for me.

I would also like to express my sincere appreciation to Prof. Dr. Hans Hirth from the Technical University of Berlin for his role as the second examiner of this dissertation, and his thorough evaluations and insightful critiques have greatly contributed to the refinement and depth of this research.

I am equally grateful for the assistance provided by colleagues, who have also become friends, as their advice and collaboration were invaluable throughout this journey. Additionally, I extend my gratitude to the practitioners who participated in the interview study and provided valuable insights into their political risk assessment processes.

Last but not least, I would like to thank my family, especially my mother, my sister, my nieces, and my friends, whose unwavering support and encouragement have been the cornerstone of my perseverance and success throughout this academic endeavor. This thesis is dedicated to my father, who has always encouraged me to push myself beyond my limits and strive for my highest ambitions. Although he is no longer here to share in this achievement, I feel his presence with me at every step of the journey.

Berlin
October 2024

Claudio Schütz

Preface

In many regions across the globe, populism has emerged as a prominent force shaping political, social, and economic landscapes. The growing prominence of populist ideologies is evident in the field of political science, while only a limited number of finance studies have addressed the economic consequences of populism. Beyond the academic realm, practitioners are also concerned with the impact of populism on financial markets and international corporations. Moreover, recent international election results highlight the relevance and timeliness of this topic.

In light of these issues, Claudio Schütz examines the impact of populism on investors' return expectations and the incorporation of political risks into pricing on international financial markets. The study employs a mixed-methods approach, integrating quantitative financial market analysis with qualitative expert interviews. The quantitative study analyzes the assumption that the uncertainty perceived by investors increases in times of populism. This, in turn, results in an increase in the required rate of return, which leads to a higher cost of equity for companies. In the qualitative section of the study, the author conducts explanatory interviews with experts in the field of political risk assessment to verify the quantitative findings and to provide a more comprehensive explanation of how populism affects the valuation of corporate investment projects.

Claudio's academic work represents a significant contribution to the theoretical understanding of the relationship between populism and financial markets. The thesis examines the impact of populism in its various forms on international financial markets, as well as the mechanisms underlying these effects. It also derives practical implications for investors, managers, and policymakers. In view of the many new insights, I am more than convinced that Claudio's publication will be very well received by both academics and practitioners. It is therefore a great pleasure for my co-editors and me to publish this thesis as the first volume in the "Studies in Finance and Accounting" series.

Berlin
October 2024

Prof. Dr. Ulrich Pape

Contents

Abbreviations

AEGM	Abnormal Earnings Growth Model
AfD	Alternative für Deutschland (Alternative for Germany)
AKP	Adalet ve Kalkınma Partisi (AK Party)
ANO	Akce nespokojených občanů (ANO 2011)
APT	Arbitrage Pricing Theory
BERI	Business Environment Risk Intelligence
CAPM	Capital Asset Pricing Model
CDS	Credit Default Swap
CHES	Chapel Hill Expert Surveys
CMP	Comparative Manifesto Project
DDM	Dividend Discount Model
EIU	Economist Intelligence Unit
EPU	Economic Policy Uncertainty
FDI	Foreign Direct Investment
FPÖ	Freiheitliche Partei Österreichs (Freedom Party of Austria)
GDP	Gross Domestic Product
GPS	Global Party Survey
IBES	Institutional Brokers' Estimate System
ICC	Implied Cost of Equity Capital
IPOs	Initial Public Offerings
M&A	Mergers and Acquisitions
M5S	Movimento 5 Stelle (Five Star Movement)
MNCs	Multinational Corporations
NPV	Net Present Value

OECD	Organization for Economic Co-operation and Development
POPPA	Populism and Political Parties Expert Survey
PREPPS	Political Representation, Parties, and Presidents Survey
RIM	Residual Income Model
Syriza	Synaspismos Rizospastikis Aristeras (Coalition of the Radical Left—Progressive Alliance)
VIX	Volatility Index
WUI	World Uncertainty Index

List of Figures

List of Tables

1 Introduction

1.1 Problem Definition

Populism has become a significant force in the global political arena in recent years, with its influence extending to political, economic, and societal spheres. By 2018, its presence in the central governments of numerous countries marked a peak in a trend of growth that spanned three decades. The rise in political importance was preceded by growing societal awareness. In 2017, the Cambridge Dictionary named "populism" the Word of the Year,[1] and prominent figures such as Pope Francis, the head of the Catholic Church, expressed concern about its rise.[2] During this time, there was also increased attention from the media and academia, resulting in a surge of literature analyzing the multifaceted impact of populism.[3]

The academic discourse on populism continues, with ongoing debates over its definition, origins, and consequences.[4] Recent central resources, such as the Oxford Handbook of Populism,[5] the Routledge Handbook of Global Populism,[6] and the Palgrave Handbook of Populism,[7] reflect the continued vitality of the field. In addition, the European Center for Populism Studies has launched the Journal of Populism Studies, highlighting the significant interest in studying the

[1] See Cambridge University Press 2017.

[2] See Caño and Ordaz 2017.

[3] See Funke et al. 2020, p. 11.

[4] See for example Aslanidis 2016, pp. 100f.

[5] See Rovira Kaltwasser et al. 2017b.

[6] See De La Torre 2019b.

[7] See Oswald 2022.

C. Schütz, *Populism and Financial Markets*, Studies in Finance and Accounting,
https://doi.org/10.1007/978-3-658-46858-3_1

various aspects of populism around the world and the need for continued research into its complex effects.

The scholarly interest in populism has seen a notable escalation across multiple disciplines, although the level of interdisciplinary engagement remains uneven across research fields. Through their comprehensive systematic review covering the years 2004 to 2019, *Hunger and Paxton* highlighted this trend, documenting a significant increase in academic articles focusing on populism. At the same time, the authors found that certain fields, such as the business sciences, have a low volume of publications on the topic,[8] suggesting a critical gap in understanding how populism affects business strategies and market behavior that warrants further exploration.

Similarly, industry practitioners have begun to explore the implications of populism for international business, including its perceived risks to financial markets. In particular, various reports have emerged analyzing the potential threats of populism to financial markets. For example, in 2017, Oliver Wyman released a publication titled "Financial Institutions in an Age of Populism", which explored the strategic implications for financial institutions in the face of the rise of populism.[9]

More recently, in January 2024, Deutsche Bank Chief Executive Officer Christian Sewing expressed concern about the far-right Alternative für Deutschland (AfD) party in Germany, highlighting the growing caution of international investors and the potential impact on the investment climate.[10] The fact that German business leaders are now engaging in political commentary is a departure from tradition and underlines a growing recognition of the potential of populism to reshape financial market trends and investment strategies. The significance of this change is reinforced by the fact that more than 70 elections will be held around the world in 2024, affecting countries that are home to more than half of the world's population.[11] This underscores the urgency of closely examining the relationship between populism and its impact on the economic landscape.

---

[8] See Hunger and Paxton 2022, p. 622.

[9] See Elliott 2017.

[10] See Kraemer and Sim 2024.

[11] See Standage 2023.

1.2 Objective and Approach

This thesis aims to address a significant gap in the literature by analyzing the impact of populism on financial markets through the perspective of political risk. Recognizing political risk is critical for investors and corporations as they navigate the complexities of the global investment landscape. For multinational corporations, it is necessary to assess the business environment in both their current countries of operation and potential investment destinations, while investors, both private and public, seek to identify international opportunities that offer the most favorable investment prospects given the inherent risks.

The heightened perception of political risk has led to a detailed theoretical and practical exploration of how various political factors influence market dynamics. By integrating multiple perspectives related to financial markets, the thesis at hand seeks to enrich the discourse on populism by framing it as a significant variable in shaping investment strategies. This research approach not only expands the academic conversation on populism, but also provides practical insights for stakeholders navigating the complexities of political risk in investment decision-making. Thus, the central research question of this thesis is: "*What are the effects of populism on investor expectations and political risk assessments in financial markets?*"

To address the research question, a mixed methods approach is chosen, combining quantitative analysis with qualitative interviews. In the quantitative part of the research, the impact of populism is assessed from a capital market perspective. It is suggested that rising populism poses significant challenges for financial market participants, in particular by complicating the formation of expectations regarding future government policies. Thus, periods of high populism lead to increased uncertainty, which in turn raises the returns required by investors and results in higher equity capital costs.

However, a comprehensive understanding of populism as a political risk factor requires more than a quantitative analysis. Therefore, the qualitative part of this thesis explores the impact of populism through interviews with experienced political risk assessment experts. The aim of these interviews is to validate the quantitative findings and shed light on the intricacies of populism's influence on asset valuations.

Applying a mixed methods approach not only leverages the distinct advantages of quantitative and qualitative research, but also facilitates an in-depth exploration by allowing each methodology to complement the other. The quantitative analysis provides a broad overview of the impacts of populism in financial markets, while the qualitative interviews offer depth, context, and a differentiated understanding of the underlying mechanisms at play. This approach ensures an examination of the subject matter, enhancing the overall interpretive depth of the research. By integrating the empirical rigor of statistical analysis with the detailed insights from scientific interviews, this thesis offers a multifaceted view of how populism functions as a significant political risk factor within the financial sector, thereby making a substantial contribution to the academic dialogue on political risk and financial market behavior.

1.3 Structure

This thesis follows a structured approach, divided into two main chapters (first level): the theoretical framework and the empirical analysis. Each main chapter contains multiple chapters (second level) that focus on specific topics, which are further divided into subchapters (third level) for in-depth exploration. Sections (fourth level) and occasional subsections (fifth level) provide additional granularity, with their specific organization detailed in the respective chapters. This layered organization allows for an examination of the research topic, moving from broad concepts to detailed specifics.

The theoretical main chapter consists of four chapters. The three initial chapters, which cover the central theoretical topics, are designed to follow a parallel structure, beginning with an exploration of basic concepts before moving on to specific assessment methods and providing an interim conclusion. Chapter 2.1 lays the groundwork by discussing the fundamentals of investment theory, with a particular emphasis on international investment decisions and the cost of equity. It covers essential theories highlighting their significance in the realm of international finance (Subchapter 2.1.1). This chapter also critically reviews various asset pricing models, offering insights into their application and limitations (Subchapter 2.1.2). An interim summary synthesizes the chapter's key themes (Subchapter 2.1.3).

Following this, Chapter 2.2 ventures into the realm of political risk, elaborating on the fundamentals of political risk assessment and its role in guiding international business strategies (Subchapter 2.2.1). It then evaluates different political risk assessment methodologies and reflects on the contributions of risk analysts to this field (Subchapter 2.2.2). The interim summary draws together the discussions from the entire chapter (Subchapter 2.2.3).

Chapter 2.3 addresses the complex phenomenon of populism, tackling the challenges of defining populism and discussing its origins and implications (Subchapter 2.3.1). It also presents methodologies for assessing the impact of populism, contributing to a nuanced understanding of its effects (Subchapter 2.3.2). An interim summary encapsulates the discussions on populism (Subchapter 2.3.3).

The final chapter of the theoretical main chapter, Chapter 2.4, consolidates insights from earlier discussions and transitions to the empirical investigation by presenting an interim conclusion. It presents a theoretic synthesis (Subchapter 2.4.1), outlines the research gap (Subchapter 2.4.2), and formulates the research question (Subchapter 2.4.3), thereby preparing the groundwork for the empirical examination.

The empirical main chapter of this thesis is also structured into four chapters. Chapter 3.1 introduces the mixed methods framework and shows the research paradigms that underpin this framework (Subchapter 3.1.1), followed by an explanation and justification of the thesis's mixed methods research design (Subchapter 3.1.2).

After this foundational chapter, the focus shifts to the quantitative research in Chapter 3.2, which is elaborated upon in four subchapters. The analysis starts with the quantitative research design, including hypotheses, variables, and the empirical model (Subchapter 3.2.1). This is followed by an analysis of the sample, detailing its construction and summarizing its characteristics (Subchapter 3.2.2). The third subchapter presents the results of various tests conducted (Subchapter 3.2.3), leading into an interim discussion that concludes this quantitative chapter (Subchapter 3.2.4).

The narrative then transitions to the qualitative research in Chapter 3.3, mirroring the main structure of the quantitative analysis. It starts with an outline of the qualitative research design (Subchapter 3.3.1), proceeds to sample analysis (Subchapter 3.3.2), and culminates in the presentation of findings and the derivation of a research framework (Subchapter 3.3.3).

Chapter 3.4 synthesizes the discussions and prospects, spotlighting the research contributions of both analyses (Subchapter 3.4.1). It further delves into the processes taken to ensure scientific rigor in this thesis (Subchapter 3.4.2), concluding with reflections on the research's limitations and suggesting avenues for future inquiries in this domain (Subchapter 3.4.3).

The thesis closes with a conclusion that summarizes the insights gleaned from both the theoretical and empirical insights, offering a summary of the thesis. Figure 1.1 presents a schematic representation of the thesis structure, illustrating the theoretical and empirical main chapter along with their respective chapters and subchapters.

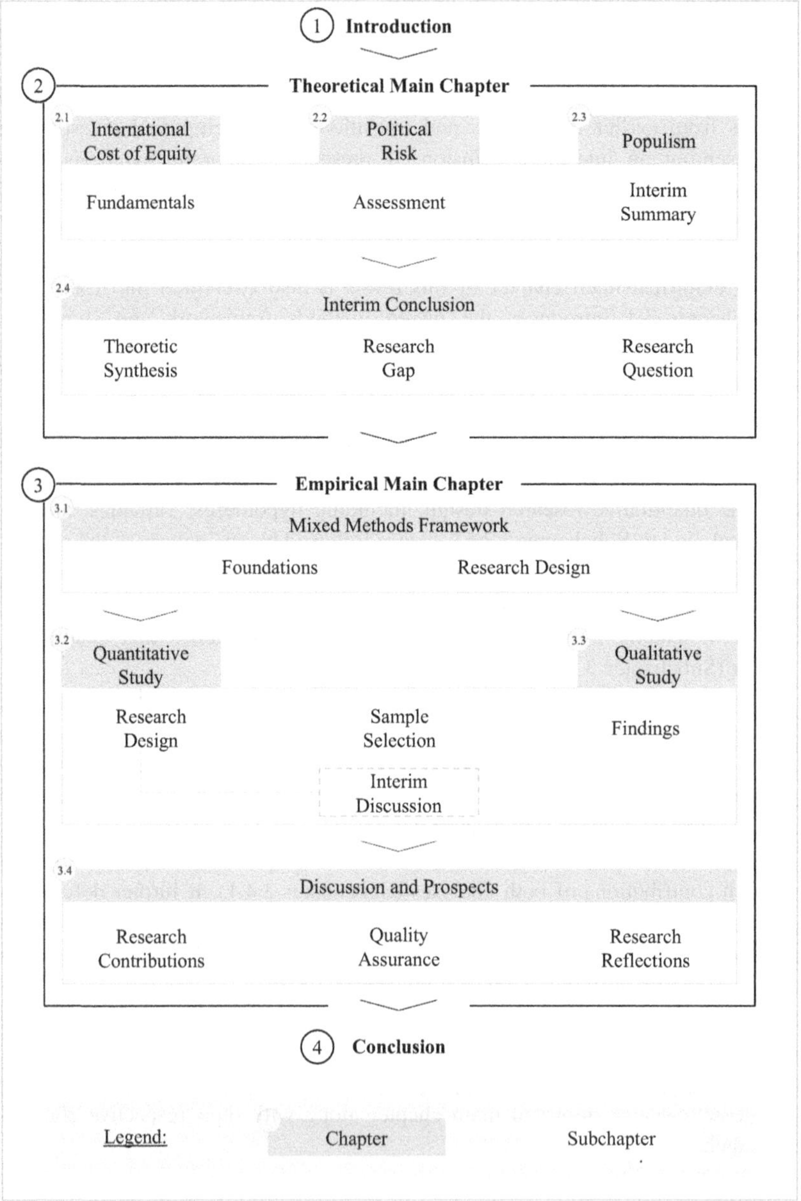

Fig. 1.1 Structure of the Thesis. (Source: Own Illustration.)

Theoretical Framework 2

2.1 International Cost of Equity

This chapter introduces the risk considerations in international finance that are essential to the later analysis of political risk assessment. It explores international equity investments and markets, setting the stage to examine the interplay between investor behavior, political risks, and market dynamics.

In the first subchapter, the focus is on international investment, with particular emphasis on capital budgeting and portfolio theory. Following this, the second subchapter introduces asset pricing models used to predict returns in global markets. These models can reveal how various factors, including geopolitical and economic changes, influence investor expectations and the perceived risk of investments in both domestic and international contexts.

2.1.1 Fundamentals

Financial markets are becoming increasingly adept at processing complex risks, including functions such as pricing, isolating, and transferring these risks. This complexity underscores the importance of accurate risk measurement, a critical factor in various applications such as setting risk limits, determining trader compensation, optimizing portfolios, and calculating the cost of capital.[1]

The first section discusses the basic principles of international equity investments and examines the implications of financial risk factors in an international context. It emphasizes capital budgeting, detailing the Net Present Value (NPV)

[1] See Holton 2004, p. 19.

C. Schütz, *Populism and Financial Markets*, Studies in Finance and Accounting,
https://doi.org/10.1007/978-3-658-46858-3_2

method and diversification strategies employed to manage risk in global markets. The following section examines the dimensions and variations of the global investment landscape. This section explores how different types of investors and investment approaches can have a significant impact on market dynamics and contribute to the changing patterns of global financial trends in international equity markets.

2.1.1.1 Conceptual Framework

This section presents a brief introduction to international investment in two subsections. The first subsection covers portfolio theory and diversification, explaining their importance in managing risk in a global investment context. The second subsection provides an overview of capital budgeting in a global context and discusses the NPV method.

2.1.1.1.1 Portfolio Theory and Diversification

An understanding of modern financial theory and the concepts of risk and uncertainty is necessary to make informed strategic decisions in global financial markets. This subsection offers a concise introduction to these concepts, emphasizing their role in global portfolio management.[2]

In investment theory, as defined by *Knight* in 1921, the term "risk" commonly refers to situations where the probabilities of different observable outcomes are known and can be quantified. In this context, risk is typically understood to relate to quantifiable factors such as fluctuations in revenue or profit. This enables decisions to be made on a probabilistic basis, which is a fundamental aspect of financial decision-making. In contrast, the term "uncertainty" is used to describe scenarios where the probabilities of outcomes cannot be determined at the time of decision-making. This renders the risks unquantifiable and more difficult to assess and manage for financial managers and investors.[3]

Risk transforms investment certainty into a spectrum of potential outcomes, each with a specific probability. Instead of a guaranteed return, risk involves

---

[2] For a more comprehensive analysis and deeper understanding of the principles and implications of international diversification in portfolio theory, refer to e.g. Eiteman et al. 2013, pp. 465 ff. The authors provide a detailed discussion of investor risk aversion, the composition and optimization of domestic and international portfolios, and the positive impact of international diversification on expected portfolio risk and return.

[3] See Knight 1921, pp. 197 ff. Some scholars, including Holton, contend that Knight's definition of risk is limited to addressing only uncertainty, failing to encompass the broader conventional understanding of risk that includes both uncertainty and potential consequences (see Holton 2004, pp. 19 ff.).

evaluating expected returns—the average outcome—and the degree of variation around this average, typically quantified with a dispersion measure such as the variance or standard deviation.[4]

Building on the concept of risk, *Markowitz's* seminal portfolio theory, introduced in 1952 and for which he was awarded the Nobel Prize in Economic Sciences in 1990,[5] focuses on how investors can optimize the balance between risk and return in their investment portfolios.[6] Portfolio risk is a measure of the uncertainty associated with the magnitude of volatility in the value of a portfolio. This volatility can be quantified using the variance, which calculates the squared deviations between the portfolio's actual returns and their expected returns.[7]

Markowitz's research underscores the importance of diversification in minimizing risk when allocating financial assets. By combining assets whose returns are not perfectly correlated, the overall risk of a portfolio can be reduced. Two main insights emerge from the researchers' theory. Firstly, there is usually a positive correlation between risk and expected return, suggesting that investors require compensation from risky securities. Secondly, diversification across asset classes, sectors and regions is an effective strategy for mitigating risk. It balances the performance of different assets, especially when those assets are not highly correlated, thereby reducing the impact of market volatility.[8]

In domestic portfolios, adding a variety of assets such as stocks generally reduces portfolio variance due to their imperfect correlation, although the benefit of further variance reduction diminishes as more assets are included. This risk reduction effect is caused by the presence of non-systematic or idiosyncratic risk, which is inherent to individual assets. Conversely, systematic risk, also known as market risk, affects all assets and cannot be fully mitigated by domestic diversification alone. This risk type can be influenced by broader economic factors, such as fluctuations in economic growth, changes in fiscal policy, and shifts in investor sentiment.[9]

The principle of diversification takes on additional implications when applied in an international context. Studies conducted by *Solnik*, later updated by *Bekaert and Hodrick*, have demonstrated the advantages of including assets from different countries in a portfolio. They found that the imperfect correlation between

[4] See Elton et al. 2014, p. 42.

[5] See Lee 1991, p. 209.

[6] See Holton 2004, p. 21.

[7] See Mangram 2013, pp. 60 ff.

[8] See Markowitz 1952, pp. 77–91.

[9] See Butler 2016, p. 466.

domestic and international stocks can significantly reduce portfolio variance. As a result, international diversification can help mitigate risks that are beyond the scope of domestic diversification.[10]

Figure 2.1 illustrates this point, showing two curves that represent the variance reduction from domestic and international diversification, respectively. The graph demonstrates that adding more international stocks leads to a more substantial decrease in overall variance compared to a portfolio consisting solely of domestic stocks. This variance reduction in both scenarios is primarily attributable to the unsystematic risk component, which can be mitigated through diversification.[11]

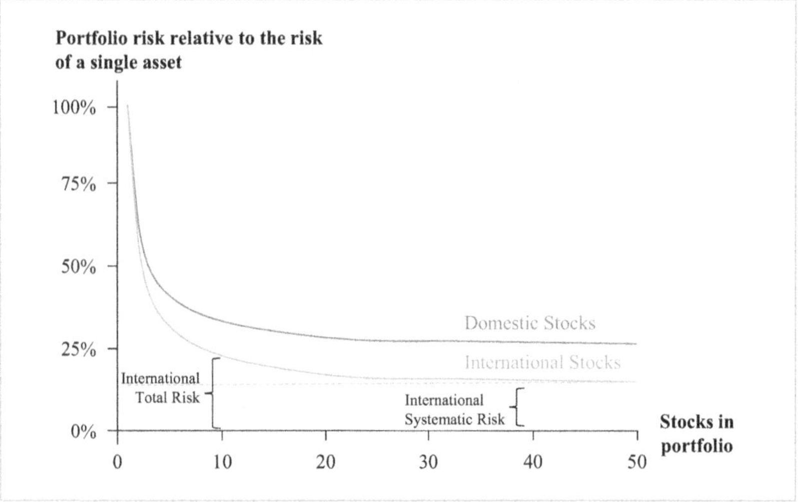

Fig. 2.1 Domestic and International Diversification. (Source: Own Illustration; following Butler 2016, p. 474, Exhibit 19.8; Bekaert and Hodrick 2018, p. 551, Exhibit 13.4.)

Although international diversification cannot completely eliminate portfolio variance due to the positive global correlation among stocks, it does reduce systematic variance relative to a purely domestic portfolio. The undiversifiable risk that remains in an international portfolio is affected by macroeconomic forces and monetary policies in various countries. Therefore, it is important to adopt a

[10] See Solnik 1974, pp. 365 ff.; Bekaert and Hodrick 2018, pp. 550 f.

[11] See Bekaert and Hodrick 2018, p. 550.

diversified investment approach to optimize the risk-return trade-off. The principle that a stock's contribution to portfolio variance depends on its covariance with other stocks in the portfolio remains valid in both domestic and international settings.[12]

The effectiveness of diversification, especially in an international context, is closely linked to diversifiable country-specific influences and correlation dynamics, which are influenced by several factors.[13] For instance, in regions such as North America and Europe, financial correlations tend to be stronger, which affects the potential for risk reduction in developed countries. In contrast, emerging markets typically exhibit more autonomous financial patterns, indicating that diversification in these environments may lead to greater risk reduction benefits, although transaction costs may be higher and market liquidity may be limited.[14] Furthermore, the nature of cross-country return correlations in developed markets, shaped by geographical proximity and trade links, differs from industry correlations. Industry correlations tend to be higher, indicating that international diversification may be more effective in reducing risk compared to industry-specific diversification.[15]

However, predicting the benefits of international diversification is not always trivial, largely due to the inherently unstable and unpredictable nature of cross-market correlations. These fluctuations pose a challenge to the effectiveness of diversification strategies,[16] particularly during global equity market downturns when increased market correlations can significantly reduce the benefits of diversification.[17]

2.1.1.1.2 International Investment Analysis

In the realm of international finance, investments offer risk and return trade-offs that provide more favorable opportunities than a purely domestic counterpart. In order to reduce the dependence on the performance of a single domestic market, it is necessary to identify opportunities with a broader investment analysis that takes into account different geographical locations, allowing investors to benefit from different economic conditions and opportunities.

---

[12] See Bekaert and Hodrick 2018, p. 551.

[13] See Bouchet 2003, p. 156.

[14] See Bekaert and Hodrick 2018, pp. 579 f.

[15] See Del Negro and Brooks 2005, pp. 3–17.

[16] See Goetzmann et al. 2005, pp. 1–3.

[17] See Longin and Solnik 2001, p. 649.

To illustrate these advantages, consider Figure 2.2, which draws on a hypothetical example from *Butler*. The shaded area of the graph shows how financial managers of multinational corporations (MNCs) can potentially increase firm value by leveraging their global reach. It displays two investment opportunity sets with downward slopes, where the MNC's set is positioned higher, indicating access to more favorable investment opportunities. This reflects higher expected returns on incremental investments compared to domestic firms, whose opportunity set lies lower, suggesting more limited and less profitable investment options. Additionally, the MNC's lower and less steep cost of capital curve suggests that MNCs can finance their international investments at a lower cost, further increasing the firm value.[18]

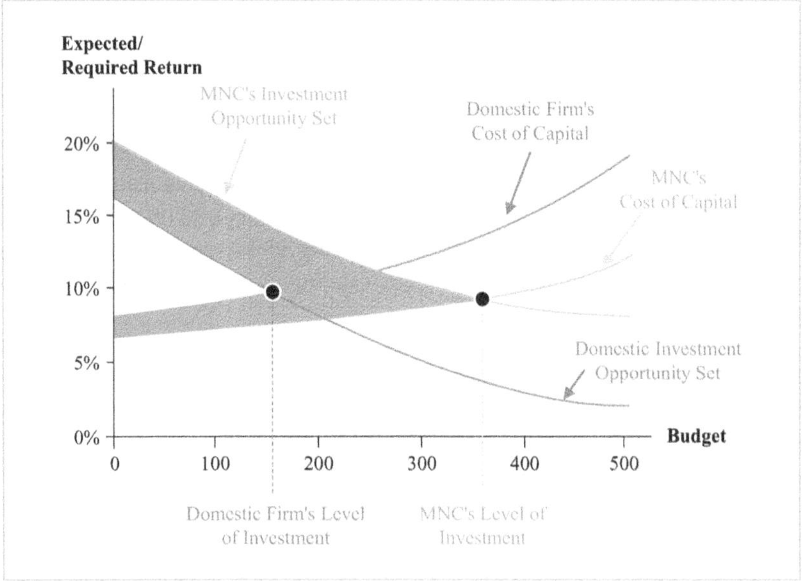

Fig. 2.2 MNC International Investment Opportunities. (Source: Own Illustration; following Butler 2016, p. 10, Exhibit 1.4.)

In order to take advantage of international investment opportunities, MNCs must navigate a more complex analysis process than they do for domestic

[18] See Butler 2016, pp. 10 f.

investments. Although evaluated using similar methods as domestic investments, foreign investment assessment must incorporate additional risk considerations such as currency risks due to the crossing of national, legal, and monetary boundaries.[19] Therefore, effective capital budgeting for international investments requires a comprehensive risk assessment, with a particular focus on country-specific factors that can significantly affect the return on financial assets.[20]

There are several methods employed in capital budgeting, including the NPV, Adjusted Present Value, Internal Rate of Return, and Payback Period.[21] Finance textbooks typically advise the use of the NPV method, which is a cornerstone of capital budgeting.[22] It determines whether the present value of a project's expected net cash flows exceeds the initial investment. To determine the NPV of a project in capital budgeting, it is necessary to define a discount rate that reflects the opportunity cost to investors. This requires an understanding of the investor's perception of risk, focusing on the need to compensate for non-diversifiable risk as outlined by the diversification principle (see Subsection 2.1.1.1.1). For example, in the context of all-equity financing, the discount rate not only represents the cost of equity, but also the rate of return expected by investors.[23] Estimating this rate properly is essential, as overestimating it can lead to profitable projects being rejected, while underestimating it can lead to unprofitable ventures being pursued. In this regard, a careful assessment of major domestic factors, including projections of tax implications, is required to ensure an accurate present value assessment.[24]

---

[19] See Cavusgil et al. 2020, pp. 1–3; Röell et al. 2022, p. 1.

[20] See Bouchet 2003, pp. 155 f.

[21] For more information see for example Bierman and Smidt 2007, pp. 43–84; Dayananda et al. 2010, pp. 1–11; Hall and Westerman 2011, pp. 217–241; Pierru and Babusiaux 2011, pp. 381–402. Other models, especially for political risk assessment in international investments, include Bekaert and Hodrick's three-step method, designed for extreme scenarios like total expropriation without compensation. While their model assumes continuous risk, it also recognizes that risks often decrease post-crisis (see Bekaert and Hodrick 2018, pp. 618 ff.). Clark, on the other hand, differentiates between sudden explicit events and ongoing changes in the approach to quantifying political risk impacts in foreign direct investments (see Clark 1997, pp. 477 f.).

[22] See Levi 2006, p. 348.

[23] See Bekaert and Hodrick 2018, pp. 544, 572.

[24] See Butler 2016, pp. 300 f.

The significance of the NPV in financial valuation is underscored by its widespread use.[25] For the international context, one prominent approach proposes to adapt the NPV framework to incorporate international risks.[26] This adaptation involves two principal strategies to accommodate the additional risks inherent in international investments. The first strategy modifies the expected cash flows to reflect country-specific risks. The process involves adjusting each year's expected cash flows (CF_t) by incorporating country-specific foreign risk factors (u_t), followed by discounting these adjusted flows to their present value using an appropriate discount rate (R).[27] This rate reflects the expected rate of return that investors generally anticipate from an investment and should be based on market values, including an appropriate risk premium added to a benchmark risk-free rate.[28] To maintain the accuracy of the valuation, it is essential that the discount rate remain unchanged in consideration of country risks, as these risks are already reflected in the cash flows. This approach provides an assessment of an investment's feasibility in an international setting, taking into account the unique challenges and uncertainties that could affect financial outcomes, such as political risk. The resulting formula is as follows:[29]

$$NPV_0 = \sum_{t=0}^{n} \frac{CF_t * u_t}{(1+R)^t} \tag{2.1}$$

The variable u_t represents a country-specific risk factor for each year t, with a value between 0 and 1 ($0 < u < 1$). This factor quantifies the likelihood of avoiding negative occurrences in the country of the investment. When there is no country-specific risk ($u_t = 1$), the expected net cash flow for year t aligns with the conventional NPV calculation, maintaining the standard framework for projecting net cash flows.[30]

The primary challenge associated with this methodology stems from determining the u_t coefficients. However, this approach has the significant advantage of being able to allocate unique coefficients that reflect varying levels of risk

---

[25] See Bekaert and Hodrick 2018, p. 572.

[26] The NPV approach is also seen critically in international contexts, with the Adjusted Present Value being the preferred methodology as it allows for the inclusion of additional terms in the valuation, such as debt subsidies (see Levi 2006, p. 347).

[27] See Bouchet 2003, p. 142.

[28] See Fabozzi and Jones 2019, p. 246; Pilbeam 2018, pp. 211 ff.

[29] See Bouchet 2003, p. 142.

[30] See Bouchet 2003, p. 142.

exposure for each period. This adaptability allows for a precise representation of a country's political, social, and economic fluctuations, encapsulating variables such as election years.[31]

An alternative strategy for evaluating investments in environments with foreign country risk is to adjust the discount rate instead of the cash flows. This approach recalibrates the rate used for discounting future cash flows to include an additional risk factor that is specific to the country of the investment. The formula for the adjusted NPV becomes:[32]

$$NPV_0 = \sum_{t=0}^{n} \frac{CF_t}{(1 + R + K)^t} \tag{2.2}$$

Within this formula, CF_t represents the expected cash flow in year t without modification for additional foreign country risk, R represents the original discount rate, while K quantifies the additional risk. To account for the additional risk, the revised discount factor $(1 + R + K)$ is increased, resulting in a decrease in the NPV of the investment.[33] For example, when K equals zero, it signifies that there is no additional risk being considered in the formula in comparison to a domestic setting.

One of the main challenges with the second approach is the absence of a solid theoretical framework to guide the selection of the appropriate adjusted discount rate. Thus, the determination of the discount rate can be somewhat subjective, reflecting some degree of arbitrariness in incorporating additional risk into the valuation.[34]

In theory, adjustments to the discount rate or cash flows should result in identical outcomes. However, the practical application of these principles encounters complexities in determining model-specific parameters.[35] In industry practices for cross-border investments, the preferred approach is to adjust the discount rate to account for both general investment risks and specific country risks. The approach of adjusting discount rates is popular because it provides a simplified method for incorporating risk into financial analysis, allowing for a single figure that encompasses all perceived additional risks.[36]

---

[31] See Bouchet 2003, p. 142.

[32] See Bekaert and Hodrick 2018, pp. 618 f.

[33] See Bouchet 2003, pp. 142 f.

[34] See Belghitar and Clark 2011, p. 250.

[35] See Bekaert and Hodrick 2018, p. 620.

[36] See Anshuman et al. 2011, pp. 41 f.

2.1.1.2 Dimensions and Variations

The investment landscape is shaped by a variety of players who impact global market dynamics. This section explores the different types of investors and their strategies, highlighting their influence on equity and debt markets, and their role in determining asset returns. These factors affect the cost of capital for companies, thereby affecting company valuations and investment decisions.

There are various types of investors, and they can be broadly categorized into several key groups, such as individual shareholders and MNCs, whose investment decisions have a direct impact on market dynamics. Additionally, institutional investors, who possess considerable influence due to their large capital bases and strategic investment approaches, include entities such as pension funds, insurance companies, banks, and mutual funds.[37]

For investors, there are several avenues through which they can gain access to global financial markets. Each of these avenues has its own distinctive characteristics, which are primarily determined by the investor's risk tolerance, investment objectives, and preference for involvement in the management of their investments. First, direct purchases of foreign securities offer a comprehensive immersion into overseas markets. However, this approach is accompanied by a number of challenges, including higher information costs, language barriers, and navigating different regulatory and tax regimes. Second, the utilization of domestic channels, such as global stocks or depositary receipts, can facilitate the investment process. These options reduce some logistical hurdles, yet still expose investors to risks, such as exchange rate volatility and differences in market valuation. Third, investing through managed funds, such as mutual funds and exchange-traded funds, offers advantages, including diversification and professional management. This strategy minimizes the need for individual stock selection and detailed market analysis, making it a more accessible option for many investors.[38]

MNCs play an important role in this landscape as they manage operations across countries and seek to optimize shareholder wealth by investing in high-return projects. Since maximizing shareholder wealth is consistent with the primary goals of firms in market economies, the perspective of the financial manager of an MNC is closely related to that of an investor.[39] This link has implications for the portfolio risk assessment framework, as it can be effectively

[37] See Bekaert and Hodrick 2018, p. 9.

[38] See Butler 2016, pp. 444–447.

[39] See Bekaert and Hodrick 2018, p. 11.

adapted and applied to assess both financial portfolio flows and Foreign Direct Investment (FDI), highlighting its adaptability to diverse aspects of investment.[40]

When expanding internationally, MNCs often begin with non-investment-based approaches such as exporting or licensing, which require limited resources. As companies gain market insight, they tend to prefer investment-based strategies, such as FDI, Mergers and Acquisitions (M&A), and joint ventures. Each strategy requires a significant resource commitment and offers different levels of control and collaboration. For example, FDI involves significant capital investment in foreign operations, which allows for direct control but also carries significant risk. Cross-border M&A, as well as joint ventures, offer the opportunity to control foreign assets and collaborate with local firms, balancing shared insights and risks.[41]

MNCs generally have a long-term investment horizon,[42] and their investment decisions are influenced not only by market dynamics, but also by the regulatory and economic policies of governments and international organizations.[43]

Governments and central banks shape the investment environment through monetary and fiscal policies that affect key financial metrics such as interest rates and exchange rates, which in turn affect asset valuations and the attractiveness of investments.[44] More specifically, governments play four essential roles within the financial system, crucial for ensuring the stability and resilience of financial markets. First, they create and enforce a regulatory framework that ensures market transparency, risk management, and fraud prevention, maintaining fairness and efficiency. Second, governments provide crucial support as lenders or guarantors to economically essential sectors, typically through mechanisms that secure financial obligations without direct lending. Third, through central banks, they manage monetary policy to control inflation and uphold financial stability, often using tools like interest rate adjustments. Fourth, they act as rescuers by deploying public funds for bailouts of vital market sectors or distressed corporations to prevent systemic failures and ensure economic continuity.[45]

International financial institutions such as the International Monetary Fund, the World Bank, and the World Trade Organization maintain stability and regulate

---

[40] See Bouchet 2003, p. 149.

[41] See Bekaert and Hodrick 2018, p. 18.

[42] See Bekaert and Hodrick 2018, p. 11.

[43] See Butler 2016, p. 31.

[44] See Bekaert and Hodrick 2018, p. 22.

[45] See Fabozzi and Jones 2019, pp. 25–36.

the global financial market, focusing on issues ranging from economic stability to poverty alleviation and trade regulation.[46]

2.1.2 Assessment

This subchapter focuses on asset pricing models, which are essential tools for measuring the impact of various market influences, including political events, on investor expectations and the assessment of financial risk. An important aspect of this exploration is the analysis of investor expectations, which determine the required rate of return and thus the cost of equity for companies. Therefore, the relationship between investor perceptions and financial metrics is of paramount importance in the field of finance, particularly in the context of capital budgeting, portfolio selection, as well as firm and stock valuation, with a particular focus on international markets.[47]

Recognizing that models in an international context often depend on assumptions about market integration, the subchapter begins by examining the key elements that influence international equity markets. Following this, the subchapter provides a comprehensive review of various asset pricing models, including Implied Cost of Equity Capital (ICC) models. The concluding section of the subchapter analyzes different versions of the ICC models in more detail.

2.1.2.1 Analytical Determinants

Considering the significant changes that have occurred in global financial markets in recent decades it is crucial to comprehend the factors that impact the valuation of international equity investments and the derivation of the cost of equity. The section first analyzes the profound impact of economic and financial integration on investment dynamics, with a particular emphasis on how these forces have restructured equity investment landscapes. Subsequently, the various factors that hinder or facilitate market integration are examined by exploring market barriers.

2.1.2.1.1 Economic and Financial Integration

This subsection expands on the previous discussions about international correlation and explores the impact of capital market integration (see Subsection 2.1.1.1.1). Market integration has a significant effect on international

[46] See Bekaert and Hodrick 2018, p. 22.

[47] See Kirby 2019, p. 105.

portfolio diversification and asset pricing, particularly on a firm's cost of capital.[48] Since the 1980s, economic and financial integration has had a profound impact on equity prices, reshaping the global financial markets. The integration of the European Union serves as a prime example of transformations in developed regions that have also affected developing nations. The liberalization of financial sectors and the development of capital markets have expanded investment opportunities, most notably in emerging markets, leading to a degree of financial openness worldwide.[49]

Estimating market integration remains a complex challenge in financial literature, with no standardized approach available. The first step is to distinguish between financial market integration and economic integration. While financial integration is often the result of market liberalization and refers to the interconnectedness of capital markets, economic integration refers to the broader interconnectedness of global economies.[50]

Numerous studies have examined the influence of global and local factors on asset returns as an indicator of market integration.[51] In theory, market integration is defined by the existence of unique global factors that determine asset prices in all markets. As a result, assets with similar risk profiles have identical expected returns regardless of their geographic location. Conversely, market segmentation persists when different factors unique to individual countries or regions affect asset pricing.[52] In environments characterized by partial market segmentation, investors have to deal with a combination of global and country-specific risks. Consequently, asset pricing in such contexts reflects a mix of local and global risk factors, which in turn affects expected returns.[53]

Emerging markets, with their unique political and economic landscapes, offer distinct diversification benefits in international portfolios; their low correlation to developed markets can significantly improve the overall risk-return trade-off, despite their inherent volatility.[54] As emerging markets continue to liberalize their financial markets, leading to greater integration with the global market,

---

[48] See Butler 2016, p. 443.

[49] See Bekaert and Hodrick 2018, pp. 3–9.

[50] See Akbari et al. 2020, pp. 2270 ff.

[51] See Akbari and Ng 2020, pp. 161 ff. Other methods have also been developed to assess market integration, for example from Bekaert et al. 2011 or Pukthuanthong and Roll 2009, providing a broader perspective on the topic.

[52] See Errunza and Losq 1985, pp. 105–124; Stulz 1981, pp. 383–406.

[53] See Arouri et al. 2012, pp. 2473–2475.

[54] See Butler 2016, pp. 335–342.

this increases the efficiency of capital allocation and risk sharing internationally. This integration is expected to reduce the cost of capital for companies in these countries, while diminishing the diversification benefits for foreign investors.[55]

However, market integration can also increase vulnerability to global financial shocks. The 2008–2009 financial crisis exemplified how highly integrated markets can facilitate the spread of financial crises across the globe.[56] Despite trends towards liberalization emerging markets have not yet reached the same level of integration as developed markets. Persistent differences in the cost of capital and diversification benefits underscore the ongoing need for research into the barriers to full market integration.[57]

2.1.2.1.2 Market Integration Barriers

In the context of financial market integration, previously explored in terms of its impact on portfolio diversification, this subsection now turns its attention to the influence of foreign investment barriers on global equity market pricing.[58]

In contrast to the recommendations of modern portfolio theory, which advocate diversifying across international markets to gain additional advantages compared to solely domestic diversification, there is a notable trend where corporate equity is predominantly held within domestic boundaries. This trend arises from a multifaceted interplay of factors that tend to favor domestic investments over international ones.[59] These barriers, which range from explicit factors like capital controls and repatriation taxes to implicit ones such as the investment climate and financial institution quality, hinder the efficient sharing of international risks.[60]

In the literature, there is no single set of barriers to foreign investment. *Bekaert,* for example, highlights legal, informational and market-specific risks as significant barriers to market integration, with different legal frameworks and information asymmetries hinder the efficient operation of global markets.[61] *Lehkonen's* research expands on the impact of financial liberalization, highlighting its differential effects on stock markets in developed and emerging economies. This study emphasizes the importance of factors such as market openness and

[55] See Akbari and Ng 2020, pp. 2276 f.

[56] See Akbari et al. 2021, pp. 2291, 2297.

[57] See Akbari and Ng 2020, p. 161.

[58] See Bekaert and Hodrick 2018, p. 584.

[59] See French and Poterba, pp. 222–226.

[60] See Akbari and Ng 2020. The concept of market integration is grounded in the principle of the law of one price (see Chen and Knez 1995, p. 287).

[61] See Bekaert 1995, p. 77.

political risk in emerging markets, as opposed to institutional stability and market liquidity in developed markets.[62]

Moreover, *Arouri et al.* have presented an alternative overview of market segmentation factors, categorizing these elements into several key groups: direct barriers, indirect barriers, global economic conditions, and behavioral finance elements. Direct barriers, including capital controls and foreign exchange regulations, explicitly restrict access to foreign assets. Additionally, indirect barriers encompass aspects like information asymmetries and political and economic instabilities that deter global investors. Global economic conditions also play a pivotal role, where factors like domestic recessions, interest rate levels, and economic growth trajectories can either encourage or impede cross-border investment flows. Furthermore, behavioral finance elements, particularly home bias,[63] significantly influence market segmentation.[64] This behavioral tendency, driven by psychological preferences for familiar markets and concerns about the potential underperformance of foreign assets, not only impacts individual investment choices but also has wider macroeconomic implications.[65] Overall, the wide range of factors highlights that while the removal of investment barriers is a crucial step towards market integration, instruments such as closed-end country funds and international cross-listings such as depositary receipts serve to connect segmented markets, but may not comprehensively address all the underlying complexities.[66]

2.1.2.2 Assessment Approaches

Building on the complexity of market dynamics in international finance, asset pricing models play a central role in predicting returns in global markets. Various models have emerged to predict returns in both domestic and international markets, incorporating a wide range of factors.[67] This section explores key asset pricing models that are essential to international equity investing. It starts by

---

[62] See Lehkonen 2015, p. 2040. An examination of how political risk influences market integration is elaborately discussed in Subchapter 2.4.1.

[63] Ardalan's review essay suggests that equity home bias, an investor's preference for domestic stocks, may be due to a mix of factors, including but not limited to investment barriers and behavioral elements. The research indicates that the bias is complex and not fully explained by any single factor, highlighting that it remains a challenging area for future theoretical and empirical investigation (see Ardalan 2019, pp. 949 ff.).

[64] See Arouri et al. 2012, p. 2473.

[65] See Lee et al. 2023, pp. 1–16.

[66] See Arouri et al. 2012, p. 2743.

[67] See Larocque and Lyle 2017, p. 69.

explaining the Capital Asset Pricing Model (CAPM) and then traces the shift towards more empirical methods such as *Fama and French's* three-factor model and the forward-looking ICC approach.

2.1.2.2.1 Capital Asset Pricing Models

The CAPM, conceptualized by *Lintner*, *Mossin* and *Sharpe*,[68] is a cornerstone of finance that is central to comprehending and estimating the cost of equity. The CAPM offers valuable insights into asset allocation by capturing the complex relationship between the risk and the expected return of equity investments. It is well-regarded for its ability to incorporate the market risk associated with general market trends into asset pricing while neglecting individual idiosyncratic risks.[69]

Based on *Markowitz's* diversification principles (see Subsection 2.1.1.1.1), the CAPM is built on strong assumptions. One key assumption of the CAPM is that all investors hold an identical mix of risky assets in equilibrium, known as the market portfolio. This portfolio includes all securities in proportion to their market value and serves as a benchmark for calculating individual security risk premiums through covariance. Following the CAPM, the expected return on an equity investment is calculated as follows:[70]

$$R_e = R_f + \beta_i \left(R_m - R_f \right) \tag{2.3}$$

According to Formula (2.3) the expected return on equity (R_e) is estimated as the sum of the risk-free rate (R_f) and the product of the security's beta (β_i), and the difference between the market's expected return (R_m) and the risk-free rate, representing the market risk premium. This equation implies that equity investors seek compensation for both the time value of money and the systematic risk associated with an investment. This systematic risk is captured with the security's beta (β_i), which is determined by:[71]

$$\beta_i = \frac{Cov(R_e, R_m)}{Var(R_m)} \tag{2.4}$$

Here, the beta (β_i) of an equity is calculated as the covariance between the security's return (R_e) and the market return (R_m), divided by the variance of the market

68 See Lintner 1965, p. 587; Mossin 1966, p. 768; Sharpe 1964, p. 425.

69 See Shih et al. 2014, p. 416.

70 See Bekaert and Hodrick 2018, pp. 566 f.

71 See Bekaert and Hodrick 2018, pp. 567 f.

return. Beta plays a significant role in assessing the relative risk of assets as it measures an assets volatility relative to the overall market. For example, if the return on a security does not correlate with the broader market, its expected return matches the risk-free rate. Conversely, security's that positively covary with the market command higher expected returns than the risk-free rate. Assets with a negative beta, which are inversely correlated with the market portfolio's return, reduce the overall portfolio variance.[72]

The appeal of the CAPM lies in its ability to isolate the risk of an asset through its beta. In essence, the CAPM states that higher risks warrant higher required returns, suggesting a linear relationship between average returns and betas. It is widely accepted as a reasonable model for estimating rates of return in capital budgeting, in part because it emphasizes the importance of diversification.[73]

However, the assumptions of the classical CAPM have been criticized for their rigidity, leading to the development of more refined models.[74] These models can be categorized into distinct streams within the literature. One stream involves modifying the CAPM's assumptions to reflect real-world conditions more accurately. For instance, *Brennan's* extension takes into account the varying tax effects on dividends and capital gains,[75] while *Merton's* model introduces a multi-beta, intertemporal framework.[76]

In the field of international finance, a second literature stream emerged during the early 1970s' financial liberalization, contrasting the domestically-focused classical CAPM. While the classical model assumes fully segmented capital markets with asset pricing and risk confined to national markets, this international stream, including contributions by *Adler and Dumas*, *Grauer et al.* or *Solnik*, led to the development of international versions of the CAPM.[77] These models diverge from the classical CAPM and advocate global market integration, which suggests uniform pricing for identical assets worldwide and promotes global diversification. By including all risky assets and adjusting for currency fluctuations, a move towards a unified financial landscape is assumed. Most importantly, returns

[72] See Bekaert and Hodrick 2018, pp. 568 f.

[73] See Butler 2016, pp. 485, 490.

[74] Since its inception, the CAPM has evolved through numerous iterations. For example, the evolution of CAPM is extensively reviewed by Celik 2012, who explores its theoretical and empirical aspects, and Shih et al. 2014, who focus on its development and practical applications.

[75] See Brennan 1970, pp. 417–427.

[76] See Merton 1973, pp. 867–887.

[77] See Adler and Dumas 1983, pp. 925–984; Grauer et al. 1976, pp. 233–256; Solnik 1974, pp. 365–378.

for similar risky assets internationally are assumed to be harmonized, allowing for consistent pricing and return expectations for these assets regardless of geographic boundaries.[78]

The analysis of global market risk and country-specific risks within an international CAPM framework demonstrates that, despite the phenomenon of globalization, national markets continue to exhibit distinctive characteristics that influence investment outcomes.[79] In recognition of the fact that, in practice, the degree of integration may vary across regions, a novel set of models has been developed that allow for partial market integration.[80] Notable developments in this area include the exploration of partially segmented markets and subsequent advancements on the impact of market barriers on asset pricing and investment decisions.[81]

2.1.2.2.2 Empirical Asset Pricing Models

Empirical asset pricing models represent a shift in asset pricing away from the theoretical founded CAPM. While theoretical models derive their estimates through logical reasoning based on a set of assumptions, empirical models, in contrast, aim to identify the specific factors that have historically influenced actual returns on markets.[82] These models adopt a data-centric approach, emphasizing the analysis of empirically observable framework to explain market pricing mechanisms.[83]

A seminal work related to this area is *Ross's* Arbitrage Pricing Theory (APT), introduced in 1976.[84] APT linearly predicts expected returns by considering various risk factors that capture systematic risk in addition to the risk-free rate. In contrast to the CAPM, which relies primarily on market beta to measure risk, APT's factor models are not limited to predetermined factors of the selection of a market portfolio.[85] Instead, risk factors in APT's can vary and are chosen subjectively based on empirical data or derived from other asset pricing theories,

---

[78] See Bekaert and Hodrick 2018, p. 569; Butler 2016, pp. 489 f.

[79] See Bali and Cakici 2010, p. 1152.

[80] See Butler 2016, p. 490.

[81] See for example Black 1974, pp. 337–352; Errunza and Losq 1985, pp. 105–124; Stulz 1981, pp. 383–406.

[82] See Sabal 2004, p. 157.

[83] See Kirby 2019, p. 154.

[84] See Ross 1976, pp. 341 ff.

[85] See Ross 1976, pp. 341 ff.

providing new insights into the factors that influence market pricing.[86] Asset prices are calculated on the assumption that arbitrage eliminates all potential profit opportunities, thereby preventing gains from any inconsistencies in prices across various assets and markets.[87]

In contrast to APT, which necessitates the a priori selection of uncorrelated factors, more recent empirical models embrace the complexities of real-world data, acknowledging the frequent interdependencies among factors. This offers a pragmatic alternative by directly identifying and analyzing factors observed in historical market data. Consequently, empirical models, though lacking strict theoretical foundations, have gradually improved in accuracy and reliability, reflecting a more robust understanding of market dynamics.[88] The absence of a theoretical foundation for these asset pricing models has constituted a significant challenge, namely in identifying the essential risk factors among the multitude that have been discovered.[89]

One notable example of an empirical multifactor approach is *Fama and French's* three-factor model, introduced in 1993, which has "become a benchmark model in the asset pricing literature".[90] It extends the market factor from the CAPM by including firm size and book-to-market factors to explain stock returns. The model is expressed as follows:[91]

$$R_j = \alpha_j + \beta_{M,j} F_M + \beta_{SMB,j} F_{SMB} + \beta_{HML,j} F_{HML} + e_j \tag{2.5}$$

In this model, R_j denotes the expected rate of return on asset j and β_j refer to the factor coefficients. The model incorporates F_M, which captures market risk similar to the CAPM, as well as F_{SMB} the size factor, reflecting the differential performance between small and large stocks, and F_{HML} the value factor, which contrasts high book-to-market stocks with low book-to-market stocks. The term α_j represents the asset's expected return independent of the three considered factors. Lastly, e_j is the error term, accounting for unique, random effects specific to asset j. This model thus segments and analyzes stocks based on size and value characteristics, alongside sensitivity to market risk.[92]

---

[86] See Butler 2016, pp. 491 f.

[87] See Sabal 2004, p. 161.

[88] See Sabal 2004, p. 162.

[89] See Maiti 2020, p. 175.

[90] Chiah et al. 2016, p. 596.

[91] See Fama and French 1993, p. 3.

[92] See Fama and French 1993, pp. 3–56.

Building on *Fama and French's* three-factor model, the landscape of asset pricing models has evolved with the introduction of additional factors in more recent studies. For example, *Carhart's* inclusion of the momentum factor marked a further development in asset pricing theory, leading to the development of the *Carhart* four-factor model. The additional factor involves the strategic buying or selling of securities based on their recent performance, referred to as the momentum factor, and expands the understanding of market dynamics beyond the scope of *Fama and French's* three-factor model.[93] Similarly, *Fama and French's* five-factor model, introduced in 2015, extends the three-factor framework by including two incremental factors. These factors are designed to reflect variations in corporate profitability and investment characteristics in stock returns.[94]

Contemporary research has uncovered more than 300 different factors, making it imperative to differentiate between those of universal importance and those that are relevant to particular market environments. This differentiation is pivotal in developing resilient asset pricing models.[95] Even well-known supporters of factor models, such as *Fama and French*, recognize the inherent limitations in the precision of expected return estimates derived from these models.[96] This illustrates that the understanding of core risk factors in equity valuation is an evolving process and has led way for alternative approaches to comprehending and predicting market dynamics.[97]

2.1.2.2.3 Implied Cost of Equity Capital Models

An innovative approach in asset pricing that diverges from factor models is the Implied Cost of Equity Capital (ICC) approach. Relying on future estimates rather than historical data, ICC is characterized as a forward-looking methodology that provides a nuanced perspective on equity valuation and risk assessment.[98]

Conceptually, the ICC mirrors a stock's expected return, derived from current market prices and future financial predictions, similar to bond yield analysis.[99] Assuming market efficiency,[100] this approach aligns a company's equity value

---

[93] See Carhart 1997, p. 57.

[94] See Fama and French 2015, p. 1.

[95] See Maiti 2020, p. 175.

[96] See Fama and French 1997, p. 153.

[97] See Maiti 2020, p. 175.

[98] See Xu 2020, p. 1.

[99] See Esterer and Schröder 2014, p. 172.

[100] In an efficient market, prices accurately mirror all accessible information, facilitating optimal investment and production decisions. This concept is categorized into three forms:

with its current share price by incorporating expected dividends, earnings, and growth forecasts into a valuation model. The model determines a stock's expected return as the implied discount factor, representing the market's projected return on the stock, by reconciling future financial projections with its current market valuation.[101]

Different valuation models have been used to calculate the ICC, with variations mainly determined by a number of factors. These include the level of valuation, whether at the company or portfolio level, and the choice of underlying financial metrics. Additionally, the models differ in their underlying assumptions in projection, which include forecast periods, estimated growth rates, and payout ratios.[102]

A significant advantage of the ICC approach is its forward-looking nature, which allows it to rely less on historical data than factor models that estimate future values based on past trends. This ex-ante method, focusing on future estimates of stock returns, addresses the imprecision highlighted in *Elton's* critique of using historical stock returns as proxies for expected returns.[103] The ICC method's independence from extensive time series data and its resilience to changes in market produces estimates with less volatility compared to those derived from historical data, providing a more stable and consistent framework for assessing equity values.[104] Moreover, the ICC utilizes available contemporaneous information, enhancing its practicality and applicability for real-time investment decisions.[105] Furthermore, it avoids the challenges of selecting a specific market portfolio based on assumptions about market integration, which is a notable issue in return-based studies like the CAPM, especially in a global context.[106]

The main objections to the ICC method, according to *Echterling et al.*, are challenges to analysts' forecasts and methodological concerns. First, they point out that analysts' forecasts, which play a crucial role in the ICC calculations, often have a noticeable optimistic bias, potentially introducing inaccuracies into the

the weak form, where prices reflect historical data; the semi-strong form, where prices adjust to publicly available information; and the strong form, where no group possesses exclusive access to information that can influence prices (see Fama 1970, p. 383).

[101] See Bielstein 2018, p. 21.

[102] See Echterling et al. 2015, p. 237.

[103] See Elton 1999, pp. 1199 f.

[104] See Hail and Leuz 2006, p. 490.

[105] See Bielstein 2018, pp. 20 ff.

[106] See Hail and Leuz 2006, p. 490.

estimation process.[107] Furthermore, the ICC method tends to favor larger firms due to its extensive data requirements, making it less suitable for a broader range of companies.[108] Another concern is the assumption that investors' expectations do not always coincide with analysts' predictions, which can lead to inaccuracies in market prices, especially in partially efficient markets.[109]

Second, methodological concerns include accounting conservatism affecting valuation models, which can lead to a conservative bias in ICC estimates. Moreover, the issue of degrees-of-freedom arises due to short, detailed planning horizons in certain valuation models and the assumption of a constant cost of capital over time, which contradicts evidence suggesting time-varying expected returns.[110]

In response to these criticisms, scholars have suggested validating ICC estimates with established risk proxies such as firm size and book-to-market ratio.[111] Additionally, mechanical forecast models have been developed that can replace analyst estimates to predict earnings expectations.[112] Moreover, to counteract the biases and inaccuracies inherent in individual models, researchers such as *Dhaliwal et al.*, *Hail and Leuz*, and *Hou et al.* have adopted a technique of averaging ICC estimates across various models. This approach aims to neutralize biases specific to each model, offering a more balanced and representative estimate of the ICC.[113] The following section will explore various valuation models that serve as the basis for the empirical variations within specific ICC models.

2.1.2.3 Implied Cost of Equity Capital Models

In the field of firm valuation, a range of models has been developed to determine a firm's intrinsic value, and, with the assumption of market efficiency, these models are also applicable for calculating the ICC. This section explores the theoretical foundations of three primary firm valuation models, each applicable for estimating the ICC at the firm level.[114] The three models being analyzed are the

---

[107] See Echterling et al. 2015, p. 248.

[108] See Hou et al. 2012, p. 505.

[109] See Esterer and Schröder 2014, p. 172.

[110] See Echterling et al. 2015, p. 245.

[111] See for example Botosan and Plumlee 2005, p. 21; Gode and Mohanram 2003, p. 399.

[112] See Li and Mohanram 2014, pp. 1152–1185.

[113] See Dhaliwal et al. 2014, p. 334; Hail and Leuz 2006, p. 495; Hou et al. 2012, p. 506.

[114] While the portfolio-level estimation of ICC also involves several models, it focuses on aggregate analyses across collections of firms. For an overview of these models see Echterling et al. 2015, pp. 240–242.

Dividend Discount Model (DDM), the Residual Income Model (RIM), and the Abnormal Earnings Growth Model (AEGM).

While these models are theoretically interconnected, their practical applications often result in significantly different valuations. This variation is due to the distinct assumptions and parameters used in each model's empirical version, resulting in differing perspectives on valuation. The purpose of this section is to present a thorough examination of the primary models, namely the DDM, the RIM, and the AEGM, by outlining their advantages and limitations. Further, the differences in their empirical adaptations are discussed briefly,[115] shedding light on their practical use in assessing the firm value and the resulting implications for the ICC.

2.1.2.3.1 Dividend Discount Model

The DDM estimates the firm value based on the premise that it is equal to the sum of all future projected dividends discounted back to their present value using the cost of equity. In practice, dividend forecasts are typically made over a finite horizon, and a terminal value is calculated at the end of that period to estimate the ongoing value of the company beyond the explicit forecast period.[116] The traditional model assumes a steady and constant discount rate over time, allowing the value of the firm to be reverse-engineered to estimate the ICC.[117] The formula at the essence of the DDM is:

$$V_0 = \sum_{t=1}^{T} \frac{D_t}{(1+R_e)^t} + \frac{D_{T+1}}{(1+R_e)^T (R_e - G_D)} \tag{2.6}$$

In this model, V_0 represents the current value of the firm and D_t reflects the dividends at time t. The cost of equity (R_e) is the discount factor in the DDM, reflecting the risk-adjusted return expected by equity investors. This model can also incorporate an adjustment for the expected growth rate (G_D) of dividends to estimate the firm's terminal value.[118]

Several adaptations of the DDM have been developed over time for empirical investigation, with significant contributions from *Gordon and Gordon* or

---

[115] Subsection 3.2.1.2.1 delves deeper into the specific models employed for the empirical analysis.

[116] See Penman and Sougiannis 1998, p. 346.

[117] See Echterling et al. 2015, pp. 237 f.

[118] See Echterling et al. 2015, p. 238.

Malkiel.[119] These adaptations primarily differ in terms of the detailed planning period and the anticipated growth rates of dividends. Although the DDM is commonly deployed, it has limitations, particularly in predicting estimates for firms that do not pay dividends and potentially undervaluing companies that reinvest earnings instead of distributing them. To alleviate these limitations, alternative accounting-based models, such as the RIM and the AEGM, have been developed. Empirical studies conducted by researchers such as *Francis et al.* and *Jiang and Lee* indicate that accounting-based models, such as the RIM, provide more accurate estimates of the firm value compared to the DDM.[120]

2.1.2.3.2 Residual Income Model

The RIM proposed by *Ohlson* and evolved from the DDM,[121] establishes a link between a company's market value, its book value, and its projected future residual income (or abnormal earnings). Unlike the DDM, the RIM focuses on valuing the company using accounting measures, particularly the residual income. The formula for estimating this measure is as follows:[122]

$$RI_t = NI_t - R_e CSE_{t-1} \tag{2.7}$$

Here, RI_t represents the residual income for period t, that equals the net income for period t (NI_t), after subtracting an equity charge, which is calculated by multiplying the cost of equity capital (R_e) with the previous period's common stock equity (CSE_{t-1}). Based on these residual income estimates the present value of the firm can be determined with the following formula, which can reverse-engineered to estimate the ICC:[123]

$$V_0 = CSE_0 + \sum_{t=1}^{T} \frac{RI_t}{(1+R_e)^t} + \frac{RI_{T+1}}{(1+R_e)^T (R_e - G_{RI})} \tag{2.8}$$

[119] See Gordon and Gordon 1997, pp. 52–61; Malkiel 1979, pp. 291–306. For an overview of versions of the Dividend Discount Models see D'Amico and De Blasis 2020, pp. 47 ff.

[120] See Francis et al. 2000, p. 45; Jiang and Lee 2005, p. 1465.

[121] See Ohlson 1995, pp. 661–687. For a detailed derivation of the Residual Income Model from the Dividend Discount Model, see Gebhardt et al. 2001, pp. 135–176.

[122] See Echterling et al. 2015, pp. 241 ff.

[123] See Echterling et al. 2015, pp. 236 f.

By adding the present value of future expected residual incomes accounting for the cost of equity capital (R_e) to its initial equity value (CSE_0) the model determines a firm's equity value (V_0). The terminal value can include a potential constant growth rate (G_{RI}) of the residual income.[124] The so-called clean surplus relation is central to this approach. It assumes that all changes in a firm's book value within a specific period are reflected either in its accounting income or in the net distributions to shareholders for that period. This principle is encapsulated in the following formula:[125]

$$CSE_t = CSE_{t-1} + E_t - D_t \tag{2.9}$$

The equation calculates the common stock equity at time t (CSE_t) by adding the previous period's common stock equity (CSE_{t-1}) to the current period's earnings (E_t) and subtracting any dividends (D_t) distributed to shareholders.[126]

The alignment of the RIM with the DDM requires adherence to the clean surplus relation, which assumes that all changes in equity are attributable solely to net income and dividends, without other adjustments. However, in practical applications, this relation is often breached due to various factors, such as changes in the number of outstanding shares, misalignments in equity bases, and differences in accounting concepts, such as comprehensive income versus net income.[127]

There are multiple empirical versions of the RIM, such as those proposed by *Claus and Thomas* and *Gebhardt et al.*, which differ primarily in their planning horizons and earnings growth assumptions used to determine the terminal value. These empirical models rely on an iterative process to determine the ICC, often using industry benchmarks and consensus forecasts to estimate earnings and terminal values more accurately.[128]

2.1.2.3.3 Abnormal Earnings Growth Model

The AEGM is closely related to the RIM, as both are theoretically grounded in the principles of the DDM.[129] Although both approaches focus on evaluating earnings, their objectives are distinct. Residual income methods concentrate on

---

[124] See Echterling et al. 2015, pp. 236 f.

[125] See O'Hanlon and Peasnell 2002, p. 230.

[126] See O'Hanlon and Peasnell 2002, p. 230.

[127] See Ohlson 2005, pp. 323–347; Penman 2005, pp. 367–378.

[128] See Claus and Thomas 2001, pp. 1629–1666; Gebhardt et al. 2001, pp. 135–176.

[129] See Ho et al. 2017, p. 561.

forecasting future levels of abnormal earnings, whereas methods based on abnormal earnings growth emphasize capturing the variability in abnormal earnings over time. The formula for calculating abnormal earnings growth for period $t + 1$ (AEG_{t+1}) is as follows:[130]

$$AEG_{t+1} = E_{t+1} + D_t * R_e - (1 + R_e)E_t \tag{2.10}$$

In this formula, E_{t+1} represents the earnings for the period $t + 1$, D_t denotes the dividends paid in period t, and R_e is the cost of equity, necessary for adjusting both the dividends of period t and the earnings from the same period (E_t). To calculate the firm value (V_0) using the AEGM, the following formula is applied, considering both short-term earnings expectations and long-term growth prospects:[131]

$$V_0 = \frac{E_1}{R_e} + \sum_{t=1}^{T} \frac{AEG_{t+1}}{R_e(1 + R_e)^t} + \frac{AEG_{T+2}}{R_e(1 + R_e)^T (R_e - G_{AEG})} \tag{2.11}$$

In this equation first the expected earnings for the next period (E_1) are divided by the cost of equity (R_e), which represents the capitalized value of the next period's earnings. The formula then adds the present value of the expected abnormal earnings growth (AEG_{t+1}) for each period up to the terminal year T. For periods beyond this terminal year, the model can include a perpetual growth rate of abnormal earnings (G_{AEG}), recognizing the company's potential for sustainable long-term growth. Thus, this approach incorporates both immediate earnings potential and the expectation of future growth.[132]

Several empirical versions of the AEGM have been developed to estimate a firm's ICC, allowing the assumptions to be tailored to specific valuation scenarios.[133] These models, such as those by *Ohlson and Juettner-Nauroth* as well as *Easton*, generally adopt a similar short-term planning period for their calculations. However, they vary in their assumptions about abnormal earnings growth, initial dividends, and abnormal earnings in the last period.[134]

---

[130] See Daske et al. 2010, pp. 3 ff.

[131] See Echterling et al. 2015, pp. 237 f.

[132] See Echterling et al. 2015, pp. 238 f.

[133] See Echterling et al. 2015, pp. 238 f.

[134] See Ohlson and Juettner-Nauroth 2005, pp. 349–365; Easton 2004, pp. 73–95. Easton's model can be further subdivided into three specific ratios: the Price-Earnings ratio, the Price-Earnings-to-Growth ratio, and the Modified Price-Earnings-to-Growth ratio.

Unlike the RIM, the AEGM does not necessarily require adherence to the clean surplus relation to produce results comparable to the DDM, assuming a constant cost of capital.[135] However, *Penman* cautions about the risks of models like the AEGM that deviate from the clean surplus relation, particularly the potential for omitting critical balance sheet information and overreliance on volatile earnings forecasts.[136] Figure 2.3 provides a comprehensive overview of the approaches introduced in this chapter.

2.1.3 Interim Summary

Chapter 2.1 consolidates the key insights from the discussion of the international cost of equity. It provides an overview of how risk considerations, which are critical to political risk assessment and broader international finance analyses, affect the international cost of equity.

Central to the risk considerations are the principles of capital budgeting and *Markowitz's* portfolio theory in the context of international investment strategies. These principles form the foundation for evaluating the impact of policy changes on investor expectations. While diversifiable risks can be managed within investment portfolios, non-diversifiable risks remain and require appropriate compensation for investors.

International diversification extends this concept by incorporating assets from varying geopolitical environments, effectively reducing the unsystematic risks specific to domestic markets while exposing investors to global systematic risks. For example, a country's political risk can be diversified by investing in assets with low correlations across financial markets, exposing investors primarily to global systematic risk.

However, the pursuit of international diversification is often complicated by market barriers such as capital controls and repatriation taxes. These restrictions impede the free flow of capital and disrupt consistent pricing across global markets, thereby increasing the cost of capital applied to international investments. Moreover, the increased overall correlation among international markets, particularly during times of global economic stress, can diminish the risk-reducing benefits traditionally associated with international diversification.

Adding to the complexity, international diversification introduces additional risks, in particular exchange rate fluctuations. Exchange rate volatility can have

---

[135] See Echterling et al. 2015, p. 238.

[136] See Penman 2005, pp. 367–378.

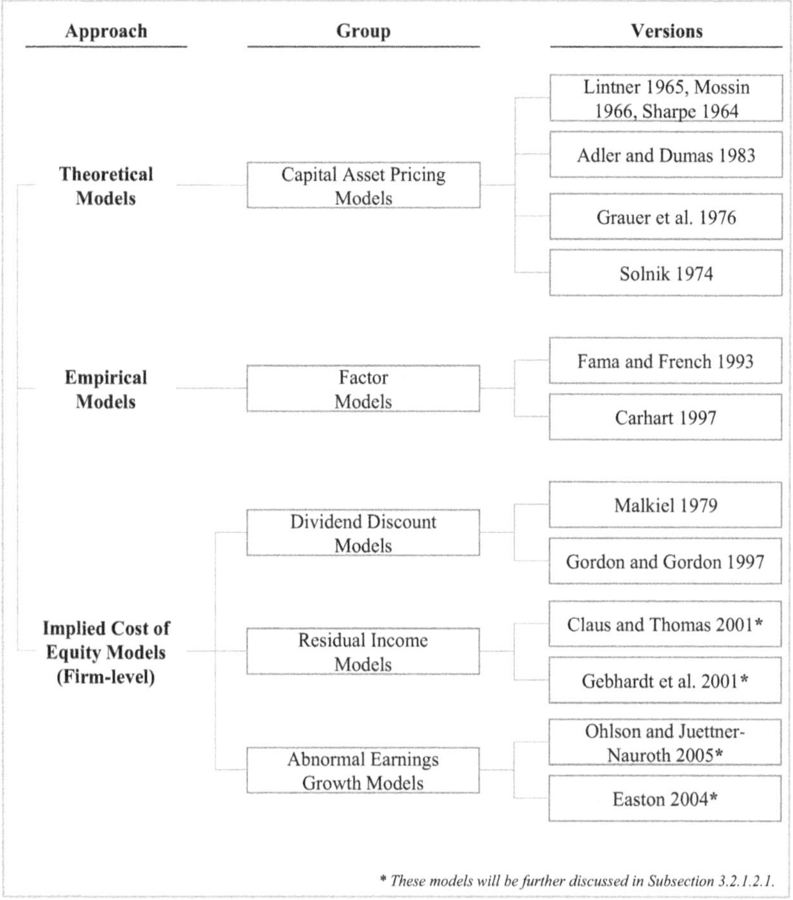

Fig. 2.3 Asset Pricing Models—Overview. (Source: Own Illustration.)

a significant impact on the profitability of foreign investments, as returns depend not only on the operating performance of the investment projects, but also on the fluctuating exchange rates between the local and investor currencies. While not the primary focus of this discussion, such risks are recognized as key factors influencing the dynamics of risk and return in global markets. Furthermore, this chapter has shown how asset pricing models, including the CAPM and the ICC, serve as fundamental tools for forecasting returns in an international context and for assessing the impact of geopolitical and economic changes on investor expectations.

In conclusion, the integration of the financial models discussed facilitates a comprehensive understanding of how economic, but especially political, uncertainties can reshape investor perceptions and alter investment dynamics. The chapter reinforces the need for investors and financial managers to incorporate these risks into their decision-making processes. The comprehensive assessments of relevant risk factors are critical for accurately determining the international cost of equity and for optimizing the risk-return trade-off in a global investment context.

2.2 Political Risk

Political risk emerges as a pivotal factor influencing international investment decisions and shaping the dynamics of financial markets. The unpredictability of political risks, combined with their potential to trigger significant market shifts, underscores the necessity for comprehensive political risk assessments.[137] Given the central role of political risk in this dissertation, this chapter aims to provide a thorough exploration of political risk, covering a wide range of dimensions and assessment methodologies.

2.2.1 Fundamentals

In the complex environment of international business and economics, political risk is a multifaceted concept, with different perceptions and classifications in academic contexts. This subchapter addresses the intricacies of political risk within the field of international business and economics.

First, various conceptual challenges, including interpretations, debates on predictability, and analysis of its intricate connection with political uncertainty, are explored. Second, it examines the diverse aspects of political risk by investigating various classifications and dimensions.

[137] See Hill 2003, p. 298.

2.2.1.1 Conceptual Framework

The concept of political risk in global business is characterized by its lack of a universally accepted definition and its interplay with political uncertainty. Initially, the term "political risk" was limited to the analysis of government actions related to nationalization or expropriation of foreign assets in the 1960s.[138] Early conceptualizations focused on government-business interactions,[139] but scholars identified limitations in these approaches. These included an overly narrow focus on adverse government actions, which resulted in a limited understanding of political risk and a tendency to view political risk as solely negative, overlooking its potential positive impacts. Additionally, there was an excessive emphasis on government factors, thereby neglecting other significant influences. The authors argue for a broader interpretation that views political risk as a dynamic entity influenced by a variety of internal and external factors, which would better reflect the complexity of international business environments.[140]

Over time, the meaning of political risk has broadened to include a wider range of interpretations and relationships.[141] A crucial aspect of the evolution of this subject is the distinction between political risk and political uncertainty.[142] Following *Knight's* framework (see Subsection 2.1.1.1.1), some academics distinguish between the two based on the measurability of risk versus the ambiguity of uncertainty.[143] Accordingly, political risk involves scenarios with quantifiable probabilities and outcomes, while political uncertainty is marked by an absence of information and is often linked to unpredictable events such as political violence or complications in assessing policy changes.[144]

In contrast, some contemporary definitions suggest that more recent understandings of political risk incorporate elements of political uncertainty, leading to their occasional interchangeable use.[145] This indicates an overlap between the

---

[138] See Bouchet 2003, p. 9.

[139] See Alon and Herbert 2009, p. 129.

[140] See for example Alon and Martin 1998, pp. 127 ff.

[141] See Bouchet 2003, p. 9.

[142] The introduction of political instability, characterized by government changes and social-political unrest, contributes to the complexity of the debate surrounding political risk and uncertainty. While distinct, these concepts often intersect, reflecting the intricate nature of their relationship (see Yi et al. 2020, p. 1051).

[143] See for example Benischke et al. 2022; John and Lawton 2018; López-Duarte and Vidal-Suárez 2010.

[144] See Benischke et al. 2022, p. 1.

[145] See for example Huang et al. 2015; Meschi 2005; Vu et al. 2017.

two concepts, particularly in international economics and business,[146] and continues the academic discourse on defining whether these concepts are distinct, overlapping, or sequential in nature amidst inconsistent terminology.[147]

Simon's defines political risk as:

> "*governmental or societal actions and policies, originating either within or outside the host country, and negatively affecting either a select group of, or the majority of, foreign business operations and investments.*"[148]

This definition is widely recognized[149] and aligns with *Fitzpatrick*, who emphasizes that political risk arises not just from discrete events but from continuous political processes.[150] *Alon and Martin* endorse *Simon's* comprehensive definition for its utility in considering political risk from various sources and levels, integrating factors from both host and home countries and considering external influences from international and global contexts. This holistic approach is particularly valuable for MNCs navigating complex political landscapes across different regions.[151] Building upon *Simon's* multidimensional definition of political risk, the next section will provide a detailed exploration of its various aspects.

2.2.1.2 Dimensions and Variations

This section examines the multifaceted nature of political risk, differentiating between its various types and levels. It situates political risk within the broader context of country risk and analyzes its implications and significance from a more holistic perspective.

2.2.1.2.1 Political Risk Levels

After discussing the challenges of defining political risk, this subsection explores its various dimensions as derived from the definition provided by *Simon*, with classifications expanded upon by *Alon and Herbert*. They identify three key dimensions based on *Simon's* definition: the impact of political risk, its origins, and its potential outcomes.[152]

---

[146] See John and Lawton 2018, p. 847; Root 1968, pp. 69–74.

[147] See Benischke et al. 2022, p. 2.

[148] Simon 1982, p. 68.

[149] See Alon and Herbert 2009, p. 129.

[150] See Fitzpatrick 1983, p. 250.

[151] See Alon and Martin 1998, p. 11.

[152] See Alon and Herbert 2009, pp. 129 ff.

The first dimension of political risk, as conceptualized by *Simon* and further developed by scholars like *Robock*, involves distinguishing between macro and micro levels, focusing on their distinct impacts and scope.[153] *Robock* describes macro-political risks as country-wide issues that affect all firms operating in a host country.[154] These can include major events, such as the overthrow of a government or a widespread economic crisis, that affect the entire business environment. Conversely, micro political risks are specific to particular firms or groups, resulting from targeted policies or local conditions. These risks have varying effects and are influenced by factors such as industry type, national origin, and dependence on local resources.[155]

Building upon this foundation, *Eiteman et al.* further refine the analysis of this first dimension of political risk. At the micro level, they focus on governance-related political risk, highlighting the complexities that MNCs face in complying with the legal and political framework of the host country. This includes navigating regulatory changes and bureaucratic hurdles. On a more macro level, they identify risks such as transfer risk, which stems from foreign exchange restrictions, and cultural and institutional risks. These include aspects such as corruption, protectionism, and the challenges of securing intellectual property rights, which can have a significant impact on business operations and profitability. In addition, *Eiteman et al.* extend the analysis beyond macro and micro risks by introducing global political risks. These include threats such as terrorism and cyber-attacks that transcend national borders and pose threats to the global operations and investments.[156]

The second dimension of classifying political risk focuses on identifying the origins of risk, underlining that the term "risk" encompasses a variety of contributing factors.[157] Building on *Simon's* definition of political risk, *Alon and Martin* present a macro-level model that categorizes sources of risk into governmental, societal, and economic dimensions. Within these dimensions, the model distinguishes between internal and external political risk factors. External factors include risks emanating from the home country, third countries, or broader global dynamics. Conversely, internal factors arise from within the host country and are influenced by its own political, social, and economic context. The model also provides various symptoms or indicators for each factor, enabling a proactive and

[153] See Alon and Martin 1998, p. 11.

[154] See Robock 1971, pp. 6–20.

[155] See Alon and Herbert 2009, p. 129; Alon and Martin 1998, pp. 11 f.

[156] See Eiteman et al. 2013, pp. 492 ff.

[157] See Miller 1992, p. 311.

comprehensive assessment of potential risks, helping to effectively identify and manage the various sources of political risk.[158]

For example, when examining political risk factors related to government, the model considers potential regime and policy change as an internal factor, while externally it evaluates the likelihood of political violence as a government-related risk factor.[159] Symptoms or indicators of internal government risk include events such as wars or revolutions, while indicators of external government risk include human rights violations. Figure 2.4 provides a detailed overview of this model and demonstrates the comprehensive approach to political risk analysis. It shows not only the government dimension, divided into internal and external factors, but also the societal and economic dimensions with their corresponding factors and symptoms.

The third dimension, as discussed by *Alon and Herbert*, relates to the potential consequences of political risk, suggesting that political risk encompasses both favorable and unfavorable outcomes, highlighting a neutral nature and the unpredictability of its consequences.[160] Scholarly perspectives in this dimension vary, with some viewing political risk as either a source of performance volatility or as a factor increasing the likelihood of adverse outcomes that could undermine projected returns. For example, *Robock* suggests that political risk may introduce business environment disruptions due to unexpected political shifts, which could significantly alter performance outcomes in either direction.[161] However, a pragmatic approach often emphasizes the negative implications of risk, associating them with possible financial losses or reduced return expectations.[162] This view prioritizes the anticipation of potential downsides over the exploration of new opportunities, a stance that finds considerable support in the existing literature.[163]

Moreover, the discourse in this dimension includes debates on what constitutes political risk. For example, specific financial challenges, such as predictable increases in foreign income taxes, may not qualify as political risk if companies and investors can plan for and mitigate their effects in advance. This distinction highlights the significance of foreseeability and adaptability in the management of

[158] See Alon and Martin 1998, pp. 10 ff.

[159] See Alon and Martin 1998, pp. 14 ff.

[160] See Alon and Herbert 2009, pp. 130 f.

[161] See Robock 1971, pp. 6–20.

[162] See Meldrum 2000, pp. 33–40; Simon 1982, pp. 62–70.

[163] See De Mortanges and Allers 1996, pp. 303 ff.; Roy and Roy 1993, pp. 92–95.

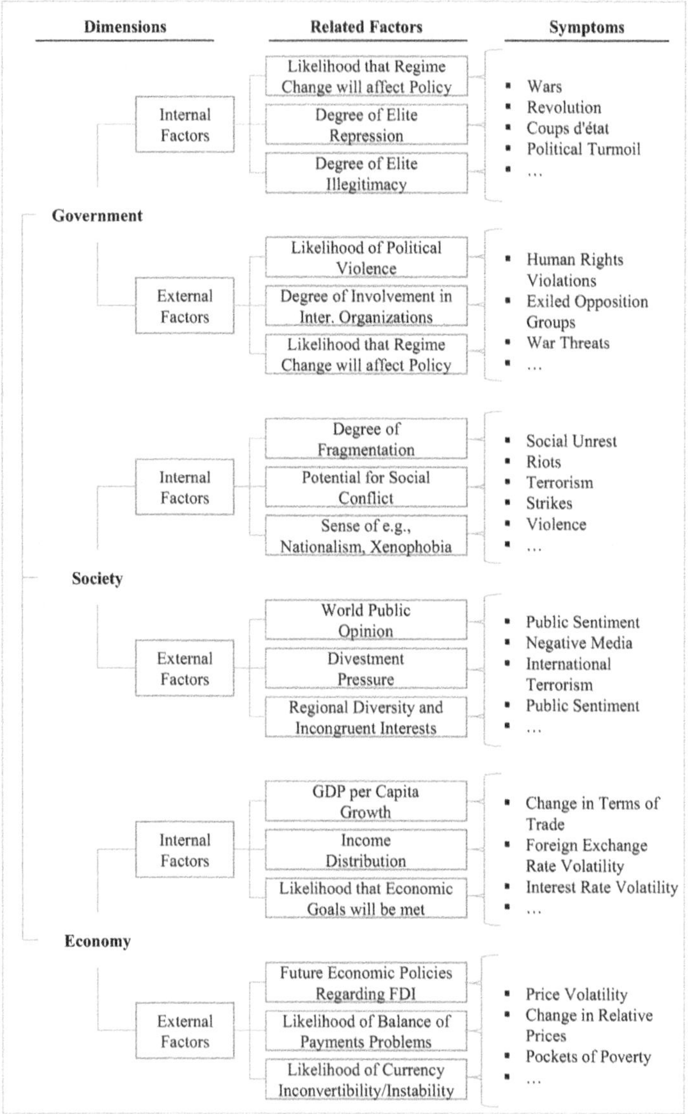

Fig. 2.4 Macro Political Risks according to Alon and Martin 1998. (Source: Own Illustration; following Alon and Martin 1998, pp. 10 ff.)

political risks, particularly with respect to investment decisions. Thus, it emphasizes that not all financial impacts resulting from political change are classified as political risks if they can be anticipated and managed.[164]

Besides the three dimensions identified by *Alon and Herbert*, other scholars have expanded the discourse to include the geographic scope of political risk. *Agmon and Findlay* argue that the economic repercussions of political power dynamics extend beyond international influence and also affect domestic firms and investors. They emphasize that political risk can affect market stability and asset valuation within a country, citing regulation as a prime example.[165]

2.2.1.2.2 Country Risk Component

After examining political risk levels in the previous subsection, this subsection analyzes how political risk interacts with broader economic and social factors, placing it within the expansive landscape of country risk. Country risk, as defined by *Meldrum*, includes the additional uncertainties encountered in international business transactions compared to domestic operations. These uncertainties arise from differences in national economic structures, policies, socio-political institutions, geography, and currencies. This broadens the perspective, moving beyond political risk to encompass the varied uncertainties present in international business, including differences in economic and financial structures.[166]

Political risk, influenced by government action or general political uncertainty, is closely linked to the economic and social elements of a country. For example, economic instability can lead to sudden changes in government policies that impact businesses, while social unrest or shifts in societal values can prompt alterations in government policies, thereby modifying the business landscape. Consequently, a comprehensive risk assessment must take into account both the direct political risks arising from government actions and the underlying economic and social conditions that could trigger these changes.[167]

Several approaches are available for analyzing this broad political environment. *Bouchet* proposes an expanded framework for country risk assessment that encompasses socio-political, economic, and environmental dimensions. Within this framework socio-political risks pertain to changes in the political landscape and alterations in governmental policies, whereas social risks include movements that could impact foreign or domestic policies. Economically, risks can

---

[164] See Butler 2016, p. 281.

[165] See Agmon and Findlay 1982, pp. 74–77.

[166] See Meldrum 2000, p. 33.

[167] See Bouchet 2003; p. 22–25; Westerman and Hall 2011, pp. 121 f.

be categorized as either macroeconomic or microeconomic, affecting the entire economy or specific industries, respectively. Additionally, natural disasters such as earthquakes are significant factors in the overall risk landscape.[168]

Researchers have developed more detailed classifications of risk types and characteristics that are essential for comprehensive risk assessment and monitoring.[169] *Miller's* approach proposes an integrated risk management strategy that addresses uncertainties collectively rather than in isolation. This broad management perspective acknowledges various interconnected uncertainties, including those that are firm-specific, industry-specific, and related to the general environment.[170]

Miller's general environmental uncertainties include social, natural, macroeconomic, political, and (government) policy uncertainties, each with distinct effects on the business environment. Social uncertainty can arise from mismatches between societal values and government and business practices, leading to political and policy instabilities. Natural uncertainties can stem from environmental factors, impacting productivity and operations, especially in sectors like agriculture. Macroeconomic uncertainty refers to the unpredictability of the economy, which affects factors such as inflation and pricing decisions for MNCs.[171]

As defined by *Miller*, political uncertainty refers to significant shifts within political regimes, embodying the risks and opportunities associated with potential or actual changes in the political system.[172] This instability can arise from conflicts, governmental overthrows, or non-violent democratic transitions. Moreover, *Miller* further distinguishes policy uncertainty, which results from the unpredictability of government actions that affect the business sector. This includes unexpected economic reforms and regulatory changes that introduce variability into economic management and affect business operations and investment decisions.[173]

---

[168] See Bouchet 2003, p. 25.

[169] Including Desta 1985, pp. 40–53; Meldrum 2000, pp. 33–40; Miller 1992, pp. 311–331.

[170] See Miller 1992, p. 313. The emphasis in this subsection is exclusively on general environmental uncertainties. For firm and industry-specific uncertainties, refer to Miller 1992, pp. 316 ff.

[171] See Miller 1992, pp. 313 ff.; Werner et al. 1996, pp. 574–576.

[172] In Miller's perspective, "risk" refers to the measurable unpredictability of a firm's outcomes, influenced by internal and external factors. "Uncertainty", however, pertains to the unpredictability of environmental or organizational variables impacting the firm, often less quantifiable (see Miller 1992, p. 312).

[173] See Miller 1992, pp. 313 f.

In contrast to political uncertainty, policy uncertainty focuses specifically on how government decisions directly affect the economic environment. The rationale for this distinction is that changes in government (political uncertainty) do not necessarily lead to changes in government policies (policy uncertainty) that affect business investment, nor does political stability inherently imply the absence of policy uncertainty.[174] Figure 2.5 depicts the five general environmental uncertainties as identified by *Miller*.

Miller emphasizes the intricate and interconnected nature of the five general environmental uncertainties. While analytically categorizing them is insightful, their overlapping nature complicates this segmentation.[175] For instance, energy deficits may result from natural causes or governmental mismanagement, blurring the boundaries between risk categories. These intricacies challenge the accurate classification of risks and significantly impact corporate operations and decision-making processes.[176]

While *Miller's* classification is widely recognized, scholars such as *Agmon* and *Bunn and Mustafaoglu* do not explicitly differentiate between political and policy uncertainties, often grouping them under the broader umbrella of political risk.[177] Furthermore, other scholars differentiate between subcategories of policy uncertainty,[178] or classify electoral uncertainty as a distinct component of political uncertainty,[179] reflecting the diversity of perspectives in this area of research.

2.2.2 Assessment

Following the exploration of the fundamentals of political risk in international business, this subchapter delves into a more focused analysis of political risk assessment. Conducting a political risk assessment shares the same objectives as country risk analysis: to identify, elucidate, and evaluate key risk factors, their origins, intensities, and emerging patterns within a particular country or region.[180]

---

[174] See Miller 1992, p. 314.

[175] See Miller 1992, p. 316.

[176] See Bouchet 2003, p. 25.

[177] See Agmon 1985, pp. 3 ff.; Bunn and Mustafaoglu 1978, p. 1557.

[178] For example, monetary policy (see Husted et al. 2020, pp. 20–36) or economic policy uncertainty (see Baker et al. 2016, pp. 1593–1636).

[179] See Julio and Yook 2016, p. 46.

[180] See Sun et al. 2021, p. 4329.

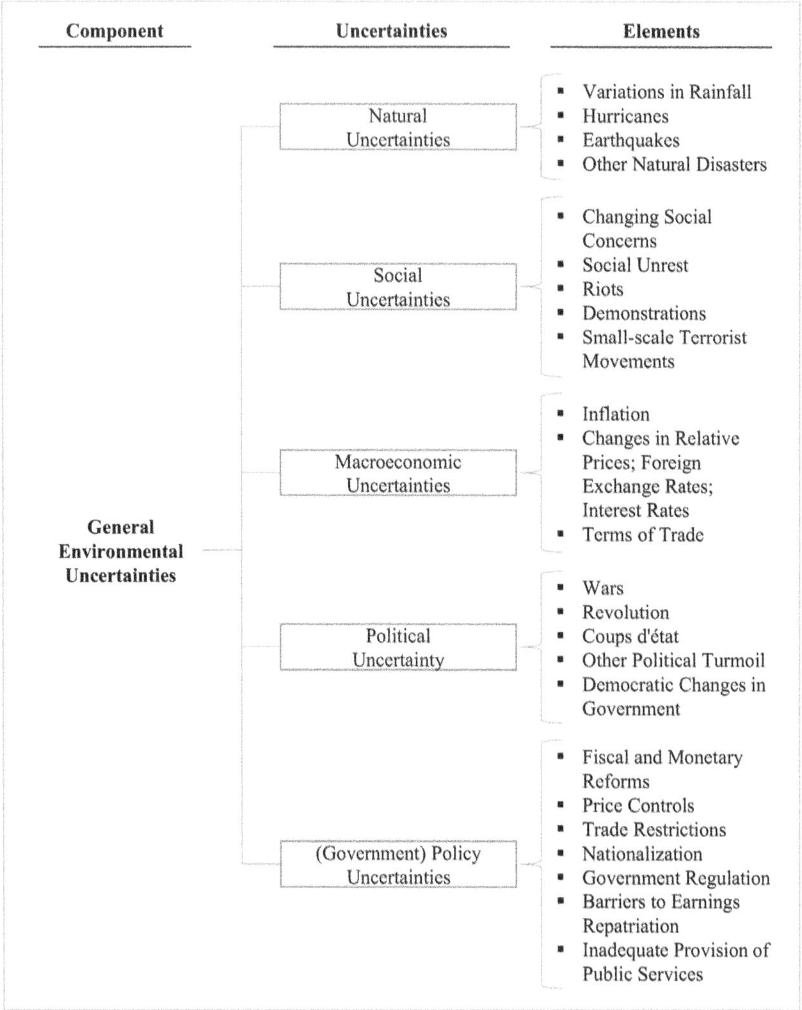

Fig. 2.5 Environmental Uncertainties Categorized by Miller 1992. (Source: Own Illustration; following Miller 1992, p. 314, Table 2.1.)

The task of assessing political risk presents inherent challenges due to its elusive and complex nature,[181] as outlined in the previous chapter.

The following sections of this thesis provide a detailed examination of political risk assessment. While not exhaustive, they provide a framework that includes relevant determinants of political risk assessment, different approaches to evaluation, and an analysis of the different perspectives of risk analysts.

2.2.2.1 Analytical Determinants

The subsequent three subsections provide a comprehensive exploration of the elements involved in assessing political risk. The first subsection examines the historical evolution of political risk, illustrating the impact of global events and market fluctuations on the identification of risk factors. The following subsection scrutinizes the diverse characteristics of political risk across different investment types, underscoring the importance of customized evaluation approaches. The final subsection traces the progression of political risk assessment methodologies from early list-based methods to today's data-driven models.

2.2.2.1.1 Temporal Influence

The evolution of political risk reflects the changing dynamics of global markets and political landscapes. This concept gained prominence in the 1960s, a period marked by significant geopolitical upheaval. Initially, the focus was on the nationalization and expropriation of foreign assets, as seen in events such as the Suez Canal crisis and in countries such as Cuba and Chile. In the 1970s, the narrative shifted to the role of FDI in the development of emerging markets. During this period, more emphasis was placed on attracting foreign investment as a catalyst for economic growth.[182]

However, the onset of the sovereign debt crisis in the 1980s presented new challenges. This era highlighted the complexities of sovereign default and credit assessment, particularly in developing countries with high debt levels, rising interest rates, and fluctuating dollar valuations.[183] As a result of the debt crises of the 1970s and 1980s, the focus of risk assessment shifted to issues of creditworthiness. This was a period of heightened awareness of how sovereign defaults and financial instability in one country could spread through the global economy, causing spillover effects throughout the global economy.[184]

---

[181] See Bekaert et al. 2016, pp. 1 f.

[182] See Jarvis and Griffiths 2007, p. 8.

[183] See Jarvis and Griffiths 2007, p. 8.

[184] See Belghitar and Clark 2011, pp. 241 ff.

The 1990s brought a further shift in the perception of political risk. The Asian financial crisis of 1997–1998 had a significant impact on global economic and financial stability, particularly in relation to currency and exchange rate issues.[185] This crisis exposed vulnerabilities in financial stability and regulatory transparency in globally interconnected yet institutionally diverse markets. This period underscored the importance of understanding political risk through a nuanced lens due to global financial interdependence, and significantly influenced the advancement of risk research by requiring more sophisticated analytical tools.[186]

With the beginning of the twenty-first century, and especially after the terrorist attacks against the United States on September 11, 2001, political risk reached new dimensions. The extensive effects of geopolitical risks have become apparent, demonstrating how isolated domestic events can have reverberating consequences throughout the world's economic and political systems.[187] Various factors, such as nationalizations in Latin America and the destabilizing effects of events like the Arab Spring, influence the contemporary political risk landscape.[188]

At the same time, new challenges have emerged, such as creeping expropriation, global terrorism, and the rise of MNCs from emerging markets, often to the detriment of foreign investors.[189] The relevance of political risk is increasingly recognized in academic research, which has intensified in response to the growing uncertainties in the global landscape and the increased impact of political events due to globalization.[190]

2.2.2.1.2 Analysis Advancements

The development of political risk assessment is intricately linked to the broader evolution of political risk. Political risk assessment has evolved from basic listings of potential governmental impacts on businesses to sophisticated analyses incorporating data analytics and technology. This development underscores the importance of political risk as a primary concern among practitioners, a theme *Baas* and other scholars have recurrently observed over the past several decades.

---

[185] See Sun et al. 2021, p. 4332.

[186] See Belghitar and Clark 2011, pp. 241 ff.

[187] See Jarvis and Griffiths 2007, p. 9.

[188] See Kirikkaleli et al. 2021, p. 328.

[189] See Kotabe and Kothari 2016, p. 729; Oetzel 2005, p. 765. Creeping expropriation refers to the gradual erosion of property rights through government measures like taxation, regulation, or legal changes, contrasting with expropriation, which involves direct government seizure of assets (see Graham et al. 2018, pp. 1785 f.).

[190] See Yi et al. 2020, p. 1055.

They emphasize the critical role of political risk assessment in the corporate world, highlighting its enduring relevance and the complex challenges it poses for businesses and investments.[191]

Jarvis and Griffiths present a comprehensive and evolving framework for political risk assessment that captures the dynamic interplay between global business and political change in four phases. Their analysis begins with a review of early political risk assessment practices dominated by the catalogue school method. This initial phase was characterized by efforts to list potential government actions that could negatively impact investments, based on the premise of near-perfect markets and viewing political factors as mere external disturbances.[192]

Subsequently, the field progressed into what has been referred to as the system-event school marking a significant shift towards understanding the relationship between political systems and market stability. Analysts began to use structural-functional analysis to predict political risk based on the characteristics of different political systems, providing a deeper perspective on political risk assessment.[193]

The third phase of political risk assessment development shifted from broad theoretical models to a more practical, method-oriented analysis. This approach focused on context-specific evaluations tailored to meet the requirements of specific industries or projects. Although this approach showed progress towards more applicable and pragmatic risk assessment, it faced challenges due to the lack of standardized methodologies and the difficulty of achieving consistent predictive accuracy.[194]

The latest advancement in political risk assessment integrates data analytics and technological progress. This approach leverages advanced risk databases and analytical techniques to forge a dynamic, interconnected comprehension of political risk. It methodically identifies and evaluates the catalysts of complex political events, offering a more flexible and predictive framework of political risk in a globally interconnected context.[195]

---

[191] See for example Baas 2010, p. 135; Jarvis and Griffiths 2007, pp. 9 ff.

[192] See Baas 2010, p. 137; Jarvis and Griffiths 2007, pp. 10 f.

[193] See Jarvis and Griffiths 2007, pp. 12 f.

[194] See Jarvis and Griffiths 2007, pp. 17 f.

[195] See Jarvis and Griffiths 2007, pp. 19 f.

2.2.2.1.3 Investment Type Exposure

Political risk significantly impacts diverse areas, including the corporate realm,[196] the sovereign sector,[197] and the financial markets,[198] impacting different stakeholders distinctively. Reflecting on this diversity, the academic study of political risk has evolved considerably. While initially focused on FDI, research since the 1990s has broadened to include a wider range of activities, such as exporting and franchising. This broader scope emphasizes the various perspectives in international investment scenarios that impact the risk assessment approach.[199]

Bouchet highlights these different perceptions of country and political risk, particularly among groups like exporters, foreign creditors, and investors.[200] In the context of FDI, investors' primary objective is to identify the best locations globally, necessitating a thorough assessment of the political and economic stability of prospective countries. For instance, when a MNC plans to establish a factory overseas, it must evaluate the risk of political changes that could impact its operations.[201] Similarly, cross-border acquisitions are influenced by various factors, such as changes in regulatory, taxation and fiscal policies, as well as the risk of asset expropriation or nationalization.[202]

In the realm of international portfolio investments, which includes investments in foreign equities and fixed-income securities, large institutional investors like pension funds, mutual funds, and insurance companies play a significant role. A critical factor for these investors is the influence of political events on the repatriation of funds, which involves assessment challenges such as the implementation of capital controls.[203]

In commercial bank loans, foreign commercial banks generally lend in the host country, the assessment shifts to evaluating the likelihood of borrower default, taking into account the impact of the political climate on the ability to repay. This involves examining factors such as government stability and fiscal policies.[204]

Exporters, although potentially a separate group, are often not distinctly categorized. Their exposures, arising from commercial or industrial activities abroad,

---

[196] See for example Faccio 2006, pp. 369–386; Shleifer and Vishny 1994, pp. 995–1025.

[197] See for example Bekaert et al. 2016, pp. 1–23; Henisz 2000, pp. 1–31.

[198] See for example Stiglitz 1993, pp. 19–52.

[199] See Kobrin 1979, pp. 67 ff.; Robock 1971, pp. 6 ff.

[200] See Bouchet 2003, pp. 13 f.

[201] See Eiteman et al. 2013, p. 487.

[202] See Cao et al. 2019, p. 440.

[203] See Cosset and Suret 1995, p. 303.

[204] See Bouchet 2003, pp. 13 f.

tend to be more like those of commercial banks.[205] In fact, *Eiteman et al.* suggest that the risk associated with exporting is the lowest related to political risk.[206]

It is important to note that the perception of political risk varies across investment types, reflecting the unique challenges and priorities of each area. However, the principles for evaluating political risk in portfolio investments can be adapted for FDI risk assessment, despite the differences mentioned above.[207]

2.2.2.2 Assessment Approaches

In the broader analysis of country risk, political risk has emerged as an increasingly vital area of focus.[208] This section assesses country and political risk methodologies, categorized into quantitative and qualitative approaches, as well as politically focused methods. Political risk assessment frequently begins with initial insights gleaned from a variety of sources, including local newspapers, radio and television broadcasts, diplomatic cables, and the experience of business professionals familiar with the country.[209]

First, the section outlines quantitative methods and highlights their data-driven nature and limitations. Next, it transitions to qualitative approaches, examining different techniques and their integration with quantitative data to yield a comprehensive risk analysis. Political risk and uncertainty metrics are also presented emphasizing specific political measures that encapsulate both the quantitative and qualitative aspects of risk assessment. While not an exhaustive compilation, the presented methodologies offer a fundamental understanding of the multidimensional landscape of risk assessment.

2.2.2.2.1 Quantitative Methods

Initially focusing on qualitative political risk analysis in the 1960s and 1970s, country risk assessment literature transitioned to a more quantitative approach in the 1980s and 1990s, particularly in predicting sovereign defaults and financial crises.[210] Quantitative approaches for analyzing country and political risk cover a range of techniques, each with its unique methodology and applicability. The choice of method for assessing political risk depends on the context and the available data. Quantitative methods can be categorized as relative or absolute

[205] See Bouchet 2003, p. 13.
[206] See Eiteman et al. 2013, p. 489.
[207] See Bouchet 2003, p. 149.
[208] See Sun et al. 2021, p. 4329.
[209] See Eiteman et al. 2013, p. 493.
[210] See Bouchet 2003, p. 16.

measures, as per *Schroeder*,[211] or as analytical or econometric approaches, as per *Bouchet*.[212]

Regression analysis and model building involve identifying variables that may impact political or country risk and testing their significance in the model. This method has been utilized in research to estimate country risk premiums and analyze their correlation with equity returns and FDI flows. Likewise, logit and probit models, which are frequently employed in cross-border lending determinations,[213] estimate the likelihood of a binary outcome, such as default or expropriation, using logistic or normal distributions.[214]

Another quantitative method is Monte Carlo simulation, which generates probability distributions and risk assessments through random sampling. It involves identifying relevant variables, determining probabilities for forecast errors, and utilizing computer simulations, providing detailed estimates of probability distributions.[215]

Discriminant analysis is another widely used technique that classifies observations into predefined groups based on predetermined characteristics. This method can contribute to the improvement of investment decision-making by sorting countries into various risk categories.[216] Thus, in many statistical approaches such as discriminant and logit analysis, country risk assessment is framed as a task of classifying countries into groups that represent different predefined levels of risk as determined by the country's economic outlook.[217]

The development of machine learning has resulted in significant progress in quantitative country and political risk assessment. The incorporation of a multi-criteria decision-making method and machine learning models has evolved the analysis and evaluation from statistical models to a more flexible and robust framework. Artificial neural networks have been utilized for predicting sovereign debt risk, as well as for broader risk assessment. Despite technological progress, choosing suitable risk indicators and weights remains a key challenge, mainly due to the lack of a well-established theoretical framework for their assessment.[218]

---

[211] See Schroeder 2008, pp. 498–501.

[212] See Bouchet 2003, pp. 115 ff. The focus in this thesis is on the econometric approaches.

[213] See Bouchet 2003, pp. 117 ff.

[214] See Solodkov and Tsyganova 2017, p. 305.

[215] See Bouchet 2003, pp. 121 f.

[216] See Bouchet 2003, pp. 115–117.

[217] See Sun et al. 2021, p. 4333.

[218] See Sun et al. 2021, pp. 4333 f.

An important challenge of quantitative approaches is that they depend on historical data for predicting future outcomes, especially across a diverse and heterogeneous sample of countries. This dependence can lead to inaccuracies in predicting future events, as previous patterns may not always be reliable indicators, especially in rapidly evolving or unforeseeable political circumstances.[219] Thus, quantitative methods can provide an overview of a country's economic and political conditions, but they may not capture all the necessary socio-political nuances. Consequently, a qualitative approach to country and political risk analysis is particularly beneficial for a comprehensive risk assessment.[220]

2.2.2.2.2 Qualitative Methods

Qualitative analysis can close some of the gaps mentioned above by delving deeply into the socio-political context, examining policies, assessing the quality of governance, and considering geopolitical tensions. Although these elements are often challenging to gauge, they are important components of political and country risk.[221] Their assessment is critical in determining how changes in a country's political or economic circumstances may affect business operations or investment returns. It involves evaluating factors such as political stability, economic practices, and social dynamics to identify potential political threats.[222]

There are two main types of qualitative political risk assessment methods: unstructured and structured approaches. Unstructured qualitative approaches are characterized by their flexible nature, allowing for adaptive exploration of political environments. An example of this is the "grand tour", where executives conduct preliminary research and engage in discussions with local government officials and business leaders. While this strategy can yield significant grassroots-level insights, it often presents difficulties in effectively incorporating selective data into the wider framework of decision-making processes. Another unstructured technique involves engaging external experts, such as scholars and political figures, who offer perspectives based on extensive experience, commonly referred to as the "old hands" or "expert system". However, it is important to note that expert opinions may be subject to personal biases, which could lead to inaccuracies in the assessment.[223]

---

[219] See Bouchet 2003, pp. 97 ff.

[220] See Solodkov and Tsyganova 2017, pp. 300 ff.

[221] See Solodkov and Tsyganova 2017, pp. 303 ff.

[222] See Bouchet 2003, pp. 70 ff.

[223] See Al Khattab et al. 2011, p. 99.

Structured methods are defined by their systematic procedures, ensuring that data collection and analysis are uniform across different scenarios. The Delphi technique, for instance, involves a panel of experts who evaluate and refine their opinions on topics such as political stability and the investment climate over several rounds. This iterative approach consolidates expert judgments into a consensus, enhancing the accuracy of the collective assessment. However, the technique may inadvertently neglect outlier perspectives in its pursuit of agreement.[224] Similarly, standardized checklists serve as a methodical tool for examining core political risk factors. They provide a comprehensive review but may not capture the nuanced insights gained from firsthand experience in the countries under consideration.[225]

Comparative rating systems, similar to the checklist method, are commonly used as a structured approach in risk assessment practices, including the assessment of credit risk. These systems allow for country comparisons based on a set of established criteria. As outlined by *Solodkov and Tsyganova*, the process of country ranking unfolds in three stages. It starts with identifying critical variables, such as political stability and economic performance metrics, to ensure a comprehensive analysis. After selecting the variables, each one is assigned a weight that cumulatively equal one. The weights are often determined using the previously discussed Delphi technique to leverage expert insights. The final stage involves calculating the index by summing the weighted factors, with a higher index typically indicating greater risk.[226]

Whilst rating systems simplify the forecasting and assessment process for international practitioners, they face challenges such as the lack of a solid theoretical basis for parameter selection and weighting, leading to potential inaccuracies. Additionally, applying uniform criteria to all countries may overlook unique national characteristics and struggle to predict extreme situations such as wars or revolutions. Furthermore, they may restrict their assessment to a limited set of indicators and exclude broader risk factors, which may result in overlooking important aspects of country and political risk.[227]

2.2.2.2.3 Uncertainty and Political Risk Metrics

This section focuses on measuring uncertainty and political risk, distinct from traditional quantitative and qualitative methods, by addressing the unpredictable

224 See De Mortanges and Allers 1996, p. 307.

225 See Bouchet 2003, pp. 79 ff.; Brüggen 2011, p. 109.

226 See Solodkov and Tsyganova 2017, p. 304.

227 See Solodkov and Tsyganova 2017, pp. 302 ff.

nature of political events and their immediate impact on markets and businesses. Specialized indices are used to estimate uncertainty, offering insights that are critical to managing risk more specifically than the broader approaches discussed above. These measures are categorized into three broad groups: general uncertainty indices, specialized measures, and political indicators, each providing unique insights into significant political shifts and their impact on financial and business metrics.[228]

Within the first category, the World Uncertainty Index (WUI) developed by *Ahir et al.* is a general index that quantifies uncertainty by analyzing the frequency of the term "uncertainty" in reports from the Economist Intelligence Unit (EIU). Covering 143 countries since 1952, the WUI provides broad cross-country and historical comparability, benefiting from the EIU's consistent examination of economic and political trends. However, one of its limitations is its reliance on a single report for each country per quarter, which can lead to sampling noise.[229]

Another measure in this category is the Chicago Board Options Exchange Volatility Index (VIX). The VIX forecasts volatility in Standard & Poor's 500 index options, reflecting United States stock market volatility and global risk sentiment. It is derived from options prices and reflects the expected fluctuation in the United States stock market, inclusive of a variance risk premium.[230] While the VIX serves as a proxy for market uncertainty, its primary focus on market factors limits its ability to evaluate non-market elements. Furthermore, its accuracy depends on market liquidity, which can reduce its reliability in emerging markets.[231]

As an alternative, the Economic Policy Uncertainty (EPU) index, developed by *Baker et al.*, provides a more comprehensive measure. The EPU index combines data from three sources: the frequency of newspaper articles discussing policy uncertainty and economic conditions, the number of federal tax code provisions set to expire, and the disparity among economic forecasts. This allows the EPU index to capture fluctuations in policy uncertainty over a wide range of time. In this way, it differs from the VIX index, which is narrowly focused on short-term market volatility. The EPU index is particularly adept at reflecting shifts in market sentiment in response to major political and economic events, such as elections or

[228] See Lei and Luo 2023, pp. 88 ff.

[229] See Ahir et al. 2022, p. 1.

[230] See Bekaert and Hoerova 2014, p. 181; Bekaert et al. 2014, p. 491.

[231] See Al-Thaqeb and Algharabali 2019, p. 2.

financial crises, thus providing a nuanced perspective on market dynamics under conditions of political uncertainty.[232]

Specialized measures, which form the second category, include *Hassan et al.'s* approach, which assesses political risk at the firm level by analyzing the content of earnings conference calls. This approach provides insights into how individual corporations perceive and manage political risks.[233] Another approach is the Geopolitical Risk index by *Caldara and Iacoviello*, which specializes in assessing global geopolitical risks, such as wars and terrorism. By monitoring the volume of news articles related to these topics, the index captures the impact of geopolitical events that may not be reflected in broader indices, thereby offering a targeted lens through which to assess the implications of geopolitical instability on global markets.[234]

The third category, political indicators, relates directly to the analysis of specific political events or phenomena and their associated risks. *Giambona et al.* identify key measures of risk within this domain, including corruption, political instability, institutional quality, and the risk of sovereign debt default.[235] Moreover, global political crises are highlighted as pivotal in gauging the overarching political uncertainty.[236] Elections, a fundamental element within this category, are recognized as significant predictors of political uncertainty, as they can lead to potential alterations in national leadership. This in turn can lead to changes in policies affecting regulation, trade policy and taxation. The uncertainty stemming from electoral outcomes offers a unique lens through which the impact of political uncertainty on financial metrics can be examined, setting it apart from other economic factors.[237] *Gala et al.* adopt this perspective, demonstrating that the unpredictability associated with electoral results and the ambiguity of future governmental policy decisions are crucial in influencing economic and market dynamics.[238] Figure 2.6 concisely summarizes the approaches detailed in this subsection.

---

[232] See Baker et al. 2016, pp. 1593 ff.

[233] See Hassan et al. 2019, p. 2135.

[234] See Caldara and Iacoviello 2022, p. 1195.

[235] See Giambona et al. 2017, p. 523.

[236] See Lei and Luo 2023, p. 87.

[237] See Julio and Yook 2012, p. 46.

[238] See Gala et al. 2023, pp. 78–81.

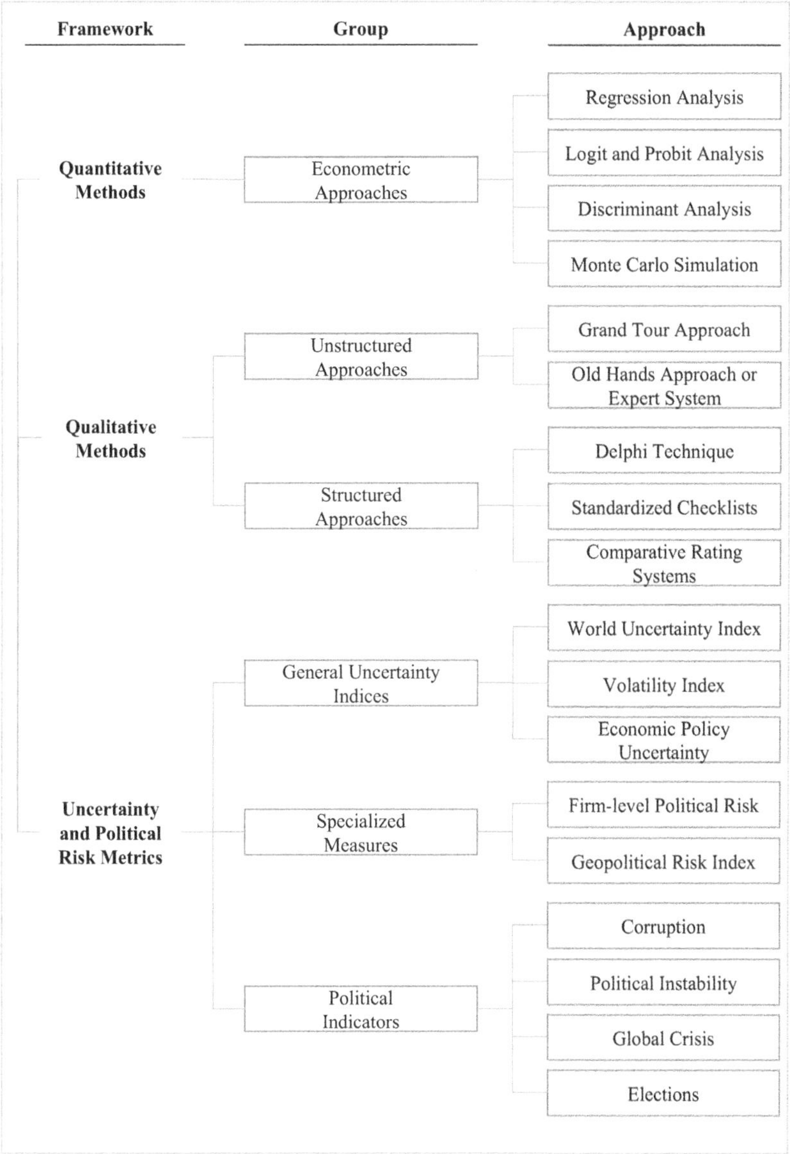

Fig. 2.6 Political Risk Assessment Approaches—Overview. (Source: Own Illustration.)

2.2.2.3 Risk Analysts

The preceding chapter outlined a range of methodologies and considerations pertinent to assessing political risk. It emphasized the necessity of a structured and holistic approach for a nuanced and precise evaluation, given the intricate nature of political risk. Specialized analysts in the field of political risk assessment possess specific knowledge of the interplay between national policies, political dynamics, and global economic trends. This expertise is essential for analyzing international markets and predicting the potential impacts on investments and operations.[239]

Schroeder categorizes these analysts into four distinct groups: official assessors, in-house assessors, specialized (proprietary) assessors, and "the market".[240] This section examines the roles, methodologies, and insights of these four groups and their importance in understanding political risk in international business within the global economic framework. The section also discusses how information from these groups can be integrated into capital budgeting decisions.

2.2.2.3.1 Official Assessors

Schroeder highlights the role of official assessors in evaluating political risks, especially in the context of international investment and lending. These assessors fall into two primary groups: multilateral agencies and bilateral agencies, each differing in approach and focus.[241] Multilateral organizations, such as the World Bank and the European Bank for Reconstruction and Development, focus on financing development programs that reinforce infrastructure and endorse emerging industries across developing nations. These programs are essential for promoting sustainable economic growth and may require sustained funding over extended periods. For example, the World Bank's Multilateral Investment Guarantee Agency provides coverage for risks such as expropriation, political violence, currency inconvertibility, and breach of contract.[242]

Bilateral agencies, including export credit agencies, assist companies in FDI or export promotion. The primary concern of these agencies is the likelihood of default that a corporation may face in specific countries. Export credit agencies

---

[239] See Jarvis and Griffiths 2007, p. 18.

[240] Schroeder's method presents a contrast to the classification system proposed by for example Radelet and Sachs, which categorizes sources of risk assessment into ratings, independent firms, investment and commercial banks, and multilateral agencies (see Radelet and Sachs 1998, pp. 11–12).

[241] See Schroeder 2008, pp. 507 f.

[242] See Bekaert and Hodrick 2018, pp. 647 ff.

determine insurance premium rates based on their evaluation of the local business climate, as well as the political and economic stability of the region.[243] The United States' Overseas Private Investment Corporation is an example of a national agency providing political risk insurance, and several similar agencies exist in other Organization for Economic Co-operation and Development (OECD) countries.[244] These government or international agency-backed political risk insurance programs serve as a deterrent to host country interference with investments. They provide contract protection and greater leverage in recovering claims from governments in the event of a political risk incident, which can include measures like asset seizure and trade pressure.[245]

Methodologically, official assessors typically employ a combination of qualitative and quantitative methods to assess risk. This involves compiling and analyzing data and applying subjective indicators to evaluate the business climate affecting financial transactions in a country. The assessment process also benefits from contributions by international and policy experts, such as academics and economists. Overall, official assessors provide a comprehensive view of political and financial risks in international transactions, balancing concerns about debt repayment with sustainable development and financial stability.[246]

Effectively integrating this information into the capital budgeting process can improve decision making and risk management.[247] Insights from government export credit agencies, historically the main providers of political risk insurance, together with private insurers, now jointly contribute to the provision of political risk insurance. By analyzing political risk insurance premiums, businesses can estimate the likelihood of political risk occurrences. Even companies that do not actively seek political risk insurance can benefit from the valuable information provided by quoted rates, which can assist in adjusting the valuation process. Government organizations may offer political risk insurance at more favorable rates than private market alternatives, providing a viable option that impacts valuation.[248]

If corporations could obtain complete insurance coverage for all risk events and receive full compensation for losses, accounting for political risk would involve adjusting the insurance premium from expected cash flows. However,

[243] See Schroeder 2008, p. 507.

[244] See Butler 2016, p. 290.

[245] See Bekaert and Hodrick 2018, pp. 647 ff.

[246] See Schroeder 2008, pp. 507 f.

[247] See Butler 2016, p. 291.

[248] See Bekaert and Hodrick 2018, p. 644.

securing comprehensive insurance coverage can be challenging due to the broad range of factors associated with political risk, which often precludes full protection of current investments.[249] Insurable political risks include expropriation due to war, revolution, civil disturbance or terrorism, frustration of contracts due to host government actions, repatriation restrictions and currency inconvertibility issues.[250]

2.2.2.3.2 In-house Assessors

Even though *Hashmi and Guvenli* highlight the common use of external political risk assessments in investment strategies,[251] the demand for firm-specific political risk analyses has led to an increase for in-house research by professional analysts. This shift stems from the inconsistency observed in assessments provided by external analysts and the distinct political risks that individual firms encounter, including those specific to their respective industries. In-house analysts tailor their evaluations to meet the specific needs of their clients, recognizing, for example, that the vulnerabilities of financial and non-financial companies can differ significantly.[252]

In-house risk assessment practices, particularly in financial firms, are deeply influenced by their individual institutional structures. These firms develop risk assessment strategies considering various factors such as domestic regulations and monitoring. For risk and return analysis, financial firms typically prefer market-based techniques to traditional accounting data. This is because market prices reflect current conditions and are responsive to short-term and long-term market changes. This approach allows to quickly adapt to changing market dynamics and prioritize a real-time understanding of risk over historical data.[253]

Conversely, non-financial or productive firms view country risk mainly through the lens of FDI. They focus on returns on their investments and the repatriation of profits. Therefore, these firms lean towards evaluation methods that highlight long-term, structural investment risks, frequently disregarding short-term market variations in favor of a more consistent and long-lasting investment perspective. Their evaluations typically rely on accounting data that analyzes and monitors investment feasibility over time.[254]

---

[249] See Bekaert and Hodrick 2018, p. 648.

[250] See Butler 2016, p. 290.

[251] See Hashmi and Guvenli 1992, p. 137.

[252] See Eiteman et al. 2013, p. 493.

[253] See Schroeder 2008, pp. 508 f.

[254] See Schroeder 2008, p. 508.

2.2.2.3.3 Specialized Assessors

The third risk assessors group is comprised of two key specialized agencies in risk assessment: credit rating and global rating agencies. These agencies evaluate different aspects of risk.[255]

Credit rating agencies specialize in assessing the likelihood of debt default by issuers, essential for both corporations and governments. Sovereign ratings, reflecting a government's fiscal health, influence the ratings of other entities within the same country. In their ratings, they consider various long-term factors, including political risk, economic structure and growth prospects, fiscal and monetary flexibility, and external liquidity and financial position.[256] The political risk component of a country's credit risk ranking can be influenced by several critical factors, including the stability of political institutions, the degree of public participation in the political process, the smoothness of leadership transitions, the transparency of economic policymaking, public security, and the impact of geopolitical risks.[257]

The criticism of credit rating agencies is focused on several key issues. These include their optimistic bias, which is particularly evident in sovereign ratings, and a prevalent herd mentality within the industry. Additionally, these agencies are often reluctant to update ratings and tend to overreact during financial crises, which can exacerbate market instability.[258]

The second group of specialized assessors, global rating entities, extends their analysis beyond sovereign risk to provide insights into a nation's overall business climate and its receptiveness to international investments.[259] Various organizations, including the Business Environment Risk Intelligence (BERI), the International Country Risk Guide, and magazine-based assessors such as Institutional Investor, Euromoney, and the EIU, use different methods to construct assessments.[260] These organizations produce assessments by leveraging a mix of financial, economic, and political indicators, often integrating expert opinions and employing systematic approaches like the Delphi technique to achieve a more balanced synthesis of viewpoints. For example, the EIU constructs a composite

---

[255] See Schroeder 2008, p. 510.

[256] See Damodaran 2022, p. 36.

[257] See Damodaran 2022, p. 41.

[258] See Damodaran 2022, pp. 43 f.

[259] See Schroeder 2008, p. 510.

[260] For a comprehensive evaluation and comparison of various political risk models, refer to the analysis presented in Howell 2014, pp. 305–316.

risk indicator for numerous countries on a quarterly basis, which encompasses political, economic policy, structural economic, and liquidity risks.[261]

The primary advantage of these ratings is their comprehensive coverage of global business risk factors, enabling broad evaluations of political, economic, and financial risks across countries.[262] This is especially useful for countries without developed bond or equity markets.[263] Moreover, these ratings provide specific numerical scores for different risk subcategories, offering detailed insights valuable for MNCs and investors.[264]

However, these rating-based methods have limitations. For example, ratings lack market sensitivity, which may undermine their reliability in predicting political events. While some evidence of predictive power exists,[265] rating services often face criticism for their slow response and inability to accurately forecast outcomes. Additionally, numerical ratings lack standardized units, such as probabilities or percentage rates. Converting these scores into relevant units is challenging due to the lack of an established methodology.[266]

In capital budgeting, it is common to use country or credit risk ratings to assess country or political risk. Investors often refer to these ratings from financial publications and research institutions to evaluate the risks of foreign investment and to guide their investment decisions.[267] *Erb et al.* investigate the relationship between country credit ratings and expected investment returns through regression analysis, utilizing Institutional Investor's semiannual country risk ratings for a large international sample. Their research revealed a significant relationship between credit ratings and returns, which they subsequently employed to establish benchmark hurdle rates for investment projects in emerging markets.[268]

2.2.2.3.4 Market-Based Assessors

Schroeder identified "the market" as a distinctive group of assessors in risk analysis, separate from traditional and formal entities such as export credit agencies, insurance agencies and rating agencies, which provide an alternative perspective. Categorizing "the market" as a distinct group emphasizes the significance

---

[261] See Schroeder 2008, p. 510.

[262] See Erb et al. 1996, p. 29.

[263] See Bekaert et al. 2016, pp. 1 f.

[264] See Bekaert and Hodrick 2018, pp. 645 f.

[265] See Bekaert et al. 2014, p. 182.

[266] See Bekaert and Hodrick 2018, pp. 645 f.

[267] See Vijayakumar et al. 2009, p. 182.

[268] See Erb et al. 1996, pp. 46–58.

of market-based assessments in comprehending political and country risk. It acknowledges that market dynamics and investor behavior shape how country risk is perceived and priced in the global financial system. In essence, market-based assessment provides a real-time perspective on political and country risk that complements the more structured approaches of other groups of assessors.[269]

"The market" comprises a wide range of participants, including individual investors, investment funds, banks, and other financial institutions. This heterogeneous group assesses political and country risk primarily through market signals and price-based measures, such as fluctuations in equity and debt prices, changes in credit ratings, and interest rate spreads. Consequently, it is a decentralized assessment method that utilizes the collective knowledge and actions of numerous market actors. The use of market signals allows valuations to be highly responsive to economic and political events, allowing risk assessment to be quickly adjusted based on current events, trends and investor sentiment. This responsiveness of market-based assessment can be advantageous, providing the ability to react rapidly to evolving threats. However, this method has potential drawbacks. Analyzing market signals can be misleading because market participants may collectively react to the same stimuli, potentially exaggerating market fluctuations due to herd behavior.[270]

A market-oriented method for evaluating political risk, especially significant for capital budgeting, involves the utilization of sovereign spreads.[271] Sovereign spreads emerge when governments issue bonds in foreign currencies instead of their own, introducing default risk due to potential foreign exchange shortages. This usually results in higher yields for these bonds compared to those issued in local currencies.[272] By monitoring fluctuations in sovereign credit spreads in the secondary market, investors can assess and contemplate the perceived risk of the country.[273]

---

[269] See Schroeder 2008, p. 511.

[270] See Schroeder 2008, pp. 511 f.

[271] See for example Damodaran 1999, pp. 1–24; Damodaran 2003, pp. 1–30.

[272] See Damodaran 2022, p. 46.

[273] See Bekaert and Hodrick 2018, pp. 628, 635.

While the spreads analysis is an important tool to assess country risk and provide a market-based, forward-looking view of a country's creditworthiness and political stability, they are not without challenges.[274] Factors such as market liquidity and investor interest can affect these spreads, potentially distorting the level of risk.[275] Furthermore, these spreads are influenced by domestic macroeconomic and fiscal conditions, which may not always allow for a clear separation of political risk. Hence, relying solely on sovereign spreads could lead to overstated cost of capital and inefficient allocation of capital due to distortions.[276]

To mitigate some of these limitations, *Bekaert et al.* introduce the concept of political risk spreads as a method to address certain limitations by isolating the political risk component from sovereign spreads. This approach utilizes regression analysis to compare sovereign spreads with various factors, among which political risk is included. The methodology enhances the accuracy and reliability of assessing political risk probabilities. Consequently, this refined method offers an improved tool for international capital budgeting, enabling a more precise evaluation of the distinct impacts of political risk on investment decisions.[277] Table 2.1 captures the key characteristics of the four risk assessors outlined in this subsection.

Table 2.1 Risk Assessors—Summary. (Source: Own Illustration.)

	Official Assessors	In-house Assessors	Specialized Assessors	Market-Based Assessors
Type	· Private, bilateral and multilateral agencies	· Financial and non-financial firms	· Credit rating and global rating agencies	· Includes investors, investment funds, banks
Role	· Evaluate political risks for international investment and insurance	· Conduct firm-specific political risk analysis	· Provide detailed political risk assessments	· Offer real-time perspective on political risk with market dynamics

(continued)

[274] See Dos Santos et al. 2021, p. 1.

[275] See Damodaran 2022, p. 48.

[276] See Bekaert et al. 2016, p. 2.

[277] See Bekaert et al. 2016, pp. 1–23.

Table 2.1 (continued)

	Official Assessors	In-house Assessors	Specialized Assessors	Market-Based Assessors
Method	· Combination of qualitative and quantitative methods	· Varies between market-based techniques and long-term focus	· Long-term assessment of financial, economic, and political indicators	· Analysis of market signals, price-based measures and sovereign and political risk spreads
Insights	· Use of political risk insurance premiums, e.g. for risk estimation	· Emphasis on industry-specific risks and market dynamics	· Coverage of global business risk factors	· Sovereign and political spreads as tool for risk assessment

2.2.3 Interim Summary

Chapter 2.2 explores political risk as a complex and multifaceted concept with significant implications for investment decisions. Initially focused on direct government actions like nationalization, the understanding of political risk has expanded to include factors such as political stability, regulatory changes, and economic policies. This evolution underscores the need for a comprehensive definition that reflects the multiple dimensions of political risk, prompting this thesis to develop a specific framework.

The definition of political risk for the purposes of this thesis encompasses its origins, impacts and potential outcomes. The origins of political risk stem from both internal actions, including government policies and social changes within a country, and external influences, including international relations and geopolitical events that can affect the investment climate. The impact of political risk is considered at a global and macro level, affecting the broader business environment through significant upheaval or reform. Micro-level effects on specific industries are considered only when explicitly stated. The potential outcomes of political risk are primarily negative, involving disruption of operations or significant loss of assets, although opportunities for market expansion or favorable regulatory changes are recognized but not emphasized unless explicitly stated.

In addition to defining the dimensions of political risk as an internal or external phenomenon that adversely affects the financial landscape, it is also important to analyze closely related concepts. Political risk is interrelated to political and policy uncertainty, and despite their theoretical distinctions, this thesis integrates these concepts under the singular umbrella of political risk, recognizing their often interchangeable application in empirical research. However, the definition of political risk as defined here remains distinct from the broader concept of country risk, which includes a wider range of factors, such as financial elements.

Based on this comprehensive definition, a sophisticated approach that goes beyond traditional data-driven quantitative methods to include qualitative methods is necessary to assess political risk. These qualitative methods are critical for predicting potential outcomes and assessing the impact of a variety of factors, such as geopolitical tensions or domestic political dynamics.

In conclusion, this thesis presents political risk as a complex interplay of multiple dimensions, inherently linked to uncertainty, and recognized as part of ongoing political processes. Understanding the dynamic nature of political dynamics is essential for investors and businesses navigating complex political terrain.

2.3 Populism

This chapter provides a comprehensive analysis of populism, divided into two main subchapters. The first subchapter explores the intricate nature of populism, including its diverse interpretations and manifestations, as well as its causes and impacts. The second subchapter focuses on the complexities of studying populism. It examines the methods and challenges of quantifying and conceptualizing populism, and presents different approaches such as surveys, content analysis, and alternative methods. Together, these two subchapters provide a detailed understanding of the characteristics of populism and the nuanced methods used to analyze it.

2.3.1 Fundamentals

Populism, despite its growing recognition as a significant political force, remains a concept shrouded in controversy. In order to unravel the complexities of populism, this subsection explores not only its various definitions and variations, but also the underlying causes and far-reaching consequences of this global phenomenon.

2.3.1.1 Conceptual Framework

Defining populism is challenging due to its application to a wide range of political movements, parties, ideologies, and leaders across different geographical areas, historical periods, and ideological spectrums. Populism's diversity spans a range of personalities and ideologies, from figures such as Donald Trump and Hugo Chávez to movements on both the radical right and the far left.[278] This term's inherent ambiguity, due to such broad application, complicates the formulation of a single, consistent definition making.[279]

For example, in news media narratives, particularly after events like Donald Trump's presidency and Brexit, there was a notable rise in the use of "populism" and "populist", especially in outlets like the New York Times.[280] The term "populist" is frequently presented with a negative connotation in media discussions, establishing a dichotomy between populism and its critics which can challenge the legitimacy of certain political figures.[281] Moreover, it contributes to the emergence of a vernacular populism understanding, highlighting the media's role in shaping public perceptions and political discourse.[282]

Similarly, in political discourse, the term "populism" is often used without a solid theoretical basis and is employed to label and discredit various movements and leaders.[283] *Mounk* observes that the term is applied in broad and indiscriminate criticism of ruling powers,[284] while *Rodrik* notes its application to a diverse array of movements.[285] *Ţăranu* highlights that it is attributed to a broader range of political and social realities than is typical for a single term.[286] These diverse applications have resulted in characterizations of populism as a "dirty political word"[287] or "a notoriously vague term"[288], highlighting its inconsistent and frequently unclear definition.

In academic discussions populism is analyzed with a range of definitions and theoretical frameworks, reflecting its complexity. Numerous categorizations have

---

[278] See Guriev and Papaioannou 2022, p. 754.

[279] See Gidron and Bonikowski 2013, p. 3.

[280] See Rooduijn 2019, p. 362.

[281] See Bale et al. 2011, p. 112; Demata et al. 2020, p. 14.

[282] See Demata et al. 2020, p. 14.

[283] See Urbinati 2019, p. 113.

[284] See Mounk 2018, p. 110.

[285] See Rodrik 2018b, p. 13.

[286] See Ţăranu 2012, pp. 131 f.

[287] Shafir 2008, p. 463.

[288] Canovan 1999, p. 2.

been suggested, adding to a more profound comprehension of the notion. These classifications often overlap, indicating that these perspectives, while distinct, are interrelated and complementary, each shedding light on different facets of populism.[289]

Scholars in political science and sociology, such as *Gidron and Bonikowski*, have developed frameworks that distinguish between different interpretations of populism. One common approach categorizes it into three conceptual areas: as a political strategy, a political style, or an ideology. This framework is crucial in illuminating the complex nature of populism, as it allows for a comprehensive analysis that ranges from the tangible manifestations of populism in political discourse and strategy to its underlying ideological foundations.[290] Subsequent subsections will further explore this three-fold classification.

2.3.1.1.1 Political Strategy

The strategic definition of populism, as articulated by *Weyland*, characterizes populism as a political strategy used by actors, such as individual leaders or political parties, to gain and exercise power.[291] This strategy involves tactics for building support and structuring political authority, with a primary focus on increasing a leader's power and influence. Populism in this context often challenges established political parties and elite factions, particularly targeting the existing "political class".[292]

Contrary to the common perception of populism as a bottom-up mass movement, the strategic approach posits it as a top-down model. In this model, a leader, central to the populist strategy, directs political influence and garners electoral support to advance personal objectives. This approach highlights the leader-centered nature of populism, where the goals and directives of the leader take precedence over organic, grassroots mobilization.[293]

Weyland's perspective views populist parties and movements as part of a broader tactic to secure power through direct public support. Populist leaders often use emotional appeals aimed at personal aggrandizement, showing a lack of commitment to firm ideologies and focusing on consolidating individual power.[294]

---

[289] See Aslanidis 2016, pp. 88 ff.

[290] See Gidron and Bonikowski 2013, p. 5.

[291] See Weyland 1999, pp. 379–401; Weyland 2013, pp. 18–32.

[292] See Weyland 2017, p. 56.

[293] See Weyland 2017, p. 54.

[294] See Weyland 1999, pp. 379–401; Weyland 2001, p. 1 ff.; Weyland 2013, pp. 18–32.

Crucially, the political-strategic definition emphasizes the direct, almost personal connection between leaders and their followers, often bypassing traditional institutional frameworks. This approach usually involves direct communication with a large, unorganized group of followers, which reduces the influence of established political organizations. Thus, populism is defined as a leader-driven approach that prioritizes the accumulation and exercise of power, often at the expense of institutionalized political processes.[295]

Gidron and Bonikowski elaborate on the definition of populism as a political strategy and identify three key aspects integral to its framework. First, they discuss policy choices, focusing on the implementation of diverse economic policies that resonate with populist objectives. Second, political organization is examined, with an emphasis on the direct support of a personalistic leader by followers who lack formal organization. Lastly, they address forms of mobilization, noting the active engagement of marginalized groups in actions that are nationalist and anti-elite in nature. Together, these aspects provide a framework for understanding populism as a strategy, detailing its approach to policy, leadership, and public engagement.[296]

However, this approach has limitations. *Rueda* criticizes the early *Weyland*-influenced approach for its narrow focus on Latin American dynamics,[297] which *Sartori* identifies as the "traveling problem"[298] due to its limited applicability beyond its region of origin. *Mudde and Rovira Kaltwasser* further elaborate on this issue, noting that the emphasis on strong personalistic leadership prevalent in Latin American studies does not translate effectively to European contexts, underscoring a significant regional discrepancy.[299]

Furthermore, the strategy-focused approach often overemphasizes the role of a charismatic leader, failing to account for forms of populism not centered around a single leader and blurring the distinction between populism and other leader-dominated systems like autocracy or fascism. Importantly, it often neglects the central role of the people, the fundamental target of populist movements.[300]

---

[295] See Jenkins 2023, p. 1.

[296] See Gidron and Bonikowski 2013, p. 14.

[297] See Rueda 2021, p. 180.

[298] Sartori 1970, p. 1033.

[299] See Mudde and Rovira Kaltwasser 2014, pp. 376 ff.

[300] See Wojczewski 2023, p. 23.

2.3.1.1.2 Political Style

Laclau significantly contributed to the perspective that views populism as a political style, emphasizing its nature as primarily a discursive approach. This approach focuses on rhetorical form and the construction of discourse rather than the content's intrinsic meaning. A key element of this approach is the deliberate division of society into opposing groups of "us-versus-them", with the understanding that these groups assume specific meanings in different social contexts. The framework places emphasis on how social or political demands are expressed, positing that the essence of populism should be identified by its unique method of discourse articulation.[301]

In this approach, populism is not regarded as a specific type of leadership or political party, but rather as a method of forming collective identities and expressing political demands. This approach challenges the view of populism as necessarily including substantive programmatic agendas. Instead, it emphasizes the adaptability and capacity of populism to operate across ideological spectrums, highlighting the varying relational connotations within the "us-versus-them" dynamic in different social contexts.[302] By prioritizing the formal framework over the substantive aspects of populism, this method enables a broader and more impartial use of the populism concept. It understands the functional dynamics of populism while avoiding essentialist biases, such as an overemphasis on charismatic authority or particular cultural practices.[303]

The interpretation of populism as a political style, however, is not without its critics. *Arditi* contends that this view conflates populism with the nature of politics itself, potentially neglecting the complexities of broader political systems.[304] Others extend this critique, pointing to an overreliance on linguistic elements while overlooking other dimensions of populism, such as its performative aspects.[305]

Based on these critiques, some scholars have shifted the focus to the performative and relational dimensions of populism, developing so-called "post-Laclauian" approaches. These approaches, developing from *Laclau's* discursive theory, integrate socio-cultural and performative aspects.[306] While still acknowledging the foundation ideas, they seek a more holistic understanding of populism, taking

[301] See Laclau 2005, pp. 33 ff.

[302] See Laclau 2005, pp. 33–44.

[303] See De Cleen 2023, pp. 19 ff.

[304] See Arditi 2010, p. 491.

[305] See Moffitt 2016, pp. 26 ff.; Sengul 2019, p. 88.

[306] See for example the "sociocultural approach" (Rovira Kaltwasser et al. 2017a, p. 73), "discursive-performative approach" (Ostiguy et al. 2020a, p. 1).

into account the role of populist leaders, the influence of the media, and cultural performance in politics.[307]

For example, *Moffitt's* approach views populism as a political style that goes beyond verbal communication, incorporating non-verbal and stylistic elements. This perspective acknowledges that populism involves both linguistic features and performative actions, such as unconventional behavior and dramatizing crises, which resonate with sentiments of discontent or alienation.[308]

Similarly, *Ostiguy* offers a dynamic, cultural-relational perspective that fuses political and socio-cultural elements. According to the researcher, populism is performative and emotionally charged, ranging from resentment to devotion towards the leader. The term "performative" refers to the expressive actions and behaviors of political actors, which are often provocative and in stark contrast to conventional politics. This approach highlights the importance of elements such as accent, language style, body language, gestures, and dress codes in understanding how populism manifests and appeals to the populace.[309] Collectively, these post-Laclauian perspectives define populism as a political style characterized not only by discourse but also by behavior, performance, and communication.

2.3.1.1.3 Political Ideology

The ideational perspective on populism, as defined by *Mudde* and later expanded upon by *Hawkins and Rovira Kaltwasser*, conceptualizes populism primarily as an ideology.[310] This approach has gained considerable prominence in the social sciences[311] and has also extended its influence into the realm of economics.[312]

From this perspective, populism is intricately woven around four interrelated concepts: ideology, the people, the elite, and the general will.[313] Central to the ideational perspective is the characterization of populism as a "thin" or "thin-centered" ideology. This approach differs from more developed "thick" ideologies like socialism or liberalism, as it focuses on a limited set of political concepts. Despite academic debates about populism's nature and authenticity as an ideology, the consensus underscores its central characteristic: a primary emphasis on the moral purity of the people in contrast to the perceived corruption of the elite.

---

[307] See Ostiguy et al. 2020b, p. 255.

[308] See Moffitt 2016, pp. 28–50.

[309] See Rovira Kaltwasser et al. 2017a, p. 73.

[310] See Hawkins and Rovira Kaltwasser 2017, pp. 513–528; Mudde 2004, pp. 541–563.

[311] See Benczes 2022, p. 110; Rooduijn and Pauwels 2011, p. 1273.

[312] See Funke et al. 2023a, p. 3250.

[313] See Mudde 2017, pp. 30–34.

Unlike the class-based cleavages of socialism or the nation-centered cleavages of nationalism, populism frames this dichotomy as a conflict of moral values, distinguishing itself in the way it defines social groups.[314] As a consequence, its scope is narrowed, emphasizing a moral divide rather than offering a comprehensive set of socio-political solutions.[315]

Populist ideology centers around the concept of the people, portrayed as a homogeneous group with moral purity and authenticity.[316] This portrayal often reflects the self-perception or idealization of the target audience, based on a sense of moral righteousness. This broad understanding of the people allows for a diverse interpretation of its members, recognizing individuals from various backgrounds as legitimate embodiments of the group.[317]

As antithesis of "the pure people", "the corrupt elite" is positioned. Typically, the elite are portrayed as morally corrupt and out of touch with the people, perceived as betraying their interests. However, the application of this distinction varies significantly, depending on the specific ideology with which thin-centered populism intersects. For example, nativist populists often exclude ethnic minorities and immigrants from the people based on ethnicity, showcasing the influence of nativism. Conversely, exclusion of the elite is often driven by moral judgments rooted in populist ideologies, even when the denunciations include ethnic considerations.[318]

The fourth fundamental element of the ideational approach to populism is the concept of the general will. It suggests that the people, perceived as morally upright and homogeneous, have collective interests and preferences. Populist policies, often presented as embodiments of "common sense", are believed to align with this general will, thus claiming to represent the voice of the people (vox populi). In contrast, these policies are often opposed to the interests of the elite, which reinforces the populist claim of being the true representative of the people's will.[319]

---

[314] See Mudde 2017, p. 39.

[315] See Mudde 2004, p. 543.

[316] See Hawkins and Rovira Kaltwasser 2019, p. 5.

[317] See Mudde 2017, pp. 32 f.

[318] See Mudde 2017, p. 33.

[319] See Mudde 2017, p. 33.

According to *Mudde*, the ideational approach to populism has four key strengths, making it a versatile and effective framework for analysis. Firstly, it offers clear distinguishability, setting definitive boundaries between populist and non-populist ideologies.[320] This clarity in political analysis is essential for distinguishing populism from similar concepts such as elitism and pluralism.[321]

Secondly, this approach could be considered useful for categorizing different populist movements systematically. It may aid scholars in identifying and classifying various forms of populism through organization and classification. This feature is particularly critical in acknowledging the spectrum within populist movements. The adaptability of the approach is demonstrated by its ability to encompass a wide range of movements and leaders, from the historical American Populist Party to contemporary figures such as Hugo Chávez and Marine Le Pen.[322] This enables an analysis on a more granular level compared to other approaches.[323]

Thirdly, the ideational approach offers a significant advantage in terms of its travelability. It has proven effective across diverse geographical and historical contexts, allowing adaptation to national and regional settings. This flexibility ensures the framework's ongoing relevance and applicability across different historical periods and regions, underscoring its usefulness as a tool for policy analysis in various global scenarios.[324]

Lastly, the ideational approach's versatility is regarded as advantageous. It can be employed across various levels of analysis, encompassing the actions and behaviors of political elites and parties as well as the attitudes and beliefs of the general population. This wide-ranging applicability facilitates a comprehensive grasp of populism, which is essential for examining how populist ideologies connect with the public and impact the decisions and policies of political elites.[325]

However, the ideational approach to populism is also subject to several criticisms. A primary concern, as noted by *Kefford et al.*, is its failure to explain why

---

[320] See Mudde 2017, pp. 34–39.

[321] Elitism contrasts with populism by valuing the elite over the masses, while pluralism differs by advocating for power distribution and consensus-building across diverse groups (see Hawkins and Rovira Kaltwasser 2019, p. 4).

[322] See Mudde 2017, pp. 34–39.

[323] See Aslanidis 2016, p. 89.

[324] See Mudde 2017, pp. 38 f.

[325] See Mudde 2017, p. 39.

individuals with populist tendencies are attracted to populist parties, thereby overlooking the significant role of populism's communicative and rhetorical appeal.[326] Another criticism focuses on the approach's simplification of the people and the elite as homogeneous groups. This simplified view may lead to a shallow comprehension of intricate social dynamics and contradicts the diverse perspectives presented by liberal and pluralist ideologies.[327]

Additionally, the ideational perspective faces scrutiny for its conceptualization of populism as a thin ideology. Critics argue that the lack of foundational populist texts and a distinct ideology leads to conceptual stretching, which weakens the term's specificity and accuracy.[328] Furthermore, comparisons of populism, as a thin-centered ideology, with more defined ideologies like elitism and pluralism have been questioned for not being on the same conceptual level.[329]

Compared to strategic and style-based approaches, the ideational perspective focuses on the ideological divide between the people and the elite. While the style-based approach emphasizes narrative and rhetoric,[330] and the strategic-based approach focuses on tactical actions, the ideational approach contributes an empirical focus that seeks to categorize and analyze populism within a well-defined framework.[331] Although these different approaches differ in focus and execution, they are not mutually exclusive and can be synergistically combined for a more holistic understanding, with the ideational approach in particular valued for its emphasis on empirical analysis and ideological constructs. Table 2.2 provides a comprehensive summary of the three approaches to defining populism discussed in this section.

---

[326] See Kefford et al. 2022, p. 1010.

[327] See Katsambekis 2022, p. 53.

[328] See De La Torre 2019a, p. 8.

[329] See Aslanidis 2016, p. 91.

[330] See Hawkins and Rovira Kaltwasser 2017, p. 514.

[331] See Kefford et al. 2022, pp. 1006 ff.

Table 2.2 Populism Approaches—Summary. (Source: Own Illustration.)

	Political Strategy	Political Style	Political Ideology
Definition	· Populism as a top-down strategy by leaders for power gain · Focus on leader-follower connections	· Populism as a discursive and performative style · Emphasizes "us-versus-them" rhetoric	· Populism as a "thin" ideology · Focus on the moral division between the people and the elite
Critiques	· Limited applicability beyond Latin America · Overemphasis on charismatic leadership	· Potential conflation with the nature of politics · Overreliance on linguistic elements, neglect of performance	· Overlooks communicative appeal of populism · Simplifies the people and the elite
Insights	· Emphasizes leadership dynamics and direct engagement with followers	· Highlights importance of discourse, identity formation · Societal division emphasized	· Centers on the moral and ethical framework of populism
Comparative Analysis	· Focuses on power dynamics and electoral tactics · Less on ideological content or discursive methods	· Stands out for emphasis on communication and symbolic construction · Contrasts with the direct power accumulation focus	· Adaptable across movements and leaders · Provides a broad framework · Focuses on ideological constructs

2.3.1.2 Dimensions and Variations

The challenge of defining populism is further complicated by the different interpretations of the term across global regions, different time periods, and various classifications including political spectrums and ideologies. *Hunger and Paxton* describe the academic study of populism as fragmented, with scholars in this field working independently. They use the metaphor of individuals "sitting at separate tables"[332] to illustrate this point.

[332] Hunger and Paxton 2022, p. 629.

For a more holistic understanding, this section offers a comprehensive examination of populism, divided into four subsections that provide a thorough exploration of populism, covering its conceptual breadth, ideological variations, historical evolution, and global scope. The first subsection expands the analysis of populism beyond the previously introduced approaches by integrating a multidimensional framework, connecting diverse perspectives for a comprehensive understanding. The second subsection illustrates how populism, as a thin ideology, intertwines with and varies based on its association with different ideologies. The third subsection explores the historical evolution and adaptability of populism, illustrating its dynamic manifestations and impact on political discourse and action across various regions and eras. The last subsection critically evaluates the extent to which populism can be considered a global phenomenon, which is significant for understanding the debates around the international scope and influence of populism.

2.3.1.2.1 Multidimensional Analysis

In the preceding subsection, fundamental approaches to populism were explored, referred to as minimal definitions because they aim to distill populism's core characteristics for empirical analysis.[333] While offering clarity and simplicity, these definitions often focus narrowly on a single aspect of populism, thereby limiting their comprehensiveness.[334]

To overcome these constraints, *Osuna* introduces a multidimensional framework that enriches the understanding of populism by incorporating a wider array of attributes. The authors' methodology builds upon several minimal definitions to encompass a more inclusive array of populism's characteristics, blending various conceptualizations. It considers populism as an ideology, a political style, and a strategy, and outlines five key dimensions along a continuum from populist to anti-populist poles.[335]

The first dimension within the framework is the antagonistic depiction of the polity, wherein populism is defined by its division of society into the morally upright people and the corrupt elites. Subsequently, the second dimension emphasizes populism's fundamental moral differentiation of political entities, positing a moral confrontation between these distinct groups. The third dimension proposes an idealized vision of society, advocating for a unified, homogenous identity that contests the pluralistic nature of democracy by sidelining those who diverge from

[333] See Osuna 2021, p. 829.

[334] See De La Torre 2019a, pp. 1–29.

[335] See Osuna 2021, p. 834.

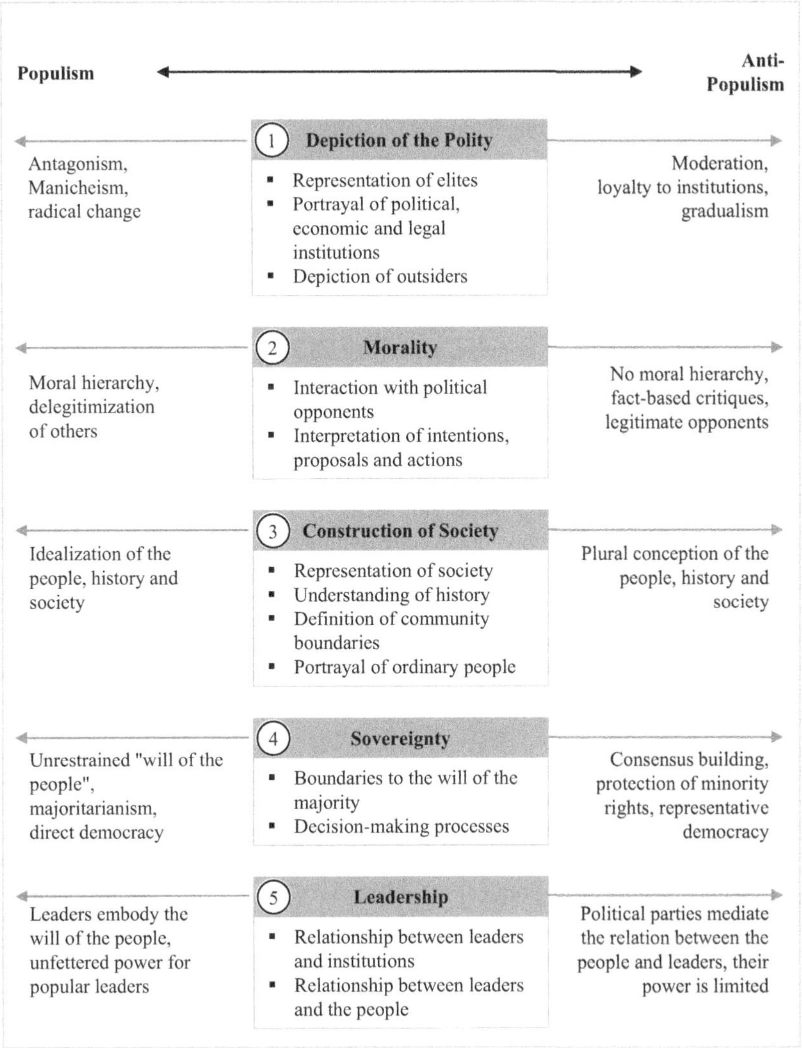

Fig. 2.7 Five-Dimensional Framework according to Osuna 2021. (Source: Own Illustration; following Osuna 2021, p. 841, Figure 1.1.)

the populist conception of the people. In the fourth dimension, populism is seen as challenging the constraints on popular sovereignty, advocating for the primacy of the people over institutional restrictions and questioning established democratic processes. The final dimension underscores the significance of charismatic leadership in populism, highlighting the role of leaders in rallying support directly from the populace, often circumventing traditional institutional channels.[336] Figure 2.7 visually encapsulates this framework.

This framework expands upon the ideational approach to populism, especially in its detailed examination of populism's antagonistic portrayal of the political domain and the moral binary between the people and the elite. By exploring the stylistic and strategic facets of populism, *Osuna's* framework provides a more complex understanding of populist narratives, aligning with strategic views that consider populism as a leadership strategy to gain power, particularly noting the significance of charismatic leadership.[337]

Therefore, the multidimensional framework captures the intricate nature of populism, enabling a more thorough investigation of its various expressions. It allows for the identification of varying degrees and combinations of populist characteristics, acknowledging the diversity within populist movements. While its practical application in measurement may have limitations, it excels in analyzing borderline cases and the range of populist attitudes, offering a refined instrument for comparative analysis. This approach favors a nuanced, gradient-based analysis over binary categorizations, serving a broad spectrum of research purposes and providing a deeper insight into the dynamics of populism.[338]

2.3.1.2.2 Ideological Spectrum

The ideational approach conceptualizes populism as a thin ideology, a term coined by *Taggart* to describe its "empty heart"[339] and "chameleonic"[340] attributes. This perspective suggests that populism lacks a deep-rooted ideological foundation and combines with other political ideologies to gain full meaning and impact. It emphasizes the tension between the people and the elite, with the interpretation of these groups varying depending on the specific populist narrative.[341] This

---

336 See Osuna 2021, pp. 836–841.

337 See Osuna 2021, pp. 834 ff.

338 See Osuna 2021, pp. 847 f.

339 Taggart 2004, p. 275.

340 Taggart 2004, p. 275.

341 See Otjes and Louwerse 2015, p. 61.

variability is determined by the core ideology that populism aligns with, providing specific meanings within particular contexts. As a thin-centered ideology, populism's nature allows it to intersect with different concepts and ideological traditions, making it appealing to different constituencies.[342] This leads to the emergence of distinct subtypes of populism, each incorporating unique ideological elements. Given the lack of a universally accepted definition of populism, scholars often recommend focusing on its specific manifestations, necessitating detailed analyses for each variant.[343]

Populism covers a diverse spectrum, encompassing a wide range of forms from economic to ethno-nationalist,[344] and adopting positions from inclusive to exclusive.[345] This spectrum transcends traditional political and ideological boundaries.[346] While subtypes of populism can be categorized as left-wing or right-wing, it is essential to recognize the multidimensionality of political attitudes. However, the left-right dimension significantly influences party positions, and populism often aligns with this traditional ideological scale.[347] Research in political science and political economy supports the distinction between left-wing and right-wing populism, providing a structured framework for comprehending the complexity of populist movements.[348]

Left-wing populism typically critiques financial elites, including international financial institutions and MNCs, especially for their role in promoting globalization. Embracing democratic socialist ideologies, these populists see the people as betrayed by elites aligned with neoliberal capitalist interests and advocate for state intervention and economic nationalism. Conversely, left-wing populists often support inclusiveness and multiculturalism in social issues, attributing economic and political inequalities to the actions of political and economic elites.[349] Examples include parties like Die Linke in Germany, the Scottish Socialist Party, and

[342] See Mudde and Rovira Kaltwasser 2013, pp. 147 ff.

[343] See Singh 2022, p. 250.

[344] See for example Doussard 2023.

[345] See for example Mudde and Rovira Kaltwasser 2013.

[346] See Cole and Schofer 2023, p. 379; Fernández-García 2021, p. 4; Peters and Pierre 2020, p. 928.

[347] See Kriesi et al. 2012, pp. 4 ff.; Van der Brug and Van Spanje 2009, p. 312.

[348] See for example Funke et al. 2023a; Huber and Schimpf 2017; Juon and Bochsler 2020; Mudde and Rovira Kaltwasser 2012.

[349] See March and Mudde 2005, pp. 23 ff.

the Socialist Party in the Netherlands, focusing on advocating for the ordinary worker and critiquing power structures favoring the elite.[350]

Right-wing populism often employs cultural rhetoric, targeting foreigners as well as ethnic or religious minorities as threats to national identity and culture and accusing political elites of protecting these minorities against the will of the people.[351] Nativism, a form of nationalism that is often associated with xenophobia,[352] is central to this ideology. It aims to preserve the nation for its native members and views non-native elements as threats. This shapes their concept of the people and the elite. Economically, right-wing populists may prioritize pragmatic policies over ideological ones, occasionally supporting pro-business policies such as low taxes and limited welfare.[353] Examples of such parties include the AfD and the Freiheitliche Partei Österreichs (FPÖ).[354]

Although left-wing and right-wing populism differ in their conceptualization of the people, they both oppose perceived elitist forces. This shared anti-elitism highlights populism's adaptability as a thin ideology that transcends traditional political divides. However, it is essential to note that these are not the only forms of populism as the ideological spectrum of populism is vast and can align with a range of political stances, ideologies, and movements.[355] Beyond the conventional dichotomy of left-wing and right-wing populism, some scholars identify other categories, such as centrist populist parties,[356] which are characterized by rejecting radical ideologies and presenting themselves as non-ideological, anti-political alternatives to mainstream parties.[357]

2.3.1.2.3 Historical Evolution

Populism has emerged as a dynamic and enduring force in global politics, adapting to various socio-economic and political contexts. This adaptability is evident in its manifestation across various regions and historical periods, shaping political discourse and global political landscapes.

Tarragoni outlines three significant historical movements that provide key insights into the enduring nature of populism in the contemporary era. The first of

---

[350] See Funke et al. 2023a, pp. 3250 ff.

[351] See Rodrik 2018b, p. 24.

[352] See March 2017, p. 286.

[353] See Mudde 2009, pp. 119 ff.

[354] See Heinisch and Werner 2019, p. 475.

[355] See Fernández-García 2021, pp. 1–15.

[356] See Petrović et al. 2023, pp. 268–290; Učeň et al. 2005, pp. 28–46.

[357] See Pop-Eleches 2010, p. 226.

these is the Narodnitchestvo movement in Russia (1860–1890), in which intellectuals sought to raise the political consciousness of peasants, whom they viewed as morally superior to the upper classes. This early populist movement aimed to empower a marginalized majority against elite domination.[358]

The second major populist movement is the emergence of the People's Party in the United States in the 1890s.[359] This political party emerged as a response to the economic challenges that farmers faced in a rapidly modernizing capitalist system.[360] It advocated for broader political participation in a landscape largely controlled by an elected oligarchy, intertwining with the broader political democratization trends of the era.[361]

Expanding on *Tarragoni's* analysis, the post-World War II era in Latin America saw the rise of populist regimes such as "Peronism"[362] in Argentina and "Varguism"[363] in Brazil. These movements centered on national self-sufficiency and the integration of the working class into the welfare state and represent a significant evolution of populism, illustrating the transition of populism from grassroots movements to governmental power.[364]

The metaphor of populist waves, commonly used to describe the rise of populism in times of crisis, captures the essence of these movements, which are characterized by charismatic leadership and mass mobilization.[365] This metaphor is limited, however, because many populist movements have had lasting effects

[358] See Tarragoni 2024, p. 48.

[359] See Tarragoni 2024, pp. 48 f.

[360] See Urbinati 2019, pp. 114 f.

[361] See Tarragoni 2024, pp. 48 ff.

[362] Peronism refers to the political ideology and movement associated with Juan Perón, who ruled Argentina during two non-consecutive periods from 1946 to 1955 and from 1973 to 1974. It is characterized by left-wing populist principles that emphasize social justice and the struggle against the landowner oligarchy and foreign influence. The concept revolves around the notion of politics being an ongoing struggle between the general public and the privileged class, primarily distinguished by their socioeconomic status (see Funke et al. 2023b, p. 35 for further details).

[363] Varguism denotes the political ideology and movement associated with Getúlio Vargas, who governed Brazil first from 1930 to 1945, and then again from 1951 until 1954. Varguism is considered left-wing populism with promised social justice, economic independence, and wealth redistribution, relying on the state's intervention to protect national interests against foreign exploitation (see Funke et al. 2023b, p. 47 for further details).

[364] See Tarragoni 2024, pp. 7–11.

[365] Demata et al. explore metaphors related to populism in British news discourse, including the wave metaphor, along with other metaphors reminiscent of natural phenomena. These metaphors collectively depict a dynamic, upward movement, similar to a wave's surge,

and have persistently evolved within the political landscape.[366] Nevertheless, this concept provides a useful framework for understanding the following examination of different phases of populism in selected regions.[367]

For instance, in Latin America, *De Lara* identifies three significant waves of populism. The "Classical Populism" of the 1930s–1970s emerged during a crisis in traditional oligarchic structures, marked by rapid urbanization and industrialization. The "Neoliberal Populism" wave shifted towards market-oriented reforms in the late twentieth century, diverging from the classical bottom-up approach. The "Radical Populism" wave, arising as a reaction against neoliberal policies, sought to fundamentally restructure societal frameworks.[368] Some scholars have suggested the emergence of a fourth wave, led by figures such as Jair Bolsonaro and Andrés Manuel López Obrador, which builds on previous concepts.[369]

Similarly, in Europe, *Goodwin* identifies four waves of national populism. The first wave, which occurred after World War II, included neo-fascist and neo-Nazi fringe groups. The second wave of populism, which began in the 1970s, included parties such as Denmark's and Norway's progress parties, which initially advocated tax cuts before shifting their focus to immigration. The third wave, which emerged in the mid-1980s, was characterized by parties such as France's Front National, which focused on ethno-pluralism and anti-immigration rhetoric. The fourth wave, in the twenty-first century, has seen the rise of parties emphasizing Euroscepticism and concerns about cultural identity, reflecting the evolving nature of societal challenges and public sentiment.[370]

The academic study of populism has also undergone distinct phases and evolved in tandem with its real-world manifestations, each marked by unique focuses and challenges. In the late 1960s, scholars initially focused on defining populism by reflecting on the characteristics observed in historical populist movements. As populist ideologies shifted in response to socio-economic changes in the 1970s and 1980s, academic research adapted by exploring how factors such as urbanization and economic crises spurred these movements. During this period, there was a particular emphasis on Latin America, where populism intertwined

---

illustrating how a political movement gains momentum and influence within populism (see Demata et al. 2020, pp. 20 f.).

[366] See De Lara 2019, p. 435.

[367] For a comprehensive analysis of the development of populism across various regions, including Africa, Australia, and the United States, refer to Rovira Kaltwasser et al. 2017b, pp. 101–267.

[368] See De Lara 2019, pp. 435 f.

[369] See for example Wajner and Wehner 2023, p. 1.

[370] See Goodwin 2019, pp. 104 f.

with rapid societal transformation. With the emergence of "Neoliberal Populism" in the late twentieth century, scholars have been challenged to understand how populist rhetoric aligned with policy, reflecting the complex evolution of populist strategies in practice. This ongoing interplay between academic perspectives and populist dynamics underscores the importance of responsive research in capturing the multifaceted nature of populism.[371]

These various waves of populism demonstrate its resilience and adaptability, as the approaches, focuses, and impacts of these movements are as diverse as the regions and periods in which they have emerged.[372] Recently, the study of populism has expanded globally, indicating a potential new wave, which is discussed in the next subsection.

2.3.1.2.4 Global Perspective

The contemporary dynamics of populism have shifted toward the study of populism as a global phenomenon, moving beyond traditional national or regional analysis.[373] This subsection examines whether modern populism, intersecting with various ideologies such as fascism, nativism, socialism, and neoliberalism, can be considered a global phenomenon.

The roots of what is perceived as global populism can be traced back to the significant developments of the 1990s. This era witnessed the rise of populist parties in Western Europe and the United States, as well as the emergence of strong populist leadership in Latin America. Scholars have described this shift as a "populist explosion"[374] or "populist surge"[375], particularly highlighted by events such as Britain's Brexit referendum and Donald Trump's presidential election in the late 2010s.[376]

Supporters of the global perspective argue that contemporary populism goes beyond traditional domestic boundaries, encompassing global and transnational dimensions. This transformation from localized voter mobilization to a broader scope, which includes international policy considerations and interactions, indicates a shift. Within this context, the current wave of global populism is typified by the simultaneous ascent of populist factions in multiple countries, exerting

[371] See Pappas 2016, p. 2.

[372] See Fuentes 2020, p. 47.

[373] See De La Torre 2019a, pp. 1–29.

[374] Judis 2016, p. 1.

[375] Mudde 2016, p. 25.

[376] See Wajner 2022a, p. 351.

growing influence over crucial government functions, including foreign policy, and contributing to the emergence of illiberal democracies in diverse regions.[377]

One characteristic of the global populism is the increasing international presence of populist leaders and movements, who seek global or transnational legitimacy. Closely linked to global issues such as migration and globalization, their discourse blurs the boundaries between domestic and international politics. This trend is particularly noticeable in regions with a history of populism, such as Latin America and parts of Europe. Contemporary populist governments are seeking international acceptance by expanding their political discourse, particularly in response to global challenges. This allows them to deepen their connection with supporters and justify their policies on an international scale.[378]

However, the concept of populism as a unified global phenomenon is challenged by scholars such as *Devinney and Hartwell*, who argue that the diversity of goals and expressions of populism across different economic systems suggests a range of localized movements rather than a cohesive global trend.[379] Populism is manifested in both liberal market and authoritarian systems, displaying distinct differences in objectives and tactics, indicating a spectrum of strategies employed by populist movements globally. Moreover, the authors contend that while certain traits, such as opposition to political and economic elites, are common to populist movements, these elements do not unite them into a single global entity. Rather, these movements act as global skeptics, each grappling with context-specific challenges to the global order.[380] *Grzymala-Busse* adds that the unified opposition to elites, while a shared trait, does not homogenize these movements globally. Instead, populism is often the result of specific historical and contextual factors, rooted in economic and cultural discontent that thrives in situations where traditional political structures are perceived as failing.[381]

Furthermore, some scholars argue that phenomena often referred to as populism, particularly in the case of radical right parties in Western Europe and politicians such as Donald Trump, are more accurately described as nativism. This distinction is crucial for understanding the ideological nuances and primary motivations of movements often classified as populist.[382]

---

[377] See Wajner 2022a, pp. 351–365.

[378] See Wajner 2022a, pp. 351–365.

[379] See Devinney and Hartwell 2020, p. 44.

[380] See Devinney and Hartwell 2020, p. 44.

[381] See Grzymala-Busse 2019, pp. 718–722.

[382] See Art 2022, p. 1005.

Related to the global populism debate is the distinction between transnational and international populism. Transnational populism emphasizes a collective people across borders, rallying against a global powerful elite, as seen in movements like Occupy or the Indignados.[383] In contrast, international populism involves temporary collaborations between nation-centered groups and does not challenge the nation-state concept, even in entities like the European Parliament.[384]

2.3.1.3 Causes

Building upon the foundational understanding of populism, this section progresses to investigate its origins. The discussion is structured into two interrelated subsections, each addressing distinct facets of the origins of populism. The initial subsection assesses economic contributors, spotlighting the influence of global financial trends, including the effects of globalization and the reduced power of nation-states, on the emergence of populist movements.

The second subsection shifts the focus to non-economic factors, such as the socio-cultural changes that have underpinned the rise of populism, focusing on the role of immigration and multiculturalism. Though not an exhaustive exploration, both these subsections together provide a comprehensive overview of drivers of populism shedding light on the multiple reasons behind its growing appeal.[385]

2.3.1.3.1 Economic Factors

This subsection investigates the influence of economic factors on the resurgence of populism, as identified by numerous scholars and economists.[386] *Guriev and Papaioannou* claim that the economic roots of the recent populist wave were triggered in particular by the global financial crisis and the simultaneous forces of globalization and technological progress.[387]

The global financial crisis of 2008–2009, marked as the most critical economic downturn since the Great Depression of the 1930s, is highlighted as one of the crucial catalysts. The crisis incited a rise in global populism, impacting not only advanced economies but also emerging markets.[388] *Mian et al.* suggest that this crisis engendered a widespread perception among the populace that they were the

[383] See De Cleen et al. 2020, p. 151.

[384] See Wajner 2022b, pp. 416 ff.

[385] See Berman 2021, pp. 71–88 for a more detailed exploration.

[386] See for example Funke et al. 2023a, p. 3249; Margalit 2019, p. 153.

[387] See Guriev and Papaioannou 2022, pp. 767–790.

[388] See Guriev and Papaioannou 2022, pp. 779–786.

ones shouldering the consequences of the economic and political elites' mistakes and misconduct.[389]

Research conducted by *Funke et al.* emphasizes how this crisis contributed to increased political fragmentation and bolstered support for far-right parties. Their findings suggest that the aftermath of the crisis, characterized by the adoption of austerity measures without adequate public spending to mitigate effects, exacerbated economic challenges for many, inadvertently driving them towards populist options. The period was characterized by a significant political shift, with traditional parties failing to gain support.[390]

Further complexities in this context are introduced by globalization and technological innovation. While globalization has spurred economic growth and development, it has also intensified the inequality gap, creating a segment of society referred to as the "globalization losers" who feel marginalized by the global economic framework.[391] This is supported by *Rodrik*, who posits that a populist backlash is foreseeable in the advanced stages of globalization.[392]

Technological transformation has widened the divide in the job market, favoring skilled "knowledge workers" while disadvantaging those with lower or outdated skills.[393] Other economic factors, such as job losses due to increased imports from low-wage countries, have exacerbated this trend.[394] Underscoring the role of economic insecurity in driving support for populist parties, *Guiso et al.* highlight how financial instability and labor market shifts are crucial factors influencing political inclinations toward populism.[395]

Overall, the financial crisis and globalization, along with technological change, have created fertile ground for the emergence and thriving of populist ideologies. These global economic shifts have had a profound impact on labor markets, trade flows, and the political allegiances of individuals and communities around the world, significantly reshaping the political landscape.[396]

---

389 See Mian et al. 2014, pp. 1 ff.

390 See Funke et al. 2016, p. 227.

391 See Guriev and Papaioannou 2022, pp. 775–779.

392 See Rodrik 2018b, p. 2.

393 See Autor et al. 2006, p. 189; Frey et al. 2018, p. 418.

394 See Autor et al. 2013, p. 2121.

395 See Guiso et al. 2017, p. 17.

396 See Guriev and Papaioannou 2022, pp. 761, 767.

2.3.1.3.2 Non-Economic Factors

To gain a comprehensive understanding of the emergence of populism, it is essential to look beyond economic factors. *Margalit* notes that while economic factors are significant, they only form a part of a larger and more intricate puzzle,[397] including socio-cultural dynamics, the impacts of immigration, and the transformative influence of new media, as *Guriev and Papaioannou* suggest.[398]

Especially culturally based explanations are increasingly recognized as important factors to understanding the appeal of populism. For example, *Inglehart and Norris* highlight the influence of long-term societal changes, such as broader access to higher education, increasing ethnic diversity, urbanization, and evolving gender roles, and how these developments have led to greater acceptance of diverse lifestyles and cultures. Yet the authors also note that the same societal shifts have fueled feelings of alienation and resentment among certain segments of the Western population, particularly white males, the elderly, conservatives, and those with less formal education.[399]

Guriev and Papaioannou suggest that immigration in particular can lead to increased perceptions of cultural and demographic changes among certain populations. Beliefs that immigrants negatively affect native employment and wages, or pose a threat to cultural identity, extend beyond economic considerations to include issues of security and social cohesion. While numerous studies have explored this relationship, the link between immigration and populism remains complex, often marked by a divergence between perceptions and the impact of immigration, which may inflame populist sentiments.[400] Indeed, it is becoming increasingly common to find that social and cultural factors, rather than economic insecurity alone, are driving the anti-immigrant sentiment that triggers populism.[401]

Furthermore, the rise of populism has coincided with the emergence of new media technologies. Social media platforms, due to their extensive reach and ease of access, have become channels for populist discourse. These digital platforms are adept at amplifying populist messages, creating echo chambers that

---

397 See Margalit 2019, p. 154.

398 See Guriev and Papaioannou 2022, pp. 790–817.

399 See Inglehart and Norris 2016, pp. 2 f.

400 See Guriev and Papaioannou 2022, pp. 797–804.

401 See Margalit 2019, p. 152.

reinforce and propagate populism.[402] Research by *Engesser et al.* demonstrates the effectiveness of these platforms in disseminating messages that emphasize the sovereignty of the people and critique the elites.[403]

Overall, the rise of populism is driven by a complex interplay of economic and non-economic factors. The diversity and variance observed in populist movements worldwide are significantly contributed to by the interactions among socio-cultural shifts, public perceptions of immigration, and the influence of digital media.

2.3.1.4 Consequences

This section presents an exploration of the impact of populism within the spheres of political and economic analysis. Politically, it evaluates the paradoxical character of populism, considering its capacity to both foster democratic progress and act as a destabilizing force that may weaken the foundational structures of democratic institutions. Economically, the section outlines the complex consequences of populist policies, examining their effects on macroeconomic stability and their broader implications for global economic patterns.

2.3.1.4.1 Political Impact

Exploring the complex relationship between rising populism and democratic systems, this subsection engages with the scholarly debate over whether populism strengthens or undermines democracy. On one hand, there is a viewpoint that populism can act as a catalyst for democratic vitality by amplifying the concerns of overlooked or marginalized communities. Advocates of this perspective argue that populism can rejuvenate democracy by realigning its focus towards the needs of the silent majority.[404] According to this line of thought, populist leaders highlight and address issues that mainstream politics often neglects, thus enhancing representation and invigorating political participation. Proponents of this view contend that it serves as a countermeasure to the vested interests of establishment elites or specific minority groups, calling for significant reforms to systems perceived as corrupt or inefficient. From this standpoint, the emergence

[402] See Gerbaudo 2018, p. 745. However, Boulianne et al. argue that offline discussions with like-minded individuals, rather than social media echo chambers, are more strongly correlated with support for right-wing populism (see Boulianne et al. 2020, p. 683).

[403] See Engesser et al. 2017, pp. 1109–1126.

[404] See Rovira Kaltwasser and Van Hauwaert 2020, p. 5. See also Bonikowski et al. 2019; Juon and Bochsler 2020; Rovira Kaltwasser 2012.

of populism is seen as indicative of a democracy responsive to the demands of its populace.[405]

On the other hand, the predominant scholarly view is that populism poses a serious threat to democratic systems challenging the basic principles, institutions, and processes of liberal democracies. Populists often perceive constitutional safeguards, minority rights, and the rule of law as obstacles to the unity of the "pure people", leading to significant changes in democratic institutions such as elections, legislatures, courts, and media.[406] By favoring the majority, populists risk marginalizing traditional democratic norms and reshaping political and regulatory frameworks to suit their agenda, thereby destabilizing established systems of governance.[407] Moreover, populism often clashes with democratic principles of autonomy, especially when it targets independent institutions such as central banks, which it views as elitist and often seeks to realign with its political goals.[408]

This group of scholars argue that populism poses a significant threat to political power dynamics. The weakening of executive constraints can enable populists to potentially seize complete control of government, stifling opposition and critical discourse. Once in power, they may engage in cronyism, using their positions for personal gain and eroding public trust in government institutions. This dynamic can have long-term effects, driving institutional change and potentially reshaping the judiciary and other independent agencies, weakening their role as checks and balances. This shift can lead to a gradual erosion or evolution of institutional structures, indicating a significant shift in the internal dynamics of these systems under populist influence.[409] If policy positions and goals are solely in the hands of populists, who claim exclusive authority to define the common goal, then the vehicles, channels, institutions, and mechanisms typically considered essential to the operation and sustainability of a liberal democracy would become unnecessary.[410]

Furthermore, the ascendancy of populists often correlates with a marked decline in institutional quality, a trend that can persist over time and adversely affect economic growth.[411] A strong democratic and legal structure is essential

---

[405] See Cole and Schofer 2023, pp. 3 f.

[406] See Benczes 2022, pp. 115 f.; Müller 2017, p. 3.

[407] See Devinney and Hartwell 2020, pp. 32 ff.

[408] See Benczes 2022, p. 116.

[409] See Devinney and Hartwell 2020, p. 43.

[410] See Benczes 2022, p. 116.

[411] See Funke et al. 2023a, p. 3249.

to foster capital accumulation necessary for continued economic development.[412] To investigate the economic effects of populist policies in contexts with weak democratic institutions, *Acemoglu et al.* developed a theoretical model.[413] Their model proposes that in response to fears of elite domination, politicians may adopt populist policies as a way to demonstrate their integrity. By positioning these policies to resonate with the median voter and distance themselves from elite interests, politicians aim to secure electoral support. However, these strategies, despite their intent, may inadvertently lead to negative economic and social consequences, including for the affluent and the general population.[414]

To conclude, while populism can address certain democratic deficits and realign political focus with public sentiment, it also poses risks to democratic structures, often leading to institutional degradation. The erosion of institutions, compounded by imperfect policy decisions, poses a challenge not only to political stability but also to the economy. The following subsection will further explore these economic consequences.

2.3.1.4.2 Economic Impact

This subsection delves into the economic ramifications of populism, offering insights distinct from its political impacts. Populist leaders often present their economic policies as reflecting the "will of the people", as noted by *Müller*.[415] However, the real-world economic outcomes of these diverse policies are varied and can exert profound immediate and prolonged impacts on national economies. These effects may not always align with the interests of the people these leaders claim to represent, including the broader electorate.[416]

Contemporary populist politicians in the United States exhibit a wide array of economic policies, spanning from progressive measures akin to those of certain Democratic administrations to the more business-centric policies characteristic of the Trump administration.[417] Historically, in the post-World War II era, Latin

---

[412] See Persson and Tabellini 2006, p. 322; Rodrik and Wacziarg 2005, p. 50.

[413] See Acemoglu et al. 2013. However, according to Kaltwasser et al. the study from Acemoglu et al. on the economic perspective of populism encounters two main challenges: firstly, it emphasizes the consequences of populism but lacks a clear framework for defining the concept itself. Secondly, it predominantly views populism as leftist or inclusionary, thereby failing to address the rightist or exclusionary forms that are prominent in various global regions (see Rovira Kaltwasser et al. 2017b, p. 14).

[414] See Acemoglu et al. 2013, pp. 771 ff.

[415] See Müller 2017, pp. 3 ff.

[416] See Weyland 2017, p. 61.

[417] See Benczes 2022, p. 110.

America's economy was notably influenced by what scholars like *Dornbusch and Edwards* and *Sachs* describe as the populist "boom and bust cycle".[418] This cycle, marked by initially appealing yet ultimately unsustainable policies, significantly shaped the economic outcomes associated with populist governments in the region.[419] Characteristics of this cycle encompass distributive, expansionary fiscal, and protectionist trade policies, often propelled by electoral demands for immediate economic advantages. Although these policies might initially foster economic growth and prosperity, their short-term orientation frequently precipitates detrimental long-term economic consequences, including inflation and financial instability, leading to economic downturns. Thus, this populist policy cycle in Latin America illustrates the dilemma between short-term economic gains and long-term economic stability, underscoring the necessity of sustainable macroeconomic policies.[420]

After the 1980s, Latin American economic strategies underwent a notable transition. The traditional patterns of fiscal irresponsibility linked with populism began to evolve, with populist leaders increasingly avoiding the macroeconomic pitfalls of their predecessors. This resulted in fewer instances of unfundable deficits and hyperinflation.[421] While massive redistribution programs leading to unsustainable macroeconomic conditions have become less common,[422] Venezuela remains an exception.[423]

In their comprehensive study, *Funke et al.* examined the economic impacts of 51 populist leaders over more than 100 years, from 1900 to 2020. The study found that countries with populist governments tend to experience significant economic costs over time. On average, 15 years into a populist regime, real Gross Domestic Product (GDP) per capita in these countries is ten percent lower than in comparable non-populist economies. Moreover, this decline in economic performance under populist governments is consistent across regions and ideological spectrums. Further, the study links populism to economic disintegration, unsustainable macroeconomic policies, and institutional erosion, including declines in trade and financial integration, increased debt and inflation, and the weakening of democratic checks and balances, judicial independence, and press freedom. These

---

[418] See Dornbusch and Edwards 1990, pp. 7–13; p. 3250; Sachs 1989, pp. 1–45.

[419] In the literature, the term "economic populism" typically refers to this phenomenon (see for example Sachs 1989).

[420] See Funke et al. 2023a, p. 3249; Sachs 1989, p. 1.

[421] See Guriev and Papaioannou 2022, pp. 817 ff.

[422] See Benczes 2022, pp. 109 ff.

[423] See Guriev and Papaioannou 2022, p. 818.

findings resonate with the earlier discussions by *Dornbusch and Edwards*, and *Sachs* on the historical pattern of boom and bust cycles under populist regimes in Latin America.[424]

Other research focusing on specific populist events, such as *Born et al.'s* study on the economic effects of populist leadership illustrated by the Brexit vote, indicates significant economic impacts. This study attributes a reduction of about 1.7–2.5% in the United Kingdom's GDP by the end of 2018 to the Brexit vote, primarily due to the anticipatory responses of households and firms to increased policy and macroeconomic uncertainty.[425]

While most research in the literature highlights the adverse effects of populism on the economy, *Rodrik* presents an outlier perspective. The author argues that under certain exceptional conditions, economic populism may yield positive results. This can occur through the easing of economic policy constraints or diminished liberal technocratic supervision, potentially leading to beneficial economic outcomes.[426]

Nevertheless, researchers such as *Mudde and Rovira Kaltwasser* contend that economic policy is no longer a defining characteristic of populism, but rather a variable aspect. This variation is consistent with the ideational approach's thin-centered definitions of populism, which implies a lack of uniformity in policy approaches among populist movements.[427]

2.3.2 Assessment

Developing an effective framework for measuring populism is paramount to its scholarly study. The approaches to assessing populism within the academic community are diverse, with some researchers prioritizing the study of populist parties or leaders, while others aim to delineate populism by delineating its fundamental characteristics, ideologies, and motivations.[428]

This subchapter covers three critical aspects of the endeavor. First, it emphasizes the importance of a precise conceptualization of populism, addressing theoretical considerations that highlight the necessity for clarity in definition and exploring how various analytical perspectives shape empirical research on

[424] See Funke et al. 2023a, p. 3251.

[425] See Born et al. 2019, p. 2722.

[426] See Rodrik 2018a, p. 1.

[427] See Mudde and Rovira Kaltwasser 2013, p. 160.

[428] See Osuna 2021, p. 832.

populism. Second, it explores the various methodologies used in quantifying populism, particularly in relation to political parties. This exploration provides an overview of survey methods and content analysis techniques, each of which offers different insights but also poses unique challenges. Finally, the subchapter critically evaluates various measures of populism, offering an analysis of their construction, applicability, and limitations. Collectively, these sections aim to provide a comprehensive overview of the current landscape of populism measurement research.

2.3.2.1 Analytical Determinants

Before discussing the different approaches to assessing populism, this section covers some important theoretical considerations. *Pappas* highlights the trend in populism research towards quantification, but cautions against premature approaches, citing *Sartori's* metaphor of "running before learning how to walk".[429] This metaphor serves as a warning against conflating different phenomena under the vague label of populism, and underscores the need for clarity in understanding its core characteristics.[430] Consequently, this section will link definitions of populism with measurement methods and explore different perspectives that influence the assessment of populism, with the aim of achieving a more conclusive analysis.

2.3.2.1.1 Measurement Difficulties

Exploring populism in academic research presents significant challenges, particularly in defining and measuring the concept. A key issue is the problem of conceptual stretching, where an excessively general definition of populism leads to imprecise conceptualizations, risking the dilution of the term to the point of meaninglessness. To maintain its analytical usefulness, it is important to focus on the core attributes of populism and avoid overly broad applications.[431]

The process of measuring populism is intricately linked to the primary difficulty that populist elements are not confined to entities explicitly labeled "populist". Instead, these elements are found across a wide spectrum of political leaders and parties, making it difficult to isolate populism as a distinct concept.[432] Moreover, individuals and groups often labeled as "populist" typically

---

[429] See Pappas 2016, p. 3. Original quote: "(...) we have started to run before having learned how to walk" (Sartori 1970, p. 1039).

[430] See Pappas 2016, p. 3.

[431] See Pappas 2016, p. 3.

[432] See Devinney and Hartwell 2020, pp. 32 ff.

resist this categorization, further blurring the lines of classification.[433] Similar challenges face the measurement of other multifaceted political constructs such as "institutions", "polarization", or "democracy", which also present definitional and methodological complexities.[434]

Moreover, the method chosen to measure populism is heavily influenced by its conceptualization—whether as a political style, a strategy, or an ideology (see Section 2.3.1.1). When viewed as a political strategy, populism is perceived as a method used by leaders or parties to gain and maintain power, focusing on increasing a leader's autonomy and influence. This perspective highlights the dynamic nature of populism and aids in understanding its impact across different political systems and historical periods. Comparative historical analysis and case studies are often used to measure populism's effects in this context.[435]

Conversely, when considering populism as a political style, it is characterized by specific ways in which political discourse is framed. This approach, as outlined by *Hawkins and Rovira Kaltwasser*, requires a broad analysis of both the rhetoric and actions of populist actors,[436] using interpretive textual analysis of speeches and public discourse as the primary research method.[437] Similarly, *Jagers and Walgrave* analyze party broadcasts to study politicians' media presentations under this framework.[438]

From an ideological perspective, populism is defined by a set of ideas about politics and society. Its broad applicability across different eras and regions highlights its versatile and context-sensitive character. This adaptability is particularly significant in the field of political science, especially in the empirical study of populism. The ideational approach is often preferred over the strategic and stylistic methods due to its inclusive nature. Unlike the strategic and stylistic approaches, which tend to concentrate on specific aspects such as charismatic leadership or the behavior and presentation of political figures, the ideational approach provides a more exhaustive analysis. It is well-suited for a variety of research methodologies, facilitating a deep dive into populist politics.[439]

Typically, when populism is understood as a political ideology, the measurement involves a detailed textual analysis of party literature, focusing on

---

[433] See Guriev and Papaioannou 2022, pp. 757 ff.

[434] See Funke et al. 2023a, p. 3253.

[435] See Gidron and Bonikowski 2013, pp. 4–16.

[436] See Hawkins and Rovira Kaltwasser 2019, p. 20.

[437] See Gidron and Bonikowski 2013, pp. 4–16.

[438] See Jagers and Walgrave 2007, pp. 319–345.

[439] See Benczes 2022, pp. 110–116; Funke et al. 2020, p. 2.

manifestos or internal documents to identify populist elements.[440] Due to the complexity and resource requirements of this type of analysis, researchers often choose to conduct in-depth studies within specific contexts. This focused approach usually takes the form of single-country studies or cross-national comparisons, allowing for a more detailed exploration of populist ideologies.[441]

In conclusion, researching populism requires careful definition and nuanced measurement, given its complex and pervasive nature across political landscapes. Whether viewed as a strategy, style, or ideology, the study of populism requires a balance between theoretical insight and empirical analysis. This comprehensive understanding is essential for academic discourse and practical political decision-making.

2.3.2.1.2 Perspective Analysis

The assessment of populism is shaped by both the definition employed and the perspective adopted. This perspective spans a wide spectrum, from personal beliefs regarding the presence of populism to expansive societal viewpoints that capture a varied range of opinions on the subject.

Populism is recognized to encompass both supply and demand aspects.[442] On the demand side, the focus has been on populist attitudes among individuals, particularly within the electorate.[443] Recent studies have increasingly explored populism on the individual level, treating "populist attitudes" as fundamental beliefs expressed through evaluations of entities aligned with populist ideologies. The primary method for studying these attitudes involves quantitative surveys.[444] However, demand-side research faces the challenge of lacking a standardized measurement approach. This complicates comparative studies and raises concerns about the validity and reliability of survey methods.[445]

Conversely, the supply-side focuses on scrutinizing the behaviors and rhetoric of political leaders and parties, involving a thorough analysis of their political actions and discourse.[446] Within political science, this can be done by employing a diverse array of methods to study political actors or parties.[447]

---

440 See Gidron and Bonikowski 2013, pp. 4–16.

441 See Gidron and Bonikowski 2013, p. 7.

442 See Axelrod 1967, pp. 51–60.

443 See Van Hauwaert et al. 2019, p. 129.

444 See for example Akkerman et al. 2014; Castanho Silva et al. 2020; Schulz et al. 2018.

445 See Van Hauwaert et al. 2019, p. 128.

446 See Celico et al. 2022, p. 1.

447 See Döring 2016, p. 536.

Many scholars emphasize the importance of analyzing populism at the party level, given the pivotal role that political parties play in shaping democratic systems. This approach provides insights into how populist ideologies and strategies influence mainstream politics, party systems, and democratic processes.[448] When targeting political parties, researchers can employ a variety of methods, including the analysis of organizational affiliations, leadership speeches, party platforms, legislative votes, and surveys of political elites and citizens. Each of these methods provides unique contributions to understanding party ideologies and identifying populist trends. Leadership speeches and party platforms provide insights into a party's populist rhetoric, while surveys mainly offer a view of populist sentiments among elites and the populace.[449]

To determine whether parties can be classified as populist, researchers often rely on indirect sources such as party manifestos, television debates, and parliamentary speeches. With the increase in available data on parties, electoral dynamics, and government composition, the importance of these indirect sources has grown.[450] Nonetheless, the degree to which various forms of party behavior or communication accurately reflect populism remains a topic of debate.[451]

Party manifestos are essential tools in political analysis, particularly for identifying populism. Providing detailed outlines of a party's policy positions, these documents serve as formal records that enhance consistency and comparability across different political landscapes. Empirical studies support the importance of manifestos, showing that parties generally deliver on a significant portion of their electoral promises.[452] This indicates that manifestos are more than mere rhetorical electoral instruments, as they reflect genuine policy agendas and potential government actions. Substantial input from a party's communications team goes into the development of manifestos, thus establishing these documents as reliable representations of the party's collective messaging. Through this authenticity, manifestos are a tool for providing consistent and reliable assessments of populist trends not only across time and region, but also within the internal dynamics of the parties themselves.[453]

However, analyzing political manifestos is not without its drawbacks. The relevance of these documents can vary considerably across regions, with public

[448] See Roberts 2017, p. 287.

[449] See Norris 2020c, p. 700.

[450] See Döring 2016, pp. 535 ff.

[451] See Meijers and Zaslove 2021, p. 377.

[452] See Di Cocco and Monechi 2022, pp. 312–314.

[453] See Di Cocco and Monechi 2022, p. 312; Hawkins and Rovira Kaltwasser 2019, p. 30.

engagement tending to be minimal in places such as Latin America.[454] Also, manifestos may not fully capture the complex or explicit populist expressions found in alternative channels of communication, such as speeches or other party publications, which may result in a more moderate representation of populist rhetoric.[455] Furthermore, focusing an analysis solely on parties is fraught with challenges due to the fluid nature of political ideologies and the varying interpretations of what constitutes populism.[456] This narrow focus on political parties risks overlooking the nuances of populist sentiments that exist within political movements or society at large.[457]

2.3.2.2 Assessment Approaches

Building on the discussion in the previous section, political parties are identified as pivotal for their role in channeling populist sentiments, illustrating the integration of populist ideologies within mainstream politics and facilitating cross-national comparative studies.[458] However, the diverse expressions of populism across political movements, parties, ideologies, and leaders—each shaped by unique geographical, historical, and ideological contexts—pose challenges for its measurement.[459]

Thus, this section advances the conversation by concentrating on methodologies for evaluating populism within political parties. It covers prevalent analytical methods, i.e. surveys and content analysis, elucidating their advantages, drawbacks, and illustrative cases.

2.3.2.2.1 Survey Techniques

This subsection explores three main survey methodologies for examining political orientations, with a focus on political parties and the complexities of populism. Defined as a structured, quantitative strategy for collecting data from a selected group of individuals or entities, survey methods aim to reflect the characteristics or behaviors of a larger population.[460] *Norris* categorizes these methodologies

[454] See Hawkins and Rovira Kaltwasser 2019, p. 30.
[455] See Pauwels 2017, p. 124.
[456] See Roberts 1995, pp. 84 ff.
[457] See Hawkins and Rovira Kaltwasser 2019, p. 6.
[458] See Di Cocco and Monechi 2022, p. 311.
[459] See Gidron and Bonikowski 2013, p. 3.
[460] See Groves et al. 2009, p. 2.

into mass surveys, elite surveys, and expert surveys, each with a distinct function in political research.[461]

The first technique, mass opinion surveys, is central to measuring public perceptions of party policies, preferences, and populist sentiments.[462] These surveys collect opinions on a variety of issues, facilitating the analysis of public sentiment on specific issues or broader ideological spectrums, such as economic policy on the left-right scale. However, designing questions can be challenging due to the potential skewing of representations by assuming equal item significance, and the ambiguity introduced by the subjective interpretation of scales such as "left" or "right".[463] For the study of populism, *Akkerman et al.* have developed a multi-item scale that significantly advances the field by evaluating individual voter attitudes on key dimensions such as popular sovereignty, anti-elitism, and a Manichean[464] outlook. Initially applied to Dutch data, this scale provides a detailed examination of populist attitudes at the personal level.[465] Its application has since expanded to include case studies and international surveys,[466] with subsequent refinements enhancing its precision and analytical scope.[467]

The second technique, elite surveys, offers insight into the beliefs and attitudes of political elites, including legislators and party activists.[468] This approach illuminates the ideological diversity within parties, from grassroots to leadership, which is essential for understanding the dynamics between party ideologies, campaign promises, and voter interactions, especially regarding populism.[469] Recent studies have included items from mass surveys in elite surveys,[470] enabling comparisons between the perceptions of both groups.[471]

The third approach, expert surveys, is indispensable for assessing party ideologies, characteristics, and policy positions. Drawing on experts' in-depth

---

[461] See Norris 2020c, p. 700.

[462] See Norris 2020c, pp. 700, 703.

[463] See Laver 2014, p. 214.

[464] The Manichean worldview is characterized by a dualistic perspective, seeing the world in terms of an absolute struggle between good and evil forces, rather than a complex interplay of nuanced, self-interested actors (see Oliver and Wood 2014, p. 953).

[465] See Akkerman et al. 2014, pp. 1324–1353.

[466] See Osuna and Rama 2022, p. 3.

[467] See for example Castanho Silva et al. 2020; Van Hauwaert et al. 2020.

[468] See Norris 2020c, p. 700.

[469] See Andreadis and Ruth-Lovell 2019, p. 113.

[470] See for example Stavrakakis et al. 2017, pp. 420–439.

[471] See Andreadis and Ruth-Lovell 2019, p. 113.

knowledge of their country's political landscape, particularly party politics, these surveys classify political entities along various dimensions, either predefined (a priori) or determined after analysis (a posteriori), thereby enhancing the understanding of party actions.[472] Originally designed to delineate the left-right political spectrum,[473] expert surveys have evolved to encompass a broad range of political dimensions.[474] Covering numerous policy areas, this method provides a comprehensive perspective by integrating expert evaluations representing multiple sources, including party manifestos and parliamentary behavior.[475]

The effectiveness of expert surveys is based on their adaptable yet standardized methodology. Standardization promotes comparability across studies, which is critical for maintaining academic integrity across different political terrains and time spans. However, flexibility is critical for the study of emerging political phenomena or situations with limited access to official documents, where expert insights illuminate the ideological and orientations of political actors.[476]

In addressing the complexities of populism, expert surveys stand out for their ability to integrate multiple aspects of party behavior, from rhetoric to leadership views. By drawing on the collective judgments of many experts, these surveys offer a comprehensive and consensus-based perspective that goes beyond the scope of qualitative case studies, making them exceptionally effective for multifaceted analysis.[477]

However, the methodology is subject to challenges beyond the complex framing of survey questions. For instance, issues may arise from the occasional scarcity of experts, particularly in specialized fields, as the need for specialists to interpret a wide range of political data narrows the potential expert pool. The response rate is also a crucial factor in ensuring the reliability and validity of survey outcomes.[478]

2.3.2.2.2 Content Analysis

In addition to the survey techniques, the second approach commonly used in political science research to investigate political parties is content analysis. Using this approach provides a systematic and objective method for examining the attributes

---

472 See Wiesehomeier 2019, p. 91.

473 See Castles and Mair 1984, p. 73.

474 See for example Benoit and Laver 2006; Döring 2016; Laver and Hunt 1992.

475 See Netjes and Binnema 2007, p. 42.

476 See Wiesehomeier 2019, pp. 90 f.

477 See Meijers and Zaslove 2021, p. 381.

478 See Hooghe et al. 2010, pp. 692 ff.

of political messages,[479] making it an indispensable tool for studying the communication of political elites, particularly through the analysis of political speeches and party manifestos.[480]

In the context of measuring populism, the process typically begins with the development of a codebook that outlines the dimensions of populism and provides a framework for subsequent analysis. Trained coders then use the codebook's criteria to analyze documents and quantify the prevalence of populism by assessing the proportion of text aligning with its defined characteristics.[481] Several authors have contributed innovative methods for measuring populism within this framework. For instance, *Rooduijn and Pauwels* utilized a two-point scale to code manifesto paragraphs,[482] while *Hawkins* employed a holistic grading approach for entire texts. Another method involves identifying key words that indicate populist style or framing, which are frequently used in party manifesto analysis.[483]

Compared to collecting data with questionnaires, this method takes advantage of the availability of existing texts, making it particularly valuable for historical research on populism.[484] Moreover, content analysis can measure populism as a concept that varies in intensity, responding to debates about whether it is a spectrum or a binary category.[485] The notion of "degreeism", as discussed by *March*, supports viewing populism on a spectrum, acknowledging the fluidity in thin-centered ideologies.[486] *Aslanidis's* research and advanced text analysis studies support this perspective, indicating a finer, more continuous understanding of populism.[487]

Although content analysis has significant advantages, it often overlooks lesser-known populist movements by focusing primarily on established parties.[488] The approach also contends with challenges such as labor intensity, coder bias, and potential inconsistencies. To address these challenges, particularly labor intensity, there has been a trend towards automated text analysis. Under this approach, computer algorithms, rather than human coders, are applied to interpret text and

[479] See Neuendorf 2017, pp. 4 ff.

[480] See Hawkins and Rovira Kaltwasser 2019, pp. 16 f.

[481] See Pauwels 2017 p. 125.

[482] See Rooduijn and Pauwels 2011, p. 1281.

[483] See Hawkins 2009, p. 1040.

[484] See Hawkins and Rovira Kaltwasser 2019, pp. 16 f.

[485] See Osuna 2021, p. 842.

[486] See March 2019, p. 52.

[487] See Aslanidis 2016, pp. 92 f.

[488] See Hawkins 2009, p. 1049.

identify relevant content based on a predefined or post-analysis dictionary.[489] An example of this approach is the use of machine learning by *Hawkins and Castanho Silva* to categorize documents such as speeches and manifestos. Automated analysis, using text examination and word frequency methods, is proving effective in increasing the efficiency of populist content detection and has the potential to improve accuracy compared to manual human coding.[490] Building on this advancement, *Rooduijn and Pauwels* conducted a comparative study to assess the efficacy of both classical and computerized content analysis in populism research. Their findings show that both methods are effective and that each provides comparable results. This highlights the adaptability of the methods in various research contexts and over time.[491]

2.3.2.3 Populist Measures

This section expands upon the foundational methodologies of surveys and content analysis, offering a detailed exploration of specific techniques designed to measure populism within these frameworks. It introduces a variety of supplementary measures that have proven effective in academic studies for capturing the essence of populism. The emphasis is placed on reproducible datasets and established measures that have been utilized in scholarly investigations to examine populism within political entities.

2.3.2.3.1 Survey-Based Methods

The preceding discussion highlighted that while both mass and elite surveys contribute valuable insights into the study of populism, expert surveys are particularly notable for their depth and breadth in analysis. These surveys integrate standardized methodologies with the flexibility needed to address various political phenomena, thereby offering a comprehensive tool for exploring the multifaceted nature of populism. This subsection introduces four key expert surveys pivotal in assessing populism at the party level, each employing distinct methodologies. These surveys either directly measure the populist stances of political parties or provide the necessary data to indirectly construct indicators of populism.

---

[489] See Pauwels 2017, p. 126.

[490] See Hawkins and Castanho Silva 2019, pp. 27–49.

[491] See Rooduijn and Pauwels 2011, pp. 1279 f.

First, the Global Party Survey (GPS) by *Norris* offers a thorough assessment of political parties worldwide, evaluating their ideological stances, policy orientations, and use of populist rhetoric, making it a valuable resource for political analysis. This comprehensive tool facilitates a deeper understanding of the dynamics and strategies within global party politics. GPS has a strong network of experts, mainly political scientists, who possess specialized knowledge of their respective countries' electoral systems and party dynamics. This expertise is complemented by insights from additional experts, particularly from smaller regions, to achieve a global analysis. In 2019, GPS engaged 1,861 experts to analyze 1,127 parties across 170 countries on 21 key aspects, such as attitudes towards democracy and authoritarianism. The forthcoming version, originally scheduled for 2023, aims to expand these aspects, providing updated insights that enable the tracking of trends, for instance, in global populism.[492]

To determine a political party's populist inclination, experts directly rated parties on a scale from zero to ten based on their use of populist versus pluralist rhetoric. A score of zero indicates a strong preference for pluralist rhetoric, which supports governance through elected officials and is grounded in the principles of minority rights, negotiation, and compromise, while also including safeguards against excessive executive power. Conversely, a score of ten indicates a preference for populist rhetoric, which challenges the legitimacy of established political structures and emphasizes the importance of the popular will. In addition, experts were asked to rate the impact of populist rhetoric at the party level, ranging from negligible (zero) to significant (ten).[493]

Second, the Chapel Hill Expert Surveys (CHES) are essential for assessing the positions of national political parties on a range of ideological, political and international issues in European and Latin American politics. CHES Europe has expanded its coverage from 14 to 32 countries over six survey waves. It assesses up to 277 parties. In 2020, CHES introduced the CHES-Latin America series, which analyzes twelve Latin American countries, paralleling the European series in scope and content.[494]

---

[492] See Norris 2020a.

[493] See Norris 2020b, pp. 9–11.

[494] See Bakker et al. 2015, pp. 143–152; Chapel Hill Expert Surveys 2022; Jolly et al. 2022, pp. 1–8.

To gauge populism using data from these surveys, researchers must adopt an indirect methodology. *Polk and Rovny*, for instance, propose that examining the prominence of anti-elite rhetoric within political parties is a useful way to identify populist inclinations.[495] This concept is quantified in the CHES dataset, where it represents the degree to which a specific party emphasizes anti-establishment and anti-elite rhetoric. On this scale, a score of zero indicates no salience at all, while a score of ten indicates extremely high salience. This approach has also been utilized by scholars like *Norris and Inglehart*, who employ the measure of anti-elite salience as a key indicator to differentiate between pluralism and populism.[496]

Third, the Political Representation, Parties, and Presidents Survey (PREPPS) provides another direct method for examining populism in Latin America by assessing the relationship between political actors' populist tendencies and their support for direct democratic mechanisms. Gathered in 2018 and 2019, the survey data covers the political positioning and democratic connections of numerous parties and presidents in 18 countries. The survey covers topics such as general left-right positions, economic policies, social issues, redistribution, foreign policy, and environmental concerns. Therefore, PREPPS is particularly valuable for its in-depth analysis of how populist actors in Latin America interact with democratic processes.[497]

Fourth, the Populism and Political Parties Expert Survey (POPPA), conducted in 2018, gathered insights from 294 experts to evaluate 250 parties.[498] The survey primarily focused on European political parties across 28 countries and evaluated aspects such as ideology, organization, and style. The variable of populism is estimated indirectly through factor regression analysis based on expert assessments of five characteristics: a party's Manichean view of politics, its perception of the public as homogenous, belief in a unified general will, prioritization of ordinary people's sovereignty, and its stance on anti-elitism.[499]

---

[495] See Polk and Rovny 2017, pp. 356–371.

[496] See Norris and Inglehart 2019, pp. 3 ff.

[497] See Wiesehomeier et al. 2019, pp. 1 ff.

[498] The next survey round was initially planned for January 2023.

[499] See Meijers and Zaslove 2020, p. 383.

2.3.2.3.2 Content Analysis-Based Methods

The previous subsection on content analysis for studying populism highlights its use in identifying political elites' ideological and rhetorical strategies. This subsection explores the Comparative Manifesto Project (CMP), a key initiative employing content analysis in political science. Since its introduction by the Social Science Research Center in Berlin in 2003, CMP has become a critical resource in the empirical study of political representation and populism.[500] The project provides a database that quantitatively evaluates the electoral programs of over 1000 political parties from more than 50 countries, with records dating back to 1945.[501]

To ensure rigorous and systematic coding, the CMP implements a comprehensive process. Initially, coders undergo extensive training, thereby improving the consistent application of coding rules. Furthermore, this training is enhanced through detailed guidance from supervisors, along with periodic retraining. Employing a two-step approach, the process begins with the division of text into quasi-sentences, followed by the categorization of these segments based on the key messages of the manifesto. To ensure comparability across parties, countries, and historical periods, coders utilize a system of 56 standard categories covering seven major policy areas.[502]

Nevertheless, the CMP encounters challenges, notably concerning data reliability issues. Consequently, to augment precision and mitigate bias, the necessity for multiple independent codings emerges, stemming from variations in coders' interpretations and the potential for coding errors.[503]

Building on CMP's data, *Stöckl and Rode* have devised a novel methodology for quantifying populism within political party rhetoric. Given that the CMP does not directly assess populism, the authors have identified specific categories from different domains within the CMP framework to proxy for populist elements. Their methodology is anchored in theoretical constructs that characterize populism by its core tenets: anti-elitism, the sovereignty of the people, the rejection of limits on the will of the people. *Stöckl and Rode* caution against interpreting

---

[500] See for example Di Cocco and Monechi 2022, pp. 311–327; Stöckl and Rode 2021, pp. 51–83.

[501] See Lehmann et al. 2023.

[502] See Mikhaylov et al. 2012, pp. 79 ff.

[503] See Mikhaylov et al. 2012, p. 79.

the presence of any single element as a definitive marker of populism. Rather, it is the synthesis of these components that suggests a populist inclination.[504]

To construct the ideologically neutral populist indicator (*POP*), *Stöckl and Rode* computed an equally weighted sum of selected CMP categories. This calculation measures the proportion of populist content in each political party's platform. Then, an aggregate measure of populism is generated at the country level, taking into account all parties and weighted according to their electoral performance.[505] This approach is vital for capturing the multifaceted nature of populism, establishing a metric that recognizes the diverse ways populist parties may conceptualize.

Similarly, the authors have developed a variable that captures the right-left ideological scale of populism (*PRILE*) through related elements derived from the CMP categories. The variable assesses parties' stances on immigration and multiculturalism, as well as the views of different constituencies within the electorate.[506] It provides a measure of political ideology, with positive values indicating right-wing populism, negative values representing left-wing populism, and zero marking the political center. An aggregate measure of *PRILE* is also created at the country level across all parties for each election considered, weighted by each party's election results, similar to the *POP* variable.

Table 2.3 presents the CMP categories, used for the *POP* or *PRILE* variables, as identified by *Stöckl and Rode*, along with brief descriptions.[507] These categories are organized into distinct domains, also derived from the CMP, and outline how each contributes to the measurement of populism and its ideological orientation.

---

504 See Stöckl and Rode 2021, p. 58.

505 See Stöckl and Rode 2021, p. 58.

506 According to Stöckl and Rode's perspective, this aspect resonates with the insights of Devinney and Hartwell 2020 and Müller 2017, who have pinpointed these issues as fundamental in differentiating various ideological strands of populism (see Stöckl and Rode 2021, p. 58.)

507 Starting with CMP version 5, variables containing an underscore "_" are included. In earlier versions, the corresponding parent variables without an underscore are used.

Table 2.3 Categories for Populism Variables based on Stöckl and Rode 2021. (Source: Own Illustration; following Stöckl and Rode 2021, p. 59, Table 2.3.)

Name	Code	Description	POP	PRILE
Domain 1: External Relations				
Anti-imperialism	per103	Negative references to imperial behavior and/or negative references to one state exerting strong influence (political, military, or commercial) over other states.	+	
Internationalism: Negative	per109	Negative references to international co-operation. favorable mentions of national independence and sovereignty with regard to the manifesto country's foreign policy, isolation and/or unilateralism as opposed to internationalism.	+	
European Union: Negative	per110	Negative references to the European Community/Union.	+	
Domain 2: Freedom and Democracy				
Democracy General: Positive	per202_1	Favorable mentions of democracy as the "only game in town". General support for the manifesto country's democracy.	+	
Direct Democracy: Positive	per202_4	Favorable mentions of the system of direct democracy, particularly in contrast to representative democracy. This includes the call for the introduction and/or extension of referenda, participatory budgets, and other forms of direct democracy.	+	
Domain 3: Political System				
Governmental and Administrative Efficiency	per303	Need for efficiency and economy in government and administration and/or the general appeal to make the process of government and administration cheaper and more efficient.	+	
Political Corruption	per304	Need to eliminate political corruption and associated abuses of political and/or bureaucratic power. Need to abolish clientelist structures and practices.	+	

(continued)

Table 2.3 (continued)

Name	Code	Description	POP	PRILE
Political Authority: Party Competence	per305_1	References to the manifesto party's competence to govern and/or the other party's lack of such competence.	+	
Political Authority: Personal Competence	per305_2	Reference to the presidential candidate's or party leader's personal competence to govern and/or the other candidate's or leader's lack of such competence.	+	
Domain 5: Welfare and Quality of Life				
Equality: Positive	per503	Concept of social justice and the need for fair treatment of all people.		–
Welfare State Expansion	per504	Favorable mentions of the need to introduce, maintain, or expand any public social service or social security scheme.	+	–
Education Limitation	per507	Limiting state expenditure on education.		+
Domain 6: Fabric or Society				
National Way of Life—General: Positive	per601_1	Favorable mentions of the manifesto country's nation, history, and general appeals.	+	+
Immigration: Negative	per601_2	Statement advocating the restriction of the process of immigration, i.e., accepting new immigrants.		+
Immigration: Positive	per602_2	Statements favoring new immigrants and against restrictions and quotas; rejection of the "boat is full" argument. Includes allowing new immigrants for the benefit of the manifesto country's economy.		–
Law and Order: Positive	per605_1	Favorable mentions of strict law enforcement and tougher actions against domestic crime. Only refers to the enforcement of the status quo of the manifesto country's law code.	+	+
Civic Mindedness: Bottom-Up Activism	per606_2	Appeals to grassroots movements of social change, banding all sections of society together to overcome common adversity and hardship, and appeals to the people as a united actor.		–

(continued)

Table 2.3 (continued)

Name	Code	Description	POP	PRILE
Multiculturalism General: Negative	per608_1	The enforcement or encouragement of cultural integration. Appeals for cultural homogeneity in society.		+
Domain 7: Social Groups				
Labor Groups: Positive	per701	Favorable references to all labor groups, the working class, and unemployed workers in general. Support for trade unions and calls for the good treatment of all employees.	+	–

Figure 2.8 summarizes *Stöckl and Rode's* methodology for generating populism variables from CMP-coded party manifestos, including the construction of country-level populist indicators.

2.3.2.3.3 Alternative Approaches

This subsection explores distinctive methodologies in populism research that move beyond traditional surveys and content analysis by merging approaches. It focuses on three distinct approaches, each combining different methods, that shed light on particular aspects of populism in politics, particularly in Europe.

The first approach, developed by *Zulianello and Larsen*, focuses on the electoral performance of populist parties in the European Parliament elections from 1979 to 2019. Covering 92 parties across the European Union, this method provides a comprehensive view of populism at the supranational level. The multi-step analysis process, which begins with the matching of existing party lists with political science literature, facilitates a broad and comprehensive identification of relevant parties. Through a subsequent literature review, both established and emerging populist parties are identified, including those in borderline categories. A particular feature of this methodology is the elaboration of a classification of parties into ideological categories such as right-wing, valence, and left-wing, based on their ideologies and policies.[508]

[508] See Zulianello and Larsen 2021, pp. 1–8.

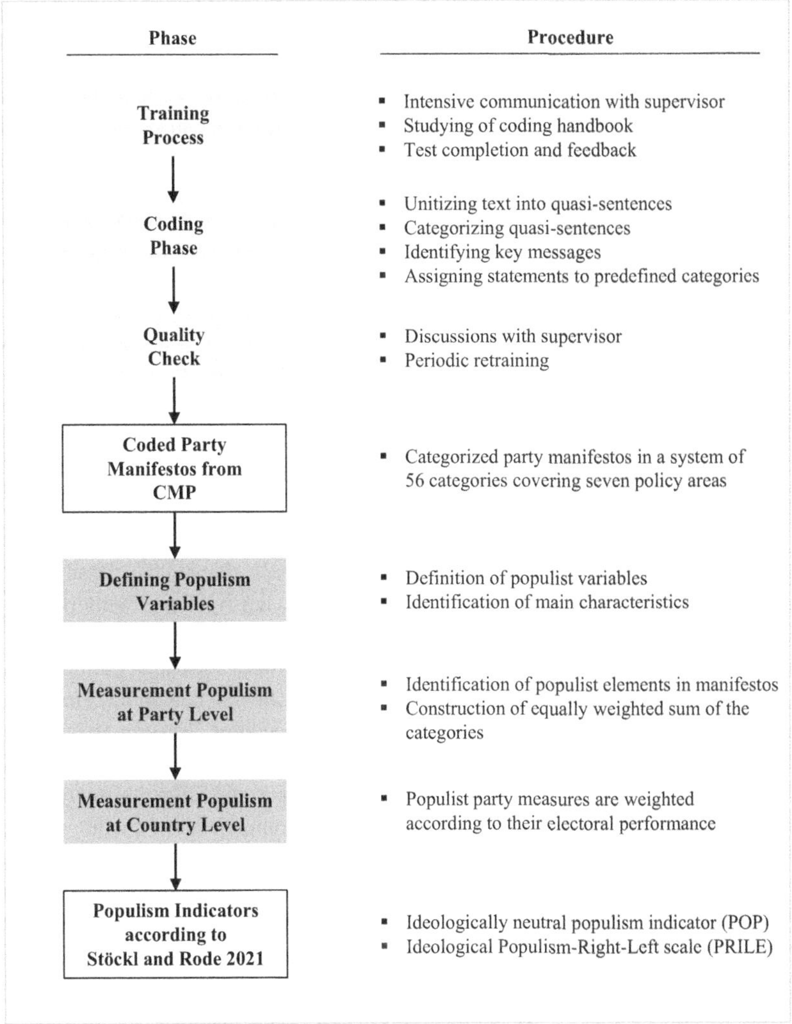

Fig. 2.8 Populism Variables Assessment according to Stöckl and Rode 2021. (Source: Own Illustration.)

The second approach, the PopuList project, takes a different but complementary approach to the study of populism. Spanning the period from 1989 to 2022, the PopuList project provides a comprehensive overview of populist parties in 31 European countries. The project categorizes political parties as populist, far-left, or far-right and evaluates their Eurosceptic positions. Central to the project's credibility is peer review by a wide range of academics, ensuring methodological rigor and comprehensive coverage. Among its contributions is the graphical representation of vote shares, adjusted for population size, which provides a visual understanding of the popularity of these parties. The latest version of the project, released in September 2023, extends to 2022 and includes updated reviews and detailed country reports, with a particular focus on borderline cases.[509]

In contrast to the comprehensive scope of the PopuList project, the third approach, Timbro's Authoritarian Populism Index, offers a more focused lens, particularly on the authoritarian aspect of populism. Timbro's index covers the period from 1980 to 2018 and specifically tracks parties that challenge the principles of constitutional liberal democracy. The Timbro report and index identified populist parties in Europe through a comprehensive process that involved reviewing authoritative lists of such parties, conducting an extensive literature review for each party, and analyzing election results. This approach enabled the classification of parties not only as populist, but also along the left-right and authoritarian-totalitarian spectrums, based on their self-identification, secondary literature, and political affiliations.[510] This index monitors the growth of European political parties that challenge the principles of constitutional liberal democracy, focusing on those that disregard democratic norms and procedures. Encompassing both European Union member states and other democratic nations, Timbro's methodology is distinguished by its qualitative assessments and in-depth analysis of each party's core ideology. Thus, it provides a comprehensive picture of the authoritarian trends within European populism.[511]

Together, *Zulianello and Larsen's* supranational analysis, the PopuList project's broad and visual approach, and Timbro's focused study on authoritarian populism each contribute uniquely to the academic understanding of populism in contemporary European politics. Figure 2.9 provides a comprehensive overview of the methods for assessing populism presented in this chapter.

---

[509] See Rooduijn et al. 2023, pp. 1–10.

[510] See Heinö 2017, pp. 3 ff.

[511] See Heinö 2017, pp. 10–12.

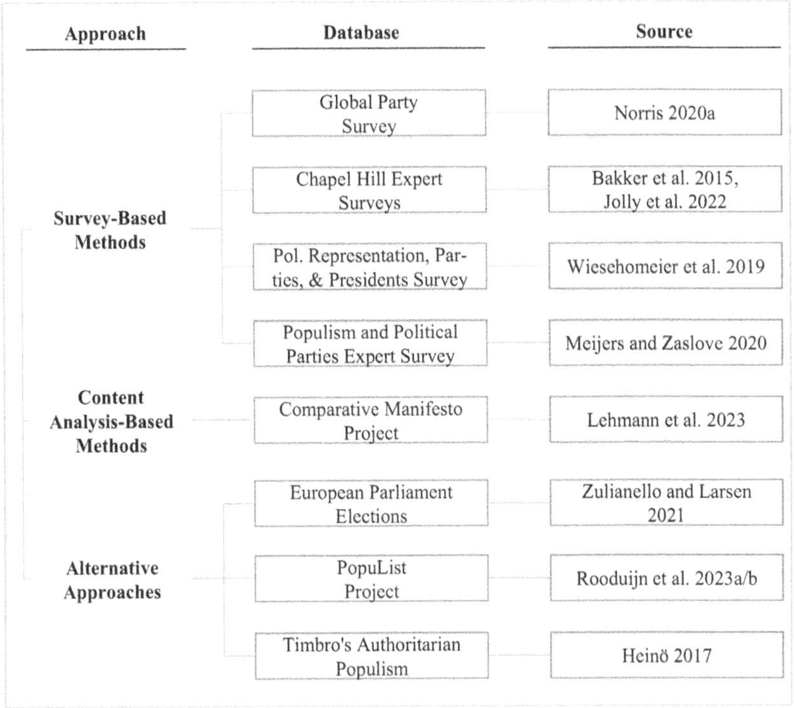

Fig. 2.9 Populism Assessment Approaches—Overview. (Source: Own Illustration.)

2.3.3 Interim Summary

Chapter 2.3 defines populism as a dynamic phenomenon that can be understood through various lenses, including as a political strategy, a political style, or an ideology. The complexity of these intersections underscores the need for a clear and consistent definition of populism. While an ideal definition would include strategic, stylistic, and ideological elements, such a multidimensional approach introduces significant empirical complexities.

Therefore, this thesis follows empirical studies that adopt the ideational perspective, which defines populism by focusing on the moral dichotomies between "the pure people" and "the corrupt elite" and categorizes it as a thin ideology. This suggests that unlike ideologies such as socialism or conservatism, which cover a wide range of social and economic issues, populism is more narrowly defined, allowing it to merge with other ideologies to form diverse manifestations.

Adopting an ideational perspective facilitates structured analysis and enhances the identification of populist characteristics for empirical analysis. More specifically, this perspective provides clarity in distinguishing populist from non-populist ideologies, systematically categorizes a variety of movements, and demonstrates broad applicability across different geographical and historical contexts. In addition, the versatility of the ideational approach is a key advantage, supporting a comprehensive analysis at multiple levels of society. This multi-level analysis is important for a deeper understanding of how populism affects both political elites and the general population, thereby addressing the complex challenges that populism poses to political systems.

The thesis examines the different methods and challenges of measuring populism, taking into account its manifold causes and consequences. Populism often appears in waves, manifesting itself strongly within national borders while also reflecting global patterns indicative of widespread socio-political sentiments. This duality underscores the complex dynamics of populism, highlighting the need for different analytical approaches to effectively capture its multifaceted nature. A range of methods, such as surveys and content analysis, are essential to explore how perceptions of populism are captured by the public and political elites, and to assess the prevalence of populist discourse in media and political communication. These approaches are necessary to capture the impact of populism and to provide a framework for quantifying populism.

In conclusion, this thesis establishes a conceptual framework for understanding populism from an ideational perspective. This framework allows for the quantification and analysis of populism, including its various variants across the political spectrum, and facilitates further exploration of populism's impact on financial outcomes, providing the foundation for the subsequent analysis within the thesis.

2.4 Interim Conclusion

This chapter transitions from the theoretical examination of investment strategies, political risk, and the influence of populism to an empirical analysis of the impact of populism on financial markets and investment decisions. The chapter sets the stage for the upcoming empirical investigation by presenting an interim conclusion, articulating a theoretical synthesis, identifying existing research gaps and deriving the research question.

2.4.1 Theoretic Synthesis

This synthesis integrates theoretical perspectives on investment strategies, emphasizing the importance of diversification and the integration of political risk into capital budgeting in the context of the challenges posed by populism. It details how these components interact within the global equity markets, impacting financial decision-making processes, shaping investor expectations, and enhancing political risk assessments.

Although theoretical models suggest that fully integrated markets would enable assets with similar risk profiles from different countries to yield comparable expected returns, real-world complexities, such as varying degrees of integration and market barriers, challenge these theoretical benefits. The discussion of market integration highlights the importance of country-specific risks, especially in markets with limited global integration. These risks, which stem from distinct political, economic, and regulatory environments, present significant challenges to the typical advantages associated with diversification. The investor's capacity to mitigate these risks is closely tied to the degree of capital market segmentation and the investor's diversification strategies. For example, a portfolio that is diversified geographically could alleviate such risks if the markets involved have low correlation. However, in situations where markets are interconnected, these risks can increase, potentially reducing the benefits for investors who focus on specific regions.

Integrating political risk into investment decision-making adds complexity. Political risk is essential in the global business landscape, though its multiple interpretations defy the creation of a universal theoretical framework. This thesis defines political risk as a multidimensional concept involving internal and external phenomena at the global or macro level, which negatively impacts the financial landscape, aligns closely with political and policy uncertainty for empirical applications, and remains distinct from the broader concept of country risk. This view recognizes political risk as the result of ongoing political dynamics rather than isolated events and emphasizes the need to account for the fluid nature of political engagements and the uncertainties within political climates.

The assessment of political risk is essential for investment decisions, as it has a significant impact on asset allocation and corporate financial planning. When integrating political risk into financial models, such as NPV, a decision must be made between adjusting the discount rate for systematic risk or modifying cash flow projections for unsystematic exposures. The decision relies on the correlation between the returns of a specific country and the global market returns.

A comprehensive assessment of political risk requires a blend of quantitative, qualitative, and politically focused analysis, using a range of measures from general uncertainty indices to specialized political indicators to closely evaluate the economic impact of political events. Risk analysts, including official assessors, in-house experts, specialized agencies, and market-based analysts, also play an essential role in providing insights for navigating the complex interplay between political events and their implications on investment strategies.

Populism presents unique challenges in political risk assessment due to its strategic, stylistic, and ideological dimensions. Its appeal is fueled by economic dissatisfaction resulting from globalization, technological advancements, and socio-cultural tensions related to immigration and multiculturalism.

The volatile nature of populism requires careful consideration in investment strategies. It has the dual potential to invigorate democratic engagement by giving voice to marginalized groups, yet it can also threaten democratic integrity by challenging established institutions. Economically, populist policies, while potentially offering immediate benefits, often lead to instability and long-term challenges, requiring a nuanced assessment of their impact. Therefore, populism has the potential to reshape political and economic scenarios.

This theoretic synthesis underscores the necessity of navigating global markets influenced by populism. It emphasizes the importance of integrating dynamic political risk assessments with investment strategies to effectively manage populist-influenced risks.

2.4.2 Research Gap

In recent years, the growing emergence of populism has raised questions about its potential impact on financial markets. Research by *Çakmakli et al.* is essential to this investigation as it provides a fundamental understanding of how the political demands of populist leaders, particularly in their criticism of and influence on central banks, affect market dynamics. According to their research, political commentaries have a significant impact on the level and volatility of market prices, especially in countries with weaker institutional frameworks. These findings demonstrate not only the disruptive capacity of populist rhetoric in the short run, but also its potential to have long-term consequences for central bank credibility and economic stability. Further, the variation in these effects across national contexts underscores the complexity of populism's impact on financial markets.[512]

Expanding on these insights, *Hartwell*'s analysis covers nine developed economies, tracing the rise of populism since 2008. The study highlights the increase in market volatility following populist electoral successes, indicating that the immediate market reaction is primarily through volatility channels. Nevertheless, the author also finds that the long-term effects of populism depend on the specific historical and national context of the populist movement, suggesting a nuanced and uneven impact on financial markets.[513]

Mueller et al. expand on this discussion by analyzing the stock market responses to the September 2022 elections in Italy and Sweden, shifting their focus from broader market indices to the performance of individual stocks. This approach reveals significant post-election uncertainty in Sweden, in stark contrast to the largely anticipated outcomes of the Italian elections. By concentrating on individual stocks rather than market indices, the study offers a more detailed view of market reactions, emphasizing how the impact of populism varies based on election results.[514]

Using a novel approach, *Stöckl and Rode* go beyond the binary distinctions of previous studies and introduce innovative measures that capture different levels of populism. Their research focuses on the short-term effects of populism on the volatility option market and shows that the success of populist parties has a significant impact on market volatility. This effect is immediately reflected in the prices of major index options around elections, with variations depending on the populist ideology in question.[515]

In spite of the extensive insights provided by these studies, several gaps remain. Primarily, they focus on short-term effects and specific electoral events, with limited geographic coverage. Moreover, most analyses have been conducted at the country level, leaving scope for a more detailed examination of individual stock performance and long-term effects. This thesis aims to fill these gaps by investigating the influence of populism on long-term investor expectations and decision-making processes, particularly in stock markets known for their sensitivity to regulatory policy.[516]

---

[512] See Çakmakli et al. 2023, pp. 1–27.

[513] See Hartwell 2022, p. 1.

[514] See Mueller et al. 2023, p. 1.

[515] See Stöckl and Rode 2021, pp. 51–83.

[516] See Ferrara and Sattler 2016, p. 2.

2.4.3 Research Question

In financial markets, the emergence of populism is a potentially pivotal political factor whose full impact on investor behavior and market dynamics has yet to be explored. This thesis builds on investment theory and political risk assessment, and then shifts its focus to a more refined investigation: the specific impact of populism on financial markets. It intends to analyze how populist parties and actors, with their distinctive appeal to the masses against the established elite, can shape investor expectations and redefine the traditional paradigms of political risk in financial environments. To accomplish this, an ideational approach to populism is adopted due to its advantages for cross-country empirical analysis and over time.

Understanding the relationship between politics and financial markets is essential. Financial markets are not isolated economic spheres, but rather a reflection of the broader political climate. Changes in government composition, policy decisions or global geopolitical events can significantly impact market volatility and financial returns. This is illustrated by the impact of these events on the performance of equity, bond, and currency markets. *Ferrara and Sattler's* research highlights the significant sway of political developments on market valuations.[517]

However, it is important to note that the impact of government economic policies on financial markets can be nuanced and sometimes overlooked. Whether directly, through strategic investment, or indirectly, through fiscal, regulatory or monetary changes, such policies shape expected return profiles and contribute to the prevailing level of uncertainty.[518] This uncertainty, in turn, can significantly impact investment decisions made by governments, businesses, and households.[519]

Measuring political uncertainty, particularly in the context of populism, can be challenging due to the intangible nature of the influencing factors. Researchers have attempted to quantify uncertainty primarily through economic policy instruments, but these measures, such as the EPU index, capture only a fraction of the complexity.[520] Adopting an electoral method as an alternative approach provides a distinctive perspective by treating political events as discrete exogenous factors, thereby differentiating political uncertainty from broader economic

[517] See Ferrara and Sattler 2016, p. 1.

[518] See Heigermoser 2020, p. 2.

[519] See Al-Thaqeb and Algharabali 2019, p. 2784.

[520] See Al-Thaqeb and Algharabali 2019, pp. 2787 ff.

fundamentals.[521] This method has been instrumental in understanding how electoral uncertainty can impact various financial metrics, such as Initial Public Offerings (IPOs) prices and volumes,[522] corporate investment strategies,[523] and cross-border investment performances.[524]

Nevertheless, the most common studies in this area tend to focus on *Baker et al.'s* EPU index.[525] The literature review by *Al-Thaqeb and Algharabali* indicates that the EPU index has a significant influence on economic behavior and corporate decision-making. EPU prompts corporations to adopt more conservative approaches, characterized by reduced capital expenditures and decreased activity in initiating new ventures such as IPOs and M&As. Furthermore, EPU leads to increased financing costs and encourages companies to hold larger cash reserves, resulting in delayed spending and investment decisions across both macroeconomic and microeconomic domains.[526]

Despite recent progress in quantifying uncertainty in relation to politics, there has been limited scholarly attention given to the multidimensional aspects of political risk, particularly the risks associated with populism. Populism introduces an element of unpredictability into financial markets, thereby challenging the very foundations of traditional economic practices. These implications extend to encompass a range of destabilizing effects on investment decisions, as well as long-term market stability and financial planning. Yet the extent and nature of populism's impact, especially when distinguishing between its different variants, has not been extensively studied.

In response to the research gap, this thesis seeks to shed light on a specific dimension of political risk: populism. The central research question, "*What are the effects of populism on investor expectations and political risk assessments in financial markets?*", aims to provide a deeper understanding of how populism affects investor behavior and market dynamics, as well as the broader landscape of political risk within financial environments. Given existing research, such as that of *Devinney and Hartwell* and *Stöckl and Rode*, which suggests that the perception of populism as a fundamental risk factor could significantly influence investor behavior and reshape market dynamics, this research is particularly timely.[527]

---

[521] See Dai and Zhang 2019, pp. 311 ff.

[522] See Çolak et al. 2017, pp. 2523 ff.

[523] See Jens 2017, pp. 563 ff.

[524] See Cao et al. 2019, pp. 439 ff.

[525] See Baker et al. 2016, pp. 1593 ff.

[526] See Al-Thaqeb and Algharabali 2019, pp. 1–11.

[527] See Devinney and Hartwell 2020, pp. 32–66; Stöckl and Rode 2021, pp. 51–83.

The primary objective of this thesis is to enhance the comprehension of how investors perceive populist gains in the financial market context. By building on the findings of previous studies, this thesis offers new perspectives on the nuanced ways in which populism is embedded in the framework of financial decision-making and risk assessment. In exploring this emerging area, the dissertation seeks to contribute an innovative analysis to the existing body of literature on finance research.

The first part of the thesis at hand examines how populism shapes investor expectations in the long run, offering a novel perspective on political risk assessment in financial contexts.[528] The second part focuses on explaining these findings and contributing to a broader understanding of populism as a potentially significant factor in political risk assessment. This second part of the research therefore seeks to develop a comprehensive framework for analyzing the complex relationship between populism, its impact on financial markets, and investor behavior that can provide fundamental guidance for academics, market analysts, and policymakers.

In summary, this thesis offers a two-fold perspective on the impacts of populism in the realm of financial markets—one that elucidates the influence on investor expectations and the other that elaborates on the broader implications for political risk assessment and market behavior.

---

[528] See Section 3.2.1.1 for an in-depth development of hypotheses, which is informed by the identified quantitative research gap.

3 Empirical Analyses

3.1 Mixed Methods Framework

This chapter outlines the rationale and design for employing a mixed methods approach to complement quantitative findings with qualitative analysis for in-depth examination. It first evaluates the philosophical basis and suitability of the approach, followed by a subchapter dedicated to the strategic choices made in employing the mixed methods approach. The overall objective is to illustrate the utility of the approach in analyzing the impact of populism on financial markets.

3.1.1 Foundations

This subchapter provides a brief overview of how research paradigms and philosophical orientations impact the selection of research methods. It clarifies that paradigms shape a researcher's approach and influence every aspect of the research process. Furthermore, it provides a selective overview of different paradigms, each with its own set of assumptions and methodological preferences. Further, the subchapter addresses the emergence of mixed methods research, highlighting the debate over its philosophical underpinnings. Ultimately, it advocates for the dissertation's mixed methods approach, emphasizing the primacy of research questions and the pursuit of a more holistic understanding afforded by the synthesis of both qualitative and quantitative methods.

C. Schütz, *Populism and Financial Markets*, Studies in Finance and Accounting,
https://doi.org/10.1007/978-3-658-46858-3_3

3.1.1.1 Research Paradigms

The process of identifying an appropriate research approach is fundamentally guided by the philosophy of science, which contends that the philosophical foundations of inquiry influence the strategic choice of methods. As *Godfrey-Smith* argues, the philosophy of science investigates the progression of scientific knowledge, which serves as a foundation for methodological decisions within diverse research paradigms.[1] These paradigms then shape the researcher's approach to a research inquiry. *Guba and Lincoln* describe a research paradigm as a fundamental worldview that guides researchers,[2] while *McGregor and Murnane* view it as a collection of assumptions and practices that form the framework of reality.[3]

The choice of a research paradigm has far-reaching implications for the entire research approach, including decisions about methodology, design, and data analysis. The research paradigm is distinguished by its ontological, epistemological, and methodological perspectives, which in turn dictate the interaction between researcher and subject, as well as the methods used to collect and analyze data.[4] Ontology, the first dimension of a paradigm, pertains to the nature of reality and analyzes the existential status of the surrounding world. It spans from realism, which assumes an objective reality, to relativism, which proposes that reality is subjective to individual perception.[5] Thus, the ontological position profoundly influences the approach to understanding reality.[6]

Epistemology, the study of knowledge acquisition and validation, is the second dimension that explores the relationship between the researcher and the subject. Two important viewpoints are considered, including objectivism, which aims to reveal universal truths, and subjectivism, which believes that knowledge is personal and interpretive, allowing only subjective impressions of reality to be tested.[7]

---

[1] See Godfrey-Smith 2021, pp. 3 ff.

[2] See Guba and Lincoln 1994, p. 150.

[3] See McGregor and Murnane 2010, p. 419.

[4] See Khan 2014, p. 225; Kivunja and Kuyini 2017, pp. 26 f.; Mayring 2022, pp. 18 f.

[5] See Mayring 2022, p. 18.

[6] See Khan 2014, p. 225; Staller and Chen 2022, p. 70.

[7] See Mayring 2022, p. 18; Scotland 2012, p. 9.

Finally, the third dimension, methodology, pertains to the comprehensive strategy and logic of the research design, including the science of appropriate methods. It evaluates the merits of different data collection and analysis techniques to shape the reliability of research findings. The methodology elected should accord with the ontological and epistemological underpinnings of the research paradigm.[8]

A variety of paradigm classifications are recognized in the social sciences, each proposing a different approach to understanding social phenomena.[9] *Guba and Lincoln* identify four major paradigms—positivism, postpositivism, constructivism, and critical approaches—that differ in their ontological and epistemological assumptions and influence the choice of the research method.[10]

Positivism is based on a realist ontology and advocates that empirical observation provides objective knowledge. By emphasizing the use of quantitative methods to produce consistent, replicable results, positivism suggests that the observer should remain detached from the object of study.[11]

Postpositivism expands upon positivism, recognizing observer bias and data imperfections as limitations. While retaining a quantitative basis, it also incorporates qualitative methods under strict controls and favors a deductive approach that seeks to falsify rather than confirm hypotheses.[12]

Constructivism adopts a relativist ontology that acknowledges the subjective nature of human perceptions and refutes the idea of an objective reality independent of them.[13] Consequently, qualitative methods are preferred by constructivist researchers to understand social phenomena in their subjective contexts.[14]

Critical approaches go beyond traditional positivism and constructivism by advocating for an objective understanding of reality shaped by social and historical factors, particularly those affecting marginalized groups. Thus, these approaches emphasize the qualitative interpretation of multiple perspectives and acknowledge the influence of both researcher and subject values on research.[15]

---

[8] See Mayring 2022, p. 16.

[9] See Okesina 2020, p. 60.

[10] See Guba and Lincoln 1994, p. 109.

[11] See Guba and Lincoln 1994, pp. 109 f.; Okesina 2020, p. 60.

[12] See Mayring 2022, p. 19.

[13] Also referred to as interpretivism see for example Abdullah Kamal 2019, p. 1389.

[14] See Mayring 2022, p. 20; Scotland 2012, p. 13.

[15] See Guba and Lincoln 1994, p. 110; Okesina 2020, pp. 60 f.

Each of these paradigms influences the researcher's methodological choices, underscoring the importance of selecting a paradigm that aligns with the research questions and objectives. In general, the paradigms of positivism and post-positivism tend to align with quantitative methods, whereas constructivism and critical approaches are often associated with qualitative methods.[16]

3.1.1.2 Methodological Synthesis

The recognition of mixed methods research as a stand-alone methodology in the late 1980s marked a fundamental advance in social science research. It established a distinct philosophical and procedural foundation, deviating from the exclusive use of either qualitative or quantitative methods.[17]

The rise of mixed methods was instrumental in bridging the methodological divide that had long been a source of debate within the social sciences.[18] This discourse tended to become what *Ross* called "science wars"[19], with strong advocates of quantitative and qualitative methods defending the superiority of their particular approach.

Nevertheless, there is also considerable controversy surrounding the concept of integrative mixed methods. Some purists contend that the philosophical underpinnings of quantitative and qualitative methods are so divergent that they should not be mixed.[20] Conversely, pragmatists recommend a research strategy that prioritizes research questions and practical outcomes over strict methodological adherence.[21] Moreover, aligned with the pragmatic viewpoint, it is emphasized that research design should consider the complexities and influences within the research context, advocating for the integration of quantitative and qualitative methods to address these concerns more comprehensively.[22]

[16] See Hesse-Biber 2022, pp. 455 f.

[17] See Staller and Chen 2022, p. 82.

[18] See Guba and Lincoln 1989, pp. 21 ff.

[19] Ross 1996, p. 1.

[20] See Cameron 2011, p. 100.

[21] See Hesse-Biber 2015, p. 775.

[22] See Staller and Chen 2022, p. 80.

This dissertation aligns with the pragmatic perspectives by adopting a mixed methods approach. Thereby, the primacy of the research questions steers the methodological decisions, favoring a flexible approach that seeks to uncover insights that might remain obscured under a monomethod approach.[23] However, this decision is not made without reconciling the different assumptions inherent in quantitative and qualitative methods.[24]

3.1.2 Research Design

This subchapter examines the structure and key decisions in mixed methods research design. Divided into three parts, the first section specifies different interpretations of mixed methods research while underscoring its distinct implementation in this thesis. The second section details various mixed methods research designs, their historical context, and explains why the explanatory sequential design was chosen in this thesis. The third section examines the design choices in mixed methods research, specifically regarding the prioritization, implementation, and integration of various methods. Additionally, it elucidates how these techniques are applied within the context of this thesis.

3.1.2.1 Definition and Application

Scholars have identified several reasons for employing mixed methods research, including verifying results through cross-validation, incorporating diverse methodologies to improve interpretation, and synthesizing insights from both qualitative and quantitative approaches to advance methodological frameworks.[25] The progression of mixed methods research is strongly influenced by scholars such as *Greene et al.* and *Johnson and Onwuegbuzie*. Their foundational work not only explained the principles of mixed methods, but also advocated for their empirical application.[26] This development has been further cemented by the establishment of dedicated journals and a burgeoning corpus of specialized literature.[27] Overall, the reliance on a mixed methods approach recognizes that

---

[23] See Feilzer 2010, p. 6; Johnson and Onwuegbuzie 2004, p. 14.

[24] See Hesse-Biber 2022, p. 456.

[25] See Creswell 1999, pp. 455 ff.

[26] See Greene et al. 1989, pp. 255–274; Johnson and Onwuegbuzie 2004, pp. 14–26.

[27] See Creswell 2016, p. 58.

each method has its own strengths and weaknesses, and that neither can provide a complete understanding on its own.[28]

Despite the abundant literature on mixed methods research, different interpretations have led to varied understandings among scholars. A review conducted in 2007, collating 19 different definitions from 21 experts, highlights the divergent interpretations of this approach.[29] *Creswell's* definition describes mixed methods as a comprehensive research strategy that includes both quantitative and qualitative methods to create a holistic research framework.[30] Similarly, *Johnson et al.* advocate for methodological integration to overcome constraints of single-method studies and yield deeper insights.[31]

In contrast, *Morse and Niehaus* propose a broader definition, suggesting that mixed methods research should include studies that blend methodologies within either the qualitative or quantitative realms, deviating from the traditional notion of combining both.[32]

Furthermore, a distinction needs to be made between mixed methods research and multimethods research. In the past, "multimethods" referred to the application of multiple quantitative data types.[33] Its current meaning has expanded to encompass the utilization of different approaches, utilized either sequentially or concurrently, but excluding the integration that characterizes mixed methods research.[34] Similarly, mixed methods differ from approaches that use qualitative data only for quantitative analysis, such as data analysis methods like content analysis.[35]

The mixed methods approach in this thesis is defined as a research strategy that explicitly involves the pairing of a quantitative and a qualitative method. This intentional combination is chosen to draw on the complementary strengths of qualitative and quantitative research to provide a richer, more nuanced analysis than would be possible using either method alone.

[28] See Staller and Chen 2022, pp. 69 ff.

[29] See Johnson et al. 2007, p. 112.

[30] See Creswell 2016, pp. 58 ff.

[31] See Johnson et al. 2007, p. 112.

[32] See Morse and Niehaus 2009, p. 20.

[33] See Creswell 2016, p. 59.

[34] See Anguera et al. 2018, p. 2758; Staller and Chen 2022, p. 83.

[35] See Creswell 2016, p. 60.

3.1.2.2 Explanatory Sequential Design

The range of mixed methods research designs is as diverse as the definitions of the approach. In the early 1980s, mixed methods research designs were heavily influenced by a positivist paradigm that often relegated qualitative methods to a secondary, supporting role.[36] Even today, there is no universal agreement on the naming or structure of these designs, with a variety of procedures emerging over time.[37] In fact, *Creswell and Clark* reported the existence of approximately forty mixed methods research designs, highlighting the expansive growth and breadth of the field.[38]

To navigate the multitude of configurations, *Creswell* has proposed a more concise categorization that focuses on commonly used designs while allowing for adaptation and exploration of new variations as research demands. This approach has resulted in a framework that includes three basic, and three advanced mixed methods designs.[39]

The three basic designs consist of the convergent design, the explanatory sequential design, and the exploratory sequential design. In a convergent approach, researchers simultaneously collect and analyze both quantitative and qualitative data separately. Aiming to compare the outcomes and identify any parallels, this approach provides a multi-dimensional viewpoint on the research query.[40]

The exploratory sequential design divides the process into two steps, beginning with qualitative data collection and analysis. This initial stage is essential for creating quantitative measures, such as surveys or experiments, when no pre-existing instruments are appropriate for the particular context of the investigation. This phase helps tailor the instruments used to the specific needs of the population being studied.[41]

---

[36] See Giddings 2006, p. 195; Hesse-Biber 2022, p. 618.

[37] See Hirose and Creswell 2023, p. 12.

[38] See Creswell and Plano Clark 2007, p. 59.

[39] See Creswell 2016, pp. 62–64.

[40] See Creswell 2016, pp. 63 f.

[41] See Creswell 2016, p. 64.

In contrast, the explanatory sequential design starts with collecting and analyzing quantitative data to establish a general understanding of the research problem. The following qualitative phase delves deeper into the topic by exploring participants' perspectives to shed light on the initial statistical findings. This design is favored for its clarity and the depth it brings to quantitative findings, although it may require more time and resources.[42]

The three advanced designs incorporate elements such as experimental frameworks or social justice perspectives. However, this thesis does not elaborate on advanced designs, as they are not necessary for addressing the research question. Instead, an explanatory sequential design is chosen to contextualize the quantitative findings with qualitative insights, as this thesis aims to investigate the factors influencing investors' risk perceptions amidst the rise of populism in financial markets. Specifically, this research design begins with a quantitative analysis of market and investor reactions to rising populism. Subsequently, it incorporates qualitative investigations of investor responses to provide a comprehensive understanding of the impact of populism on financial markets. In fact, according to *Dewasiri et al.*, such an explanatory sequential design is prevalent in finance-related mixed methods research, underscoring its relevance and utility in capturing the nuanced effects of political phenomena on economic behavior.[43]

3.1.2.3 Design Elements

In the context of mixed methods research, the study's direction is determined by specific decisions on the design elements, besides the particular design chosen. These choices are guided by the study's objectives, the research questions it aims to address, and the dominant methodological discourse within the academic field.[44] *Ivankova et al.* outline decisions on three key elements that need to be made in relation to the degree of emphasis on quantitative versus qualitative methods (priority), the sequencing of data collection and analysis (implementation), and the points at which these methods are integrated (integration).[45]

The element of priority in mixed methods research refers to the weight given to quantitative or qualitative approaches. It is influenced by the focus of the researcher, the needs of the research target, and the complexity of the topic.[46] The thesis operationalizes the approach through the explanatory sequential design

---

[42] See Ivankova et al. 2006, p. 5.

[43] See Dewasiri et al. 2018, p. 8.

[44] See Onwuegbuzie 2012, p. 478.

[45] See Ivankova et al. 2006, pp. 9–11.

[46] See Ivankova et al. 2006, pp. 9 f.

described previously. Starting with a quantitative assessment to establish a baseline understanding of market responses to populism. The subsequent qualitative phase, which builds on the initial analysis, is central to the thesis and aims to uncover the deeper relationships and contextual factors that quantitative data alone cannot reveal. This qualitative phase is not merely an attachment, but rather the core of the investigation, as evidenced by the significant amount of coverage devoted to the qualitative analysis and its findings. By emphasizing qualitative research, a comprehensive understanding of populism's impact on investor sentiment and market dynamics is established, providing insights with practical relevance for policymakers, companies and investors.

The second design element, implementation, pertains to the sequence of data collection and analysis, both quantitative and qualitative.[47] The explanatory sequential design chosen for this thesis involves data collection in two distinct stages. First, quantitative data is gathered and analyzed. Then, the qualitative phase begins, examining the implications of the quantitative findings. The study's objectives dictate the sequence, with qualitative data collection deferred until quantitative data analysis is complete.

According to *Ivankova et al.'s* model, the third design element, integration, refers to the stages in the research process where the quantitative and qualitative approaches converge.[48] This can occur at various stages, from the initial phase of the research process, where objectives are defined and research questions are formulated, to the final phase, where results are compared in an integrative phase.[49] In this thesis, integration is a central process that takes place at several stages: first, in the specification of research objectives; second, in the design of the qualitative research phase through the consideration of quantitative findings; and finally, in the synthesis of findings from both qualitative and quantitative strands to formulate comprehensive conclusions that contribute to a holistic analysis. Figure 3.1 presents an overview of the mixed methods research approach, including its design and key design elements.

---

[47] See Greene et al. 1989, p. 255.

[48] See Greene et al. 1989, p. 270; Ivankova et al. 2006, p. 11.

[49] See Ivankova et al. 2006, p. 11.

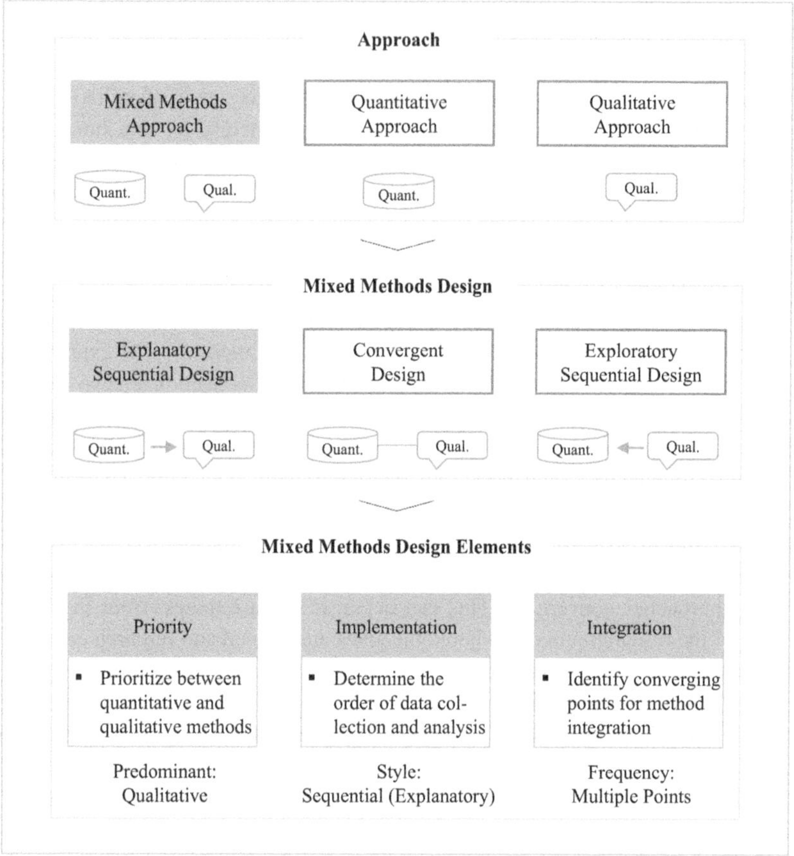

Fig. 3.1 Mixed Methods Design—Overview. (Source: Own Illustration.)

3.2 Quantitative Study

This chapter of the thesis introduces the quantitative study that focuses on the impact of populism on financial markets.[50] It first establishes the research framework, outlines the quantitative approach, and details the analytical process. This includes deriving hypotheses, identifying key variables, and constructing the

[50] See also Schütz and Pape 2024, pp. 1 ff.

regression model, laying a solid foundation for the analysis. The next subchapter covers the process of sample selection and description. Following this, the core findings are presented, which reveal the effects of populism on market behavior and investor expectations. The chapter concludes with an interim discussion.

3.2.1 Research Design

This subchapter presents the quantitative research approach to investigate populism's impact on financial markets. It begins by formulating hypotheses to set the stage for the analysis. Subsequently, the key variables relevant to the study are identified and examined. Finally, the regression model designed to systematically investigate the relationship between populism and market responses is presented.

3.2.1.1 Hypotheses Development

This section focuses on developing hypotheses regarding the influence of populism on financial markets. The analysis aims to elucidate the specific ways in which populism influences investor behavior and market dynamics, leading to the development of two hypotheses.

First, the impact of populism on the political landscape and its effect on investors' required returns is analyzed. The focus is on how populism influences the cost of equity, a critical financial metric in strategic decision-making, representing the risk-adjusted return required by investors.[51] In this regard, the analysis refers to the theoretical framework for asset pricing in politically uncertain environments, as established by *Pástor and Veronesi.* By demonstrating the complex relationship between government-induced uncertainty and its impact on asset pricing in a general equilibrium setting, these models find that political uncertainty leads investors to demand a risk premium. They also elaborate on how political uncertainty stemming from government policy decisions can significantly affect investor behavior and market dynamics. Furthermore, the models provide a conceptual framework for government decision-making processes and their impact on investors facing uncertainty about future policy directions. Most relevant to this study, these models emphasize the central role of the risk premium associated with political uncertainty.[52]

Building on these insights, various empirical studies have delved into the effects of politically induced uncertainty on asset pricing, focusing mainly on

[51] See Chapter 2.1 for more information.

[52] See Pástor and Veronesi 2012, pp. 1219–1264; Pástor and Veronesi 2013, pp. 520–545.

equity markets. These studies often use tools such as the EPU index[53] or examine specific instances of political uncertainty, such as leadership transitions[54] or political scandals.[55]

In drawing on these findings, the thesis at hand focuses uniquely on the specific implications of populism. *Devinney and Hartwell* emphasize the need to recognize the distinct risks associated with the rise of populist parties, suggesting that investors may increasingly consider these developments as significant risk factors in their decision-making processes.[56] Following their argument, this study examines how populism induces political uncertainty, i.e., the economic risk posed by unclear future government policies and regulations. It proposes the concept of a populism risk premium, a heightened rate of return required due to the added element of political uncertainty brought by populism.

Recognizing the differentiated impact of political dynamics on financial markets, the focus of this study shifts to how populism specifically increases uncertainty for investors. Populist regimes are characterized by unpredictable policy shifts,[57] often anchored in unsustainable macroeconomic policies with potential long-term economic consequences.[58] They also tend to challenge or weaken established democratic institutions, adding another layer of complexity. This tendency not only makes it difficult to quantify the economic impact of institutional changes but also undermines the institutional framework,[59] reducing investor confidence.[60] Consequently, market participation decreases, and investment opportunities contract.[61] In this context, the study posits that the increasing influence of populist parties introduces a distinct form of political uncertainty, prompting investors to reevaluate risks and pursue greater long-term returns. This leads to the formulation of the first hypothesis:

---

[53] See for example Brogaard and Detzel 2012, pp. 3–18. For a literature overview on the impact of EPU on stock market returns, see Al-Thaqeb and Algharabali 2019, pp. 5 f.

[54] See Li et al. 2018, pp. 215–222.

[55] See Liu et al. 2017, pp. 286–310.

[56] See Devinney and Hartwell 2020, p. 33.

[57] See Bartha et al. 2020, p. 71.

[58] See Funke et al. 2023a, p. 3250. For an analysis of the economic impact of populism see also Subsection 2.3.1.4.2.

[59] See Benczes 2022, pp. 109 ff. For an analysis of the political impact of populism see also Subsection 2.3.1.4.1.

[60] See La Porta et al. 1997, p. 333.

[61] See Georgarakos and Pasini 2011, p. 693.

H1: There is a positive relationship between the rise of populism and the risk-adjusted returns required by investors.

Second, the quantitative analysis examines the effects of different forms of populism, distinguishing between left-wing and right-wing populism.[62] While left-wing populism often emphasizes anti-business sentiments and promotes multiculturalism and inclusion,[63] right-wing populism typically focuses on cultural issues and targets minorities as threats to national identity and security.[64] The study proposes that investors may be more skeptical of left-wing populism due to its association with state market regulation and income redistribution,[65] while some right-wing populists are perceived as more business-friendly.[66] This leads to the formulation of the second hypothesis:

H2: Investors are more skeptical of the electoral success of left-wing populism than right-wing populism.

To summarize, these two central hypotheses regarding the impact of populism on financial markets explore the notion of a populism risk premium and differentiate the effects of left-wing versus right-wing populism on investor behavior and financial decision-making. The subsequent section will focus on operationalizing these hypotheses.

3.2.1.2 Variables

A detailed examination of the key variables central to the research hypotheses is presented in this section. It includes a comprehensive analysis of these variables, detailing their measurement methodologies, relevance, and justifications for their inclusion. The analysis begins with an assessment of variables that gauge investor return expectations and progresses to an evaluation of indicators for measuring populism. To enhance the robustness of the study, a set of control variables at both the firm and country level are also discussed in this section.

---

[62] See Subsection 2.3.1.2.2 for a more detailed distinction between different varieties of populism.

[63] See Stavrakakis and Katsambekis 2014, p. 132.

[64] See Rodrik 2018b, p. 196.

[65] See Cole and Schofer 2023, p. 1.

[66] See Funke et al. 2023a, p. 3256.

3.2.1.2.1 Implied Cost of Equity Capital

Among the various methods for calculating expected returns, the Implied Cost of Equity Capital (ICC), as presented in Section 2.1.2.3, distinguishes itself significantly from traditional models such as the Capital Asset Pricing Model (CAPM) and *Fama and French's* three-factor model. While the CAPM and the three-factor model rely on historical data to determine risk premiums based on past performance, the ICC approach is inherently forward-looking, utilizing current market prices and future earnings forecasts to determine expected returns. By providing a forward-looking perspective, ICC models enable an assessment of how populist political shifts influence risk assessments and market dynamics. Academic support from scholars such as *Lee et al.*, *Li et al.*, and *Pástor et al.* underscores the effectiveness of these models in revealing economic relationships that are often obscured by measures based on realized returns.[67]

Building on this argument, the ICC is constructed as an average of both residual income models and abnormal earnings growth models, providing a comprehensive measure of risk assessment and market expectations. More specifically, this study employs the four most commonly utilized models to derive this ex-ante metric:[68] *Claus and Thomas's* model (*ICC_CT*), *Gebhardt et al.'s* model (*ICC_GLS*), *Ohlson and Juettner-Nauroth's* model (*ICC_OJ*), and *Easton's* model (*ICC_ET*).[69] Each of these models integrates analysts' earnings forecasts with current stock prices to determine the ICC. However, they differ in their foundational assumptions and methodologies, such as the forecast horizon and growth expectations.[70]

The first model, *ICC_CT*, is a residual income-based valuation approach that aims to capture the current share price by considering various financial factors. The calculation of *ICC_CT* takes into account the cost of equity, present book value, forecasted earnings, and earnings growth. The following formula at the core of this model is solved for *ICC_CT*.

---

[67] See Lee et al. 2011, pp. 1–38; Li et al. 2012, pp. 1–49; Pástor et al. 2008, pp. 2859–2897.

[68] See Mishra and O'Brien 2019, p. 74.

[69] See Claus and Thomas 2001, pp. 1629–1666; Gebhardt et al. 2001, pp. 135–176; Ohlson and Juettner-Nauroth 2005, pp. 349–365; Easton 2004, pp. 73–95.

[70] See Rjiba et al. 2021, p. 6. See also Section 2.1.2.3 for a discussion on different ICC models.

$$P_o = B_o + \sum_{t=1}^{5} \frac{(E_t - ICC\_CT * B_{t-1})}{(1 + ICC\_CT)^t} + \frac{(E_5 - ICC\_CT * B_4)}{(ICC\_CT - g_{lt})(1 + ICC\_CT)^5} \quad (3.1)$$

Here, P_o represents the current share price, and B_0 is the book value of equity per share as of the most recent fiscal year-end. The term E_t denotes the median analyst earnings forecast for period t. If a three, four, or five-year-ahead earnings forecast is not available within the Institutional Brokers' Estimate System (IBES), a methodology similar to that proposed by *Boubakri et al.* or *Xu* is employed.[71] In this case, a missing forecast is extrapolated by using the previous year's forecast along with the long-term growth projection from IBES (g_{lt}^{IBES}).[72]

Consistent with the assumption of the clean surplus relation,[73] the *ICC_CT* model facilitates the calculation of future book values of equity using current book values, expected earnings, and dividends.[74] In particular, the future book value of equity is calculated using the clean surplus relation, assuming an average payout ratio based on data from the last three years.[75] Residual income for period t (RI_t) is computed by deducting the cost of equity charge from the forecasted earnings using the formula:

$$RI_t = E_t - ICC_{CT} * B_{t-1} \quad (3.2)$$

The model maintains a fixed explicit forecast horizon of five years. After this period, the forecasted residual earnings are expected to grow at the long-term growth rate (g_{lt}). This long-term growth rate is determined as the greater of two values: Either the difference from the risk-free rate (rf) based on ten-year country-specific government bonds minus three percent to approximate the real risk-free rate prevailing in the economy, or zero ($g_{lt} = \max(rf - 0.03; 0)$).[76]

71 See Boubakri et al. 2014, p. 330; Xu 2020, p. 55.

72 This is accomplished using the following formula: $E_{t+1} = E_t\left(1 + g_{lt}^{\text{IBES}}\right)$.

73 See Formula (2.9): $B_t = B_{t-1} + E_t(1 - d)$.

74 See Kryzanowski and Rahman 2009, p. 172.

75 $B_t = B_{t-1} + E_t(1 - d)$. See also Subsection 2.1.2.3.2 for more information on the clean surplus relation.

76 See for example Botosan and Plumlee 2005; Gode and Mohanram 2003.

The second model, *ICC_GLS*, also incorporates a residual income-based approach for estimating investor expectations and is derived by solving for the value of *ICC_GLS* using the following formula:

$$P_o = B_o + \sum_{t=1}^{5} \frac{(froe_t - ICC\_GLS) * B_{t-1}}{(1 + ICC\_GLS)^t} + \sum_{t=6}^{11} \frac{(froe_t - ICC\_GLS) * B_{t-1}}{(1 + ICC\_GLS)^t} + \frac{(froe_{12} - ICC\_GLS) * B_{11}}{ICC\_GLS * (1 + ICC\_GLS)^{12}} \tag{3.3}$$

This valuation model relates the current share price (P_0) to the book value of equity per share at the most recent fiscal year-end (B_0), and projected return on equity ($froe_t$). The model operates in three distinct stages, estimating the future book values of equity as in the *ICC_CT* model.[77] The initial stage involves establishing a five-year forecast horizon. During this stage, the company-specific return on equity ($froe_t$) for the first years is estimated using median analysts' earnings forecasts (E_t). Here, $froe_t$ is defined as:[78]

$$froe_t = \frac{E_t}{B_{t-1}} \tag{3.4}$$

In the subsequent stage, the model linearly adjusts the projected return on equity to match the industry return on equity $\left(froe_t^{Ind}\right)$ by the twelfth year.[79] This industry return on equity is calculated as a ten-year rolling average, following the *Fama-French* 48 industry classifications[80] and excluding firms with a negative return on equity. This stage captures the concept of mean reversion, which suggests that individual company performance will gradually converge with that of its industry peers over time. In the final stage, the return on equity is projected to remain constant. This adheres to the principle that companies tend to stabilize and mirror broader industry trends over the long term.[81]

[77] The duration of the first and second stage in this process may slightly differ, allowing for variations in the length of each phase.

[78] See Echterling et al. 2015, p. 239.

[79] The formula for t from 6 to 11 is used: $froe_t = \frac{1}{7} * \left(froe_t^{Ind} - froe_{t-1}\right) + froe_t$.

[80] See Fama and French 1997, pp. 153–193.

[81] See Gebhardt et al. 2001, p. 136.

The third cost of equity estimate, the *ICC_OJ* model, adopts the abnormal earnings growth approach. The valuation formula for the *ICC_OJ* model is structured as follows:

$$P_o = \frac{E_1}{ICC\_OJ} + \frac{E_1(g_{st} - ICC\_OJ(1-d))}{ICC\_OJ(ICC\_OJ - g_{lt})} \tag{3.5}$$

In this model, the current stock price (P_o) is expressed in terms of E_1,which is the one-year forward earnings estimate, g_{st} is the short-term earnings growth rate based on the growth from the first to the second earnings estimate ($E_2 - E_1$), and g_{lt} is the long-term growth rate, defined similarly to the *ICC_CT* model. Moreover, the dividend payout ratio d is an average based on data from the last three years.[82] For the model to be applicable, the second earnings estimate must exceed the first.

The fourth model for estimating the ICC, *ICC_ET*, is based on the abnormal earnings growth approach. This model is derived from the *ICC_OJ* framework and operates under the assumptions of non-dividend payouts and a zero long-term growth rate. The *ICC_ET* model is represented by the following equation:

$$ICC_{ET} = \sqrt{\frac{E_2 - E_1}{P_0}} \tag{3.6}$$

In Formula (3.6), P_0 is the current share price, while E_1 and E_2 represent the earnings forecasts for one and two years ahead, respectively. The model implicitly incorporates the growth rate within the two-year-ahead earnings growth projections, reflecting the expected change in earnings without the influence of dividends or long-term growth. Similar to the *ICC_OJ* model, the second earnings estimate must be greater than the first for the *ICC_ET* model to be solvable.[83]

Each of these four models provides unique insights into investors' return expectations while maintaining a shared sensitivity to the accuracy of input data, such as analysts' earnings forecasts and growth rates. The relevance and effectiveness of each model can vary significantly depending on the financial context and the specific characteristics of the analyzed firms. To obtain a more balanced estimation, this thesis utilizes a method that averages the estimates derived from all

[82] See Gode and Mohanram 2003, p. 407.

[83] See Boubakri et al. 2014, p. 330.

four models aligning with recommendations from prior literature.[84] This approach can mitigate potential biases or limitations inherent in any single model. The average ICC for company i in year t is denoted by $ICC\_AVG_{t,i}$, and the formula is as follows:

$$ICC\_AVG_{t,i} = \frac{ICC\_CT_{t,i} + ICC\_GLS_{t,i} + ICC\_OJ_{t,i} + ICC\_ET_{t,i}}{4} \tag{3.7}$$

By integrating the results from all four models, this approach ensures a comprehensive assessment of the ICC, resulting in a more reliable estimation as a proxy for investor expectations.

3.2.1.2.2 Populism Measures

Building upon the discussion of populism assessment from Subchapter 2.3.2 this subsection provides insight into the advantages and methodology used to measure populism in this study, following the approach outlined by *Stöckl and Rode*.[85] The study integrates their populism indicator (*POP*) and their ideological measure of populism (*PRILE*). Furthermore, following *Stöckl and Rode's* study, an interaction term between *POP* and *PRILE* (*POPxPRILE*) is included to examine the combined effect of populism and political ideology on investors' risk perceptions.[86]

By focusing on this approach and assessing populism at the party level through content analysis, several key enhancements to the study are introduced. First, the approach of measuring populism at the party level provides direct insights into the ideologies that are likely to influence policy decisions. Analyzing party manifestos becomes a practical method for understanding a party's intentions and future actions, as parties generally act in accordance with their manifestos. This form of analysis offers a systematic and objective way to mitigate subjectivity and potential biases that can be inherent in survey methods (see Section 2.3.2.2).

Second, *Stöckl and Rode's* approach goes beyond a one-dimensional view of populism. By analyzing the core aspects of populism according to the ideational approach (see Subsection 2.3.1.1.3), and treating it as a continuous variable, this method provides a more nuanced understanding of the populist leanings

---

[84] See for example Attig et al. 2013; Belkhir et al. 2017; Chen et al. 2009; El Ghoul et al. 2011; Hail and Leuz 2006; Rjiba et al. 2021.

[85] See Stöckl and Rode 2021, pp. 51–83.

[86] The variables are specified in Subsection 2.3.2.3.2.

within political parties.[87] This perspective is essential for analyzing how populism can affect market dynamics and investor expectations and allows for a deeper exploration of the connections between populist politics and economic outcomes.

Third, this approach utilizes the extensive database of the CMP, grounding the analysis in a strong empirical foundation that covers a wide range of political parties and countries throughout a significant historical period.[88] The approach not only allows for examining of the progression of populism over time but also provides critical insights into the lasting effects of populist politics on the investment climate. Using historical data from manifestos, the approach allows for comparative analysis across political systems, which enhances the global applicability of the research and is essential for understanding the different effects of populism on expected returns in different national contexts.[89]

3.2.1.2.3 Control Variables

In addition to the ICC measures and the populism variables, it is important to consider a range of control variables at both the firm-level $\left(ContF_{i,t}\right)$ and country-level $(ContC_{c,t})$ to ensure a thorough analysis of the impact of populism on the firms' cost of capital. In the context of cross-country ICC comparisons, where numerous factors can significantly influence the relationship, these variables ensure a more accurate assessment.[90]

At the firm level, the first control variable to be considered is the size of the firm $\left(SIZE_{i,t}\right)$, measured by the natural logarithm of a firm's total assets at the end of the previous fiscal year. This approach is grounded in *Diamond and Verrecchia's* findings, which highlight the relationship between larger firms and lower risk premia due to greater information disclosure.[91] As such, a negative correlation between firm size and the ICC is expected.[92]

---

[87] See Stöckl and Rode 2021, p. 58.

[88] See Lehmann et al. 2023.

[89] See Stöckl and Rode 2021, p. 58.

[90] See for example Campbell et al. 2012; Chen et al. 2009; Hail and Leuz 2006; Houston et al. 2015. No unique set of control variables exist, when analyzing the cost of equity. Garzón-Jiménez and Zorio-Grima 2020 provide a comprehensive literature review comparing 22 articles, highlighting variations in included control variables (see Garzón-Jiménez and Zorio-Grima 2020, Table 3, pp. 12 f.).

[91] See Diamond and Verrecchia 1991, p. 1325.

[92] See for example Belkhir et al. 2017, p. 161; Boubakri et al. 2014, p. 332; Gode and Mohanram 2003, p. 405.

Second, the leverage ratio $(LEV_{i,t})$, a measure of financial risk, is also included as a firm-level control variable. The variable reflects the financial stability of the firm and is defined as the book value of total debt divided by the market value of equity. It is suggested that high leverage, which is often associated with an increased risk of financial distress, should have a positive impact on the cost of equity.[93]

Third, the book-to-market ratio $(BTM_{i,t})$ is included in the analysis as an additional firm-specific control variable. This ratio, which is calculated by dividing the book value of equity by the market value of equity accounts for differences in growth prospects and accounting practices. The equity's book value comprises stockholder's equity, deferred taxes, and investment tax credit, reduced by preferred stock capital. Previous research indicates a positive correlation with the ICC.[94]

Fourth, return on assets $(ROA_{i,t})$ is incorporated to control for financial performance. This variable, calculated as net income before extraordinary items divided by total assets at the beginning of the year, is expected to have an inverse relationship with the ICC.[95]

Fifth, analyst forecast bias $(FBIAS_{i,t})$ is included to account for international differences in forecasting practices.[96] This variable is determined by the difference between the median EPS forecast and the actual EPS normalized by the median EPS forecast.[97] It is expected to have a positive coefficient, suggesting that optimistic forecasts may lead to a higher ICC and emphasizing the importance of forecasting accuracy in equity valuations.[98]

Finally, the study also includes the historical volatility of stock returns $(RVAR_{i,t})$, as a control variable at the firm level. The motivation for including the historical volatility of stock returns instead of the beta factor is the inherent complexity and problematic assumptions associated with beta estimation, particularly with respect to the integration of capital markets.[99] The estimation of historical stock return volatility is based on fluctuations in stock returns over

[93] See Belkhir et al. 2017, p. 161; Botosan and Plumlee 2005, p. 35; Gode and Mohanram 2003, pp. 404 f.

[94] See Hail and Leuz 2006, p. 511. The inclusion of this variable in ICC approaches has been a subject of debate in the literature (see for example Gode and Mohanram 2003, p. 406).

[95] See for example El Ghoul et al. 2021, p. 251.

[96] See Easton and Sommers 2007, p. 983.

[97] See Belkhir et al. 2017, p. 161; Hail and Leuz 2006, p. 498; Rjiba et al. 2021, p. 7.

[98] See Botosan and Plumlee 2005, p. 48; Hail and Leuz 2006, p. 498.

[99] See for details Section 2.1.2.1.

the past twelve months. Previous studies have predicted a positive correlation between this variable and the cost of equity.[100]

Transitioning the focus to the country level, this study uses two additional variables to differentiate the impact of populism from broader economic conditions: the GDP growth rate $\left(GDP_{c,t}\right)$ and the inflation rate $\left(INFL_{c,t}\right)$. The GDP growth rate, which serves as a measure of economic development, is hypothesized to have an inverse relationship with the cost of equity. This suggests that robust economic growth correlates with lower equity costs. Conversely, the inflation rate, which indicates the rate at which consumer prices increase, is expected to have a positive relationship with the cost of equity.[101] Table 3.1 provides a detailed overview of the control variables, including their definitions and expected correlations, as well as the respective data sources.

Table 3.1 Control Variables. (Source: Own Illustration.)

	Definition/ Description	Source	Ex.
Firm–level Controls			
SIZE	Size is defined as the natural logarithm of a firm's total assets.	Compustat	–
LEV	Leverage is defined as total debt (the sum of long-term and short-term debt) divided by the market value of equity. The market value of equity is the net number of all common shares outstanding at year end (without treasury shares) multiplied by the adjusted closing share price.	Compustat	+
BTM	Book-to-market ratio is defined as book value of equity scaled by the market value of equity. The book value of equity is the sum of the stockholder's equity plus deferred taxes and investment tax credit minus the preferred stock capital.	Compustat	+
ROA	Return on assets is defined as net income before extraordinary items scaled by total assets at the beginning of the year.	Compustat	–

(continued)

[100] See for example Hail and Leuz 2006, p. 496.

[101] See Belkhir et al. 2017, p. 161; Gungoraydinoglu et al. 2017, p. 176.

Table 3.1 (continued)

	Definition/ Description	Source	Ex.
FBIAS	The one-year-ahead analyst forecast bias is measured as the median EPS forecast for year one minus the actual EPS for the forecast date scaled by the median EPS forecast for year one.	IBES	+
RVAR	Volatility of stock returns over the previous twelve months.	Compustat	+
Country–level Controls			
GDP	The annual GDP growth rate in percent at the country level (Code: NY.GDP.MKTP.KD.ZG).	World Development Indicators	–
INFL	The inflation rate measured as the annual change in consumer prices at the country level (Code: FP.CPI.TOTL.ZG).	World Development Indicators	+

3.2.1.3 Regression Model

To analyze the impact of populism on the ICC, while considering the previously identified variables, various empirical models can be considered. This section evaluates various alternatives to set the stage for introducing the chosen analytical framework.

3.2.1.3.1 Analytic Panel Models

Panel data models are key tools for analyzing datasets that track the ICC in firms across varied international contexts over time. Panel data merges the characteristics of time series with cross-sectional data, playing a crucial role in assessing fluctuations over time and between different entities.[102] When dealing with panel datasets, such as those in this thesis, it is of importance to choose an appropriate panel data model. There are three common types of panel analysis with different characteristics and implications: pooled regression models, fixed effects models, and random effects models.[103]

The pooled regression model treats all units as homogeneous and extends multiple linear regression to panel data scenarios. It is based on the assumptions of linearity, exogeneity, homoscedasticity, non-autocorrelation, and full rank of variables. When these conditions are met, it can provide efficient and consistent

---

[102] See Greene 2019, pp. 415 ff.

[103] See Greene 2019, p. 413.

estimates, assuming the random variable's conditional density is consistent across entities over time. However, potential endogeneity is a limitation that can lead to biases in the estimates, often due to issues such as self-selection, simultaneity, or measurement error.[104]

The fixed effects model is effective at capturing variations within an entity over time, by isolating and controlling for time-invariant characteristics that influence the dependent variable. To apply the fixed effects approach, the dependent variable must be consistently measured for each unit across at least two different time points, ensuring uniform meaning and scale. Furthermore, the predictor variables should demonstrate variability in their values during these periods for a substantial portion of the sample. This variability is essential as it reflects stable, non-random differences, either over time or across different entities. These requirements ensure that the fixed effects model can capture the dynamic relationships in the data, making it a robust tool for analyzing variations within entities over time.[105]

The random effects model is suitable when variations across entities are assumed to be random and not correlated with independent variables. The model considers the variation in unobserved effects across entities as random and unrelated to the independent variables of the model, which accounts for the stochastic variability in unobserved characteristics. Given that this model assumes that the error component is random, it is particularly appropriate for studies in which cross-sectional units are randomly selected from a larger population.[106]

For models that consider heterogeneity across units or over time, both fixed effects and random effects models provide valuable insights.[107] The key difference between the random effects and fixed effects models lies in how they treat observed and unobserved variables. Applying the random effects model assumes that these variables are uncorrelated, implying that the unobserved factors are random and independent of the observed variables. In contrast, the fixed effects model permits potential correlation between observed and unobserved variables, treating the unobserved variables as fixed components within the model. This makes the fixed effects model more suitable for scenarios where unobserved variables are believed to be fixed and possibly correlated with observed variables.[108]

[104] See Das 2019, pp. 468 ff.

[105] See Allison 2009, pp. 6–27.

[106] See Das 2019, pp. 457, 487, 497.

[107] See Das 2019, pp. 471 f.

[108] See Allison 2009, p. 9.

3.2.1.3.2 Research Model

In order to further examine the differences between panel data models, this subsection focuses on their application in assessing the impact of populism on the ICC for firms in an international context. Aligning the chosen model with the specific objectives of this study and the nature of the underlying data set is emphasized as an important factor in ensuring the effectiveness and accuracy of the analysis.

When evaluating the models—pooled regression, fixed effects, and random effects—each offers a unique perspective and analytical strengths for studying the influence of populism on equity costs. While the pooled regression model provides primary insights, it may oversimplify the complex dynamics of the ICC, which is expected to vary substantially across firms and countries. On the other hand, the random effects model provides a broader analysis, but it operates under the assumption that unobserved effects are random components unrelated systematically to the firms' characteristics.

As the aim of this research is to analyze the impact of populism, a dynamic predictor, on the ICC, the fixed effects model is particularly useful. Its strength lies in its ability to deal with unobserved heterogeneity in a dataset characterized by diversity and uneven data distribution across firms and countries.

Empirical research, notably studies focusing on political factors,[109] political risk,[110] and the impact of parliamentary disagreement on the cost of capital,[111] supports the suitability of the fixed effects model for analyzing political influences on financial indicators. Specifically, the research on parliamentary disagreement by *Heigermoser and Maier* serves as a methodological foundation for this investigation, demonstrating the effectiveness of the model in similar contexts.[112] Consequently, to analyze the relationship between populism and investors' return expectations, this study employs the following fixed effects regression, which captures both inter- and intra-country variations in populism and their respective effects on the cost of equity:

$$\begin{aligned} ICC\_AVG_{t,i} = {} & \beta_1 POP_{c,t} + \beta_2 PRILE_{c,t} + \beta_3 POPxPRILE_{c,t} \\ & + \gamma_1 ContF_{i,t} + \gamma_2 ContC_{c,t} \\ & + IndustryFE_k + CountryFE_c + TimeFE_t + \in_{i,t} \end{aligned} \tag{3.8}$$

[109] See Ben-Nasr et al. 2012, pp. 605–646.

[110] See Mishra 2023, pp. 615–644.

[111] See Heigermoser and Maier 2020, pp. 1–72.

[112] See Heigermoser and Maier 2020, pp. 15 f.

Here, $ICC\_AVG_{t,i}$ represents the average of the firm-specific cost of equity estimate. $POP_{c,t}$ is the general populism indicator, while $PRILE_{c,t}$ captures the populist ideology. The interaction term $POPxPRILE_{c,t}$ is included to capture the combined influence of these variables on the investors' risk perception. Control variables at the firm level are denoted by $ContF_{i,t}$, and those at the country level are represented by $ContC_{c,t}$.

To control for time-invariant factors, omitted variables, and unobservable heterogeneity, the model includes three types of fixed effects: industry ($IndustryFE_k$), country ($CountryFE_c$), and year ($TimeFE_t$), where k, c, and t represent industries, countries, and years, respectively. *IndustryFE* accounts for unique industry-specific trends and characteristics, ensuring that variances in equity costs attributable to industry differences are adequately controlled for. The 48-industry classification scheme proposed by *Fama and French* is used to that end.[113] Country-specific elements, including economic, cultural, and political influences, are accounted for by *CountryFE*, effectively isolating the impact of populism from other national variables. *TimeFE* compensates for global economic trends and temporal variations, ensuring that annual fluctuations unrelated to populism do not distort the results. The model nearly universally includes robust standard errors clustered at either the firm or country level to address potential issues of heteroskedasticity or within-panel serial correlation.

This fixed effects approach, tailored to the needs of the study, combines country, time, and industry fixed effects with firm and country level controls and robust standard errors. Therefore, the model's ability to generate reliable insights by accounting for unobserved heterogeneities and data complexities when analyzing the impact of populism on firms' ICC is enhanced.

3.2.2 Sample Selection

This subchapter outlines the creation and analysis of the international research sample used for the analysis. The first section details the construction of the sample, including data sources and selection criteria. While the second section presents summary statistics of the dataset, providing initial insights into the research.

---

[113] See Fama and French 1997, pp. 153–193.

3.2.2.1 Sample Construction

To analyze whether variations in exposure to populism can explain international differences in the cost of equity, a comprehensive compilation of relevant data from multiple sources is conducted. The primary data used to create the populism variables was sourced from the Comparative Manifesto Project (CMP), developed by *Lehmann et al.*[114] Complementing this, election-related information comes from the ParlGov database of *Döring et al.*[115]

Country-level macroeconomic data, essential for the control variables, are obtained from the World Bank database.[116] For robustness tests, sovereign Credit Default Swap (CDS) spreads based on five-year contracts from Refinitiv and the EPU index developed by *Baker et al.* are also included.[117]

Firm-specific financial information is extracted from Compustat and Refinitiv, supplemented with analyst earnings-related data from Institutional Brokers' Estimate System (IBES). Using these databases, the study constructs an international sample of available common stocks, influenced by data availability at the firm level and populism parameters at the country level. Excluded are firms that are not major listings, those not listed on the domestic stock market, or those with a security type other than equity. Furthermore, stock names that include terms such as "warrant" are also filtered out.[118]

While numerous financial measures are required to estimate data-intensive ICCs and control variables, the most significant limitation in this analysis is the lack of earnings forecasts, which are essential for estimation. The average ICC is calculated for firm-years where at least two out of four valuation model estimates are available. To mitigate the influence of outliers, model-specific ICC estimates are capped at one hundred percent, and all continuous variables are winsorized at the first and ninety-ninth percentiles.[119] Given that most countries hold elections in the third quarter, the ICC is computed at the end of each year, with the expectation that election results will have been priced in by then.[120] To avoid look-ahead bias, data availability is ensured by maintaining a time window of at least seven months.[121] Following previous literature, the study focuses primarily on elections that lead to a change in the chief executive role of the government, thus

[114] See Lehmann et al. 2023. See also Subsection 2.3.2.3.2.

[115] See Döring et al. 2022.

[116] See World Bank 2023 and also Table 3.1.

[117] See Baker et al. 2016.

[118] See for example Campbell et al. 2010, p. 3089; Ince and Porter 2006, p. 477.

[119] See Drobetz et al. 2018, p. 32; Li et al. 2022, p. 2; Xu 2020, p. 4.

[120] See Heigermoser and Maier 2020, p. 7.

[121] See Li and Mohanram 2014, p. 1155.

concentrating on presidential elections in presidential systems and parliamentary elections in parliamentary systems.[122]

The final sample comprises firm-year and country-year observations for 25 countries, mainly OECD members, with exceptions such as Croatia and Romania, covering the period from 1995 to 2021. The distribution of the 165 covered elections varies across countries, from a minimum of four in Romania to a maximum of eight in countries such as Austria and Spain. Overall, the dataset comprises 39,071 observations categorized by firm-year and 512 observations classified by country-year. The United States has the highest number of firm-year observations (19,128), followed by the United Kingdom (3,569) and France (2,644), indicating significant representation from these economies. In contrast, Croatia and Slovenia have much smaller contributions, with 31 and 30 firm-year observations, respectively. The data coverage on a country-year basis is relatively consistent for each country, averaging around 20 country-years, with some exceptions such as Canada or Romania.

This dataset, detailed in Table 3.2, provides a broad temporal and geographical span. It establishes a foundation for examining the effects of populist electoral outcomes on investors' risk expectations.

[122] See for example Gungoraydinoglu et al. 2017, p. 173; Julio and Yook 2012, p. 52.

Table 3.2 Sample Overview. (Source: Own Illustration.)

	Elections Included			Observations	
	No. of Covered Elections	Year of First Election	Year of Last Election	Firm-Years	Country-Years
Australia	8	1998	2019	562	21
Austria	8	1995	2019	307	24
Belgium	7	1995	2019	617	24
Canada	6	2000	2015	1,157	15
Croatia	6	2000	2016	31	16
Czech Republic	6	1998	2017	50	19
Denmark	7	1998	2019	455	21
Finland	7	1995	2019	1065	24
France	5	1997	2017	2,644	20
Germany	7	1998	2021	2,459	23
Greece	8	1996	2019	372	23
Hungary	6	1998	2018	49	20
Ireland	5	1997	2016	284	19
Italy	6	1996	2018	1,231	22
Netherlands	8	1998	2021	1,067	23
New Zealand	8	1999	2020	64	21
Norway	6	1997	2017	715	20
Poland	7	1997	2019	451	22
Portugal	8	1995	2019	247	24
Romania	4	2004	2016	41	12
Slovenia	5	2004	2018	30	14
Spain	8	1996	2019	959	23
Sweden	6	1998	2018	1,517	20
United Kingdom	7	1997	2019	3,569	22
United States	6	2000	2020	19,128	20
Total	**165**			**39,071**	**512**

3.2.2.2 Summary Statistics

Within this section, a detailed examination of the data used for the quantitative analysis of this thesis is presented. Table 3.3 provides comprehensive descriptive

Table 3.3 Key Variables Descriptives. (Source: Own Illustration.)

	Mean	Std. Dev.	Min	Q1	Median	Q3	Max
Cost of Equity Estimate							
ICC_AVG	0.11	0.097	0.0001	0.047	0.077	0.13	0.82
Populism Variables							
POP	28.7	5.34	4.92	26.0	29.2	31.2	46.1
PRILE	–8.33	8.16	–32.8	–14.3	–7.48	–2.67	11.1
POPxPRILE	–247.6	268.8	–1,217.3	–397.7	–236.2	–86.6	685.1
Firm–level Controls							
SIZE	7.49	1.88	1.82	6.14	7.46	8.75	13.9
LEV	1.05	2.04	0.00	0.19	0.57	1.13	30.8
BTM	0.58	0.42	0.006	0.26	0.48	0.81	2.00
ROA	0.03	0.12	–0.87	0.013	0.041	0.076	0.47
FBIAS	0.14	1.23	–13.9	–0.12	0.038	0.30	22.1
RVAR	0.10	0.066	0.010	0.061	0.085	0.12	3.88
Country–level Controls							
GDP	0.019	0.024	–0.11	0.015	0.022	0.030	0.25
INFL	0.019	0.012	–0.045	0.013	0.018	0.026	0.14

statistics for the key variables, including mean, standard deviation, minimum, first quartile, median, third quartile, and maximum. This provides a thorough understanding of central tendency and dispersion for each primary variable, which lays the foundation for a deeper exploration of the relationships and patterns within the data in the following chapters.

Focusing on the ICC, the *ICC_AVG* synthesizes the approaches of *ICC_CT*, *ICC_GLS*, *ICC_OJ*, *ICC_ET* and averages 0.11. The estimates range from nearly zero to 0.82, highlighting the significant diversity in the cost of equity across a wide array of international firms.

Concerning populism, *Stöckl and Rode's* proposed populism indicator (*POP*) captures the level of populism at the party level, regardless of its ideological orientation. At a mean of 28.7, *POP* suggests a significant presence of populist elements across the political spectrum in the parties studied. The standard deviation of 5.34 indicates a moderate variation in populism levels, which is indicative of the different levels of populism in political parties internationally. The populism right-left index (*PRILE*) provides insights into the ideological direction of populism. A negative mean of –8.33 on the *PRILE* suggests a tendency toward left-wing populism in the dataset. Additionally, the interaction term between *POP* and *PRILE* reveals the intricate relationship between the level of populism and its political stance, as demonstrated by its negative mean and wide range.

Regarding the firm-level control variables, the natural logarithm of a firm's total assets (*SIZE*) has a mean of 7.49 ($1,789.64 million) and a wide range, indicating the diversity of firm sizes within the sample. The sample companies have, on average, marginally higher debt levels than equity values, as reflected in the leverage ratio (*LEV*) of 1.05. On average, firms' assets are valued at slightly over half of their market value, with a book-to-market ratio (*BTM*) mean of 0.59. The return on assets (*ROA*) varies widely, ranging from –0.87 to 0.47, underscoring significant differences in profitability between companies. The analyst forecast bias (*FBIAS*), with an average of 0.14, indicates a slight tendency towards optimistic earnings forecasts, with a considerable range (–13.9 to 22.1), highlighting different levels of earnings predictability and market sentiment. Lastly, the volatility of stock returns (*RVAR*) over the past year averages at 0.10, denoting a moderate level of variation in the stock returns of the companies in the sample.

Finally, the country-level controls, which include the GDP growth rate (*GDP*) and inflation rate (*INFL*), each with an average of 0.019, reflect the broader economic context of the sample. These indicators display a range of economic conditions, with the GDP growth rate varying from contraction at –0.11 to growth at 0.25, and the inflation rate oscillating between deflation at –0.045 and inflation at 0.14. This range demonstrates the diverse economic environments in which the sampled firms are operating.

3.2.3 Findings

This subchapter examines whether variations in exposure to populism affect investors' risk assessments and proceeds through several stages of analysis. Initially, a correlation analysis examines the relationship between populism and the ICC and extends to assessing correlations with firm-specific factors and country-level indicators. The next phase includes a univariate analysis that segments the sample based on variables related to populism and compares the cost of equity estimates across different groups defined by their measures of populism. Subsequently, a multivariate analysis is conducted to scrutinize the effects of populism under varied model specifications, thereby distinguishing its influence from other factors. The final section concludes with robustness tests using different models and methodologies to ensure the consistency and reliability of the results, thereby providing a comprehensive view of how populism affects investors' risk perceptions and the cost of equity in an international context.

3.2.3.1 Correlation Analysis

This section discusses the main findings of the correlation analysis. Table 3.4 presents the results of the Pearson correlation analysis that examines the relationship between populism and the ICC, using different measurement approaches, namely the average (*ICC_AVG*), median (*ICC_MED*), and specific ICC models (*ICC_CT*, *ICC_GLS*, *ICC_OJ*, and *ICC_ET*). Moreover, the correlations with numerous firm-specific factors and country-level economic indicators and the ICC estimates are shown.

Table 3.4 indicates a consistent, positive, and statistically significant correlation between *POP* and the ICC across several measures—including average, median, and model-specific values—suggesting that an increase in populist sentiment may be associated with a higher ICC.

The controls at the firm level exhibit correlations that are largely consistent with the expectations outlined in Subsection 3.2.1.2.3. Firm size (*SIZE*) displays a negative correlation with ICC, which can be interpreted as the market rewarding the perceived stability and lower risk associated with larger firm size with a lower cost of equity. The positive correlation between book-to-market (*BTM*) ratio and ICC aligns with the anticipated outcomes. Conversely, the negative correlation

Table 3.4 Correlation Analysis. (Source: Own Illustration.)

		Average Estimates		Model-Specific Estimates			
	Ex.	ICC_AVG	ICC_MED	ICC_CT	ICC_GLS	ICC_OJ	ICC_ET
POP	+	0.051***	0.053***	0.040***	0.082***	0.026***	0.012**
SIZE	–	–0.310***	–0.297***	–0.281***	–0.274***	–0.180***	–0.250***
LEV	+	0.010*	0.012**	–0.007	–0.010*	0.082***	0.045***
BTM	+	0.151***	0.150***	0.085***	0.132***	0.246***	0.152***
ROA	–	–0.132***	–0.120***	–0.024***	–0.066***	–0.249***	–0.404***
FBIAS	+	0.071***	0.073***	0.039***	0.059***	0.135***	0.072***
RVAR	+	0.200***	0.190***	0.091***	0.123***	0.355***	0.400***
GDP	–	–0.031***	–0.031***	0.022***	–0.018***	–0.122***	–0.088***
INFL	+	0.041***	0.033***	0.060***	0.028***	0.018***	0.027***

Note: The superscripts ***, **, and * next to the correlation coefficients indicate significance at the 1%, 5%, and 10% levels, respectively.

between return on assets (*ROA*) and ICC is consistent with the expectation that more profitable firms, or those that use their assets more efficiently, are viewed as less risky, resulting in a lower cost of equity. The positive correlation between analyst forecast bias (*FBIAS*) and the ICC suggests that markets may be factoring in the possibility of over-optimistic earnings forecasts by analysts. This may indicate an adjustment for perceived risk in the reliability of information available to the market. Additionally, the return volatility (*RVAR*) shows a strong positive correlation with ICC, which aligns with the expectation that higher volatility is associated with higher risk, leading to an increased cost of equity.

In macroeconomic terms, inflation (*INFL*) has a positive correlation with ICC in all models, suggesting that higher inflation is associated with an increase in the cost of equity. On the contrary, the negative correlation between GDP growth (*GDP*) and the ICC, which holds in all models except the *ICC_CT* model, is consistent with the notion that economic growth tends to reduce perceived risk and thus the cost of equity.

However, the analysis reveals some anomalies. The leverage ratio (*LEV*) displays a non-significant or weakly significant negative correlation with the ICC in some models, which is contrary to the common expectation that higher leverage correlates with higher risk and therefore a higher cost of equity. This finding suggests that the relationship between leverage and the cost of equity may be affected by other mitigating factors that were not accounted for in the models.

Overall, the correlation analysis results suggest that a comprehensive approach is essential for a more balanced and reliable assessment of how populism may affect investor risk assessments. This approach should integrate various ICC measurements with a thorough analysis of firm-level data and macroeconomic indicators to understand the influence on the cost of equity.

3.2.3.2 Univariate Analysis

Expanding on the initial correlation analysis, this section conducts a univariate statistical analysis by dividing the sample into annual subsamples based on two primary indicators of populism. The study assesses the impact of the populism and separates it from the underlying ideological influence. Using a methodology similar to that of *Belkhir et al.* and *Rjiba et al.*,[123] this analysis enables a comparison of medians and means across various cost-of-equity estimates, including

[123] See Belkhir et al. 2017, p. 163; Rjiba et al. 2021, p. 8.

average (*ICC_AVG*), median (*ICC_MED*), and those calculated from specific valuation models (*ICC_CT*, *ICC_GLS*, *ICC_OJ*, and *ICC_ET*).[124]

The reported results in Table 3.5 are drawn from univariate tests comparing estimates of the cost of equity stratified by levels of populism (*POP*) and the populism right-left index (*PRILE*).

Table 3.5 Results Univariate Analyses. (Source: Own Illustration.)

	Populism Indicator (POP)			Populism Right-Left Index (PRILE)		
	Low	High	Diff.	Right-Wing	Left-Wing	Diff.
	(1)	(2)	(2) – (1)	(3)	(4)	(4) – (3)
ICC_AVG	0.103	0.116	0.013^{***} (12.92)	0.100	0.121	0.021^{***} (19.71)
ICC_MED	0.097	0.109	0.012^{***} (11.85)	0.095	0.112	0.017^{***} (16.76)
ICC_CT	0.126	0.155	0.029^{***} (13.23)	0.108	0.170	0.062^{***} (27.09)
ICC_GLS	0.049	0.068	0.019^{***} (14.07)	0.052	0.068	0.016^{***} (10.42)
ICC_OJ	0.122	0.123	0.001^{*} (1.94)	0.123	0.124	0.001 (0.65)
ICC_ET	0.110	0.112	0.002^{***} (3.02)	0.111	0.114	0.003^{***} (3.92)

Note: The t-statistics are reported in parentheses. The superscripts ***, **, and * indicate significance at the 1%, 5%, and 10% levels, respectively.

For the *POP* index, a consistent pattern emerges from the annual classification into High *POP* and Low *POP* groups: firms in the High *POP* category show higher cost of equity estimates than those in the Low *POP* category in all models. For example, in the *ICC_AVG* model, the High *POP* group has an average cost of equity of 11.6%, while the Low *POP* group has 10.3%, a statistically significant difference at the 1% level (t-statistic: 12.92). Similarly, in the *ICC_CT* model, the High *POP* group has an average cost of equity of 15.5%, which is 2.9% higher than the Low *POP* group's average of 12.6%, also significant at the 1% level (t-statistic: 13.23). These consistent results across models suggest that greater

[124] Variations in cost of equity estimates across models arise from distinct assumptions. For instance, the *ICC_CT* model assumes constant residual earnings growth, while the *ICC_GLS* model predicts convergence with industry standards over twelve years using historical data (see Botosan et al. 2011, p. 1098).

exposure to populism leads to a higher cost of equity. This supports the first hypothesis (H1), which posits a correlation between increased levels of populism and an increase in the ICC.

To analyze the relationship between PRILE and the cost of equity estimates, the sample is categorized into annual groups based on left-wing and right-wing populism. The results of the *ICC_AVG* model show that the group subject to left-wing populism has an average cost of equity of 12.1% compared to 10.0% for the right-wing group, with a significant difference of 2.1% at the 1% level (t-statistic: 19.71). This trend is consistent across most *ICC_OJ* models, except for the model, where the difference is not statistically significant. These findings suggest that, in almost all model estimations, groups exposed to left-wing populism experience a higher cost of equity on average, supporting the second hypothesis (H2) that the cost of equity is influenced by the ideological direction of populism.

The univariate analysis provides a fundamental basis for comprehending the impact of populism and its ideological orientation on the cost of equity. However, it is important to note that this approach has inherent limitations, such as potential confounding variables and the challenge of establishing causality. Therefore, it is necessary to extend the exploration into a more rigorous statistical framework. In the following sections, a multiple regression analysis with fixed effects is employed to account for unobserved heterogeneity, control for a wider range of variables, and examine the temporal dynamics involved.

3.2.3.3 Multivariate Analysis

This section extends the analysis to explore the relationships observed between increased populism and a higher cost of equity. To this end, a multivariate approach with fixed effects is used to scrutinize the resilience of this relationship, taking into account a broad spectrum of variables that may influence equity costs, following the foundational regression model.[125]

The analysis is executed through a series of firm-level fixed effects regression analyses, presented in four different models, the results of which are reported in Table 3.6. Each model introduces more sophisticated controls and fixed effects, refining the precision of the outcomes. All models maintain a consistent sample of 39,071 firm-year observations, with clustering at the firm level to ensure robust standard errors.

[125] See Section 3.2.1.3.

Table 3.6 Firm-Level Fixed-Effects Regression Analysis. (Source: Own Illustration.)

		Model 1	Model 2	Model 3	Model 4
	Ex.	ICC_AVG	ICC_AVG	ICC_AVG	ICC_AVG
POP	+	0.093*** (11.74)	0.109*** (6.62)	0.102*** (6.10)	0.086*** (5.14)
PRILE	–		–0.117** (–2.09)	–0.199*** (–3.50)	–0.149** (–2.51)
POPxPRILE			0.163*** (3.83)	0.212*** (3.95)	0.169*** (3.04)
SIZE	–			–0.349*** (–15.53)	–0.348*** (–13.19)
LEV	+			0.049*** (6.31)	0.049*** (6.26)
BTM	+			0.202*** (23.63)	0.187*** (21.29)
ROA	–			–0.091*** (–9.51)	–0.092*** (–9.56)
FBIAS	+			0.014** (2.34)	0.012** (2.04)
RVAR	+			0.023** (2.86)	0.033*** (3.78)
GDP	–			–0.024*** (–5.06)	–0.021 (–2.44)
INFL	+			0.037*** (7.10)	0.034*** (3.30)
Time Effects		No	No	No	Yes
Country Effects		No	No	No	Yes
Industry Effects		No	No	No	Yes
Observations		39,071	39,071	39,071	39,071
Cluster		Firm-level	Firm-level	Firm-level	Firm-level

Note: The reported beta coefficients are standardized, and the t-statistics are reported in parentheses. The superscripts ***, **, and * indicate significance at the 1%, 5%, and 10% levels, respectively.

Model 1 serves as the baseline, examining the direct relationship between populism (*POP*) and the average cost of capital (*ICC_AVG*) without including additional control variables or fixed effects. The coefficient for populism (*POP*) is statistically significant at the 1% level and demonstrates a highly significant positive effect, with a coefficient of 0.093 (t-statistic: 11.74), indicating that an increase in populism is associated with a rise in the cost of equity.

Model 2 extends the analysis by incorporating the populism right-left index (*PRILE*), which quantifies the ideological orientation of populism, and the interaction term *POPxPRILE*. The negative coefficient of the *PRILE* index (–0.117, t-statistic: –2.09) indicates that a right-wing ideological orientation of populism is associated with a decrease in equity costs. Conversely, left-wing populism, represented by negative values of *PRILE*, is associated with an increase in equity costs. The positive coefficient for the interaction term *POPxPRILE* (0.163, t-statistic: 3.83) suggests that when high levels of populism are combined with a right-wing ideological orientation, the cost of equity is amplified.

In Model 3, company-specific controls, including *SIZE*, *LEV*, *BTM*, *ROA* and *RVAR*, are introduced to adjust for the financial characteristics and risk profile of the companies. In addition, country-specific economic indicators such as *GDP* and *INFL* are included as controls to isolate the impact of populism from other financial and macroeconomic variables. Overall, the estimated coefficients of the control variables on the firm and country levels have the predicted signs and are mostly statistically significant at the 1% level. For example, the coefficient associated with *SIZE* is significantly negative (–0.349, t-statistic: –15.53), suggesting that larger firms tend to have a lower cost of equity. Conversely, the coefficient for *LEV* is positively significant (0.049, t-statistic: 6.31), indicating that higher leverage is associated with a higher cost of equity. Within this model, the coefficients for the variables related to populism remain significant. *POP* has a coefficient of 0.102 (t-statistic: 6.10), *PRILE* has a coefficient of –0.199 (t-statistic: –3.50), and *POPxPRILE* has a coefficient of 0.212 (t-statistic: 3.95), confirming that the relationships observed in the previous models are not confounded by the included control variables.

Model 4, the main model, retains all the variables from Model 3 and introduces fixed effects for time, country, and industry. These effects are necessary to control for unobserved heterogeneity and potential confounding influences. Time effects adjust for global economic trends, country effects adjust for national differences, and industry effects adjust for industry-specific risks to ensure that results are not confounded by other systematic variations across time, geography, and industry.

The significant results of the previous models remain valid. More specifically, *POP* has a positive coefficient of 0.086 (t-statistic: 5.14) and this outcome is also economically significant. Given that the median market capitalization in the sample is approximately $1.673 billion, an increase in the ICC of 86 basis points is equivalent to an average of $14.39 million in additional equity financing costs. The *PRILE* index again displays a significant negative coefficient of –0.149 (t-statistic: –2.51), *POPxPRILE* and the term shows a positive coefficient of 0.169 (t-statistic: 3.04). Importantly, these coefficients reassure that the introduction of time, country, and industry effects in Model 4 does not diminish the significance of the populism variables, underscoring the substantial impact of the magnitude and ideological direction of populism on financial valuations. The firm and country-specific controls retain their expected signs and significance levels, reinforcing the robustness of the model. The following section will delve deeper into the robustness of these findings by conducting additional tests to ensure the validity of the conclusions drawn from this multifaceted analysis.

3.2.3.4 Additional Analysis

This section presents a set of additional tests that analyze the impact of populism on investor return expectations. The results are summarized in Table 3.7 and span six different regression models. Each model incorporates a range of methodological nuances and alternative measures to bolster the validity of the main findings reported in the previous section.

Model 1 revisits the firm-year regressions, retaining all control variables at the firm and country levels, considering the three levels of fixed effects, and incorporating firm-level clustering of errors. Uniquely, this model excludes companies located in the United States, which account for approximately 49% of the sample, to mitigate potential overrepresentation bias. Analyzing the remaining 19,943 observations, the impact of populism (*POP*) on the average ICC (*ICC_AVG*) remains significant with a coefficient of 0.059 (t-statistic: 3.23). The impact of the ideological dimension of populism (*PRILE*) also remains significant, with a negative coefficient of –0.166 (t-statistic: –3.00). Furthermore, the interaction term *POPxPRILE* shows a significant positive coefficient of 0.166 (t-statistic: 2.91), indicating that high levels of populism combined with right-wing populist ideology amplify the increase in the cost of equity.

Table 3.7 Robustness Tests. (Source: Own Illustration.)

		U.S. Firms Exclusion	Alternative Cost of Equity Estimates		Country Regression	Credit Risk	EPU Inclusion
	Ex.	Model 1	Model 2	Model 3	Model 4	Model 5	Model 6
		ICC_AVG	ICC_MED	DY	ICC_AVG	CDS	ICC_AVG
POP	+	0.059*** (3.23)	0.081*** (4.77)	0.042** (2.16)	0.168*** (2.90)	0.119*** (2.95)	0.075*** (3.75)
PRILE	–	–0.166*** (–3.00)	–0.148** (–2.44)	–0.104* (–1.68)	–0.281** (–2.09)	–1.186 (–1.55)	–0.122* (–1.72)
POPx PRILE		0.166*** (2.91)	0.164*** (2.89)	0.081 (1.41)	0.256* (1.89)	1.132 (1.54)	0.151** (2.28)
SIZE	–	–0.302*** (–7.54)	–0.334*** (–12.68)	0.261*** (6.50)	–0.081* (–1.71)	–0.017 (–0.27)	–0.385*** (–13.20)
LEV	+	0.057*** (4.24)	0.048*** (6.15)	0.054*** (3.78)	–0.010 (–0.37)	–0.156 (–1.04)	0.049*** (6.05)
BTM	+	0.160*** (13.63)	0.180*** (20.29)	0.234*** (21.60)	–0.017 (–0.21)	–0.221 (–1.25)	0.199*** (20.27)
ROA	–	–0.080*** (–6.51)	–0.085*** (–8.38)	0.159*** (10.08)	–0.253** (–3.21)	–0.097 (–0.97)	–0.089*** (–8.21)
FBIAS	+	0.012 (1.31)	0.014** (2.23)	0.030*** (3.26)	–0.030 (–0.46)	–0.013 (–0.17)	0.010 (1.57)
RVAR	+	0.011 (0.87)	0.033*** (3.86)	0.081*** (6.87)	0.077 (1.13)	0.500 (1.22)	0.039*** (3.93)

(continued)

Table 3.7 (continued)

		U.S. Firms Exclusion	Alternative Cost of Equity Estimates		Country Regression	Credit Risk	EPU Inclusion
	Ex.	Model 1	Model 2	Model 3	Model 4	Model 5	Model 6
GDP	–	–0.029** (–2.49)	–0.020** (–2.26)	–0.002 (–0.19)	–0.071 (–1.15)	–0.060 (–0.79)	–0.012 (–1.21)
INFL	+	0.038*** (3.12)	0.028*** (2.69)	–0.012 (–0.94)	0.288*** (3.17)	–0.085 (–0.65)	0.008 (0.61)
EPU	+						0.016* (1.81)
Time Effects		Yes	Yes	Yes	Yes	Yes	Yes
Country Effects		Yes	Yes	Yes	No	No	Yes
Industry Effects		Yes	Yes	Yes	Yes	Yes	Yes
Observations		19,943	39,071	23,958	512	289	32,324
Cluster		Firm-level	Firm-level	Firm-level	Country-level	Country-level	Firm-level

Note: The reported beta coefficients are standardized, and the t-statistics are reported in parentheses. The superscripts ***, **, and * indicate significance at the 1%, 5%, and 10% levels, respectively.

Model 2 maintains the primary regression framework but transitions to using the median ICC (*ICC_MED*) as the dependent variable, based on the full sample of 39,071 firm-level observations. Consistent with previous findings, this model confirms the positive impact of populism with a *POP* coefficient of 0.081 (t-statistic: 4.77) and the negative association with *PRILE*, having a coefficient of –0.148 (t-statistic: –2.44). Additionally, the interaction term *POPxPRILE* shows a significant positive coefficient of 0.164 (t-statistic: 2.89), reinforcing that the combined influence of high levels of populism and right-wing populist ideology amplifies the effect of populism on the ICC.

In Model 3, the cost of equity is proxied by the dividend yield (*DY*), following *Pástor et al.*,[126] while retaining consistent control variables and fixed effects. By substituting the ICC with the *DY*, the analysis based on 23,958 firm-level observations, explores whether the observed influences of populism on investor return expectations hold when using a proxy that primarily reflects current income rather than future expectations. The results align with previous models, however, the interaction term shows no significance compared to the other models.

Shifting to a country-level perspective, Model 4 aggregates data into country-year median values, similar to *Hail and Leuz*.[127] Based on 512 country-level observations, the results confirm a significant positive impact of populism on the cost of equity, with a coefficient of 0.168 (t-statistic: 2.90) and a negative association with a *PRILE* coefficient of –0.281 (t-statistic: –2.09). The interaction term *POPxPRILE* again shows a positive coefficient of 0.256 (t-statistic: 1.89).

Model 5 complements the focus on the impact of populism on stock markets by examining the impact of populism on sovereign credit risk via CDS spreads across 289 country-level observations. The results show a significant coefficient of 0.119 for *POP* (t-statistic: 2.95) and a negative coefficient for *PRILE* of –0.186 (t-statistic: –1.55), indicating that right-wing populism reduces sovereign credit risk, whereas left-wing populism is viewed as exacerbating it. The interaction term *POPxPRILE* has a positive coefficient of 1.132 (t-statistic: 1.54), though its significance is marginal. This suggests that while there is an indication that the combined effect of high levels of populism and right-wing ideology may increase sovereign credit risk, the result is not robust.

Lastly, Model 6 incorporates the EPU index from *Baker et al.*[128] to disentangle the effects of populism from broader political uncertainty. The model, based on 32,324 firm-level observations, shows a significant positive effect of populism

[126] See Pástor et al. 2008, pp. 2859–2897.

[127] See Hail and Leuz 2006, p. 493.

[128] See Baker et al. 2016, pp. 1593 ff.

on *ICC_AVG* with a coefficient of 0.075 (t-statistic: 3.75), indicating that populism increases the cost of equity, even after accounting for political uncertainty. Furthermore, the effect of *PRILE* remains negative with a coefficient of –0.122 (t-statistic: –1.72), while the interaction term *POPxPRILE* continues to show a positive coefficient of 0.151 (t-statistic: 2.28).

In all six models, the control variables, *SIZE*, *LEV*, *BTM*, *ROA*, *RVAR*, *INFL*, and *GDP*, at the firm and country levels, mostly reflect the expected relationships with the response variables. The supplementary analysis conducted in this subchapter through various models and adjustments further supports the substantive effect of populism on investors' return expectations, which will be discussed in detail in the next subchapter.

3.2.4 Interim Conclusion

This subchapter consolidates the findings from the quantitative analyses presented in the previous subchapter to draw initial conclusions about the impact of populism on the cost of equity and investor return expectations. These findings are essential for understanding the interplay between populism-induced political dynamics and financial markets. The core of the study revolves around testing two hypotheses: first, that populism is positively related to the cost of equity, suggesting that the rise of populism leads to higher risk-adjusted returns required by investors; and second, that this effect is more pronounced for left-wing populism compared to right-wing populism.

In line with the first hypothesis, a statistically significant relationship between rising populism and higher equity costs is observed across various tests, model specifications, and measures, including correlation, univariate, and multivariate analyses. This pattern is not only consistent, but also robust. Taken together, these analyses suggest that populism, with its associated policy uncertainties, significantly increases the cost of equity for firms. The validity of this relationship is further confirmed through various robustness tests, such as alternative measures of the cost of equity, including the median ICC and the dividend yield. Moreover, the consistent impact of populism on the cost of equity, even when controlling for general political uncertainty, highlights the independent and significant influence of populism. This indicates that populism adds an additional layer of complexity to financial market dynamics.

This wide applicability across different model specifications suggests that the observed impact of populism goes beyond specific measurement contexts and is a broader economic phenomenon. Furthermore, this trend persists across various geographic contexts, even when excluding United States firms, highlighting the global significance of the findings. The analysis also includes country-level regressions and examines the impact of populism on sovereign credit risk, as indicated by CDS spreads. This comprehensive approach enables an investigation into how populism may impact financial markets beyond equity pricing, including its potential effect on sovereign creditworthiness.

The testing of the second hypothesis reveals a more nuanced and complex relationship between populism and the cost of equity based on ideological orientation, thus only partially supporting the hypothesis. There is some support for the hypothesis that left-wing populism leads to higher equity costs compared to right-wing populism. However, the interaction term shows a significant positive coefficient in many models, indicating that high levels of populism combined with a right-wing stance amplify the cost of equity. This interplay, apparent across multiple models and metrics, suggests that the market's response to populism is multifaceted, driven by both the degree of populism and its ideological orientation.

Overall, the quantitative analysis underscores a significant impact of populism on investors' return expectations, revealing the intricate relationship between populism's ideological orientation and the cost of equity. This relationship holds even after controlling for a wide range of control variables, including firm-specific characteristics as well as macroeconomic factors. Including time, country, and industry fixed effects in the regression models further refines the analysis, allowing for a more precise estimation of the impact of populism while controlling for potential external influences.

Despite the robust findings, it is important to acknowledge the potential limitations, such as the challenge of establishing causality. While the analyses demonstrate correlations, further research is needed to explore the causal mechanisms through which populism influences investor perceptions and financial markets. Additionally, the challenging nature of the ideological findings underscores the need for further research. The qualitative study that follows, aims to further explore the impact of populism on financial markets and how different ideologies are perceived in financial markets.

3.3 Qualitative Study

Following up on the quantitative results, this chapter employs a qualitative analysis as the second phase of the mixed methods approach, aiming to understand how increased populism affects investor return expectations and financial markets.

Organized into three subchapters, this part of the thesis will address the important considerations inherent in qualitative research. The first subchapter will cover the method of data collection, which will be discussed in the next subchapter and set the foundation for the subsequent analytical strategies. The following subchapter will detail the data analysis and interpretation methods. Finally, the composition and rationale of the research sample is explained, emphasizing the importance of this aspect as it is influenced by both the collection and analysis methods.

3.3.1 Research Design

This subchapter outlines the qualitative study's research design, focusing specifically on the pivotal elements of data collection and analysis. The data collection methods are fundamental to the ensuing analysis, ensuring the study's elements build upon one another to create a cohesive and comprehensive representation. Reflecting the cyclical nature of qualitative research, data collection and preliminary analysis are presented as mutually reinforcing processes that continually enhance each other throughout the investigation.

The first section provides insight into the method of data collection, where interviews are identified as a pivotal approach to investigate the relationship between populism, financial markets, and investor behavior. The section explores various interview formats and details the structure of the interview guide. Additionally, the section discusses the transcription process, emphasizing the importance of converting interviews into data suitable for analysis.

The second section introduces the *Gioia* Methodology, acclaimed for its contribution to methodological rigor. It outlines the core principles and foundational assumptions of this approach. This section also describes the systematic coding and thematic analysis that transform raw data into a robust data structure. The subchapter concludes by exploring how this methodology assists in constructing a theoretical framework that effectively connects data and theoretical concepts.

3.3.1.1 Data Collection

Data collection is a systematic process for gathering information to address research questions. The accuracy of this process is crucial as inadequate data can lead to inconclusive or misleading results. The appropriateness of various collection techniques varies by research context, and no single approach can be universally applied. According to *Mwita*, several factors, including research objective and data type, impact the decision of the data collection selection.[129] This variety of factors results in diverse approaches that can be applied to similar research inquiries.[130]

Creswell identifies four primary methods for collecting qualitative data, including engaging in fieldwork, using observation, conducting interviews, and analyzing documents. Among these, the interview data collection approach has become a primary method for generating knowledge, especially in the social and human sciences.[131] As one of the most widely used tool in qualitative research, scientific interviews are focused conversations designed to elicit detailed information and narratives from participants through strategic questioning. The exchanges held in the interviews serve as fundamental data sources that can be examined to derive meaningful insights about the research questions.[132]

Considering the objective of this thesis to explain the complex interplay between populism, financial markets, and investor reactions, it was paramount to obtain insights directly from those deeply entrenched in the field. Because of the explanatory goal of the study and the aim of uncovering new concepts and their interrelationships, interviews were chosen as the data collection method. They present a unique opportunity to probe deep into the personal beliefs, perspectives, and lived experiences of each participant and are well-suited to capturing the complexities of subjective experiences.[133] This makes interviews an appropriate data source for this research topic.

After acknowledging the significance of selecting interviews as a method of data collection, it is necessary to further examine the complexities of the interview approach. Over time, researchers have continually refined, adapted, and redefined the definition of an interview, leading to various interpretations and

---

[129] See Mwita 2022, p. 533.

[130] See Adams et al. 2014, p. 1; Gehman et al. 2018, p. 284.

[131] See Creswell 2018, pp. 55 ff. For more information on the different qualitative data collection methods, as the following chapter only focuses on scientific interviews, see also Denzin and Lincoln 2018, pp. 309 ff.; Flick 2022, pp. 69 ff.

[132] See Brinkmann 2018, pp. 1016 f.

[133] See Roulston and Halpin 2022, p. 669.

approaches. Given the continuously changing nature of qualitative interviews, some scholars suggest considering them as a family of methods rather than a singular, monolithic approach.[134] The following subsection seeks to clarify the various forms and adaptations of the interview and to provide a better understanding and appreciation of its versatility and depth. Subsequent subsections will examine the advancement and significance of modern interview techniques, highlighting the specific methodology employed in this thesis.

3.3.1.1.1 Degree of Structure

When using interviews as a tool for data collection, researchers must make several choices. One central decision in this process revolves around the choice of the interview type. Various forms of interviews exist,[135] each with distinctive data collection techniques and textual material.[136]

Interviews can vary greatly in their degree of structure, ranging from structured to unstructured. On one end, there are structured or standardized interviews, similar in approach to surveys. These interviews are characterized by predetermined questions that aim to ensure comparability and potential quantification of responses across participants.[137] However, they carry the risk that interpretations beyond the predetermined structure may be overlooked, potentially hindering the researcher's understanding of the interaction. Traditionally favored for their consistency, structured interviews have been a cornerstone of research methods, but the trend has shifted to more flexible and dialogic forms of qualitative research interviewing.[138]

Conversely, unstructured interviews, which represent the other end of the spectrum, aim to minimize preconceived notions and structures. In these interviews, the interviewer may have particular topics in mind, but the conversation is permitted to flow naturally, directed by the interviewee's responses. This format allows respondents to articulate their own inquiries, concerns, and perspectives using their preferred language and frames of reference. It is worth noting that interviews can never be entirely unstructured, as the interviewer will always have some objectives guiding the dialogue.[139] An example of a relatively unstructured

---

[134] See Roulston and Halpin 2022, p. 668.

[135] See for example Hopf 2004, pp. 203–209 for an overview.

[136] See Mayring 2022, p. 42.

[137] See Roulston and Halpin 2022, p. 675.

[138] See Brinkmann 2018, p. 999.

[139] See Brinkmann 2018, pp. 999 ff.

interview is the life story interview, which focuses on eliciting significant influences, experiences, and themes from an individual's life perspective. In these interviews, the role of the interviewer is less about asking specific questions and more about facilitating the narrative, allowing the participant to tell their story in a more natural way.[140]

In between these two extremes are semi-structured interviews, which have become popular in the human and social sciences[141] and are often equated with qualitative interviews.[142] This type combines the premeditation of structured interviews with the spontaneity of unstructured interviews. Semi-structured interviews rely on a set of open-ended questions that guide the discussion, yet leave enough flexibility for the conversation to evolve organically based on the interviewee's responses. At the same time, semi-structured interviews ensure a level of uniformity in the questions posed, which allows for robust theory building through consistent comparison of responses and cases. This format also balances the structure of the interview with the flexibility to follow up on points of interest raised by the interviewee. The interviewer can contribute as a more prominent knowledge-producing participant and also steer the conversation to areas relevant to the research project.[143]

With these considerations in mind, semi-structured interviews were chosen for this study because they provide a balanced approach that combines the benefits of both structured and unstructured interviews: Semi-structured interviews provide the necessary structure to ensure consistency and comparability of the data, yet are adaptable enough to capture the depth and richness of each participant's perspective on the impact of populism on financial markets and investor responses.

---

[140] See Roulston and Halpin 2022, p. 676. For more information on scientific interviews see also Brinkmann 2018, pp. 997–1038; Gubrium and Holstein 2001, pp. 75 ff.; Hopf 2004, pp. 203–209.

[141] See Roulston and Halpin 2022, p. 675.

[142] See Warren 2001, p. 83.

[143] See Roulston and Halpin 2022, pp. 676 ff.

3.3.1.1.2 Guide Construction

The adaptability of the interview guide is a hallmark of semi-structured interviews and distinguishes them from rigid questionnaires, where the respondent's understanding may remain unexplored.[144] This flexibility allows for modifications based on the specific dynamics of individual interviews, sometimes necessitating the rephrasing of questions.[145] The interview guide may also include follow-up questions for further discussion if participants do not address them directly.[146]

The semi-structured interview approach adopted in this dissertation was carefully developed using an interview guide as the central research instrument. Developing the guide required careful consideration of multiple important factors. First, it was imperative to approach the participants' experiences without presumptions. To adhere to best practices, suggestive or dichotomous questions that allow for limited responses or that might steer responses in a particular direction were avoided.[147] Instead, the guiding principles were to engage with predominantly open-ended questions, allowing for a natural and comprehensive sharing of narratives, using sequencing questions from general to specific, and addressing only one topic at a time.[148]

The final interview guide outlined is organized into four comprehensive sections. Each section is subdivided into more detailed segments, complete with primary questions and corresponding follow-up questions. The introductory section aims to establish rapport and present the research context, ensuring a comfortable dialogue atmosphere. Participants were first asked to provide consent for the interview to be recorded, followed by preliminary questions that explored their professional background and experience with political risk in the financial sector.

The second phase of the interview explored the concept of political risk. Interviewees were encouraged to describe their interpretation of political risk in the financial context. The subsequent discussion aimed to assess the perceived impact of political risk by measuring its importance from the perspective of various market participants. Moreover, this section sought to identify the factors that might induce political risk within the global finance landscape.

The focus of the discussion then shifted to the central theme of the dissertation: populism. Participants were first asked to consider the implications of

---

[144] See Mayring 2022, p. 34.

[145] See Roulston and Halpin 2022, p. 677.

[146] See Roulston and Choi 2018, p. 237.

[147] See Kaczynski et al. 2014, p. 133.

[148] See Roulston and Halpin 2022, p. 676.

populism for political and economic environments. Follow-up questions dealt for example with its impact on democratic institutions, the resilience of political systems, and the influence of populist policies on economic stability. Delving into the subject, the dialogue unpacked the basic characteristics of populism, exploring possible different short- and long-term effects and how these might change with the political leanings of populist movements. In the next stage, the focus shifted to the financial sector's response to populism. This included examining how populism might affect risk assessment and investment strategies. Topics covered included the varieties of populist movements, the risk-mitigation strategies available to investors, and the changing dynamics of these approaches as populism rises.

In the final phase, participants were given a chance to share any concluding thoughts or additional insights, ensuring an exhaustive collection of viewpoints on the complex relationship between populism and financial market dynamics. Figure 3.2 outlines the interview guide structure, featuring the five leading questions (L1–L5) and the respective backup questions, alongside the various stages of the interview process.

Identifying interaction issues or misunderstandings at the early stages of the research process enables researchers to reflect whether adjustments to their study design or interview questions are necessary. Despite adequate preparation, unpredictability is inherent in interviews as responses cannot be predicted in advance. Factors such as the mutual perceptions of the interviewer and interviewee, the knowledge of the research topic, and the framing of questions and responses can significantly influence the course of the interview interaction. Therefore, conducting pilot interviews to test interview questions may prove beneficial.[149]

In the context of this dissertation, these recommendations were taken into account. The initial version of the interview guide was subsequently tested in a feasibility interview, which helped refine question scope and wording. Although it was not recorded, this pilot interview was crucial in improving the interview guide. Additional revisions were made after the first two actual interviews. Certain questions that covered multiple topics were refined or removed, and several other questions were categorized as follow-up questions. Additionally, the order of the questions was rearranged due to the extensive debates surrounding the understanding of populism. The definition of populism was moved to a later position, while questions related to understanding political risks were placed at the beginning.

[149] See Roulston and Choi 2018, p. 240; Roulston and Halpin 2022, p. 677.

Introductory Part

Start | Recording Confirmation | Personal Background

Political Risk/Uncertainty

- L1: How do you define political risk in a financial context?
  - How relevant are political risk factors from an investor/corporate perspective in the assessment of (investment) risk?
- L2: What are the effects of political risk in a financial context?
  - What events or factors can cause political risks?
  - How relevant are these factors?

Impact of Populism

- L3: What impact has populism on the political landscape?
  - How does increasing populism affect democratic institutions?
  - How does populism affect a country's political risk/uncertainty?
- L4: What impact has populism on the economic landscape?
  - What (economic) policies do you associate with populist parties?
  - What effect does increasing populism have on the macroeconomic stability?
- L5: How does increasing populism impact the risk assessment of investors/ financial market participants?
  - How do you define populism?
  - How does the underlying populist ideology influence the effect?
  - How does the impact differ in terms of short- and long-term effects?
  - How does the impact differ depending on whether populist parties are likely to be in the opposition or join the government?
  - How do investors weigh the potential impact of populism against other political or economic risks?
  - How do investors factor in political risks, such as populism, into their (investment) decision-making?
  - What are some of the key opportunities and threats for investors that have emerged as a result of the rise of populism?

Conclusion

Other Insights/ Questions | Next Steps | End

Fig. 3.2 Interview Guide—Overview. (Source: Own Illustration.)

3.3.1.1.3 Format Specification

Once the interview type and guide have been determined, the following decision involves selecting the interview format. Traditionally, qualitative research has relied primarily on face-to-face interviews. However, advances in technology have provided researchers with additional options for data collection, such as videoconferencing or telephone interviews. In fact, online interviews have become a popular choice.[150]

Nonetheless, the acceptance of online interviews is controversial within the research community.[151] *Seitz* advises against their use due to technical difficulties like dropped calls, as well as potential interference with reading body language and nonverbal cues.[152] Conversely, *Jenner and Myers* highlight the advantages of online interviews. These include more convenient scheduling for participants, greater geographic diversity in sample selection, and the ability to receive visual feedback when video is enabled. It is noteworthy that the study revealed participants' disclosure levels in online interviews were comparable to those in physical, in-person interviews.[153] Considering these divergent viewpoints, this dissertation implemented the use of online video interviews due to their numerous advantages. Among these, a key advantage is the capability to engage a more extensive and diverse participant base, unrestricted by geographical barriers.

The virtual format of interviews necessitates comprehensive preparation. As *Roulston and Choi* suggest, interviewers should demonstrate several essential skills for successful interviews, such as attentive and respectful listening, challenging questioning, and reflective analysis of the evolving interview dynamics, which require practice and self-reflection.[154]

3.3.1.1.4 Transcription Process

After conducting the interviews, transcription is the next step in qualitative research, particularly essential for subsequent data analysis. Academic consensus underscores the importance of this process, which converts oral dialogues into textual data for in-depth examination.[155] Although recording interviews is common, transcription presents its own set of challenges. Frequent issues include

[150] See Salmons 2014, pp. 2 ff.

[151] See Roulston and Halpin 2022, p. 673.

[152] See Seitz 2016, p. 229.

[153] See Jenner and Myers 2019, p. 165.

[154] See Roulston and Choi 2018, p. 238.

[155] See Mayring 2022, p. 132.

the misinterpretation or mishearing of phonetically similar words, which can unintentionally introduce errors into the transcripts.[156]

In the context of this dissertation, the transcription process acknowledges these risks and prioritizes their mitigation. The recordings were transcribed using Whisper, an automatic speech recognition system.[157] Although artificial intelligence has improved the efficiency of such tools in recent years, it is still not a full-proof solution. Therefore, scholars recommend reviewing and correcting any differences in the auto-generated transcripts to ensure the accuracy of the original content.[158]

To address concerns of some interviewees who did not want to be recorded, the captioning feature of the video software was used to create a preliminary transcript with their permission. The resulting raw data, along with consistent interview notes, formed the basis of the final transcript. These additional notes provide an organized documentation of the topics covered and the context of the conversation, allowing for a thorough reconstruction of the interview setting and reducing potential recall bias later. Recognizing the potential for errors due to the hybrid approach, participants were asked to review and correct any inaccuracies to ensure the integrity of the data. Irrespective of the transcription method used, the editing phase was a crucial part of the research process for this project.

Maintaining participant confidentiality is critical in the transcription process. This encapsulates the agreed-upon conditions for handling and disseminating participant information, emphasizing the concealment of their identities.[159] It implies the methodical removal of personal identifiers to meet the ethical requirement of participant anonymity.[160] In this dissertation, confidentiality principles were strictly adhered to, specifically in the transcribing phase. The data was consistently anonymized during data cleaning, analysis, and reporting, ensuring a strong commitment to ethical research standards. Figure 3.3 summarizes the systematic data collection process described in this section, encompassing the use of semi-structured interviews, guide construction, interview format choices, and transcription methods to ensure accuracy and participant anonymity.

---

[156] See Flick 2018b, p. 90.

[157] See OpenAI 2022.

[158] See Roulston and Halpin 2022, p. 678.

[159] See Sieber and Tolich 2013, pp. 155–158.

[160] See Kaiser 2012, p. 461.

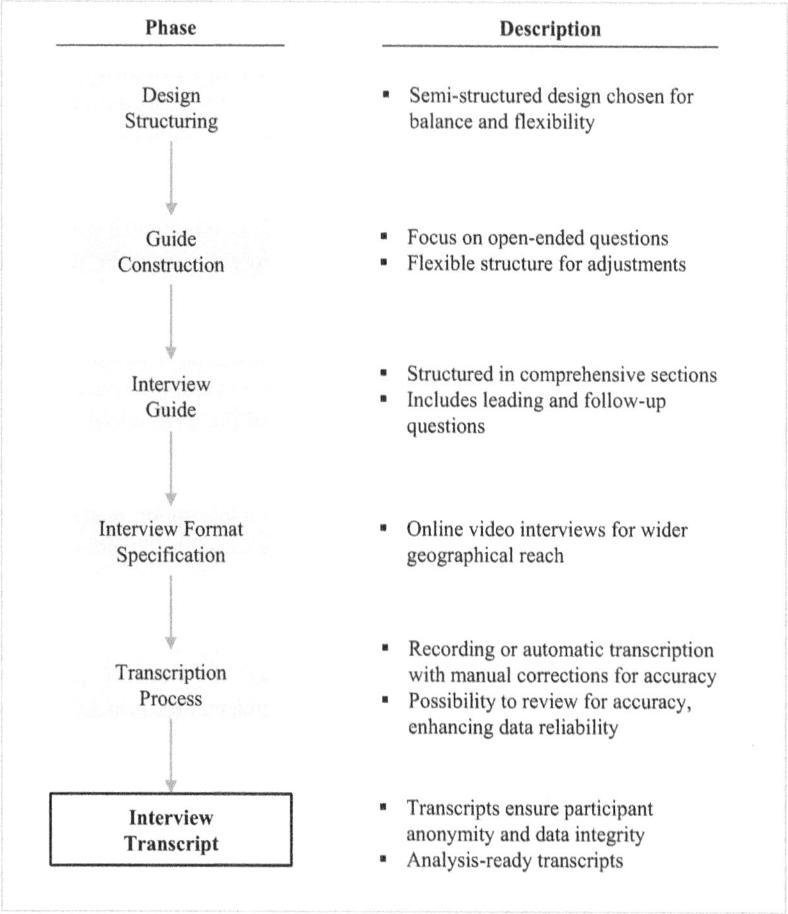

Fig. 3.3 Data Collection Approach—Summary. (Source: Own Illustration.)

3.3.1.2 Data Analysis

The preceding discussion of the data collection strategy through interviews sets the stage for the subsequent steps of data analysis and evaluation. Many qualitative and interpretive researchers challenge the traditional separation between data collection and analysis, advocating for a more integrated approach to interviewing and analysis within qualitative research.[161] Nevertheless, for the purposes of clarity and coherence, this dissertation delineates these processes in separate sections.

This section focuses on the methods of data analysis that are critical to the integrity of research. Both qualitative and quantitative research aim to ensure the robustness of study findings, albeit through different approaches. Quantitative research utilizes deductive reasoning, statistical tools, and a systematic connection between hypotheses, data presentation, and conclusions, whereas qualitative research relies on inductive reasoning to explore and understand complex realities. This divergence in the research approach has historically led to criticism of qualitative methods, with skeptics questioning the core foundations of their findings due to perceived shortcomings in scientific rigor.[162]

Amidst criticism that necessitated improvement, systematic and reliable qualitative research methods that aim to produce convincing conclusions with greater rigor were developed.[163] Against this backdrop, the *Gioia* Methodology presents a systematic technique to meet the demand for increased methodological rigor in theory development. This methodology is a structured yet adaptable approach to data coding and theory building that is recognized for its consistent process.[164]

The upcoming subsections will examine the *Gioia* Methodology as an advanced Grounded Theory approach, highlighting its methodological strengths and qualitative research applications. The first subsection delves into the basic principles of Grounded Theory, followed by an exploration of the *Gioia* Methodology's refinement of these principles for data coding and theory building, confirming its significant role in qualitative research and its suitability for this dissertation.

---

[161] See for example Langley 1999; Lincoln and Guba 1985.

[162] See Gioia et al. 2013, pp. 16 f.

[163] See Welch and Piekkari 2017, p. 716.

[164] See Gioia et al. 2013, pp. 15–31.

3.3.1.2.1 Grounded Theory Foundation

Grounded Theory, established in the 1960s by *Glaser and Strauss*, is a methodological approach to generating theory from data through systematic collection and analysis.[165] Its appeal lies in its strong empirical foundation and its particular relevance to organizational research.[166] *Mayring* emphasizes the importance of Grounded Theory as a technique for qualitative textual analysis.[167] The applicability of this approach extends to fields traditionally dominated by quantitative research,[168] including management and accounting.[169] Moreover, the iterative nature of the method is conducive to qualitative interviews, where continuous data analysis informs and refines ongoing data collection.[170]

Applying Grounded Theory within mixed methods research further enhances its applicability to further research domains,[171] especially those that are primarily quantitative.[172] This versatility is fundamental to the analytical approach of this thesis, which uses Grounded Theory as its core methodological foundation, offering qualitative insights to enrich the quantitative aspects.

Since its inception, Grounded Theory has evolved into various strands, from exploratory to systematic, with the original model serving as a foundation for many adaptations.[173] Among these approaches, the *Gioia* Methodology originated with *Gioia and Chittipeddi* was developed through subsequent studies and refined in a series of publications from 2004 to 2021.[174] In its current form, this methodology offers a well-established and rigorous qualitative framework for analyzing data and developing concepts.[175]

---

165 See Glaser and Strauss 1967.

166 See for example Corbin and Strauss 2008; Gioia et al. 2013; Glaser 1978.

167 See Mayring 2022, pp. 40 ff. for a comparison with other approaches such as content analysis.

168 See Guetterman et al. 2019 p. 182.

169 See Azmi et al. 2019, p. 1.

170 See Foley et al. 2021, p. 1.

171 See Charmaz and Belgrave 2012, p. 360.

172 See Guetterman et al. 2019, p. 179.

173 Various Grounded Theory methodologies stem from distinct ontological and epistemological stances, aligning with different philosophical research paradigms. For an extensive analysis, see Levers 2013 and for comprehensive descriptions of the various forms of Grounded Theory, see for example Flick 2018a.

174 See Gioia and Chittipeddi 1991, pp. 433–448. For refined versions, see, for example, Gioia et al. 1994; Gioia and Thomas 1996.

175 See Gioia 2021, p. 20.

Applying the Grounded Theory based *Gioia* Methodology, this thesis aims to provide interpretive insights that expand theoretical understanding, adhering to the qualitative tradition of generating grounded, substantive theory. This methodology ensures a thorough and systematic examination of data, as the iterative data analysis process is tailored to capture the complexity of organizational phenomena through continuous comparison of participants' perspectives.[176]

3.3.1.2.2 Core Assumptions

The *Gioia* Methodology surpasses a standard method and attains the form of a methodology by the means of its three philosophical foundations. The first premise posits that organizations are not static entities, but rather are constructed as dynamic processes that are continually shaped by their members' interactions. This aligns with social constructivism, acknowledging that the perceived reality of organizational existence is the result of collective human action and interaction.[177]

The second assumption argues that individuals within socially constructed organizations possess intrinsic knowledge of their roles and activities. This challenges the researcher's perspective by emphasizing the expertise of organizational members, indicating that researchers should not overshadow informants' narratives with their own constructs or theories. This approach positions researchers as "glorified reporters"[178], whose primary task is to convey the experiences and perceptions of the informants' interpretations of their socially constructed reality.[179]

---

[176] See Magnani and Gioia 2023, pp. 1 ff.

[177] See Magnani and Gioia 2023, p. 2. See also Section 3.1.1.1 for a discussion on philosophical foundations.

[178] Gioia et al. 2013, p. 17.

[179] See Gioia et al. 2013, p. 17.

The third assumption shifts the research focus from seeking absolute answers to generating plausible and defensible explanations for organizational phenomena. This approach requires a clear connection between data and theoretical conclusions.[180]

Collectively, these three assumptions shape the *Gioia* Methodology as a comprehensive framework that respects the complexity of organizational life, emphasizes the credibility of informants' knowledge, and focuses on constructing theories that are grounded in empirical reality.[181] The assumptions underlying this approach led to a methodology that prioritizes the perspectives of informants and recognizes their deep understanding of their organizational roles. Since researchers cannot fully experience the organizational world firsthand, they strive to accurately represent it by using the language and concepts familiar to those within it. Yet in order to extend the utility of the research beyond its immediate context, a theoretical view is also applied to identify concepts and connections that may be hidden from the informants themselves. This dual view ensures that the findings are both authentic to the informants' experiences and valuable in a broader theoretical context.[182]

3.3.1.2.3 Data Structure

Building on these foundations, the *Gioia* Methodology is characterized by a multi-layered data structure that supports the research process and substantiates the researcher's conclusions through systematic data coding and analysis. Using this framework, the researcher's observations are presented in a concise manner, showing how informant-based codes relate to researcher-based themes and dimensions.[183] It allows researchers to present results from different angles and substantiate their conclusions by connecting data with theory. This joint depiction enhances the qualitative soundness that characterizes sophisticated qualitative research.[184]

[180] See Gioia et al. 2013, pp. 17 f.

[181] See Gioia et al. 2022, pp. 232 ff.

[182] See Gioia et al. 2022, pp. 232 ff.

[183] See Gioia et al. 2013, p. 18; Magnani and Gioia 2023, p. 2.

[184] See Gioia et al. 2013, p. 19.

The analytical process of the *Gioia* Methodology begins with a first-order analysis that catalogs the informants' insights into a wide range of categories that account for the informants' understanding of their work. During the initial stage of data collection, it is possible to identify between 50 and 100 first-order categories after conducting the first ten interviews. Even though this multiplicity of categories can initially seem overwhelming and disordered, presenting the researcher with a complex array of data that lacks immediate coherence, navigating this complexity is an essential part of the research process, where a period of disorientation precedes the emergence of clarity.[185]

Proceeding to the second-order level of analysis, the perspective shifts to the researcher, who acts as a knowledgeable agent refining these informant-derived categories into a coherent set of theoretical themes.[186] At the third-order level of analysis, the second-order themes are condensed into broader aggregated dimensions and a larger narrative.[187] This analytical process ensures the conscious integration of new data with existing literature, aiming to introduce new concepts while taking into account existing knowledge to avoid premature theoretical assertions.[188] Through this phase of analysis, new questions and directions for exploration emerge, especially as subsequent interviews focus on the evolving concepts and potential connections within the data.[189]

With a comprehensive set of first-order codes, second-order themes, and aggregate dimensions established, the data structure provides a representation of the analytical progression from raw data to codes, from codes to themes, and finally to dimensions.[190] This robust data structure systematically organizes the findings and supports the transition to the methodology's final phase: constructing a cohesive framework that integrates emergent concepts into a unified model.

---

[185] See Gioia et al. 2013, p. 20.

[186] See Gioia 2021, p. 22.

[187] Some authors refer to this step as extension of the second-order analysis see for example Gioia 2021, p. 25.

[188] See Gioia et al. 2013, p. 20.

[189] See Gioia 2021, p. 25. This approach aligns with "theoretical sampling", where data collection is driven by the evolving theoretical framework and will be further described in Section 3.3.2.1.

[190] See Gioia 2021, p. 23.

3.3.1.2.4 Framework Development

The *Gioia* Methodology results in creating a Grounded Theory model that displays the dynamic connections between emerging concepts and theoretical constructs. This approach responds to the critique that qualitative research does not effectively showcase the linkage between data and theory. Thus, the focus remains on creating a robust inductive model that is grounded in the data and theoretically encapsulates the informants' experiences.[191]

This research approach is designed to verify existing theoretical frameworks, thereby aligning new research with established academic understanding. It also extends these frameworks by providing detailed insights into known concepts. Moreover, it innovates by introducing new concepts and theoretical frameworks that enhance the understanding of the research topic. To support these findings, scholars may enhance their analyses with tables, figures, and appendices to provide a compelling foundation for their theoretical conclusions.[192]

Magnani and Gioia delineate the research trajectory of the *Gioia* Methodology as an iterative process that initiates with inductive reasoning, grounded in firsthand accounts from participants, and progresses toward abductive reasoning in its later phases. Abductive reasoning entails the interpretation of data to formulate conclusions that seamlessly connect empirical findings with theoretical insights. The shift towards abduction necessitates the recontextualization of primary concepts into an expansive theoretical narrative, culminating in the development of second-order themes and aggregated dimensions. This methodological transition is crucial for the construction of a theoretical framework that not only accurately reflects the collected data but also offers coherent, overarching explanations for the observed phenomena. The synergistic application of inductive and abductive reasoning throughout this methodology fosters the development of a theory that is empirically robust and extends meaningfully current scholarly debates.[193] Figure 3.4 outlines the qualitative data analysis process for the qualitative study derived in the previous phases, from coding and theme development to the synthesis of a theoretical framework.

---

[191] See Gioia et al. 2013, p. 21.

[192] See Magnani and Gioia 2023, p. 3.

[193] See Magnani and Gioia 2023, pp. 3 ff.

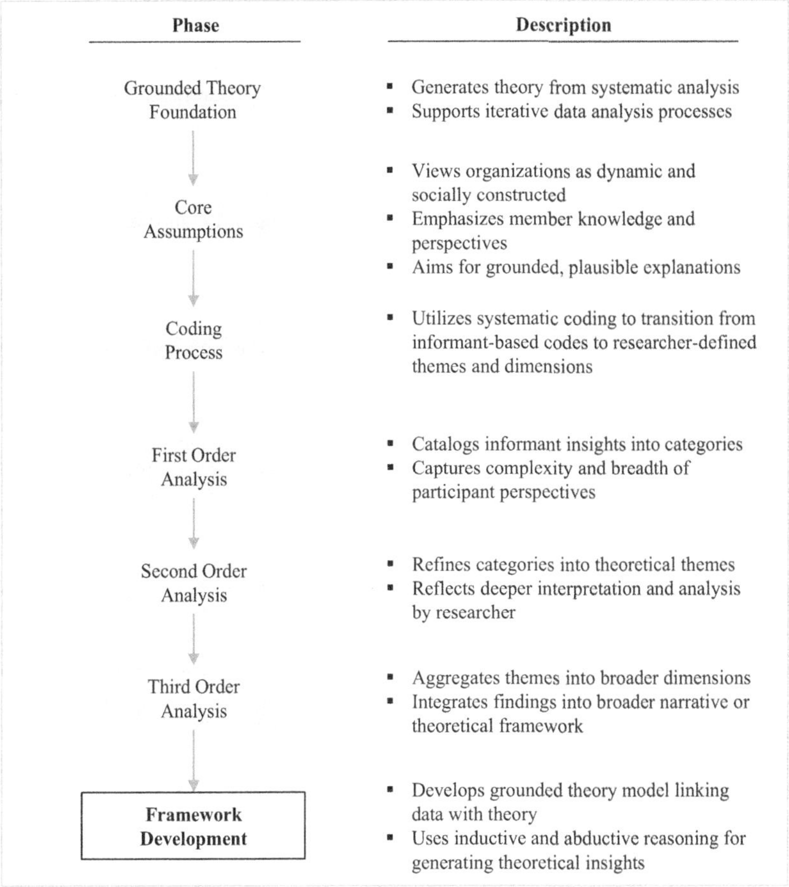

Fig. 3.4 Data Analysis Approach—Summary. (Source: Own Illustration.)

3.3.2 Sample Selection

The previous sections of the thesis have demonstrated the importance of scientific interviews and the *Gioia* Methodology as integral components of the research design, highlighting their capacity for adaptation during the research process. This adaptability is reflected in the sampling strategy, which is characterized by an iterative cycle that refines the data collection in line with the ongoing analysis, thereby strengthening the emergent theory. The following sections present an in-depth analysis of the sampling procedures that guide this research. The first section covers the basics of sampling methodologies, examining the differences between techniques, and highlighting the central role of saturation in qualitative research.

In the subsequent section, the practical implementation of these concepts is presented, detailing the multi-stage sampling process applied in this thesis. The section outlines the systematic approach taken to identify and engage professionals in various financial and professional services sectors with different roles and functions related to political risk assessment, aiming at a comprehensive assessment of the impact of populism.

The following section provides an analysis of the composition of the sample, revealing the diverse academic and professional backgrounds of the participants. It also describes the progression of the theoretical sampling process as it evolves throughout the research. Furthermore, the expansion of the categories relevant to the sample is explained, and the theoretical sampling method is illustrated as an effective approach for enhancing the understanding of political risk analysis in the financial sector.

3.3.2.1 Qualitative Sampling

Sampling is crucial in connecting theoretical concepts and empirical research, offering an economical strategy for deriving insights from a segment of a larger population. There are two primary sampling techniques: probability sampling and non-probability sampling. While probability sampling allows for statistical representation by giving each member of the population an equal chance of being selected, non-probability sampling relies on the discretion of the researcher to select participants.[194]

[194] See Adams et al. 2014, pp. 72 f.

Probability sampling is a fundamental part of quantitative research, allowing for broad representativeness and generalizability. In contrast, non-probability sampling is central to qualitative research, where the emphasis is on gaining an in-depth understanding of a chosen phenomenon through a specifically selected group. For qualitative research, the selection of smaller, more focused groups is paramount, as these participants have specific knowledge or experiences relevant to the research questions. This method aims to uncover nuanced insights rather than generalize findings numerically.[195]

Sample size in qualitative research is not regulated by a standard rule but by the requirements of the study, such as the discipline, design, and desired level of comprehension. For instance, Grounded Theory approaches depend on theoretical sampling, where researchers gather and scrutinize data until saturation is reached, the point at which new data do not contribute additional insights.[196] Saturation is a subject of significant debate in qualitative research due to its role in validating the thoroughness and credibility of a study. Theoretical saturation is particularly important because it indicates the stage at which the data represents the constructs of a theory and verifies that the theoretical concepts are well contextualized and dimensionalized.[197] Supporting this, *Guest et al.* describe saturation as the point at which the theoretical model becomes stable and additional data do not provide new information.[198]

In the application of Grounded Theory methods, achieving theoretical saturation relies on theoretical sampling, which is necessary to construct a strong theoretical framework.[199] This technique involves simultaneous data collection and analysis, guiding further data gathering and enabling a comprehensive and dynamic exploration of emerging concepts. It enables researchers to dynamically engage with the data and explore emerging concepts in depth, without being constrained by predefined selection criteria. The iterative nature of this approach fosters a responsive development of theory as the research unfolds, leading to a deeper engagement with the subject matter and a more nuanced and thoroughly justified theoretical framework.[200]

---

[195] See Beitin 2012, p. 248.

[196] See Roulston and Halpin 2022, p. 672.

[197] See for example Hennink et al. 2017; Saunders et al. 2018; Sim et al. 2018.

[198] See Guest et al. 2020, p. 1.

[199] See Conlon et al. 2020, p. 954; Foley et al. 2021, p. 1.

[200] See Corbin and Strauss 2008, pp. 28 ff.; Glaser and Strauss 2012, pp. 45 ff.

Another technique that can be relevant to Grounded Theory research is purposive sampling. It is a technique characterized by the selection of information-rich cases according to predetermined criteria at the beginning of the sample selection study. This approach, as explained by *Conlon et al.*, is versatile and involves selecting extreme cases, typical cases, cases with maximum variation, highly engaging cases, and pivotal cases that elucidate the relationships relevant to the research questions.[201] Despite its distinct approach, purposive sampling can guide subsequent data collection in Grounded Theory research, providing foundational insights that inform further data collection.[202]

After selecting a sampling strategy and identifying participants, who can provide relevant perspectives related to the research questions, the subsequent task is recruitment. This phase typically utilizes a range of techniques, from leveraging networks to distributing flyers to sending mass emails or letters. The overarching goal is to engage participants who can meaningfully contribute to the depth and breadth of the study and ensure a comprehensive exploration of the research topic.[203]

3.3.2.2 Sampling Strategy

For the qualitative study, a stratified approach to sampling was applied, beginning with purposive sampling and moving to theoretical sampling as the research progressed. This method was designed to enhance the research objective of elucidating the mechanisms through which market reactions to populism occur.

In the initial phase, purposive sampling was used to target individuals whose experiences could shed light on the research objective. The focus was placed on experts in political risk assessment—key actors in the financial valuation sphere that assess the potential impacts of political events on companies, investments, and the broader economic landscape. Recognizing the complexity of this domain and aiming to refine the selection process further, the study incorporated *Schroeder's* framework for classifying the risk analysis domain.[204] This step allowed for a more targeted approach in identifying in-house assessors within financial institutions, prioritizing those who employ market-centric methodologies for political risk evaluation as outlined in Section 2.2.2.3. Consequently, this phase saw the purposeful selection of six individuals from the asset management

201 See Conlon et al. 2020, p. 956.

202 See Ligita et al. 2020, p. 119; Palinkas et al. 2015, p. 533.

203 See Roulston and Halpin 2022, p. 672.

204 See Schroeder 2008, pp. 507 ff.

and investment banking sectors, chosen for their direct involvement and expert insights into navigating political risk within global investment landscapes and financial advisory services.

The selection of individuals from these two sectors was based on *Conlon et al.'s* criteria for identifying representative cases that provide foundational insights for the subsequent theoretical sampling phase.[205] To identify potential interviewees, the professional networking platform LinkedIn was used. The platform's search function allowed for filtering of profiles based on various characteristics. Basic search terms included "political risk", "policy risk", and "policy analysis".

To further refine the participant selection, the study applied more specific filters based on job function, seniority level by targeting individuals in senior or managerial positions, language proficiency by requiring English, and focusing on professionals with at least six years of experience in their field. Based on the large number of potential candidates, the focus was narrowed down to the first 500 profiles that showed significant relevance to the field of political risk analysis. Participants were selected based on additional criteria, including contributions to relevant academic or professional literature and the centrality of political risk analysis within their professional priorities. Individuals were then contacted in order of relevance, with each receiving a personalized message highlighting the importance of their contribution to the research study.

In the following phase, theoretical sampling was employed to guide the research towards a broader exploration of political risk. This method's flexibility allowed for a data-driven approach, revealing significant themes within the initially targeted sectors. The analysis of the initial interviews highlighted the need to explore additional areas for a comprehensive understanding of political risk. Consequently, four specific roles were identified as critical to the assessment of political risk: strategists and analysts, economic researchers, risk managers, and policy advisors.

---

[205] See Conlon et al. 2020, p. 947.

The first role refers to the group of strategists and analysts who develop and interpret political risk strategies and provide expert advice on how to navigate and mitigate the complexities inherent in global political landscapes. The second role, identified as economic researchers such as policy and macroeconomic specialists, integrates economic theory with practical market insights to provide strategic recommendations by analyzing economic trends and policy shifts. The third role, risk managers, is responsible for identifying and managing investment risks associated with specific countries or sectors. They play a crucial role in enhancing financial stability by providing guidance on risk management to protect investments from the volatility of political and economic changes. The fourth role, policy advisors, encompassing policy consultants and government affairs specialists, serves as a conduit between the financial sector and public policy. This group assesses the impact of government policies on financial markets and advises on compliance with regulatory standards.

Introducing additional layers of information based on the identified roles increased the complexity and depth of the theoretical framework, requiring a refined approach to sampling as the research progressed. The iterative nature of sampling and analysis during this phase enriched the understanding of the categories, refined their conceptual definitions, and elucidated the connections between them. As the study progressed, the categories' characteristics became more distinct, allowing for a more focused theoretical sampling strategy and a more advanced theoretical framework. This phase concluded with the attainment of data saturation after 20 interviews, suggesting that additional data collection was unlikely to yield new insights.

In the final validation phase, two additional interviews were conducted with distinguished experts in political risk assessment who had made significant contributions through professional publications and held influential roles within their organizations. This phase aimed to confirm that the developed model accurately reflected the collected data and was supported by a sample broad enough to encompass a comprehensive range of experiences and perspectives on political risk assessment. The careful implementation of this procedure has confirmed the study's findings, supporting its reliability and comprehensiveness. Figure 3.5 depicts the sequential sampling process, from selecting the methods to achieving data saturation and validating the theoretical framework.

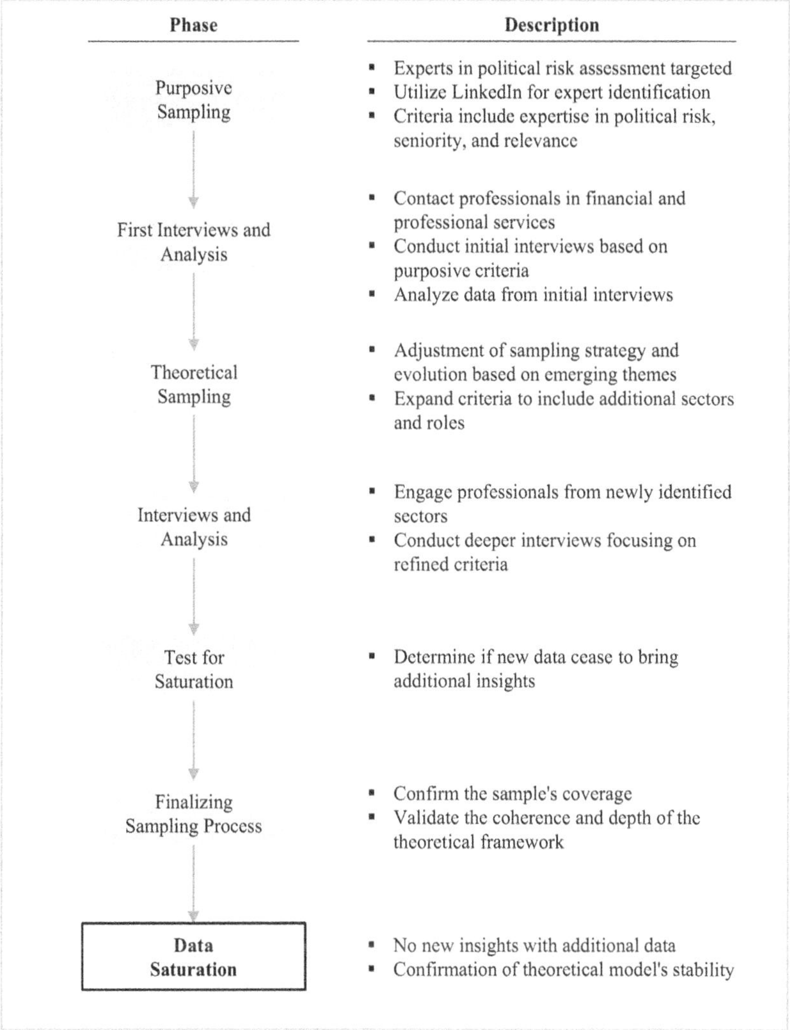

Fig. 3.5 Sampling Strategy—Summary. (Source: Own Illustration.)

3.3.2.3 Overview

This section outlines the composition of the sample and provides an analysis of respondents' academic backgrounds, categorization into expertise roles identified through theoretical sampling, and sector-specific political risk expertise.

The recruitment process took place from February to June 2023 and targeted 298 experts in the field. This initiative resulted in 22 in-depth interviews, accumulating over 14.5 hours of recorded conversations, ranging in length from 23 to 57 minutes each. The systematic selection strategy, from purposive to theoretical sampling, resulted in a diverse cohort of political risk specialists uniquely qualified to explore the impact of populism on investment decisions and financial markets. This rigorous selection of experts is a key factor in determining that the study's findings are a robust reflection of the complex relationship between political trends and financial dynamics.

Regarding the academic qualifications of the 22 respondents, the sample is diversified beyond economic disciplines in response to the needs of theoretical sampling, including political science, international relations, and other fields to provide a more comprehensive understanding of the research topic. Of the interviewed professionals, seven hold degrees in political science and international relations, five in economics, another five in business and finance, and the remaining five have diverse academic backgrounds, including history. It is noteworthy that all participants hold at least a master's degree, with five holding a Ph.D., underscoring the high educational level of the sample.

As outlined in the sampling strategy, participants were selected to represent four key professional roles critical to the assessment of political risk. The participant composition included nine strategists and analysts, five economic researchers, five risk managers, and three policy advisors.

Examining the sectors of the 22 interviewees reveals a diverse range of expertise and focus areas. These individuals can be classified into five sectors based on their professional domains and contributions. As discussed in the previous section, the initial phase of the selection process involved purposive sampling, resulting in the purposeful selection of six individuals from the asset management as well as investment banking and financial services sectors. During the subsequent stages, the sample was extended, ultimately including four individuals from asset management and another four from investment banking and financial services in the final selection process.

Additionally, five specialists in risk management, insurance, and reinsurance were chosen for their focused expertise in crafting strategies to counter disruptions induced by political risk. This subset highlights the importance of political risk insurance in protecting businesses from the financial instability caused by political turmoil, which is integral to determining insurance premiums and coverage options.

The study also benefits from insights provided by five participants from research, ratings, and intelligence agencies who are leaders in issuing credit ratings and economic forecasts. Their analysis of political conditions, government stability, and policy trends is vital for providing actionable intelligence to clients, particularly in politically volatile regions.

Finally, four professionals from consulting and advisory services contribute their expertise in strategic planning and international expansion, with a focus on political risk analysis. Their involvement offers a comprehensive view of how political trends can affect business strategies and market positions, underscoring the importance of political risk assessment in global business planning. Table 3.8

Table 3.8 Qualitative Research Sample. (Source: Own Illustration.)

	Degree	Academic Background	Professional Role	Sector
Expert 1	Master	Economics	Economic Researchers	Asset Management
Expert 2	Ph.D.	Interdisciplinary & Specialized Studies	Economic Researchers	Asset Management
Expert 3	Master	Political Science & International Relations	Strategists and Analysts	Risk Management, Insurance, and Reinsurance
Expert 4	Master	Business and Finance	Economic Researchers	Asset Management
Expert 5	Master	Interdisciplinary & Specialized Studies	Strategists and Analysts	Risk Management, Insurance, and Reinsurance
Expert 6	Master	Business and Finance	Economic Researchers	Asset Management
Expert 7	Master	Economics	Economic Researchers	Research, Ratings, and Intelligence
Expert 8	Master	Political Science & International Relations	Strategists and Analysts	Consulting and Advisory Services
Expert 9	Master	Political Science & International Relations	Strategists and Analysts	Consulting and Advisory Services

(continued)

Table 3.8 (continued)

	Degree	Academic Background	Professional Role	Sector
Expert 10	Master	Economics	Risk Managers	Risk Management, Insurance, and Reinsurance
Expert 11	Ph.D.	Political Science & International Relations	Strategists and Analysts	Risk Management, Insurance, and Reinsurance
Expert 12	Master	Political Science & International Relations	Strategists and Analysts	Consulting and Advisory Services
Expert 13	Master	Interdisciplinary & Specialized Studies	Strategists and Analysts	Research, Ratings, and Intelligence
Expert 14	Master	Business and Finance	Risk Managers	Investment Banking and Financial Services
Expert 15	Master	Interdisciplinary & Specialized Studies	Risk Managers	Research, Ratings, and Intelligence
Expert 16	Ph.D.	Interdisciplinary & Specialized Studies	Policy Advisors	Investment Banking and Financial Services
Expert 17	Master	Economics	Strategists and Analysts	Consulting and Advisory Services
Expert 18	Master	Business and Finance	Policy Advisors	Risk Management, Insurance, and Reinsurance
Expert 19	Master	Political Science & International Relations	Strategists and Analysts	Investment Banking and Financial Services
Expert 20	Ph.D.	Political Science & International Relations	Policy Advisors	Research, Ratings, and Intelligence
Expert 21	Ph.D.	Economics	Risk Managers	Investment Banking and Financial Services
Expert 22	Master	Business and Finance	Risk Managers	Research, Ratings, and Intelligence

summarizes the academic qualifications, roles, and sectors of the 22 participants included in the research project.

3.3.3 Findings

In this subchapter, the findings of the qualitative analysis are discussed.[206] This dissertation follows the contemporary recommendation of *Gioia* to introduce the research framework early in the exposition, before elaborating on the data structure and coding procedures, in order to facilitate a clearer understanding of the scope of the findings.[207] Therefore, first, the research framework is presented, highlighting the aggregated dimensions identified, the related second-order themes, and their interrelationships.

Subsequently, the thesis explores the framework's underlying category system in depth. This part of the thesis is structured, reflecting the five aggregated dimensions on the section level and their respective second-order themes on the subsection level. Each section introduces the dimensions and closes with a table detailing both the concepts, supported by illustrative quotes, and the associated themes. The analysis then focuses on the themes on the subsection level analyzing the underlying concepts.

3.3.3.1 Framework Overview

Based on scientific interviews and data analysis using the *Gioia* Methodology, a multi-level research framework that provides a comprehensive understanding of the complex relationship between populism, financial markets, and investor behavior was generated. The research framework, which is illustrated in Figure 3.6, aims to investigate the relationship between populism and its impact on various facets, contextual factors, and most notably, financial markets and investor behavior.[208]

---

[206] The interviewees shared their individual insights, these do not reflect the official position of their current or past employers.

[207] See Gioia 2021, p. 27.

[208] The graphical representation provided here is intended solely for illustrative purposes and does not adhere to a strict logical or chronological sequence (see Subsection 3.4.3.1.2 for a critical examination). It is also important to note that the framework only shows the first two levels of analysis, as categories are not included in Figure 3.6 and will be discussed individually in the following analysis.

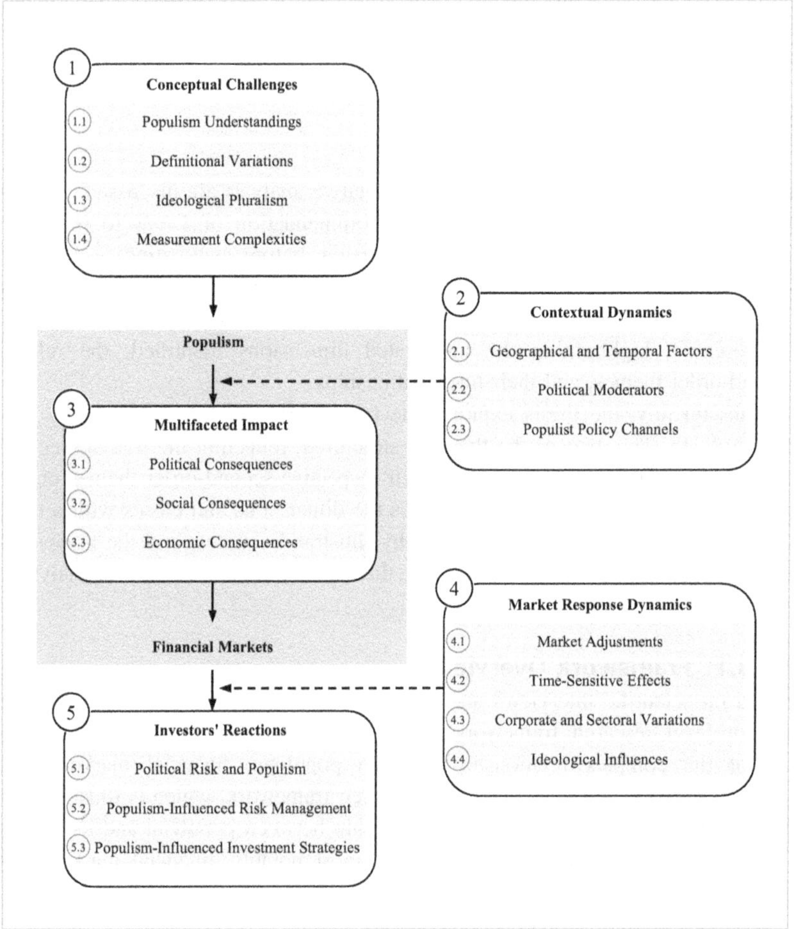

Fig. 3.6 Research Framework. (Source: Own Illustration.)

This framework is segmented into five aggregated dimensions, with each encompassing a broad area of inquiry further subdivided into themes and concepts.[209] Instead of regarding each layer in this framework as a separate entity, it is crucial to perceive them as interconnected components. It is only by examining the interplay between the dimensions, themes, and concepts that the framework can provide a holistic understanding, from populism's conceptual foundations to its broader societal impacts, market reactions, and investor responses.

Beginning with the first dimension, "Conceptual Challenges", this section explores the complex notion of populism through four distinct themes. The first theme "Populism Understandings" introduces the debates surrounding the definition and ambiguities of populism, highlighting the lack of clarity that also exists in the practical discourse. This theme further delves into how populism has evolved in perception over time and examines the skepticism associated with the term. The second theme, "Definitional Variations", explores the various definitions that were provided, ranging from an anti-establishment to an economic focus. "Ideological Pluralism", the third theme, analyzes the intersectionality of different varieties of populism, its position within the political spectrum, and the extremes and diversities within populist movements. This examination aids in further conceptualizing populism. The fourth theme, "Measurement Complexities", addresses the challenges of quantifying populism due to the differing perceptions, inconsistencies in methods employed, and the limited availability of data, which may introduce bias. Notably, the underlying themes in this broad dimension influence each other significantly and lay the foundation for the subsequent dimensions.

After establishing the conceptual foundation, the subsequent dimension "Contextual Dynamics" analyzes the environment in which populism flourishes. More specifically the contextual factors that either influence or are influenced by the persistence of populist sentiments are explored. The first theme, "Geographical and Temporal Factors", investigates how the impact of populism varies among countries and over time, highlighting the dynamic nature of populism. The second theme, "Political Moderators", focuses on e.g., political structures, governance models and other political factors that moderate the impact of populism. Furthermore, this dimension includes the theme "Populist Policy Channels", which examines the multiple channels through which populism influences politics, whether through participation in government, through opposition politics,

---

[209] In the following, the expression "aggregated dimension" will be abbreviated to "dimension" for ease of reading, and "second-order themes" will be referred to as "themes", while "first-order concepts" will be called "concepts".

or outside the mechanisms of governance. In summary, the second dimension establishes the framework by which the effects of populism can be assessed. It provides a foundation for comprehending the ways in which populism influences political, economic, and financial markets.

The third dimension, "Multifaceted Impact", interacts with its predecessors and aims to detail the consequences of populism on society. Its objective is to scrutinize the very multidimensional real-world consequences of populist movements on various societal aspects, including politics, society, and the economy. The theme of "Political Consequences" includes the general political unpredictability associated with populism, but also its impact on political institutions, the political landscape, the erosion of democracy, and the implications for governance. While the negative elements associated with populism dominate, positive political consequences of populism are also elaborated. Additionally, the second theme, "Social Consequences", explores the broader social ramifications of this phenomenon, such as societal polarization and social unrest. Finally, the last theme "Economic Consequences" examines economic implications, including macroeconomic policy, nationalist economic strategies, and the effects of essential reforms associated with populism. The outcomes discussed in the third dimension are consequences of the rise and spread of populism, given the conceptualization and context derived in the previous dimensions. Overall, these outcomes, in turn, impact market responses and investor behavior, which form the next dimension.

Considering the unique structure of financial markets, the fourth dimension, "Market Response Dynamics", shifts the attention to evaluate how financial markets at macro and micro levels react to the changes introduced by populism. The first theme refers to the impact of "Market Adjustments" on the dynamics of populism. Not only are different market segments explored, but also how markets react by adjusting, adapting, and sometimes normalizing the presence of populists. Further populism's influence in global markets is analyzed. The second theme, "Time-Sensitive Effects", provides an overview of the various short- and long-term effects, as well as the contextual responses that accompany them. The third theme of this dimension "Corporate and Sectoral Variations" focusses then on the varying impact of populism on different business sectors and corporate structures, focusing on possible regulatory shifts or economic policies that specific sectors or MNCs might encounter. The final theme, "Ideological Influences", examines how, for some, the market reactions to populism depend on its ideological basis, while others mention blurred ideological lines, suggesting that market reactions and impacts may vary depending on the different populist ideologies. The market reactions presented are closely linked to the consequences of populism in the third dimension and the understanding of different investor reactions elaborated in the following dimension.

The last dimension "Investors' Reactions" addresses the changes caused by populism in financial decision-making for investors. The first theme, "Political Risk and Populism", examines the evolving importance of political risk in the financial landscape, with a particular focus on the transformative impact of populism. The following theme, "Populism-Influenced Risk Management", discusses how populism has transformed risk management, highlighting the need for prompting a nuanced approach to assessing its unpredictable influence on markets and political events such as elections. It investigates how the emergence of populism affects risk assessment by discussing its unpredictable nature and the shifts it poses to investors in political risk analysis. Within the last theme, "Populism-Influenced Investment Strategies", it is analyzed how populism reshapes investment strategies due to its effect on asset values and investor behavior prompting varied investor responses. As investors' decisions are influenced by the market's proposed responses to populism, their decisions are shaped by the preceding dimensions, resulting in the culmination of the entire research framework.

Subsequent sections will provide a detailed examination of each dimension by expanding on its second-order themes, as well as more specific first-order concepts on the subsection level. This systematic approach not only deepens the analysis but also illuminates the complex impacts and interactions involved.

3.3.3.2 Conceptual Challenges

The "Conceptual Challenges" dimension examines the basic principles of populism, exploring its definition, historical evolution, and interpretations through four themes. For a detailed overview of the first dimension of the research framework, see Figure 3.7, which provides a visual representation of its themes and concepts along with illustrative quotes.

Within the first theme, "Populism Understandings", the first concept, "Definitional Ambiguities", identifies the varying definitions and interpretations of populism among stakeholders. The following concept, "Modern Perception", documents shifts in the perception of populism throughout history. "Term Relevance Debate" provides a critical review of the common application and interpretation of populism. Concluding this theme, "Media Influence" investigates how media shapes public perceptions of populism.

Moving on to the second theme, "Definitional Variations", the concept of "Contested Perceptions" presents populism not only as an ideology but also as a potential strategy used by political entities. The subsequent concept "Economic

1

Second Order Themes	First Order Concepts	Illustrative Quote
1.1 Populism Understandings	Definitional Ambiguities	*"I do not have a strict definition at hand." (E21: 23).*
	Modern Perception	*"(....) a lot has changed around how populism is perceived and has evolved." (E9: 39).*
	Term Relevance Debate	*"Because it is the word. The word is like "reform". What does reform mean? Nothing." (E15: 51).*
	Media Influence	*"You could have a party or a leader or presidential nominee that are named populist by, say, certain media outlets, but (....) what is the bias of these media outlets." (E15: 35).*
1.2 Definitional Variations	Contested Perceptions	*"Discussing definitions for me it is a political strategy more than an ideology. So, you maybe use it to gain a support from your electorate, but maybe it is a cover up." (E11: 25).*
	Economic Focus	*"Populism is something which increases the chances of decisions against the interest of the economy." (E21: 23).*
	Interpretational Differences	*"(....) populism the term itself carries a lot of weight, a lot of sentiment is, and the sentiment is decidedly negative." (E14: 17).*
1.3 Ideological Pluralism	Populist Ideology Intersections	*"So, there is a difference, but I think the underlying ideology is not so important." (E11: 37).*
	Populist Extremes	*"I think people do not naturally always look at it that way, but any populist extremes are bad, and I do not make a difference there." (E9: 29).*
	Political Spectrum Position	*"My point was that sometimes populism is cross-ideological (....)." (E1: 60).*
	Ideological Varieties	*"I think it is not clear. I mean you definitely have center populists as well." (E3: 47).*
1.4 Measurement Complexities	Metric-Related Challenges	*"I think because people could not really agree on the definitions of things. I think that what makes populism, (...) difficult is that the definition is different in everyone's minds. And then it becomes difficult to quantify because you cannot pin down what exactly it is." (E4: 66-67).*
	Methodological Concerns	*"You're going to be reducing your observations significantly by only looking at elections because it is not always elections, it is changing government and changing regime sometimes." (E6: 28).*
	Contextual Interpretations	*"It's very complicated because you have always sort of interaction today (....). We are moving to a new one [world order], more molecular, and it is going to lead to a lot of crises." (E10: 44).*
	Analytical Biases	*"I did not like, that when you are looking only at one type of populism, and you are not looking at other types of populism. And that, that is bias." (E15: 58).*

Fig. 3.7 Conceptual Challenges of Populism—Overview. (Source: Own Illustration.)

Focus" assesses populism from an economic perspective and the final concept of this theme, "Interpretational Differences", presents a discussion on the varying perceptions of the term "populism".

Within the theme of "Ideological Pluralism", the first concept of "Populist Ideological Intersections" analyzes the overlaps and divergences among populist movements. The subsequent concept of "Populist Extremes" evaluates the ideological differences between far-left and far-right populist movements, while noting potential similarities. Then, the concept of "Political Spectrum Position" assesses the placement of populist movements within the traditional political spectrum, considering the alignment of diverse ideologies with similar agendas. The theme concludes with the concept of "Ideological Varieties", which addresses the fact that populism is not limited to the edges of the political spectrum, as there are also centrist populists.

The final theme of this dimension, "Measurement Complexities", includes the concept of "Metric-Related Challenges", which discusses the concerns that arise from different definitions when attempting to quantify populism. "Methodological Concerns" assesses the challenges involved in creating reliable models for measuring populism, especially when limited to electoral data. The subsequent concept of "Contextual Interpretations" suggests that a comprehensive measurement of populism may require consideration of deeper systemic factors. Lastly, the concept of "Analytical Biases" highlights the potential pitfalls of research biases in capturing the essence of populism.

3.3.3.2.1 Populism Understandings

Defining populism poses a challenge, whether in academia or in practice, particularly when considering financial markets. In their responses, interviewees express varying views about "populism", including its connotations and usefulness as a descriptor ("Definitional Ambiguities"[210]). The challenge for analysts, practitioners, and scholars when using the term populism or attempting to determine its impact on financial markets is underscored by the lack of clear definition and understanding (e.g., E21: 23[211]). The imprecise nature of the term requires

---

[210] In the subsequent analysis of various themes, a consistent format is employed where each concept is introduced at the end of an introductory sentence, denoted by its name enclosed in brackets.

[211] In the reference system "E21: 23", the letter "E" stands for "Expert" and is followed by a number to indicate which expert is being referenced, in this case, the twenty-first. The number after the colon, in this instance, "23", refers to the particular paragraph of that expert's transcript.

dependence on historical comparisons and visual recognition rather than a precise definition, suggesting that populism is recognized by its presence (E11: 21). Another interviewee acknowledges the multi-layered complexity of the term, expressing the difficulty in fully understanding it (E7: 24).

Populism has evolved over time, leading to changes in how it is perceived ("Modern Perception"). The term "populism" has gained popularity (E5: 17), but its meaning remains contentious (E15: 29). There is some agreement that the term's usage has expanded or been modified from its initial meaning, adding to its ambiguity in contemporary use (E9: 39; E15: 29).

Skepticism exists regarding the term's usefulness ("Term Relevance Debate"). Comparisons with vague terms such as "reform" have been made (E15: 51; E16: 11), raising doubts about the relevance of the term, which can be interpreted differently depending on the context. Some label the term as "a term of abuse" (E16: 17), while others perceive it as a "catch-all" for things that are disliked (E4: 81–82). This leads to a wide range of movements classified as populist. The lack of a shared understanding of the term could impede meaningful discussions due to the resulting conceptual ambiguity (E20: 29).

The media's role is significant in promoting and distorting the concept of populism ("Media Influence"). Interviewees believed that some media outlets display bias when branding particular movements or leaders as "populist" (E15: 35). There is a perception that the term "populism" has been excessively used or misapplied, particularly given claims of its increasing prevalence (E12: 44).

3.3.3.2.2 Definitional Variations

Interviewees propose different understandings of populism ("Contested Perceptions"). Debates arise around whether populism should be considered solely a political strategy or also an ideology, with opinions varying between viewing it as a tactic for electoral success and perceiving it as a collection of beliefs or ideals (E11: 25; E12: 21). Opinions are also divided on the nature of populism. Populism can be linked to various factors, including disruptions in the political landscape, the "world of technocrats created since the 70s and 80s" (E15: 44), and anti-establishment movements that seek to eliminate established structures (E20: 36). It is also suggested that defining populism exclusively in terms of anti-establishment sentiments avoids normative debates (E20: 15).

Some scholars emphasize the economic aspect of populism when defining it, highlighting the importance of comprehending its impact on fiscal stability and policymaking ("Economic Focus"). Populism's connection to policies that can be unpredictable (E14: 40) or unrealistic (E9: 21) often diverges from traditional economic interests (E21: 23), resulting in significant challenges. These challenges include heightened inflation and substantial increases in governmental spending (E3: 49–50).

The interpretation of populism varies significantly due to its flexible nature, allowing for different perspectives. As a result, multiple definitions have been proposed depending on the context. Populism is generally viewed negatively (e.g., E14: 17), although there are those who take a different view (e.g., E5: 20). In fact, one expert suggests that populism may not necessarily have negative connotations and may genuinely represent people's interests. Notably, the expert argues that differences in the definition of populism may be partly due to the location of the practitioner (E15: 47), suggesting that perceptions may be influenced by geography. Various distinctions are made between global manifestations of populism, with a particular focus on trends such as those associated with Donald Trump and the Brexit, as well as dynamics for example in Latin America (E8: 13).

3.3.3.2.3 Ideological Pluralism

The dialog surrounding populism, as inferred by the experts, evokes a complex environment characterized by ideological pluralism and a blurring of the conventional political spectrum ("Populist Ideology Intersections"). It is a landscape in which the boundaries of left-wing and right-wing populism often overlap, suggesting a fundamental convergence in their core characteristics, regardless of their ideological banners. This convergence is emphasized by noting the similarities that exist between seemingly different populist movements, regardless of whether they are represented by a "red star banner" (E5: 20) or any other symbol. Another expert echoes the sentiment that the underlying ideology may not be of significant importance (E11: 37).

This does not mean, however, that populism is devoid of extremes ("Populist Extremes"). Some voices express concern about the harmful potential of both far-left and far-right populism, emphasizing that extremes, regardless of their direction, can be harmful (E9: 29). This sentiment is consistent with the broader notion that the ideological root of populism, whether from the left or the right, may sometimes be less influential than the practical, technocratic implications of its policies (E2: 20).

This calls into question the traditional labels and frameworks used to categorize populism ("Political Spectrum Position"). One expert emphasizes that populism often operates beyond these conventional political spectrums (E1: 60). For another expert, it is clear from the analysis of different regions that there is a spectrum of populism ranging from the left in Chile to the right under leaders such as Bolsonaro in Brazil and Trump in the United States (E4: 43–44). A third expert suggests that the traditional political spectrum may not adequately capture the nuances of populism, leading to complexities in assessing policies that may appear to be left or right but are adopted by opposing sides (E6: 64). In addition, it is argued that the political landscape of the United States provides an illustrative case, showing that while parties such as the Republicans and Democrats may differ in their strategies, there is a common populist undercurrent that advocates for the broader distribution of societal benefits (E8: 9, 15).

The experts also disagree on the varieties of populism that exist ("Ideological Varieties"). In addition to left-wing and right-wing populism, one expert identifies centrist populism as another form (E3: 47). A second expert uses the emergence and mainstreaming of the "green movement" in Europe to illustrate the multi-faceted nature of populism. The expert claims that the shift of green politics in Europe from the fringe to the center demonstrates how populism can revolve around broader socio-political issues based on popular sentiments and concerns rather than conventional party-based ideologies (E15: 56–57).

3.3.3.2.4 Measurement Complexities

When it comes to the task of quantifying populism, one of the main concerns is the inherent difficulty in defining populism accurately ("Metric-Related Challenges"). This ambiguity arises from different perceptions, leading to inconsistencies in quantification and modeling (E4: 66–67). While some datasets exist that attempt to measure populism, their reliance on a universally accepted definition often proves problematic. These datasets can be either too inclusive or too exclusive, leading to potential oversights or exaggerations (E15: 60). Another issue arises when individuals attempt to sidestep this challenge by relying on pre-existing datasets without critically examining their underlying definitions (E11: 49).

A further layer of complexity is added by the limitations of data collection and analysis methods ("Methodological Concerns"). For example, a narrow focus on electoral outcomes can lead to a truncated understanding of populism, as political shifts do not always occur during electoral cycles (E6: 28). Unique settings, such as Argentina's primary electoral system, underscore the importance of understanding local political processes to identify emerging populist sentiments (E6: 24). Questions of causality and the interaction of variables remain additional challenges (E11: 27).

Beyond issues of definition and measurement, some experts see populism as a symptom of broader sociopolitical shifts ("Contextual Interpretations"). This may indicate a systemic political weakness or a widening disparity between the general populace and the privileged elite (E2: 34). Moreover, it is argued that populism does not exist in isolation, as it interacts with other monumental variables, such as the effects of climate change or shifts in global power structures (E10: 44).

Finally, it is a major concern that biases could affect analyses and measurement ("Analytical Biases"). For instance, limiting the analysis to a single type of populism may unintentionally introduce a bias (E15: 58). Another form of distortion is called the "transparency bias", which refers to the potential for greater attention to be paid to the risks in open societies, with their distinctive political processes and press freedoms, and for the dangers posed by opaque societies to be underestimated (E1: 39).

3.3.3.3 Contextual Dynamics

The "Contextual Dynamics" dimension includes three themes that study the diverse manifestations of populism. It analyzes the various forms of populism as influenced by geographic, temporal, and political factors, and examines how populism affects and is affected by politics. For a comprehensive understanding, Figure 3.8 presents a visual depiction of the primary themes of this dimension, along with the associated concepts, supported by illustrative quotes.

The first theme, "Geographic and Temporal Factors", explores the spatial and historical dimensions that influence the nature and manifestations of populism. The first concept, "Country-Specific Manifestations", is devoted to how different countries exhibit different levels of issues for local reasons. The following concept, "Global Populist Agendas", shows how populist policies differ, resulting in different agendas for left- and right-leaning governments. Concluding this theme, "Temporal and Regional Trends" examines the global and historical fluctuations of populism, emphasizing the role of phenomena such as globalization and regional dynamics. These concepts highlight the unique dynamics and characteristics of populism in specific regions and provide a lens for identifying how different factors can cause populism to manifest differently in various settings.

Transitioning to the second theme, "Political Moderators", focuses on the structural and institutional elements that can either mitigate or reinforce populist trends. Beginning with "Political Structures", this first concept delves into the influence of varied political systems on the ascent of populist entities. The next concept, "Institutional Resilience", focuses on how institutions provide checks and balances against populism. The following concept, "Governance Models", analyzes how the nature of governance, whether authoritarian or democratic, affects vulnerability to populist ideologies. Concluding this theme, the "External and Economic Constraints" concept addresses how international institutions and economic obligations shape national political trajectories.

2

Second Order Themes	First Order Concepts	Illustrative Quote
2.1 Geographical and Temporal Factors	Country-Specific Manifestations	*"But in some cases, in some countries, because of local reasons, it could be extremely bad." (E15: 44).*
	Global Populist Agendas	*"But the policies themselves that kind of resonate with the population are going to be different depending on what the population is. And so, we see very different policies coming out of (....) left leaning populist governments versus right leaning populist governments." (E4: 44).*
	Temporal and Regional Trends	*"So, we had a populist wave here for sure for the past ten years or so, and I think such waves, they will somehow disappear again after a while, unless these parties [and] people, (...) achieve a stronghold on the political power, and they can maintain it." (E11: 45).*
2.2 Political Moderators	Political Structures	*"[The] first step is selecting a government, so how likely we are to have a populist government. And that's obviously going to be a little bit of a higher hurdle in a more multi-party system." (E20: 19).*
	Institutional Resilience	*"I think the French electoral system does not favor a candidate (....). So, it is clear when you have a runoff, it favors the centrist candidate." (E11: 57).*
	Governance Models	*"You have always so many interactions, you have contacts that are different, but I would say, for me, an independence of the main institution is always a guarantee of at least long-term stability and the implementation of policies." (E10: 60).*
	External & Economic Constraints	*"You have an institutional setup in Europe that you do not have in Latin America. So, I think that's one of the main differences when analyzing both regions." (E12: 40-41).*
2.3 Populist Policy Channels	Governance Role	*"And then the next one is, which policy domains can they affect? Are they just going to affect migration? Well, that's a socio-political topic. From a market's point of view, that's very tolerable. That's not a big event. Are they going to occupy the finance ministry and drive industrial policy? That's a very different story. Or God forbid, you know, run a central bank or something like that." (E2: 12-13).*
	Policy Rhetoric and Actions	*"But when they are in power, they are (....) also pursuing some very, very problematic policies as well. I think it is almost every time." (E11: 33).*
	Non-Governance Influence	*"I think as long as they are in opposition, (....) they tend to polarize the political debate a lot. And it is very simple messages and easy solutions." (E11: 33).*

Fig. 3.8 Contextual Dynamics of Populism—Overview. (Source: Own Illustration.)

The final theme, "Populist Policy Channels", assesses the ways in which populist ideologies are reflected in politics and governance. The "Governance Role" concept offers insights into the positioning and influence of populist groups, whether in government or in opposition. Subsequently, the concept "Policy Rhetoric and Actions" contrasts the dichotomy between populist rhetoric and its actual implementation. The last concept, "Non-Governance Influence", reveals how mainstream political factions can amplify populist tenets and expand their influence outside of the governance structure, even without a populist government in place.

3.3.3.3.1 Geographical and Temporal Factors

Populism has had waves of success and decline globally and throughout history, which consequently affected its economic, political, and social consequences. To understand this phenomenon, it is crucial to acknowledge its inherent variability across national contexts, the diverse populist agendas that arise in individual countries, and the temporal cycles and contextual factors that shape populism within specific regions or nations, as discussed in this theme.

Firstly, it is essential to address the underlying diversity of populism across different nations ("Country-Specific Manifestations"). This concept stresses that populism is complex in its origin and requires a country-specific analysis rather than broad assumptions. National contexts can have an impact on the consequences of populism, as certain countries and situations may have localized factors that result in notably harmful outcomes (E15: 44). Experts consistently emphasize the significance of a case-by-case evaluation of populism's influence, which cannot be regarded as an universal phenomenon (E2: 26; E12: 40; E14: 38; E15: 41; E21: 41). Comprehending the differences in economic factors and non-economic elements is crucial (E15: 68), as well as having a comprehensive understanding of each country's unique characteristics and overall situation across multiple dimensions (E20: 17). A one size fits all approach can be both reductionist and misleading. Therefore, a case-by-case approach provides a more precise and nuanced comprehension of the impact of populism, highlighting that drawing general conclusions from specific political risk events can obscure judgment (E22: 14).

Parallel to this variability is the recognition of diverse populist agendas that span the globe ("Global Populist Agendas"). Consequently, even though populist movements may have a shared oppositional position, the specifics of their solutions can be very divergent. Some experts suggest that populism can lean either to the left or right of the political spectrum, and its influence is often predicated on the unique socio-political histories and realities of each country. This diversity stems from how individual populations resonate with populist messages, be they left-leaning or right-leaning (E4: 44). A central element driving populist movements is anti-establishment sentiment, which varies considerably from country to country (E20: 17).

Finally, it is crucial to consider populism and its impact within the context of temporal waves and broader global trends, as well as regional trends ("Temporal and Regional Trends"). Populism tends to ebb and flow, with periods of substantial sway followed by phases of reduced impact. Possible factors contributing to the rise of populism include globalization leaving segments of the population behind, inducing them to be responsive to populist agendas (E11: 45, 47). For instance, one interviewee places this current wave in the context of recent historical events, pointing to a shift from the post-Cold War neoliberal consensus to a period in which populism has become a more dominant political force (E18: 31–32). Other participants recognize socio-economic differences as the driving force behind populist waves (E15: 40).

Despite discernible trends on a global scale, regional dynamics can exhibit significant differences beyond temporal variations. Regions such as Africa, Latin America, and Eastern Europe are frequently cited as examples (E15: 68). For instance, in Africa, tribal tensions may be driving developments (E7: 41), while in Latin America, fiscal cycles and historical populist tendencies play a role (E7: 43; E10: 64–65) and long-standing populist trends can be observed (E18: 31). Additionally, the economic landscape reinforces regional differences, where short-term economic strategies may be countered by deeper structural reforms, each leading to different consequences (E8: 28).

3.3.3.3.2 Political Moderators

Populism can fuel uncertainty and interact with the established political landscapes of nations in a variety of ways. When examining the broader political context, institutional and political structures primarily influence the impact of populism. Specifically, the complex connections between political systems, governance mechanisms, and electoral procedures can either facilitate the growth of populist movements or prevent them.

The political and electoral systems play a crucial role in shaping the behavior of populists ("Political Structures"), either enabling or hindering their success based on structural factors (E20: 19). Generally, frequent electoral cycles combined with the potential for unstable power transitions could exacerbate populist disruptions (E7: 22). In multi-party systems, a variety of political voices can create an environment conducive to populist ideologies, but the United States' two-party system also shows susceptibility to populist influences, as demonstrated by internal shifts within the Republican Party (E15: 54; E18: 35). In contrast, it is claimed that France's electoral system, which favors centrists, often hinders the rise of populism (E9: 31; E11: 57).

The strength of a nation's institutions is crucial in building resilience to populism ("Institutional Resilience"). Institutions that maintain their integrity and adherence to the rule of law over time act as a buffer against the potential harm of transient populist trends, ensuring long-term stability (E10: 38, 60). Strong checks and balances, such as those found in many mature Western democracies, serve as barriers. The French constitution exemplifies this by strongly resisting unrestrained power, even within its presidential form (E9: 15). Recent events, such as the Trump administration in the United States or the Brexit, underscore that even developed democracies are not resistant to populist influences (E8: 9). However, their institutional robustness typically allows them to resist, confront, and occasionally absorb populist movements, as evidenced by the resilience of the United States in maintaining democratic ideals through challenging times (E11: 31). Additionally, institutional flexibility plays a crucial role in this discussion, particularly when addressing potential threats to the system, such as corrosion (E15: 54). Notably, countries with established governance structures that have not undergone leadership transitions can create uncertainty by failing to signal upcoming changes in governance. This lack of clarity can leave stakeholders unprepared, hindering proactive responses (E15: 22, 24).

The role of different political governance models also acts as a political moderator affecting the influence of populism ("Governance Models"). Authoritarian regimes tend to suppress the growth of populist movements in the absence of democratic checks and balances, suggesting a less fertile ground for populism to thrive (E15: 67). While both democracies and autocracies can exhibit long-term stability, this might not necessarily continue during periods of transition (E10: 29). Several experts suggest that younger democracies are more prone to experience an increased prevalence of populist movements, particularly during times of political realignment or when faced with fragmented democratic frameworks (E11: 45; E13: 6). The implications of populism in these scenarios can be significant. For instance, elections could escalate into violence, putting political stability at risk (E12: 15). Furthermore, any advancements made can swiftly be undone by a shift in political leadership (E4: 40–41).

Beyond national borders, external entities play a major role in mitigating the effects of populism ("External and Economic Constraints"). Supranational organizations such as the European Union offer an extra layer of governance that can temper the effects of populism. During the eurozone crisis from 2009 to the late 2010s, the institutional structure of the European Union efficiently directed policies, in contrast to the responses of regions like Latin America (E12: 40–41). The governance of the European Union maintains stability, despite some member states, such as Hungary and Poland, facing populist challenges (E10: 62). Furthermore, European Union membership necessitates fiscal compliance, requiring countries to adhere to pre-established financial parameters (E12: 33). Economic factors, such as national debt ratios, can restrain populist government actions. These governing bodies are obligated to ensure fiscal responsibility, generate revenue, and oversee expenditures. In the context of the European Union, Hungary's management of the Union's budget highlights the existing financial oversight (E12: 34; E22: 26).

3.3.3.3.3 Populist Policy Channels

The impact of populism is complex, influenced by the channels through which populists can influence both politics and the economy. The role of populists in government and opposition, as well as the gap between their rhetoric and their actual actions, play an important role in determining this impact.

Central to understanding this influence is the position of populist parties within the governing structure ("Governance Role"). The way financial markets and analysts respond to populism is largely determined by the governance position of the populists. Their influence varies depending on whether they are junior coalition partners or primary government leaders. Additionally, the portfolios controlled by these parties affect their ability to exert power. For example, a nationalist party in charge of foreign policy may be of considerable concern to financial market participants due to potential geopolitical shifts (E9: 33). Furthermore, the scope of their influence is also policy-specific; while their involvement in migration policies might be less concerning, their control over critical economic areas such as the finance ministry or central bank could lead to substantial market repercussions (E2: 12–13).

It is important to differentiate between populism as a mere rhetorical tool and its application in actual policy-making processes ("Policy Rhetoric and Actions"). When populist parties ascend to power, they frequently encounter the intricate realities of governance, challenging their initial commitments and strategies. They may adopt either a moderate stance or implement potentially radical policies that have far-reaching consequences (E9: 15). While in power, populist strategies can disrupt traditional institutional frameworks, sometimes leading to problematic policies (E11: 33). The decision by the United States to withdraw from the climate agreement during the Trump administration was a significant example of this strategy (E17: 26). This is supported by the fact that established parties generally resist populist extremism or oversimplified solutions (E11: 37). Although the rhetoric can be powerful and, at times, challenge conventional norms, there remains a noticeable disjunction between campaign promises and post-election actions (E16: 13). Populist politicians, such as President Trump with his promise to build a wall along the United States-Mexico border, may not necessarily follow through on their campaign pledges (E20: 21). It is therefore crucial to critically evaluate the rhetorical promises against the actions taken (E10: 37). Post-election, concerns about populists may be unfounded, as their policies may not be as extreme as anticipated (E5: 26). Over time, a noticeable pattern has emerged where populist parties, upon strengthening their power, become more moderate in their political approach (E14: 42).

Expanding the scope of analysis beyond direct governance reveals additional pathways through which populism can exert influence ("Non-Governance Influence"). Populist entities, even when not in control of the government, can significantly shape political discourse and outcome, for example by assuming roles in the opposition (E9: 15). From these positions, they can significantly shape discussions, often advocating for simplified solutions (E11: 33). The rise of a powerful populist entity can cause shifts in traditional parties, prompting them to adopt or align with populist themes to maintain voters' support. One expert suggests that this trend is evident in regions such as the Nordic countries, where traditional parties have shifted towards populist narratives, particularly on issues such as immigration (E11: 41). Erdogan's Adalet ve Kalkınma Partisi (AKP) party in Turkey serves as another example, demonstrating a shift where non-populist parties engage in populist tactics to remain in power (E8: 19; E11: 45).

3.3.3.4 Multifaceted Impact

The third dimension, referred to as "Multifaceted Impact", clarifies the various consequences of populism in political, social, and economic domains. This dimension includes three comprehensive themes, each representing a perspective for exploring the macro-level impact. For a more detailed examination, see Figure 3.9, which graphically depicts the key themes and related concepts of this third dimension of the research framework. Further exploration of these themes and concepts is detailed in the subsequent subsections.

The initial theme, "Political Consequences", assesses the manner in which populism interacts with political structures and institutions. Within this theme, the first concept, "Political Unpredictability", addresses the uncertain and often pragmatic nature of populist policies. Then it delves into the analysis of how populism can reduce institutional independence and influence spheres such as the judiciary and monetary policy within the concept of "Institutional Impact".

3

Second Order Themes	First Order Concepts	Illustrative Quote
(3.1) Political Consequences	Political Unpredictability	*"I do not necessarily think of it as being tied to any specific set of policies." (E4: 43-44).*
	Institutional Impact	*"What they both tend to do is they erode the institutional independence or institutional independence. Let's say they tend to erode the power of technocrats." (E8: 21).*
	Political Landscape	*"The impact is the fragmentation of the political system (...), but the main effect is actually not the political system but the political party system." (E12: 25).*
	Democratic Outlet	*"That is why it is popular with the public because it, it responds to certain frustrations." (E15: 41).*
(3.2) Social Consequences	Social Unrest	*"So, for example, (....), you get the right-wing reaction, and they go to war politically speaking, and then now you get this serious social unrest. (....) That's a risk. If it disrupts your business, if it means you can no longer safely operate, if it damages your property, then that is a political risk." (E3: 34-35).*
	Societal Polarization and Fragmentation	*"(...) and it also decreases cohesion within society (...). It could become more extreme; (....) increasing risk of confrontation (....) within the context of the country." (E15: 34).*
	Economic Ripple Effects	*"But since the protests started happening, you have seen a lot of changes to the political environment that have made it less appealing to investors in some ways." (E4: 30-31).*
(3.3) Economic Consequences	Economic Policy Unpredictability	*"[W]hen you're talking about a populist government there is like fears that they would invoke more unorthodox economic policies which would then result in a lot of different concerns about being able to do business operations." (E19: 15).*
	Macroeconomic Policies	*"(....) [A]nd in terms of expenditures, again, it can vary. So similarly, increasing pension spending, increasing wages in the public sector, things that are low hanging fruit." (E13: 9).*
	Nationalistic Strategies	*"And probably also more domestically oriented rather than international oriented. This could kind of be visible in different ways. So, for example, providing more subsidies to domestic industries and putting tariffs on imports from specific countries. I think it is more domestically oriented rather than internationally." (E21: 30).*
	Reforms and Opportunities	*"You have [Narendra] Modi who has been extremely strong on certain institutional reforms which improve the efficiency of the economy but of course there is a significant kind of Hindu nationalist components in the governing party (...)." (E1: 45).*

Fig. 3.9 Multifaceted Impact of Populism—Overview. (Source: Own Illustration.)

The following concept, "Political Landscape", analyzes the impact of populism on the broader political landscape. Subsequently, the concept of "Democratic Outlet" discusses the appeal of populism as a response to public frustration.

The second theme, "Social Consequences", focuses on the societal impact of populism, with the first concept, "Social Unrest", discussing potential disruptions caused by populist-driven policy decisions. The following concept, "Societal Polarization and Fragmentation", analyzes how populism plays a role in intensifying societal divisions, amplifying extreme voices, and increasing confrontations, ultimately deepening divisions in society. The final concept in this theme, "Economic Ripple Effects", emphasizes the ways in which social consequences can interact to affect economic conditions.

The analysis then proceeds to the "Economic Consequences" theme, which focuses on the economic implications of populist movements. Within this third theme, the concept of "Economic Policy Unpredictability" illuminates how populism intensifies economic uncertainty and may not always provide realistic solutions. The discussion then centers on the concept of "Macroeconomic Policies", revealing how populist administrations can inflate public spending, leading to potential long-term economic repercussions. The following concept, "Nationalist Strategies", examines how populism tends to prioritize domestic and protectionist economic policies. The third theme concludes with the concept of "Reforms and Opportunities", which examines the potential for positive economic change that could be driven by populist movements.

3.3.3.4.1 Political Consequences

Populism has been acknowledged as a transformative force of great impact on the global political stage. The analysis of this theme begins by exploring the inherent unpredictability of rising populism and then examines its broader implications for institutions and the domestic and international political landscape. It also considers populism's central role as a political outlet.

One of the most notable features of populism is its inherent unpredictability, which in turn poses challenges for traditional policy frameworks and governance conventions ("Political Unpredictability"). The interviews reveal that populism is generally not defined by a distinct policy set (E4: 43–44), but rather by the absence of a specific policy program (E15: 45). Instead, the term "populist policy" is often used without a clear definition, sometimes confusing the popular with the populist (E12: 30). This ambiguity about what constitutes populist politics leads some to see it as a style or rhetoric rather than a consolidated policy program (e.g., E16: 11). Nonetheless, it is widely believed that while there are some inherently populist policies, such as those rooted in xenophobia, many policies can adopt a populist veneer depending on the situation (E17: 16, 18). Consequently, populism varies in unique ways across different countries, reflecting their distinct political scenarios, leading to significant policy variations globally (E20: 17). This unpredictability, however, is not only of concern to investors, but also to those who value political predictability, potentially leading to increased political risk (E14: 8–9).

Adding to this unpredictability is another dimension: the potential inexperience of populist leaders, which further increases uncertainties in both governance and policymaking (E13: 9, 13). This inexperience frequently results in ambiguous policy directions that can shift based on prevailing public sentiments, further amplifying risk perception (E15: 32). A consistent trait running through populist movements is their anti-establishment nature. Movements that challenge the existing political structure inherently threaten the status quo, potentially leading to shifts in regulatory and policy environments (E20: 38). Further complicating the picture is populism's often-observed lack of strategy. Instead of a coherent plan, populism prioritizes popular sentiments over the intricate trade-offs of policymaking, seeming more like an unorthodox approach (E2: 18). One interviewee emphasized the lack of clear strategies in several populist movements, citing the Italian Movimento 5 Stelle (M5S) as an example (E13: 9). Despite its apparent lack of a long-term strategic vision, populism often demonstrates pragmatism, with populists showing a capacity for highly practical decision-making that can override ideological commitments when deemed necessary (E8: 21, 23).

Beyond unpredictability, the most important political feature of populism, according to the interviewees, is the erosion of institutional independence ("Institutional Impact"). Populism tends to undermine technocrats, leading institutions to favor the immediate political agenda over established norms, with both left-wing and right-wing populists eroding institutional integrity to align more closely with government objectives (E2: 26; E8: 21, 23). Populist trends in contemporary times pose a threat to democratic institutions and have the potential to produce disruptive outcomes. The attack on the United States Capitol on January 6, 2021, serves as an example of the real-world implications of this phenomenon, and fears of democratic systems transitioning to hybrid or authoritarian regimes are growing (E17: 26, 28).

In this context, the judicial system is a major target for the institutional degradation of populism. This process usually begins with the appointment of judges and slowly spreads to other political institutions. The goal is to manipulate judicial mechanisms, such as ensuring that populist leaders do not face legal consequences (E11: 29). This trend is apparent in numerous new European democracies where populist parties can alter constitutions with supermajorities, resulting in regulatory changes, media manipulation, and the erosion of judicial independence (E11: 31).

Central banks and their monetary policies are also affected by populism. As populist governments come into power, they jeopardize the autonomy of central banks, which could destabilize monetary policy (E19: 15, 23). Although populist agendas may be a driving force behind policy shifts, personal or religious beliefs of leaders may also play a role. For instance, an expert highlights the case of Turkey, where central bankers were ousted from their positions to consider adjustments in interest rates, causing significant institutional turmoil with broader economic consequences (E10: 53, 55–56).

The institutional reach of populism is not limited to this. Among the institutions affected are also statistical and economic agencies, which face challenges to their credibility under populist administrations. One of the challenges is the risk of data manipulation, which affects confidence both domestically and internationally (E19: 47).

Populism's influence extends beyond specific areas, profoundly reshaping the national and international political landscape ("Political Landscape"). Central to this transformation is the disruption of the political party system, with increased fragmentation and the rise of populist parties (E12: 25; E15: 34). The detachment and volatility in party loyalty within political parties indicates that voters are shifting away from traditional affiliations and becoming more receptive to new political movements and voices (E12: 26). As a result, the political spectrum is being redefined, allowing emerging entities to challenge existing political norms (E18: 36). Importantly, populism is not limited to new parties. Established parties, such as the British Tory Party, are not immune from its effects, with significant populist factions occasionally overshadowed by the party's mainstream image (E12: 28). Moreover, the influence of populism on longstanding political parties may result in internal disputes, as exemplified by the Brexit scenario in the United Kingdom, highlighting the disruption that populist movements can cause within conventional party frameworks (E11: 39).

However, the impact of populism extends beyond the political landscape, as its effects permeate into other areas beyond mere party dynamics within a national context. Although immediate transfers of power to populist parties may be rare in some countries, their impact on the party system is significant and can occur through several channels. For example, populist parties often manifest their influence through legal complications, especially in countries with coalition governments, where such fragmentation makes it difficult to achieve majorities and impedes policymaking processes (E16: 21). Nonetheless, the governance landscape, which has traditionally relied on political compromise and collaboration, is also susceptible to the complexities of populism. Situations of gridlock arise when different political parties control different branches of government, leading to inaction and obstruction of policymaking (E13: 7). With the emergence of populist sentiments, traditional negotiation approaches have been disrupted. The United States is a prime example of the challenges faced by Democrats in engaging with a fragmented Republican party, resulting in difficulties in achieving bipartisan deals (E18: 36).

The influence of populism on the international arena is also relevant, reflecting how populism is reshaping global politics, diplomacy, and international institutions. International relations, particularly with major players like the United States, have experienced declining trust attributed to the unpredictable behavior and actions of populist leaders. For instance, governments with populist tendencies, such as the Trump administration, have put a strain on international relations and questioned established norms (E9: 17). Those governments often mistrust multilateral institutions such as the International Monetary Fund and prefer bilateral arrangements, resulting in new geopolitical dynamics that also involve trade-offs and complexities (E10: 45; E19: 27).

While populism is often viewed critically, it can also serve a constructive role in democratic systems ("Democratic Outlet"). Despite its disruptive perception, populism provides an outlet for public frustrations and desires, thus demonstrating its positive political impact. It serves as a mechanism that allows for the expression of dissatisfaction with existing political and economic modalities and prevents extreme scenarios such as those seen in authoritarian regimes (E3: 45). This argument is substantiated by highlighting the fact that the appeal of populism stems primarily from its capacity to address the public's discontent. Populist politics often arises as a response to established systems, reflecting widespread dissatisfaction with the functioning of the political economy within conventional frameworks (E15: 41; E20: 15). Leaders advocate policies that promise significant change and contrast strongly with prevailing norms, often rallying against perceived enemies or threats (E5: 17).

3.3.3.4.2 Social Consequences

Populism, as revealed in numerous interviews, has also multifaceted impacts on social dynamics. Depending on the circumstances, populism can act as a double-edged sword, capable of generating both unity and discord, such as social unrest and violence.

In certain political environments, the rise of left-wing populists can provoke a reactionary response from right-wing populist groups ("Social Unrest"). This fluctuation between opposing populist powers can intensify into what one expert metaphorically describes as a "political war". This escalating dynamic can lead to heightened social unrest, presenting real challenges for businesses and investors in such regions, including potential operational disruptions and property damage (E3: 34–35). For example, one expert notes that the emergence of a left-wing populist in Venezuela has triggered a reactionary response from the right-wing, resulting in direct confrontation when both sides mobilize their supporters. Alternatively, populism can also pave the way for peaceful avenues of dissent. Chile serves as an example, where mass unrest eventually led to constitutional reforms that provided a democratic platform for the population to voice its dissatisfaction, potentially restraining violent manifestations of unrest (E3: 40–43).

Yet not all populist movements or their outcomes are confined to institutional structures. Sometimes political discourse spills over into the streets, resulting in violence. In such cases, governments often struggle to maintain control as the basic institutions are threatened (E14: 11). Brazil provides an additional example of this phenomenon, where the ambiguity surrounding the results of the country's 2022 general election has resulted in social turmoil and an assault on federal government facilities (E10: 31).

In addition to the physical chaos of protests and violence, populism casts a long shadow of polarization over society ("Societal Polarization and Fragmentation"). Societies can become artificially fragmented by magnifying marginal voices and marginalizing moderate perspectives through confrontational rhetoric, which exacerbates division. When populist narratives target specific groups or political entities, it increases the risk of violent confrontation and decreases cohesion within the society (E15: 33–34). The digital sphere amplifies this phenomenon. Although most people have moderate views, online platforms disproportionately reinforce extremist voices, pushing the moderate consensus into obscurity and undermining societal cohesion (E17: 26).

These social upheavals can have economic repercussions ("Economic Ripple Effects"). This link can be seen in countries that, despite their progress toward developed market status and reputations for stability, face issues of investor confidence due to political upheaval caused by protests. Such disruptions in the social landscape can make these countries less attractive for investment, highlighting the business implications of social unrest (E4: 30–31).

3.3.3.4.3 Economic Consequences

Populism's impact on the economy remains a topic of much debate, with experts attributing diverse and profound effects, both positive and mostly negative. A key concern associated with populism, similar to its political consequences, is its economic unpredictability ("Economic Policy Unpredictability"). Populist messages often identify structural problems but offer solutions that are frequently one-dimensional and thus likely to be economically unfeasible (E15: 41). Populism, with its diverse ideological foundations, frequently leads to unconventional or disruptive strategies, particularly in terms of economic policies. There is a widespread view that populist governments tend to pursue more unorthodox economic policies. For instance, some consider the Trump administration to be a mix of unorthodox and orthodox economic policies (E2: 12). Concerns particularly emerge when populist governments enact non-traditional economic policies, from imposing capital controls and stringent regulations that deter foreign investment to adopting cryptocurrencies as national currency, as illustrated by El Salvador, potentially harming business operations (E19: 15, 27).

Several experts have linked populism to a specific set of economic policies ("Macroeconomic Policies"). In response to the need to satisfy constituents, populist governments tend to endorse increased spending as a means of short-term economic stimulus, such as raising public sector wages or enhancing pension benefits (E13: 9). The reasoning behind this approach often arises from populist governments' urgency to address societal discontent, even if these fiscal loosening measures are short-lived or merely aimed at a temporary boost in popularity (E4: 59; E11: 27, 29). Rushed policies may receive immediate approval, but they may not align with a country's long-term economic strategy. Tempted by quick gains, populist leaders may advocate temporary measures that, while popular, may lead to long-term economic challenges (E10: 48–49). This perspective is reinforced by observations that populist administrations influence fiscal decisions, often escalating spending without clear financing strategies (E3: 48; E22: 22, 24). For instance, the Chilean government increased spending to appease the population in the face of social tensions (E4: 28–29). The Turkish government's unconventional growth strategies are another example of this phenomenon (E10: 48–49). Moreover, the economic infeasibility frequently linked to populism is highlighted by the unfulfilled pledges of leaders such as Jair Bolsonaro, who was Brazil's 38th president from 2019 to 2022, and Alberto Ángel Fernández, who has been Argentina's president since 2019 (E10: 47). The potential economic instability resulting from such fiscal decisions induces an inherent danger. Boosting public spending without a well-defined plan threatens to undermine the economy's long-term stability (E9: 43; E11: 27; E13: 6).

Furthermore, multiple interviewees have proposed that populism often aligns with a nationalist economic approach ("Nationalistic Strategies"). A widespread perspective indicates that populist movements tend towards a more domestically focused approach, frequently avoiding international partnerships in favor of localized efforts (E21: 30). Economic strategies influenced by populism demonstrate increased involvement in prioritizing domestic interests, potentially resulting in actions such as subsidies for domestic industries or import tariffs on particular countries. Yet the nature of these strategies varies globally, with policies ranging from tax adjustments to nationalization (E14: 22). Protectionism is a hallmark of populist economics as it is a recurring theme in populist regimes. However, such policies can lead to confrontations that disrupt the functioning of central banks, albeit at later stages of implementation (E6: 9–10). Such policies may result in increased public spending leading to economic inefficiencies as the government's control over the economy intensifies (E11: 21, 27). According to one expert, this protectionist stance often stems from both left- and right-wing populist narratives (E17: 28) that emphasize self-reliance and reluctance to engage in global markets. Notably, another expert posits that right-wing populists find nationalistic strategies particularly relevant, whereas their left-wing counterparts tend to prioritize social goals (E22: 20).

Another dimension of populism's nationalist economic approach is in the areas of immigration and trade. A restrictive immigration policy is often synonymous with populism, an outlook that many global businesses see as detrimental to economic growth (E16: 17). This sentiment is reinforced by the perceived absence of pro-immigration or pro-free trade populist movements (E18: 39–40). Restrictions on people's movement can exacerbate economic pressures. Companies are forced to revamp their previously efficient global supply chains and confront increasing wage pressures, as observed in the United Kingdom (E18: 32).

However, the economic narrative of populism is not always negative ("Reforms and Opportunities"). In certain contexts, populist leaders have been able to introduce significant economic reforms. Governments influenced by populism have the potential to positively change narratives by implementing reforms from fiscal adjustments to improving the business climate and potentially attracting foreign investments (E4: 36–39). Multiple experts have noted that India's Prime Minister Modi has enacted measures aimed at reducing bureaucracy, enhancing transparency, and fostering foreign investment, all within the framework of a populist nationalist narrative (E1: 45; E8: 30). The concept of anti-corruption also remains a prominent theme for many populist movements. The Italian M5S and Greece's Synaspismos Rizospastikis Aristeras (Syriza) have advocated for similar narratives with the intention of purifying political systems of corruption. Thus, the rise of populism can sometimes be linked to broader economic and governance reforms (E13: 7; E14: 18).

3.3.3.5 Market Response Dynamics

The "Market Response Dynamics" dimension explores how domestic and global markets respond to populist trends, organized into four themes. Figure 3.10 provides a visual representation of the themes, related concepts, and illustrative quotes that form the fourth dimension of the research framework. Additional information is provided in the following subsections.

The initial theme, "Market Adjustments", analyzes the financial market elements affected by populism. Within this theme, the concept of "Segmental Responses" assesses the reactions of specific market segments, such as stocks, bonds[212] and currencies, to the rise of populism. The subsequent concept, "Learnings and Adaptation", reflects on market reactions to populist events and the evolving understanding of these effects over time. While the next concept, "Local and Global Impact", contrasts the impact of populism on local versus global markets based on regional significance.

The second theme, "Time-Sensitive Effects", concentrates on the temporal aspect of market reactions to populism. It is divided into "Short-Term Responses" and "Long-Term Responses" to separate immediate from longer-term market effects. Moreover, the concept of "Event-Driven Shifts" analyzes the variations in market reactions based on different events or contexts.

In the third theme, "Corporate and Sectoral Variations", the focus shifts to the impact of populism on various business sectors. The concept of "Regulatory Changes" centers on shifts in government rules that affect business operations, while the subsequent concept of "Economic Policy Exposure" analyzes exposure concerns regarding how companies are affected by a country's financial and economic decisions. The third concept centers around "Sector-Specific Implications" and presents populisms impact on selected industries.

The last theme, "Ideological Influences", scrutinizes market reactions based on the ideological tenets of populism. It features the first concept, "Populist Ideology Responses", which examines how investor perceptions vary depending on the ideological orientation of populism for both the left and the right. The subsequent concept, "Election-Driven Responses", examines the market's impact for different ideologies due to the potential risks associated with post-election policy shifts.

---

[212] In the following discussion, references to bonds specifically pertain to government bonds. References to corporate bonds will be explicitly labeled as such.

(4)

Second Order Themes	First Order Concepts	Illustrative Quote
(4.1) Market Adjustments	Segmental Responses	*"When it comes to market prices that is a different story and it is very difficult to assess the impact of populism on equity prices. It is a lot easier to assess populism on foreign exchange and interest rates." (E6: 13).*
	Learnings and Adaptation	*"There is a lot of these analytical questions to get right. And (....) you can see that the market has frequently gotten some of these steps a little bit wrong and frequently it gets them right." (E2: 13)*
	Local and Global Impact	*"So, in practice, that means that obviously the US elections are always a very big one [a]nd then you also have a few large European countries and then some emerging markets (....)." (E2: 10).*
(4.2) Time-Sensitive Effects	Short-Term Responses	*"It depends on the situation in general. I would say they are short-term consequences because the market adjusts. But the market can adjust to a level which remain unfavorable and come through with a risk premium to be paid for along the time." (E22: 38).*
	Long-Term Responses	*"So yes, in many cases, I would say it is often that populism goes for these perceivable easy solutions, which if you follow mainstream economics (....) could have negative impact on a mid-long-term perspective." (E5: 29).*
	Event-Driven Shifts	*"I think that the pandemic definitely marked an important point where market prices reaction to populism changed dramatically (...)." (E6: 13-15).*
(4.3) Corporate and Sectoral Variations	Regulatory Changes	*"What could happen is that (....) there are going to be any big political policy changes that might change basically the regulatory regime." (E12: 17).*
	Economic Policy Exposure	*"If you break it down to a sectoral level, I think populism can represent opportunities for certain sectors. And if you are a very export-oriented sector, that is probably not a good place to be." (E11: 23).*
	Sector-Specific Implications	*"So, in a sense like if you were an oil investor in Russia versus Venezuela the mechanism of populism was very different, but the outcome is the same." (E1: 43).*
(4.4) Ideological Influences	Populist Ideology Responses	*"If you had the populist on the left, it is not good for capital markets." (E22: 16).*
	Election-Driven Responses	*"The businesses tend to be super happy. I feel like financial markets tend to react positively when a right populist is elected." (E3: 59-60).*

Fig. 3.10 Markets Response Dynamics—Overview. (Source: Own Illustration.)

3.3.3.5.1 Market Adjustments

The impact of populism on financial markets is manifold. The complexity lies not only in the general reactions of these markets to populist governance, but also in the nuanced reactions of different market segments ("Segmental Responses"). When examining various market segments, equity markets are particularly responsive to political shifts, often undergoing rapid adjustments in reaction to changing circumstances. However, assessing the impact of populism on equity prices presents greater challenges compared to interest rates (bonds) and currencies, as equity markets are highly volatile to the remarks of populist leaders (E6: 13). Of particular concern are instances where leaders make unorthodox statements or take unexpected decisions that could challenge existing monetary policy or trade norms. These unpredictable statements cause disruptions in the markets, often leading to rapid reactions from investors (E19: 33–34). Although some market segments may appear less affected by populism in the equity sector, populist policies can still have a significant impact on market outcomes, such as the implementation of new taxes or subsidies (E21: 16–17).

Compared to equity markets, bond markets exhibit a varied response to populism. One expert suggested that investors may turn to bonds as a safer option amid populism-induced uncertainty (E1: 10). However, populist governments have led to higher risk premiums in some countries, affecting bond yields (E19: 14). An example can be observed in the Italian bond market, which experienced upheaval when the Italian M5S and Lega Nord coalition came to power in 2018, as their unconventional ideas raised concerns about Italy's future ability to manage its debt, leading to a sharp rise in Italian bond yields (E16: 13). The lasting impact of populism on bond markets lies in the potential erosion of investment confidence. A single default can have a significant and lasting impact on a country's risk premium (E19: 34–35), and political risk can be priced into bond yields for extended periods (E16: 25).

Currency markets can also be sensitive to populist sentiment (E19: 34) but were less focused in the interviews. The extent to which geopolitical risks can affect currencies depends on the nature of the event and the channel through which its effects are transmitted (E19: 15). For example, tensions between global powers could have a direct impact on their respective currencies, with emerging markets more exposed than developed markets (E21: 19).

Markets frequently display initial misinterpretations of populist policies, oscillating between disproportionate panic and unwarranted optimism ("Learnings and Adaption"). This reaction highlights the crucial role of communication in bridging understanding between political movements and financial markets, thus effectively shaping risk perceptions (E2: 13). Over time, markets tend to adjust to the realities of populist governments, reflecting a gradual normalization process as these governments establish their presence (E9: 41). For instance, in Italy, markets have grown more accustomed to the Meloni-led government of populist parties, suggesting an adjustment to the new political landscape (E2: 26). Despite the confrontational rhetoric often associated with populist leaders, they may enact policies that ultimately support the business sector, illustrating a complex relationship between political attitudes and practical governance (E3: 68; E8: 36). However, markets swiftly respond to policies viewed as hostile towards business or market interests, rapidly integrating these perceptions into the valuations of currencies, equities, and bonds, underscoring the importance of political climate on market dynamics (E17: 14; E19: 12).

Nevertheless, an over-reliance on the broad appeal of populist rhetoric, coupled with an optimistic belief in the unwavering effectiveness of institutions, poses significant risks. This complacency disregards the potential for systemic vulnerabilities that can arise from populist policies, underscoring the need for a vigilant and informed market response (E1: 42–43).

When analyzing the market impact of populism, the element of surprise cannot be neglected. There are numerous examples in recent history, such as the political rise of Donald Trump or the political changes in Argentina, where markets were caught off guard by unexpected election results, leading to pronounced market reactions (E6: 26). That said, not all populist victories lead to market adjustments. There are cases where the market was largely unaffected by a populist victory because it had already been priced in (E9: 9). For example, the election of Bolsonaro in Brazil did not cause significant market turmoil as the outcome was expected (E6: 23; E9: 23). The reliability of polls is a factor to consider. If the polls align with market expectations, the victory of a populist government may not result in significant market shocks (E6: 26; E9: 11).

The geographical context also plays a key role in the impact of markets ("Local and Global Impact"). While the rise of populist forces in smaller nations may not resonate much on a global scale, large economies can cause significant movements in global markets when influenced by populism (E2: 10; E22: 34). For example, populist events in countries like Turkey can dramatically affect local markets but may leave markets in countries like the United States largely unaffected (E22: 14).

3.3.3.5.2 Time-Sensitive Effects

Understanding the impact of populism on financial markets requires an investigation of temporal mediation factors. According to the interviews conducted, this influence is categorized into three primary time frames: short-term reactions, intermediate to long-term effects, and context-dependent responses.

In short-term market analysis, financial markets rapidly adjust to changes caused by populist ideologies ("Short-Term Responses"). Quick adjustments to potentially unfavorable levels that may require a continuous risk premium were mentioned (E22: 38). The interviews also revealed that policies implemented by a populist leader generally take time, implying that these changes may have limited relevance for short-term investors (E14: 38). One expert notes the tendency of markets to inadvertently overlook long-term challenges when they should rationally be taken into account (E11: 55). Another interviewee emphasized the unpredictable nature of market reactions, using the quick market rebound following Trump's election as an example of how short-term reactions may not always indicate long-term outcomes (E21: 45).

In terms of intermediate to long-term impacts, an even more complex picture emerges ("Long-Term Responses"). Different market segments—equity, bond, and currency markets—demonstrate distinct temporal reactions. While currency markets tend to react in the short term, equity markets take a medium-term view, and bond markets prefer a longer time frame. One expert pointed to a medium-term impact of populism, often covering a period of six to 24 months (E2: 22). The dual nature of populist policies, which can bring immediate socioeconomic benefits but also risk negative economic outcomes in the medium to long term, was noted (E5: 20, 29). Concerns were raised regarding the prolonged sustainability of economic surges caused by populist practices and the handling of consequent predicaments (E8: 25–26). The significance of examining the lasting institutional effects of populism, which could set new long-term trends, was emphasized (E10: 26). Moreover, it was highlighted that long-term viewpoints are frequently deemed more perceptive than short-term perspectives (E10: 38).

Context-sensitive responses were also discussed ("Event-Driven Shifts"). Major global events, such as the COVID-19 pandemic, have altered the traditional patterns of market responses to populism. Volatility and the subsequent rally following Trump's election were compared to more recent market responses to populist events in the United Kingdom. This highlighted a change attributed to different fiscal environments before and after the pandemic (E6: 13–15).

3.3.3.5.3 Corporate and Sectoral Variations

When considering the multifaceted impact of populism on financial markets, populist policies can affect industries differently. This impact can vary greatly, presenting both obstacles and opportunities for companies across multiple sectors.

Examining how populism interacts at the sectoral and firm level, firms express concern about the regulatory impact of populist governments ("Regulatory Changes"). As part of the so-called elite, companies may typically find themselves at odds with populist agendas (E3: 56). As a result, under populist regimes, the regulatory environment could experience significant changes with implications specific to each sector. The business environment may become more challenging as populist governments often take a more interventionist stance, as evidenced by the trend towards direct government intervention at the sectoral or institutional level, which further complicates the business climate (E21: 27). For example, populist agendas can lead to the establishment of sector-specific tax policies that align with their respective governments' ideological leanings (E21: 16).

Furthermore, populist influence can potentially impact central banking decisions and lead to subsidies for certain industries. Although this intervention could benefit certain business sectors, it may result in market inefficiencies. Export taxes are an example of unconventional measures that are characteristic of populist governance (E19: 23). This increasingly volatile regulatory landscape poses a growing challenge for companies navigating uncertain economic conditions, as MNCs are particularly concerned about how populism could change policies, such as taxation, that affect their operations (E12: 15, 17).

Complementing the regulatory shifts, populist governments often implement changes in economic policies ("Economic Policy Exposure"). For example, nationalistic policies aim to strengthen local economic capacity by changing market norms in favor of domestic industries, potentially disadvantaging foreign firms (E5: 22). The effect on firms may vary depending on how they diversify their operations. Global companies operating in diverse political environments may experience heightened exposure, yet their international presence across multiple countries can serve as a buffer against regional risks (E18: 14). In contrast, companies with operations concentrated in just a few countries may suffer significant consequences in the case of political disruptions in those regions (E17: 10). Trade dynamics may shift as a result, with export-driven sectors potentially encountering protectionist trade barriers, while domestically-oriented sectors may confront reduced competition and increased government support (E11: 23). In global organizations, populism can create hurdles that impede the movement of personnel and the exchange of information, ultimately hampering the operational agility of international corporations and creating tangible obstacles (E18: 51).

Several sectors have been identified to be especially exposed to populism ("Sector-Specific Implications"). The energy and natural resources sectors, especially oil and gas, are acutely susceptible to populist policies, where fears of nationalization strongly influence investor behavior and shape stakeholder expectations (E5: 24; E19: 41). Notably, both right-wing and left-wing political ideologies can lead to similar adversities for investors, as seen in the oil industries of Russia and Venezuela (E1: 43).

Strategic industries, particularly those in the technology and high-tech sectors, can also be significantly impacted (E5: 24). The impact of populism on global economic dynamics is especially pronounced in sensitive areas of national security, such as advanced microchips, where the rivalry between major powers, including China and the United States, underscores this effect (E18: 27–28).

Furthermore, the influence of populism has extended to non-strategic industries that have historically been insulated from political sensitivities may not remain immune to populist challenges (E18: 25). For example, manufacturing sectors, often associated with lower-skilled workers, may find themselves on the target of increased government intervention (E21: 34–35).

3.3.3.5.4 Ideological Influences

The interviews with experts indicate that the influence of populism on financial markets is significantly shaped by its ideological orientation. Different views on how markets react to left-wing versus right-wing populism were highlighted, revealing nuanced interpretations and responses to these ideological distinctions ("Populist Ideology Responses"). Left-wing populism is commonly considered anti-capitalist and has traditionally been believed to introduce detrimental elements into capital markets (E22: 16, 40). However, recent developments present a more sophisticated picture. Notably, left-wing populist governments in countries such as Brazil and Mexico have demonstrated a willingness to adopt relatively moderate fiscal positions, challenging conventional understandings (E6: 33, 36). On the opposite end of the ideological spectrum, right-wing populism, as evidenced in countries like the United States, tends to favor nationalistic policies. The key focus seems to be on potentially growth-restrictive policies, particularly in areas such as immigration and trade (E1: 54; E5: 22).

When it comes to how these populist movements are interpreted in the financial sphere, differences emerge. According to one expert, financial markets tend to view left-wing populism as more predictable because of its immediate consequences, such as potential tax increases or the threat of asset nationalization (E1: 41–42, 44). In contrast, right-wing populism presents challenges regarding its unpredictable fiscal policies, as evidenced by tax cuts without corresponding reductions in government spending (E6: 31–32).

Market reactions to the electoral successes of left- or right-wing populists underscore the complexities inherent in populist ideologies, revealing nuanced dynamics within financial markets ("Election-Driven Responses"). One expert suggests that there is a tendency for markets to react more positively when right-wing populists come to power (E3: 59–60). However, a counter-narrative suggests that left-wing populism can lead to more market-friendly outcomes in specific contexts (E6: 63). It is noticeable that while many experts stress the impossibility of categorizing populism according to its ideological roots (E19: 29; E22: 16), others mention different market reactions to different forms (E8: 34).

3.3.3.6 Investors' Reactions

The final dimension, "Investors' Reactions", covers the ways investors navigate and potentially adjust to the ascent and influence of populism unfolding through three overarching themes. Figure 3.11 depicts the themes and related concepts that make up the fifth dimension of the research framework, with more detailed discussion in the following subsections.

Beginning with the theme entitled "Political Risk and Populism", the focus is on comprehending the facets of political risk connected to populism. The first concept "Finance-Related Political Risks" within this theme delves thoroughly into the complex considerations involved in evaluating political risk, ranging from market perceptions to the wider geopolitical context. Expanding on the preceding concept, "Populism-Induced Political Risk", analyzes the increasingly prominent role of populism in market risk assessments. To complement this theme, "Political Risk Developments" looks at the evolution of political risk over time, with a focus on the impact of populism.

The second theme, "Populism-Influenced Risk Management", focuses on the challenges and intricacies introduced by populism in risk management, emphasizing its impact on investments and the evolving political landscape. The concept of "Risk Assessment Impact" explores how rising populist movements globally are shaping risk assessment, creating unique challenges and changing dynamics in the economic sphere. The following concept of "Risk Prediction Method Adaptations" emphasizes the importance of refining risk prediction models to navigate the complexities of populism, focusing on accurately quantifying risks and avoiding simplifications amid global concerns. To conclude this theme, "Political and Electoral Dynamics" examines how populist electoral campaigns and their impact on global financial markets influence the predictability of elections.

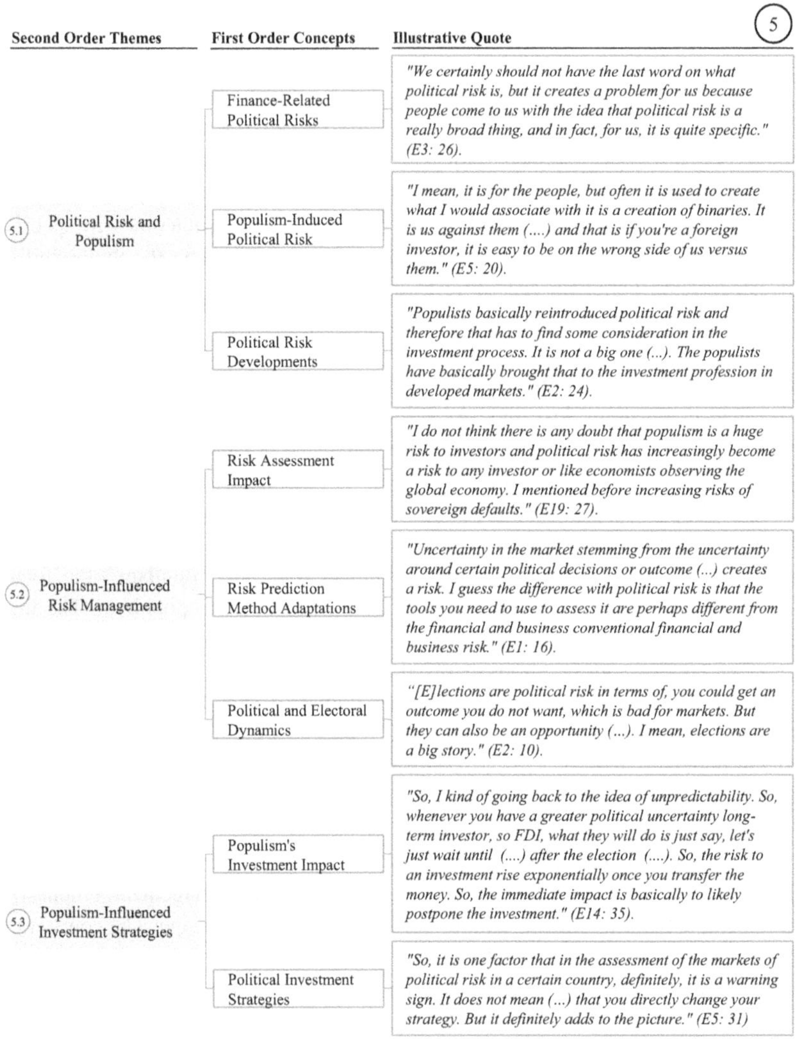

Fig. 3.11 Investors' Reactions to Populism—Overview. (Source: Own Illustration.)

Lastly, the theme of "Populism-Influenced Investment Strategies" outlines how populism is shaping the investment landscape, highlighting the need for adaptive strategies that take into account its complex dynamics. The concept of "Populism's Investment Impact" focuses on the implied unpredictability that leads to different investment responses. Subsequently, the concept of "Political Investment Strategies" offers insights into how populist events shape investment approaches, requiring comprehensive assessments of political shifts and their policy implications.

3.3.3.6.1 Political Risk and Populism

Within the dynamic financial landscape, the assessment of political risk has become critical for investment decisions as the perception and impact of the subject has undergone significant transformations. This is demonstrated by exploring the complex definition and nature of political risk, its historical development in financial markets, and the current challenges and changes brought about by populism.

The interpretation and understanding of political risk are manifold and often varies according to the professional context in which it is assessed ("Finance-Related Political Risks"). In general, two main lenses through which political risk is viewed can be distinguished on the basis of the interviews: one is from the perspective of the insurance industry, and the other focuses on the impact of risk on market prices. In the insurance industry, political risk's definition is precisely specified to prevent litigation and to differentiate between insurable events and unpredictable outcomes (E3: 21, 26, 74). Within this context, political risks are classified into areas such as expropriation, political violence, and currency-related issues (E5: 8–10). On the other hand, the financial market's understanding of political risk is driven by its impact on asset prices. It has traditionally been defined as changes in laws, regulations, or policies that could affect the value of an investment (E20: 6). However, some experts broaden this definition to include any political event that could potentially affect asset prices (E4: 11–12). From their standpoint, a line is often drawn between the academic definition of political risk and its practical implications. Some assert that the market has already internalized risks arising from regulatory and policy changes and therefore do not consider them to be political risks (E1: 17–18). Moreover, it is paramount to recognize that assessing political risk involves not just anticipating potential downsides but also identifying instances where political changes may lead to financial opportunities (E2: 6).

Exploring the complexity of political risk from a financial perspective, its inherent nature is complex and multifaceted. Such risk can involve a wide range of factors and, at times, even overlap with other types of risk. Moreover, certain risk elements may remain in the background, only to emerge abruptly in response to certain triggers or catalysts (E11: 17; E21: 53). From a global perspective, political risk is not restricted to domestic events. Actions or decisions by international entities can create risks in other markets, underscoring the interconnectedness of domestic political risk with broader geopolitical concerns and spillover effects (E1: 19–20). For example, political turmoil in one country could trigger institutional challenges in neighboring countries (E15: 44). Thus, political risk can be broadly characterized as any local or international event or development that significantly affects market prices (E17: 10; E21: 6).

The rise of populism has notably reshaped the landscape of political risk for investors, positioning it as a pivotal concern within the investment domain ("Populism-Induced Political Risk"). Insights from the interviews underscore populism as a significant factor affecting investment decisions, primarily due to its tendency to cast foreign investors and market participants in adversarial roles, thus amplifying uncertainties (E5: 20). This perceived adversarial positioning contributes to a climate of apprehension, with fears centered around asset expropriation and the potential for unorthodox economic policies (E4: 50; E14: 17). Investors' wariness towards populist governments is compounded by concerns over stricter regulations and increased taxation. This cautious stance transcends ideological boundaries, underpinned by apprehensions regarding non-traditional economic strategies often adopted by populist regimes (E4: 61–62; E16: 17; E21: 51).

Additionally, the combination of populism and nationalism heightens the "us-versus-them" dichotomy and negatively affects the environment for foreign investors by increasing perceptions of risk. While foreign investment may be initially perceived positively, difficulties can arise in the areas of asset security, contract enforcement, labor relations, and profit repatriation (E14: 26, 27). The example of Argentina, where populist policies have affected foreign-owned assets, illustrates the concrete challenges faced by foreign investors in such regimes (E5: 18).

Populism's presence as a political risk factor can be substantial within the overall risk analysis ("Political Risk Developments"). It has brought political risk into sharper focus in investment decisions, particularly in developed markets where these risks were once seen as more relevant to emerging markets (E2: 24). One expert notes that the long-term "legacy" of populism is its potential to lead institutions in developed economies down a path of instability and uncertainty. As a result, the rise of populism has made what was once considered unlikely a plausible scenario and reintroduced political risk as a relevant concern in developed countries (E2: 16). Over the past, investing in developed markets has been seen as a protection against political uncertainties. However, the emergence of populism has brought a new element of unpredictability, compelling investors to review risks that were previously underestimated or overlooked (E1: 13; E12: 54).

3.3.3.6.2 Populism-Influenced Risk Management

The rise of populism has added layers of complexity to the process of assessing risks, necessitating the need for robust risk prediction frameworks ("Risk Assessment Impact"). Populism's unpredictability poses a direct challenge to investors (E2: 12; E19: 27). Initial reactions to populism tend to be negative, primarily because it introduces volatility and unpredictability, both generally considered undesirable in the investment domain (E14: 32). Echoing this sentiment, another expert pointed out that once a government takes an unconventional or perceived irresponsible step, it instills a lasting doubt in the minds of investors about future policy decisions (E16: 29). The persistent existence of populism in the political risk landscape appears to be certain. As one expert put it, the social and economic changes driving populist movements are expected to persist, ensuring that the discontent driving these movements will remain (E16: 23). Although populism is considered one among various political risks, such as weak governance and geopolitical conflicts, some interviewees believe that its significance on markets are profound (E13: 17; E22: 6).

Given these challenges and the evolving nature of populism, it is vital to adapt to assess these risks ("Risk Prediction Method Adaptations"). Navigating the complexities and uncertainties involved in assessing populist risks underscores the need for clearly defined risk prediction frameworks. Assessing political versus financial risks requires sophisticated tools, which adds further complexity to evaluation (E1: 16). Several experts stress the imperative of moving beyond mere predictions and advocating for a proactive approach (E12: 67; E15: 60). Nevertheless, integrating these risks into financial analyses poses a challenge in the absence of proven quantitative methods (E21: 49). Despite the challenges, there is widespread consensus on the importance of developing a reliable metric to assess populism, which would improve the understanding of its impact on financial markets and investor perceptions (E4: 70; E10: 35). Notably, experts caution that devising such measurements presents its own challenges based on their firsthand encounters (E4: 66; E8: 13; E20: 15). An additional considerable challenge is identifying the "populist element" amongst numerous overlapping risks. It is notably complex to isolate a single populist variable amidst global concerns such as climate change and geopolitical tensions (E5: 36). This complex web of global issues is further described, introducing the term "polycrisis" to define this state (E5: 31). Simplistic metrics and vague definitions may erroneously include unrelated factors, potentially leading to distorted views of actual threats (E12: 61–62).

When assessing populism, it is also relevant to note how it is linked to political events, such as elections ("Political and Electoral Dynamics"). Populism has significantly influenced the dynamics of elections, making their outcomes highly unpredictable and, as a result, altering how investors approach and assess them. Once viewed as regular occurrences with known risk profiles, these elections have become a "big story" (E2: 10), adding layers of uncertainty and representing both potential risks and returns for investors. Populism, by its very nature, brings an element of uncertainty to electoral outcomes as it tends to break away from conventional political trends (E19: 43). Therefore, the potential for market disruptions increases when populist parties gain more traction compared to when the main electoral rivalry involves centrist parties (E22: 12). The rising probability of populist parties coming to power has amplified their significance in the eyes of investors (E19: 45). This shifting political landscape may create surprises or lead to unforeseen events, which might be less manageable than familiar risks (E14: 33). However, it is important for effective risk management and assessment to recognize that the influence of populism extends beyond just electoral outcomes. As noted by an expert, unexpected political transitions, such as the resignation of Liz Truss after only 44 days in the United Kingdom, can also significantly affect market dynamics and influence investment strategies (E6: 26–27).

3.3.3.6.3 Populism-Influenced Investment Strategies

Populism can have a significant impact on the investment landscape, leading to new decision-making processes and strategies. The complex relationship between populism and investment primarily centers on its impact on asset valuation, strategic planning, and investor response.

Different types of investors react variably to populism based on their individual risk preferences ("Populism's Investment Impact"). The unpredictability of populism can cause long-term investors, especially those involved in FDI, to delay investment activities. This delay stems from a preference for stable political environments, such as post-election phases or periods of consistent government policy (E14: 35). Conversely, portfolio investors, who do not have physical assets in the markets, tend to quickly adjust their positions and exit when political risks exceed their risk tolerance (E14: 16, 36). Despite the unpredictability associated with populism, some investors adjust their risk strategies and maintain their investments. For instance, some investors scrutinize the broader institutional context of an economy before deciding, while others choose to divest (E1: 34–35). Some argue that avoiding markets due to populism may not be the appropriate approach, emphasizing the importance of understanding the dynamics of populism for long-term investments (E6: 62–63). Moreover, well-established investors often suggest a sustained commitment to markets, even amidst risks (E1: 36). As populism gains prominence, there is a noticeable decrease in its overt influence on markets, signifying a deeper comprehension of its ramifications (E9: 39, 41).

Navigating the impact of political change, particularly with the rise of populism, on both local and global markets can also affect investment strategies ("Political Investment Strategies"). The assets included in an investment portfolio can impact the approach taken to address political changes associated with populism (E4: 35). While domestic events, such as the rise of extremist parties, primarily influence local assets, events with global implications can affect international markets (E21: 10). Political changes, particularly in influential nations such as the United States, possess broader implications in comparison to emerging markets (E21: 14). There, institutional instability can lead to significant changes in the direction of a country during elections, especially when there is a change in leadership. Yet these changes primarily affect the domestic political landscape (E4: 17).

Strategically, the impact of populism becomes clearer over the mid-to-long term horizon. While immediate economic indicators may drive short-term investment decisions, the political climate influenced by populism can significantly impact long-term strategic investment decisions (E21: 47). Populism can be considered a relevant indicator for assessing political risk within a country (E5: 31), requiring investors to consider multiple factors such as social stability and ethnic dynamics, especially in the run-up to elections (E10: 27). A shift in risk perception from traditional party politics to a focus on populist trends highlights the changing market dynamics (E12: 52).

However, when evaluating the strategic implications of post-election populist parties, it is crucial to conduct a thorough analysis of multiple potential scenarios. The focus should not only be on the potential of a populist party to gain power, but also on its ability to influence policy. It is not only their electoral triumph that is relevant, but also the policies they propose and their practicality (E2: 12; E14: 24). Ultimately, the assessment of political events such as elections and their potential impact on policy changes will become more important determinants of market strategies (E3: 82; E12: 77, 90). In this context, obtaining reliable data to analyze the political risks associated with populism will be crucial for effective investment decisions (E20: 10).

3.4 Discussion and Prospects

This chapter presents an in-depth analysis of empirical research discussing the complex dynamics between political risks associated with populism and financial markets, as well as investor reactions. By comparing the key findings of the quantitative and qualitative studies with related academic research, this enhances the understanding of how rising populism and subsequent shifts in the political landscape have significant financial implications. The chapter is divided into three subchapters. In the first subchapter, the main theoretical and practical contributions are presented. The second subchapter addresses additional quality controls for the empirical tests. In the third subchapter, the limitations of the thesis are discussed, both to qualify the scope of the findings and to suggest possible avenues for future research.

3.4.1 Research Contributions

This subchapter outlines the theoretical and practical contributions of studying the influence of populism on financial markets. The section on theoretical contributions examines the impact of populism on financial markets and equity costs, providing empirical insights that advance the academic discourse. Following this, the practical contributions offer guidance for investors, financial managers, and policymakers navigating the challenges posed by populist movements and parties in the financial landscape.

3.4.1.1 Theoretical Contributions

This section evaluates the theoretical contributions of the thesis. The qualitative framework established in earlier sections represents a significant theoretical advancement, offering a new perspective on the interaction between populism, financial market dynamics, and investor behavior. While this fundamental insight sets the stage, it will not be further explored here. Instead, it provides the foundation for the more detailed analyses that follow.

The first subsection examines the theoretical contributions regarding the impact of populism on financial markets. It analyzes how populist movements reshape market dynamics and influence investor decisions. The second subsection focuses on the cost of equity. This part scrutinizes how populism impacts firms' financial strategies and alters investors' perceptions of risk, prompting a reevaluation of the cost of equity.

3.4.1.1.1 Populism and Financial Markets

This thesis advances the understanding of how populism influences financial markets by exploring the interplay between populist politics and market dynamics, contributing a novel perspective to the existing body of academic literature. The research highlights three main theoretical contributions regarding the impact of populism on financial markets: the significant impact of populism on investor behavior, the specific mechanisms by which populism affects markets, and the complexity regarding the ideological impact of populism.

The first theoretical contribution of this thesis is the systemic and enduring effects of populism on investor behavior. This concept is labeled the populism risk premium, which highlights how investors adjust their expected returns in response to the risks associated with increasing populism. The quantitative study surpasses previous research by *Stöckl and Rode*, and *Hartwell*,[213] by focusing on over 39,000 firm-years of stock market data for a detailed analysis. Unlike *Hartwell's* approach, which relies on retrospective country-level realized returns, this study employs an ex-ante expected return metric that more accurately captures investor expectations and risk assessments at the firm level.[214] Moreover, by utilizing stock market data in lieu of options market data as analyzed by *Stöckl and Rode*, the study markedly expands the sample size and incorporates countries with a significant populist influence, such as Hungary. This enhances the identification of the nuanced effects of populism on broader financial markets.

The quantitative study's methodological approach further includes industry-specific controls, refining the analysis and overcoming the shortcomings of prior country-level analyses that may overlook the nuanced impacts of populism across different sectors. This approach, refined by qualitative insights from the derived framework, indicates that populism can have varying degrees of influence. This can range from affecting tax policies due to nationalistic motivations to causing disproportionate effects in certain sectors through unpredictable regulatory changes. These methodological enhancements are crucial for accurately assessing populism's diverse effects on the financial landscape.

Building on the empirical foundations set by *Hartwell* and *Stöckl and Rode*,[215] this thesis deepens the understanding of how populism influences financial markets, extending beyond mere methodological advancements. While *Hartwell's* research suggests that short-term market volatility typically increases following

[213] See Hartwell 2022, pp. 1 ff.; Stöckl and Rode 2021, pp. 51–83.

[214] See Subsection 2.1.2.2.3.

[215] See Hartwell 2022, pp. 1 ff.; Stöckl and Rode 2021, pp. 51–83.

the electoral success of populist parties,[216] and *Stöckl and Rode* focus on short-term fluctuations using options market data,[217] this thesis shifts the perspective by revealing the profound impact of populism on long-term risk perceptions of stock market investors. The study shows that changes in populist sentiment induces investors to adjust their expected returns, suggesting a broader and more persistent influence of populism on financial markets than previously recognized. Additionally, the thesis expands on the effects of populism by demonstrating its influence on CDS spreads, which are indicators of investors' perceived risk of sovereign default. These findings corroborate those of *Pan et al.* who found that economic and political uncertainties contribute to higher CDS spreads, signaling an increased perception of risk.[218]

The second major theoretical contribution of this thesis explores the complex mechanisms by which populist movements influence financial markets. It highlights three key areas based on the research framework: each serves as an example of how populism affects financial systems, illustrating different aspects of this complex relationship.[219]

One example is the contextual impact of populism, which reveals a multifaceted influence that varies significantly with the unique conditions of each country. The research framework outlined in this thesis emphasizes the necessity of an analysis approach that considers each country's unique economic and sociopolitical conditions. It lays the groundwork for incorporating country-specific elements, such as the electoral system and development status, which can shed light on contextual nuances for a more comprehensive analysis of populism's effects. *Hartwell* supports the view that market performance is tied to the specific conditions in which populist movements operate, and also highlights the contextual nature of their influence.[220] Similarly, scholars argue that the impact of other political indicators, such as the EPU index, depends on country-specific factors such as economic stability and the size of its stock market.[221]

Another example regarding the mechanisms of populism's influence on financial markets is detailed by examining various channels through which populism exerts its influence. This exploration, embedded within the theoretical framework, underscores the critical role of populist parties' strategic positioning in

[216] See Hartwell 2022, p. 1.

[217] See Stöckl and Rode 2021, pp. 51, 65.

[218] See Pan et al. 2024, p. 144.

[219] See Section 3.3.3.1 for a description of the entire theoretical framework derived.

[220] See Hartwell 2022, p. 1.

[221] See for example Christou et al. 2017, pp. 92–102.

shaping economic and foreign policies. These findings are drawn from scientific interviews that emphasize the profound influence of such positioning, whether populist parties find themselves in opposition, as part of a governing coalition, or in outright leadership. This analysis proposes how these parties maneuver policy effects across economic sectors, demonstrating the sophisticated ways in which populism can influence market dynamics through different policy channels.

These diverse and complex channels through which populism influences politics are further highlighted in broader academic discussions. The overall narrative suggests that populists do not merely occupy government positions, but profoundly reshape policy directions—a trend that has been well documented in recent years.[222] Populist parties demonstrate a capacity for strategic cognition by amassing significant electoral power, allowing them to exercise veto power or form influential coalitions as junior partners. Notably, even without formal government positions, their growing support puts pressure on mainstream parties to align more closely with populist ideologies.[223] For instance, populist movements can influence established parties towards their positions, even without being in power.[224] *Abou-Chadi and Krause's* study provides an example of this, examining how radical right-wing parties gaining parliamentary seats change mainstream parties' perspectives on multiculturalism in 23 European nations.[225] This suggests that financial market analysis should focus not only on populists coming to power, but also on populist electoral successes in general, highlighting the importance of measures that can capture different levels of populism, as they show that the influence of populism extends beyond scenarios where populists lead the government.

The research framework provides another example of how theoretical knowledge about the mechanisms of populist influence can be extended. It indicates that financial markets adjust their pricing strategies in response to historical populist events, implying a market learning process that enhances resilience and predictive capabilities against future populist developments. This, in turn, reveals that financial markets react not only to the immediate consequences of populists coming to power, but also to their broader electoral successes.

The third essential theoretical contribution of this thesis is the exploration into the ideological distinctions within populist movements and their impact on financial markets. The quantitative study cannot provide conclusive evidence that

---

[222] See Guriev and Papaioannou 2022, p. 807.

[223] See Guriev and Papaioannou 2022, p. 762.

[224] See Schumacher and Van Kersbergen 2016, p. 300.

[225] See Abou-Chadi and Krause 2020, p. 829.

investors are more skeptical of left-wing populism when forming long-term return expectations, as suggested by *Stöckl and Rode's* findings for short-term analysis. Instead, caution is warranted, as the qualitative part of the research highlights the controversial and complex nature of the left-right divide in populism. Differences emerge in how financial markets interpret populist movements and the associated market reactions to populist leaders are varied and complex, with both ideologies potentially causing similar adversities for investors. The blurring of conventional political spectrums suggests a convergence in core characteristics between left- and right-wing populism, making the underlying ideology less significant than the practical implications of their policies. Furthermore, experts identify additional variants of populism, such as centrist and green populism, further illustrating its multifaceted nature.

The controversial nature of the left-right divide in populism is also debated in the broader academic community. *March* presents two prominent views on the interaction between populism and ideology. The first view suggests that ideology overshadows populism, highlighting the significance of conventional right-left distinctions. The second perspective posits that populism takes priority over ideology, emphasizing commonalities among populist parties and maintaining that their fundamental nature persists irrespective of their ideological orientation.[226] Even though the prevailing argument suggests that ideological tendencies dominate over populism, leading to political alliances that traditionally converge around these ideological markers, recent shifts challenge this narrative. The rise of "post-ideological" populist movements, such as Italy's M5S and the Czech Republic's Akce nespokojených občanů (ANO), disrupts the conventional binary framing of left and right.[227] In this evolving context, *Aslanidis* argues that populism may not always have a consistent ideological foundation, regardless of their left or right orientation. This perspective highlights the difficulty of identifying policy positions that are universally agreed upon across diverse populist groups[228] and calls for careful consideration in both categorizing and analyzing different varieties of populism.

3.4.1.1.2 Populism and the Cost of Equity

Political factors can not only have a significant impact on financial markets but can also influence corporate financial strategies. While it remains inconclusive

[226] See March 2017, pp. 282–303.

[227] See Fernández-García 2021, p. 1.

[228] See Aslanidis 2016, pp. 90 f.

whether the quantitative findings solely reflect market inefficiencies in information assimilation, the research suggests an increase in the cost of equity following the electoral rise of populist entities, possibly in response to increased perceived uncertainty. These findings indicate that populism represents a distinct and non-diversifiable political risk, underscoring its importance in investor pricing models and enhancing the understanding of factors influencing stock prices, while also highlighting the potential importance of populism in assessing the cost of equity.

This thesis contributes to the scholarly discussion on the variations in the cost of equity capital across countries, building upon the foundation laid by previous multinational studies. It focuses on areas that have received less attention, expanding on prior studies that have shown how political dynamics, such as scandals,[229] or changes in leadership,[230] play a crucial role in shaping the cost of equity, beyond the more general effects of EPU.[231] This research extends the scope of understanding of the variability of the cost of equity capital on a global scale by specifically examining the impact of populism.

To further explore this relationship, this subsection critically examines the relationship between populism and the cost of equity within the analytical framework established by *Boubakri et al.*, who argue that political institutions can significantly influence the cost of equity through both direct and indirect mechanisms.[232] This subsection refers to their framework to analyze how the rise of populism might similarly impact these channels—specifically, the exacerbation of information risks, the impairment of investor risk-sharing, and the impact on legal institutions, stock market development, and corporate governance—enhancing the understanding of the specific effects of populism on the cost of equity.

Boubakri et al. identify the first direct channel as the impact of political institutions on information risk. Strong political institutions typically enforce transparency and regulatory measures so investors can expect fewer sudden changes in policy agendas, which reduces unpredictability that reduces information asymmetry, thereby lowering the cost of equity.[233]

In the context of populism, this information channel is particularly vulnerable. The findings of this thesis suggest that populist leadership may intensify transparency issues, exacerbating information risk by restricting access to critical

229 See Liu et al. 2017, pp. 286–310.

230 See Li et al. 2018, pp. 215–222.

231 See for example Chan et al. 2021, pp. 1–45; Christou et al. 2017, pp. 92–102; Li 2017, pp. 41–56.

232 See Boubakri et al. 2014, pp. 326–344.

233 See Boubakri et al. 2014, p. 327.

economic data and widening the information gap between firms and investors. For example, a major concern is that populist governments may undermine the trustworthiness of national statistical agencies. This could lead to an environment characterized by less reliable economic indicators, which would further complicate investment decision-making processes for investors.

Similarly, from an academic perspective, several studies have analyzed how populism can increase information risk by undermining trust in traditional sources of information, destabilizing public belief systems, and weakening institutions such as universities and the press.[234] *Bronk and Jacoby* note that this uncertainty makes future predictions and best practices unreliable.[235] For *Brubaker*, the spread of misinformation empowers populist leaders to position themselves as the sole arbiters of truth.[236]

The second direct channel discussed by *Boubakri et al.* focuses on the influence of political institutions on investor risk-sharing. Effective political institutions act as a mechanism to increase trust, improve legal efficiency, and strengthen anti-corruption measures, which in turn increases investor participation, refines risk-sharing mechanisms, and ultimately reduces the cost of equity.[237]

Populism can severely impact this channel by eroding trust and confidence in political and legal institutions. The rise of populism often disrupts established norms through its unpredictability and rapid policy changes as discussed in the qualitative part of this thesis. Typically, populist forces advocate policies that are abrupt and opaque, thereby reducing the stability and predictability that are essential to the efficient functioning of financial markets. This instability manifests in various ways, including bypassing established channels for policy announcements and efforts to manipulate media narratives. This, in turn, can lead to a decline in investor activity, particularly in turbulent markets disrupted by sudden populist policy changes. As a result, optimal risk-sharing is hindered as investors and market participants are hindered from making informed decisions, thereby discouraging investor participation in the market and increasing the cost of equity.

Boubakri et al. suggest that political institutions can influence a firm's cost of equity through three indirect channels, with the first being their impact on legal institutions. Strong political governance strengthens the enforcement of property

[234] See Hartwell and Devinney 2021, p. 9.
[235] See Bronk and Jacoby 2020, p. 3.
[236] See Brubaker 2017, p. 357.
[237] See Boubakri et al. 2014, p. 327.

rights and investor protections, which in turn lowers the cost of equity by securing investor interests.[238]

Populism, however, can undermine the integrity and efficacy of legal systems, introducing uncertainties that destabilize investor confidence. In particular, populist regimes often undermine the integrity of legal systems, thereby shaking investor confidence in the reliability of legal frameworks and the enforcement of contractual obligations. As this fundamental trust erodes, investors demand higher returns to compensate for their increased risks, leading to a higher cost of equity. In addition, the rise of populist parties raises fears of policy changes that could threaten property and contractual rights, further increasing investor uncertainty and consequently their required rate of return.

The second indirect channel outlined by *Boubakri et al.* involves political institutions contributing to stock market development, thereby affecting the cost of equity. The authors argue that stable and transparent political environments bolster investor confidence, which enhances market liquidity and lowers the cost of equity.[239]

The research framework derived in this thesis suggests that populist governments may adopt policies that directly interfere with stock markets, such as introducing strict controls on foreign investment or influencing the operations of regulatory bodies. Such interventions can create instability and uncertainty that affect stock market development. This reduction in liquidity exacerbates information asymmetries and reduces investor participation, factors that can contribute to a higher cost of equity. Consequently, in order to attract investors, firms may need to offer a higher return on equity, thereby increasing the cost of equity. Particularly in a volatile environment, companies may find it difficult to raise capital as investors' perceptions of risk are heightened. This is especially relevant for emerging markets, where the maturity and resilience of the stock market is still developing, making them more susceptible to the disruptive influences of populism.

The third indirect channel identified by *Boubakri et al.* involves the impact of political institutions on corporate governance. Where political institutions are

---

[238] See Boubakri et al. 2014, pp. 327 f.

[239] See Boubakri et al. 2014, pp. 327 f.

strong, corporate governance is generally more robust, leading to a more equitable distribution of control within firms and lower risks of insider expropriation, thereby reducing the cost of equity.[240]

The results of this thesis suggest that the impact of populism on corporate governance can be profound. Populist movements, with their anti-establishment stance, can affect the typical mechanisms of corporate governance. For example, certain populist policies may tend to nationalize dominant industries, advocate protectionist measures that favor domestic firms, or push for regulatory changes if existing frameworks are perceived to favor select groups or foreign interests. These policy decisions can alter the operating framework for companies, potentially reducing the decision-making autonomy of corporate boards and executives and causing shifts in established governance structures. Such policy changes can affect the cost of equity, although the exact impact depends on the country's socio-political landscape and level of economic development. However, it is also relevant to note that the interviews also suggested that certain populist agendas may support anti-corruption measures that, if implemented effectively, could improve governance and ultimately reduce the cost of equity.

Overall, this thesis argues that the emergence of populist trends increases the cost of equity by leveraging the channels identified by *Boubakri et al.* Their framework applied to populism reveals how its emergence can amplify these effects by introducing additional risks and uncertainties through its impact on information risk, investor risk-sharing, legal institutions, stock market development, and corporate governance. While the multifaceted effects of populism may be mitigated by strong institutions or specific country conditions, the overall context suggests that populism could utilize one or more of these channels to affect the cost of equity. Nevertheless, given the complex and often unpredictable nature of populism, not all populist channels exert the same influence, underscoring the importance of nuanced, context-specific analysis, which was also addressed in the research findings. Figure 3.12 summarizes the discussed channels identified by *Boubakri et al.* through which populism could affect the cost of equity.

---

[240] See Boubakri et al. 2014, pp. 327 f. For a detailed examination of the impact of populism on political corporate social responsibility theory and practice, see Al-Esia et al. 2024, pp. 373–408.

Route	Description	Populism's Impact
Direct Channels		
Information Risk	Political institutions promote regulatory measures and transparency, reducing unpredictability and lowering information asymmetry	Disrupts established norms, increases unpredictability and information risks, raises equity costs
Investor Risk-Sharing	Political institutions foster trust and judicial efficiency, improving market participation and risk distribution	Erodes trust in institutions, fragments markets, and increases required investor returns
Indirect Channels		
Legal Institutions	Political institutions strengthen enforcement of property rights and investor protections, reducing investment risks	Compromises the integrity of legal systems, increases legal uncertainties, raises equity costs
Stock Market Development	Political institutions enhance market stability and transparency, increasing investor confidence and market liquidity	Creates policy instability, disrupts market operations, reduces liquidity and increases cost of equity
Corporate Governance	Political institutions ensure robust corporate governance, minimizing insider risks and lowering equity costs	Challenges governance structures, potentially nationalizes industries or alters regulatory frameworks, increasing governance risks

Fig. 3.12 Cost of Equity Channels according to Boubakri et al. 2014. (Source: Own Illustration.)

3.4.1.2 Practical Implications

Both the literature review and empirical research indicate that populism may have a significant impact on the financial landscape. However, closer examination of the practical implications of these observations is needed. This section, therefore, explores the potential consequences of populism's influence, including the challenges it poses for investors and financial managers, as well as its implications for companies and policymakers.

3.4.1.2.1 Investors Considerations

This subsection discusses the implications of populism from an investor perspective[241] and highlights the need for investors to recalibrate their risk assessment models in light of the uncertainties created by the rise of populist movements. The quantitative analysis in this thesis indicates that investors tend to demand a higher premium for risks that result from populist electoral successes and that are perceived as non-diversifiable. This adjustment in expected returns highlights the importance of considering populism in financial modeling and investment strategy.

The qualitative findings of this thesis further illustrate how populism is reshaping the investment landscape and complicating the traditional understanding of political risk. Both practitioner interviews and a review of the academic literature underscore that the financial impact of populism varies significantly across regions, influenced by local contexts and regional dynamics. Moreover, the global synchronicity of the populist rise,[242] particularly in the aftermath of the 2008 financial crisis, suggests a widespread reassessment of investment strategies in response to a phenomenon that has been described as "swift and synchronized"[243] across borders.

Another dimension for investors to consider is the concept of spillover effects, which can be associated with various political phenomena, including populism. These effects occur when policy changes in one country can influence policy directions and political climates in other countries,[244] a dynamic reminiscent of historical patterns observed with ideologies such as communism.[245] The thesis also builds on the notion of populist contagion, which has been observed in other settings, such as the concept of the EPU,[246] and describes a more direct and rapid cross-border influence. This is exemplified by the global responses to major populist events, such as the election of Donald Trump and the Brexit

[241] From the perspective of foreign investors, the implications of populism can be considerably more complex. Foreign investors may face additional challenges when populism is articulated through an "us-versus-them" narrative, which casts them as potential adversaries. These challenges include the possibility of increased tax burdens and the risk of asset confiscation.

[242] For an evaluation and analysis of the subject matter, see Subsection 2.3.1.2.4.

[243] Guriev and Papaioannou 2022, p. 754.

[244] See Devinney and Hartwell 2020, p. 49.

[245] See Hartwell 2018, p. 599.

[246] See Al-Thaqeb and Algharabali 2019, p. 5.

vote. These instances illustrate how populist successes can inspire similar movements around the world, challenging investors to rethink the traditional benefits of diversification in a tightly interconnected global market.[247]

The increasingly indistinct boundaries between traditionally "stable" developed markets and "volatile" emerging markets, compounded by the unpredictability of populism, require a reassessment of investment strategies. The susceptibility of developed markets to political upheaval, once thought to be a characteristic only of emerging markets, highlights the changing nature of global investment risk. The interdependence of equity markets has led to disruptions in one market being quickly transmitted to others, reducing the effectiveness of diversification strategies.[248] This shift highlights the increasingly global nature of investment risks, where the traditional differentiation between developed and emerging markets is becoming less distinct.

This interconnected nature of equity markets requires the development of adaptive diversification techniques to manage intensified systemic risk.[249] Since there are no specific financial instruments designed to hedge against the uncertainties of populism, investors must devise individual hedging strategies. This requires a comprehensive view of the impact of populism and the development of customized risk models that take into account companies, sectors and countries that are less susceptible to populist trends. To navigate the politically charged investment climate, investors can pursue a strategy of identifying safe havens, which are assets that demonstrate consistent return patterns despite market fluctuations during politically volatile periods.[250] Examples of potential safe havens from political risk include assets such as crude oil, crypto currencies, and precious metals.[251]

3.4.1.2.2 Corporate Considerations

The insights presented in this thesis have important implications for corporate strategy, particularly for financial managers of MNCs operating in diverse geopolitical landscapes. Populism has become a multifaceted challenge not only in

[247] See Devinney and Hartwell 2020, p. 33.

[248] See Connolly et al. 2005, p. 161.

[249] See for example Arshanapalli and Doukas 1993; Asgharian and Nossman 2011; Koutmos and Booth 1995.

[250] See Baur and Lucey 2010, p. 217.

[251] See Bouoiyour et al. 2019, p. 6076.

international markets but also within corporations' home countries.[252] This phenomenon requires a thorough comprehension of how financial policy, which aims to optimize firm value through strategic financing and investment decisions, must adapt to growing political exposures.

The essence of financial strategy is determining the optimal mix of equity and debt, structuring debt maturities, selecting appropriate capital markets for funding, and accurately assessing risks, including those arising from political developments. Populism can shift investor expectations, potentially escalating equity costs, directly impacting corporate financing and investment strategies. Recognizing populism's impact allows financial managers to better navigate the complex political risk landscape and incorporate these considerations into their decision-making processes. Populism introduces a potential politically non-diversifiable risk, demanding a higher risk premium from investors, which in turn increases the cost of equity financing for companies. The heightened political risk can deter investment, suggesting a critical need for companies to reassess their investment strategies in populist contexts.

Beyond the investment entry phase, MNCs face post-investment populism vulnerabilities, subject to host government policy shifts that may favor local interests over foreign commitments. These shifts can redirect investments, impacting both the domestic economy and the investing firm's strategy. Populism's capacity to reshape institutional frameworks adds another layer of uncertainty, altering operational dynamics for corporations.[253]

Additionally, the rise of populist parties presents opportunities for corporations to align with changing political dynamics, potentially securing competitive advantages such as government contracts. This emphasizes the significance of adaptability and strategic foresight, enabling businesses to navigate and flourish in uncertain terrains shaped by populism.[254]

This raises the question of how corporations should adapt to the rise of populism. *Devinney and Hartwell's* research underscores the importance of balancing global reach and local engagement in formulating corporate responses to populism. According to the authors, MNCs may switch between global strategies and local affiliations depending on their ties to local contexts. In situations where there is mild populist sentiment, MNCs with a global focus may move towards localization strategies, while stronger populist pressures could lead them

---

[252] See Devinney and Hartwell 2020, pp. 56 ff.

[253] See Devinney and Hartwell 2021, pp. 95 f.

[254] See Hartwell and Devinney 2024b, p. 2.

to regional diversification. Local MNCs, which are involved in both global and local commitments, face the challenge of balancing these dual objectives.[255]

In addressing populist challenges, *Devinney and Hartwell* propose a strategic framework that includes anticipation, forestalling, and absorption strategies. Anticipation involves forecasting potential challenges, as demonstrated by the proactive measures taken by companies during the Brexit uncertainty. Forestalling emphasizes preemptive actions to mitigate risks, such as diversification, public relations efforts, political lobbying, and strategic positioning. The absorption strategy integrates political risk management into the operational framework through joint ventures, preemptive FDI, or vertical integration to manage and mitigate risks effectively.[256]

Devinney and Hartwell observe the evolving nature of corporate strategies in response to populism, marking a shift from a globalized approach to deep local integration. This transition from "Think Global, Act Local"[257] to "Think Global, Be Local"[258] emphasizes the requirement for corporations to embed themselves in local contexts and illustrates a strategic pivot for financial managers and corporations necessitated by the contemporary populist surge.

3.4.1.2.3 Policy Considerations

This subsection discusses policy considerations in the context of populism's impact on the investment climate and corporate decision-making, drawing on findings from both the qualitative and quantitative study. The emergence of populist regimes often heralds significant shifts in the political landscape, affecting investor confidence and altering the business environment. The need for policymakers to understand the drivers of investment hesitancy following populist victories to promote a stable investment atmosphere are also addressed.

Institutional strength is essential since strong institutions not only facilitate consistent governance, but also serve as the pillars of a favorable investment environment.[259] Robust institutions ensure reliable governance and act as the foundation for a thriving investment climate. These institutions mitigate informational asymmetries, streamline business operations, and enhance the attractiveness of economies for investment, both domestically and internationally.[260]

---

[255] See Devinney and Hartwell 2020, pp. 32 ff.

[256] See Devinney and Hartwell 2020, pp. 57 f.

[257] Devinney and Hartwell 2020, p. 57.

[258] Devinney and Hartwell 2020, p. 57.

[259] See Globerman and Shapiro 1999, p. 513; Peng et al. 2008, pp. 920 ff.

[260] See Meyer et al. 2009, p. 61; Stevens et al. 2016, p. 945.

However, populism poses a significant threat to the autonomy and functionality of foundational institutions, such as judiciaries and central banks, by casting doubts on their impartiality and effectiveness. This, in turn, affects the decision-making processes of various economic actors, including businesses, investors, and financial institutions, as they prioritize stable and predictable political landscape. The integrity and stability of a country's political and institutional framework often dictate its attractiveness as an investment destination.[261]

Beyond the immediate effects on institutions, the impact of populism is far-reaching and characterized by its cyclical nature and historical patterns of waves. *Funke et al.* argue that the recurrence of populism can be compared to the concept of serial default,[262] in which countries experience repeated crises over different periods of time.[263] Additionally, their study reveals that populist leaders tend to hold onto power for longer periods than non-populist leaders, with an average tenure almost twice as long. This extended time in office underscores the significant and lasting impact that populism can have on a nation's political landscape.[264]

Addressing the challenges posed by populism can unlock new avenues for investment and economic growth, especially in regions where private investment is essential for development. Policymakers have a pivotal role in this process by shaping regulatory frameworks, tax policies, and overarching macroeconomic policies.[265] Ensuring policy stability and predictability is of central importance, as it allows investors and businesses to effectively adapt their strategies in response to, or in anticipation of, political and economic changes.

An examination of the origins of populism is also necessary for formulating responsive policies. Populist movements often arise from economic inequality, political disenfranchisement, cultural shifts, and a perceived divide between the general populace and the political elite. Addressing these underlying causes, *Guriev and Papaioannou* proposed several potential government responses, including strengthening social safety nets, combating tax evasion, and addressing corruption and abuses of market power in the global economy. Additionally, promoting participatory democracy tools, such as town hall meetings,

[261] See Boubakri et al. 2014, p. 326.

[262] See Funke et al. 2023a, p. 3262.

[263] See Reinhart and Rogoff 2004, p. 53.

[264] See Funke et al. 2023a, p. 3251.

[265] See Kaviani et al. 2020, p. 838.

coupled with an improved digital communication strategy for mainstream political parties, can help to more closely connect the broader public with political entities.[266]

Collectively, the research underscores the importance of political stability and a predictable policy environment in fostering favorable conditions for economic growth and investment. The rise of populism and the consequent political shift not only indicates dissatisfaction with current political establishments but also exposes potential areas for reform. By implementing targeted policy adjustments and strengthening institutional robustness, policymakers can foster a more stable and attractive environment for investors.

3.4.2 Scientific Quality Assurance

The research project was executed with diligence and a strong emphasis on quality and scientific rigor. A structured approach was followed to maintain the integrity of the research throughout the process. The following sections explore the procedures implemented to uphold scientific quality. First, specific criteria used to assess the quality of this mixed methods research are outlined. Subsequently, additional quality assurance measures taken during the data collection and analysis phases of both the quantitative and qualitative components of the project are presented.

3.4.2.1 Mixed Methods Quality Criteria

Assuring the quality of mixed methods research approaches requires careful consideration of several complex factors. It is essential to determine how to evaluate each method, which may require distinct assessment criteria. Furthermore, it is imperative to set benchmarks and establish quality standards for mixed methods. This process should include, for example, assessing the need for integration of methods, their ability to incorporate different research methodologies, and the effectiveness of their application.[267]

---

[266] See Guriev and Papaioannou 2022, pp. 818 f.

[267] See Flick 2018b.

In mixed methods research different sources of evaluation criteria exist. For example, *Bryman* identifies three potential quality dimensions: The "Convergent Criteria" involves applying identical standards to both the quantitative and qualitative aspects of the research. The "Separate Criteria" suggests utilizing distinct standards for the quantitative and qualitative segments. Finally, the "Bespoke Criteria" advocates creating custom-made criteria for mixed methods research.[268]

Several attempts have been made to establish specific, tailor-made quality criteria for conducting mixed methods research studies.[269] In this thesis, the six quality criteria proposed by *Hirose and Creswell* are utilized, and this section explains their significance and how their quality was upheld. The criteria highlight justifying mixed methods, setting varied objectives, detailing data types, categorizing designs, showcasing integrated visuals, and assessing combined analysis insights.[270]

According to *Hirose and Creswell*, the first quality criterion assumes that since mixed methods research is still a relatively new methodology in some fields, valid research practice requires providing a rationale for selecting mixed methods research over other approaches to investigating research questions.[271] In this thesis, the mixed methods approach was chosen to investigate the influence of populism on financial markets since it allows to balance the objectivity of quantitative data with the depth and nuance of qualitative data. Thus, this thesis provides a more comprehensive understanding of the intricate relationship between populism and financial markets, which a singular method fails to achieve. For example, a purely qualitative study cannot quantify the economic impact of populism on financial markets and focuses on a deeper understanding rather than the measurable impact of significant political change. Additionally, the quantitative results would not provide the insights gained from the scholarly interviews, especially regarding the relevant factors of populism, such as country-specific effects, to gain a better understanding of the relationship. Moreover, the qualitative insights helped clarify the inconclusive quantitative findings on the ideological impact of populism, revealing the controversial and complex nature of the left-right divide.

[268] See Bryman 2006, p. 112.

[269] See Mayring 2022, pp. 173–183.

[270] See Hirose and Creswell 2023, p. 12.

[271] See Hirose and Creswell 2023, p. 19.

The second quality criterion requires the formulation of at least three research questions or objectives.[272] Building on this premise, the research in this thesis is tailored around three central research objectives, in addition to the overarching research question. The first objective aims to discern whether shifts in populist influences result in investors adjusting their return expectations. Second, the focus shifts to investigating whether and how certain populist ideologies can impact these adjustments. The third research objective seeks to uncover the underlying factors and driving motives behind these observed patterns in order to provide a holistic perspective on the prevailing dynamics.

Hirose and Creswell's third criterion demands a clear distinction between the sources and characteristics of the quantitative and qualitative data used in the study.[273] Within this thesis, comprehensive analyses of data types, tools and formats for qualitative data collection (see Subchapter 3.3.1), as well as quantitative data analysis methods (see Subchapter 3.2.1), are outlined separately, following this criterion.

The fourth criterion requires the identification and labeling of the mixed methods design type, accompanied by an appropriate diagram. Although there is no widely accepted convention for labeling and categorizing mixed methods designs,[274] the design chosen based on *Creswell and Clark's* categorization is the explanatory sequential design.[275] Its objective is to complement the collection and analysis of quantitative data with qualitative data to provide a more detailed account of the quantitative results (see Subchapter 3.1.2). Following the format prescribed by *Ivankova et al.*[276] a mixed methods graph is displayed in Figure 3.13. The figure provides a structured overview of the mixed methods research process in three columns: The first column describes the various stages of the research, distinguishing between quantitative and qualitative components. The middle column, labeled "Procedure", outlines the specific activities performed at each stage, including data collection and analysis methods. Finally, the "Result" column presents the outcomes of each phase, highlighting elements such as samples, empirical findings, interview transcripts, and the resulting framework.

---

272 See Hirose and Creswell 2023, pp. 19 ff.

273 See Hirose and Creswell 2023, pp. 20 f.

274 See Hirose and Creswell 2023, p. 21.

275 See Creswell and Plano Clark 2018, pp. 4 ff.

276 See Ivankova et al. 2006, pp. 3–18.

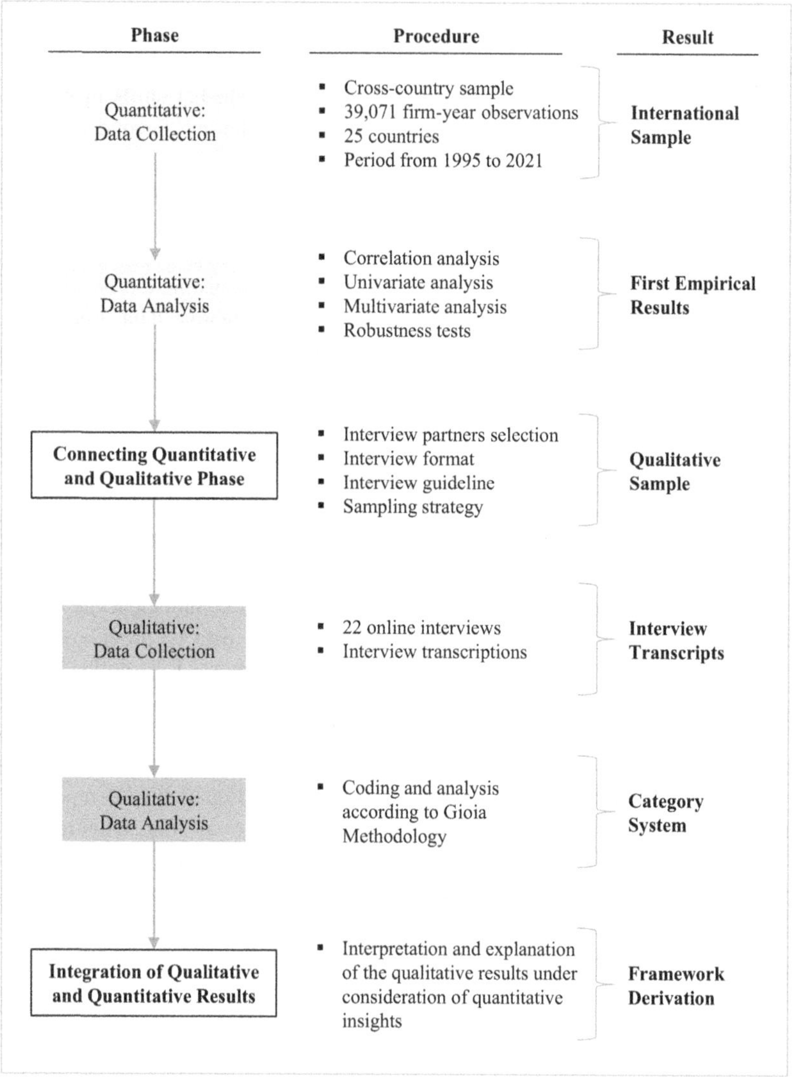

Fig. 3.13 Sequential Explanatory Design. (Source: Own Illustration; following Ivankova et al. 2006, p. 16, Figure 1.)

Hirose and Creswell's fifth criterion concerns to the essential aspect of integration. Mixed methods studies initially gathered both quantitative and qualitative data without emphasizing integration.[277] Nevertheless, integration has progressively been discussed in mixed methods research in various forms.[278] In this thesis, integration unfolded in multiple stages, including the utilization of a qualitative approach to explicate quantitative results or the discussion of quantitative and qualitative results (see Subchapter 3.4.1).

Hirose and Creswell's final criterion requires a discussion of how value and meta-inferences are derived from integrative analysis.[279] This criterion suggests that the integration process extends beyond mere consolidation of information by considering the synthesis of methods, findings, or implications. The goal is to reach a meta-inference that links multiple findings, some derived from qualitative data analysis, others from quantitative data analysis.[280] This thesis addresses these requirements in several points of the thesis. A comprehensive analysis was constructed by integrating methods and findings in a coherent manner. For instance, while quantitative findings demonstrated the theoretical connections between the rise of populism and increased uncertainty, qualitative findings delved into the details and unpacked the multiple influences on this relationship. By integrating these findings into the existing literature to derive theoretical and practical contributions, the meta-inferences were both established and innovative.

3.4.2.2 Quantitative Research

Although adherence to quality criteria for mixed methods is essential, it is important to emphasize that the quantitative component of the research underwent further quality assurance, such as additional robustness testing (see Section 3.2.3.4). This section expands on these quality assurance practices, with a particular focus on the populism-centric measures introduced by *Stöckl and Rode*[281] and delves into the empirical model employed to ensure a comprehensive understanding of the methodological rigor applied.

---

[277] See for example Greene et al. 1989.

[278] See Hirose and Creswell 2023, p. 12.

[279] See Hirose and Creswell 2023, p. 24.

[280] See Schoonenboom 2022, pp. 17 ff.

[281] The characteristics and limitations of ICC measures are discussed in detail in Section 2.1.2.3.

3.4.2.2.1 Populism Variables

Given that the difficulties of measuring populism have been mentioned several times in this thesis, the validity of *Stöckl and Rode's* measures of populism is discussed below. According to the authors' analysis, their populism index captures the essence of populism in party platforms empirically and they assert that it lacks strong bias toward any particular political ideology.[282] Compared to other indicators of populism, including those revealing cultural and economic divisions,[283] recent rhetoric measures from populist leaders,[284] and the dynamics of economic left-right positions,[285] the variable performed favorably in the tests of the authors.[286]

Furthermore, the authors' right-left scale populism measure closely aligns with several indicators related to populist ideology. The authors argue that their index is deemed appropriate for assessing political ideologies as it effectively monitors the rise and fall of populist discourse, avoiding the limitations of conventional categorizations that simply classify parties as populist or non-populist.[287]

In addition to the evaluations conducted by *Stöckl and Rode*, this thesis presents an additional analysis of their variables through an illustrative approach. A visual examination in Figure 3.14 depicts the political parties from the 2021 German federal election, plotted according to their level of populist intensity and ideological position. The y-axis shows the level of populism for each respective party, while the x-axis shows its ideological location. According to *Stöckl and Rode's* framework, the graph shows, among other things, that the AfD emerges as the most populist party. In addition, from an ideological perspective, Die Linke is the most left-wing populist entity, while AfD anchors the far right. This classification, based on the populism measures developed by *Stöckl and Rode*, broadly reflects the general perception of the parties.

---

[282] See Stöckl and Rode 2021, p. 58.

[283] See Inglehart and Norris 2016, pp. 1–52.

[284] See Norris 2020b, 2020c.

[285] See Meijers and Zaslove 2020, 2021.

[286] See Stöckl and Rode 2021, p. 58.

[287] See Stöckl and Rode 2021, p. 58.

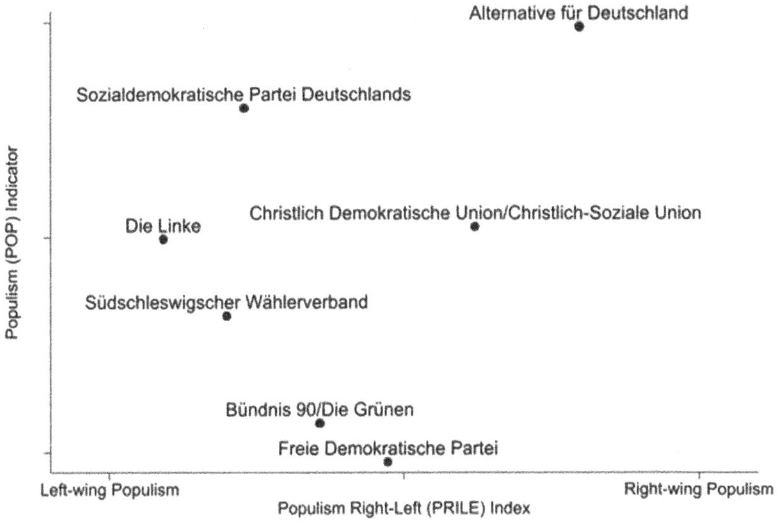

Fig. 3.14 Populism Variables Test. (Source: Own Illustration.)

3.4.2.2.2 Fixed Effects Model

Beyond examining individual variables, the empirical model itself underwent systematic testing to ensure its robustness and reliability. The fixed effects regression model (Equation (3.8), page 140), was selected for the quantitative study based on the theoretical groundwork detailed in Section 3.2.1.3. This model sufficiently considers time-invariant components, unobserved heterogeneity, and omitted variables, while incorporating country, year, and industry dummies. Furthermore, to mitigate potential heteroskedasticity or anticipated within-panel serial correlation, almost all the regressions have been adjusted by utilizing robust standard errors that have been clustered.

The primary benefit of the fixed effects approach is its capability to consider all predictors that are constant over time, regardless of whether they are observed or unobserved. Despite its merits, the fixed effects method relies on the critical assumption that time-consistent predictors exert uniform effects across all instances. Thus, variables whose effects vary across occasions must be entered directly into the model.[288]

[288] See Allison 2009, p. 3.

Additionally, it is worth noting that in many cases, estimates derived from fixed effects models may have significantly larger standard errors than their counterparts from random effects models. Larger standard errors result in larger p-values and, consequently, larger confidence intervals. This is due to the fact that estimates derived from random effects models incorporate information from both within-individual and between-individual variation. Fixed effects models, in contrast to random effects models, solely consider within-individual variation and do not take into account any information about between-individual differences. Consequently, in scenarios where predictor variables exhibit significant differences between individuals but negligible temporal variation for each individual, the precision of estimates from fixed effects models is likely to be substantially reduced.[289]

Given the limitations of this approach, this analysis examines the suitability of the random effects model, which allows for time-invariant characteristics, as a viable alternative. To assess the comparative adequacy of this model, the *Hausman* specification test, a formal hypothesis testing method, is used to examine the fit between these model types. In essence, the *Hausman* test assesses the correlation between the unique errors and the regressors. The null hypothesis posits that the expected value of the error term u_{it} conditional on the regressors X_{it} is zero ($H_o : E(u_{it}|X_{it}) = 0$). Conversely, the alternative hypothesis contends that the expected value of the error term u_{it}, given the regressors X_{it}, is not zero ($H_1 : E(u_{it}|X_{it}) \neq 0$).

Based on the data utilized in this thesis, the *Hausman* test results led to the rejection of the null hypothesis, which posits that there is no correlation between the individual effects and the regressors in the model. This rejection implies that the random effects model, suggested under the null hypothesis as more suitable, is less preferred in this context. Consequently, the fixed effects model is more suitable for this research because it effectively accounts for the correlation between individual-specific errors and the regressors, providing a more precise estimation of the relationships being examined.[290]

3.4.2.3 Qualitative Research

Similar to the quantitative study, quality assurance was implemented for the qualitative research project, with specific attention given to the interview process.

---

289 See Allison 2009, pp. 17 ff.

290 See Hausman 1978, pp. 1251–1271.

In interview research, it is often emphasized that the information elicited during interviews must be reliable.[291] Maintaining interview integrity is especially essential in evaluating the credibility of qualitative research.[292] Focusing on data integrity is not limited to the data collection phase, but also extends to the data analysis phase. Accurate and authentic representation of participants is important at this analytical stage, where researchers must actively avoid personal bias and potential misinterpretation.[293] The following subsections will delve into the strategies adopted to uphold these standards.

3.4.2.3.1 Interview Process Quality

To ensure the integrity and validity of research findings, it is necessary to conduct high-quality interviews that adhere to key principles. *Rubin and Rubin* proposed four pivotal criteria to enhance the quality of interviews: authenticity, balance, accuracy, and detail.[294] These criteria were rigorously followed in this thesis, facilitating the capture of detailed insights critical to the study's methodology.

The initial criterion according to *Rubin and Rubin* highlights the authenticity of interviews. The authors assert that to ensure interviews are genuine and valuable, interviewers should rely predominantly on first-hand knowledge. They promote the selection of interviewees who have directly dealt with the subject, rather than individuals speaking from others' experiences.[295] In this research project, the first criterion of authenticity was closely followed. Those with first-hand involvement in assessing various political risks within financial markets—including strategists and analysts, economic researchers, risk managers, and policy advisors—and extensive professional experience were selected based on purposive and theoretical sampling. Using this strategy ensured genuine insights rather than second-hand accounts or generalized observations.

The second criterion emphasizes the importance of balance and thoroughness in interviews and underscores the need to capture multiple viewpoints for comprehensive understanding. The authors suggest that interviewers should be observant to prevent any significant informational gaps and incorporate a broad range of perspectives on the subject matter.[296] Adhering to this criterion, in this research project efforts were made to ensure that the interviews were both comprehensive

[291] See Weiss 1995, p. 147.

[292] See Flick 2018b, pp. 26 ff.

[293] See Roulston and Halpin 2022, pp. 17 f.

[294] See Rubin and Rubin 2012, pp. 64 ff. For further insights see Flick 2018b, pp. 54 ff.

[295] See Rubin and Rubin 2012, pp. 71 f.

[296] See Rubin and Rubin 2012, pp. 70 f.

and provided a balanced view. In order to obtain a broad range of viewpoints on the consequences of populism, diverse groups of risk analysts' perspectives were consulted to produce a comprehensive comprehension of the subject (see Section 2.2.2.3).

In their third criterion *Rubin and Rubin* stress accuracy and credibility, underscoring the need for reliable and valid interviews. They recommend transcribing interviews immediately and conducting thorough questioning when appropriate, while maintaining transparent reporting practices.[297] Following these guidelines, interviews were promptly transcribed. To ensure transparency in the research, careful documentation of methods and clear reporting of results, coding processes and the inclusion of illustrative quotes to substantiate themes were considered.

The fourth criterion proposed by *Rubin and Rubin* emphasizes the importance of obtaining rich and detailed insights from interviews. The authors advise interviewers to ask clear, precise questions using exploratory techniques that encourage respondents to provide richer and more detailed descriptions.[298] By closely adhering to these standards for in-depth interview responses, a rigorous and systematic preparation was conducted. Each interview question was designed to be precise and clear to minimize the possibility of ambiguity. To avoid potential misconception of answers, a set of questions and follow-up questions was developed and tested in a pilot interview. This process helped to refine the guide, which is a key instrument in the collection of qualitative data.

3.4.2.3.2 Data Evaluation

To further ensure the quality of the conducted research in evaluating qualitative data, several key areas were addressed. Regarding the data analysis methodology used in this study, the *Gioia* Methodology, the authors emphasize a number of points to consider. They express concern that researchers tend to employ a formulaic approach, replicating the framework of prior studies, which can hinder originality and creativity. *Gioia et al.* assert that their methodology was designed to be flexible, to promote adaptability to different scenarios, and to encourage innovation. They claim that overlooking this adaptability not only limits the innovative prospects inherent in the methodology, but also circumvents its core objective of establishing a strong link between empirical data and theoretical foundations.[299] In this thesis, *Gioia's* Methodology guided the analysis and

---

[297] See Rubin and Rubin 2012, pp. 70 f.

[298] See Rubin and Rubin 2012, pp. 70 ff.

[299] See Gioia et al. 2013, pp. 25 f.

evaluation of the data but was not used as a static approach. Its inherent adaptability was used to make clear connections between the data and the framework developed.

Another potential drawback of evaluating qualitative research is over-reliance on expert viewpoints, as identified by *Sandbergh*.[300] This is particularly relevant when deriving first-order concepts to replicate informant statements. However, relying solely on informant experiences can present challenges as it may lead to becoming too closely aligned with their beliefs and adopting their perspective, which can cause a narrow view and hinder sound reasoning. To avoid this *Magnani and Gioia* suggest that when assigning labels to quotations, one should continually question how these labels were developed using the data and how the empirical evidence supports the concepts being developed.[301] Demonstrating commitment to these principles, the dissertation presents empirical findings through direct quotes from experts, linking them to the underlying concepts and corresponding themes. For improved reader comprehension, graphical illustrations are utilized to demonstrate this analytical process. This allows readers to track the development from data to theory, providing a coherent thread of reasoning.[302] Furthermore, the coding process was subject to review, as the assignment of labels to quotations was an iterative approach. After the first coding round, labels were re-examined and checked against the raw data to ensure empirical consistency, improve label accuracy, and ensure fidelity to the underlying data.

3.4.3 Research Reflections

3.4.3.1 Limitations

Any research endeavor, no matter how carefully conducted, is bound to encounter certain limitations that may affect the interpretation and generalizability of the findings. These limitations are examined in this section in order to provide a transparent assessment of the scope and implications of the quantitative and qualitative aspects of the research.

3.4.3.1.1 Quantitative Constraints

This subsection outlines the primary limitations of the quantitative study, which include measurement concerns, definitional complexities, methodological choices,

---

[300] See Sandbergh 1997, p. 203.

[301] See Magnani and Gioia 2023, p. 3.

[302] See Gioia 2021, p. 22.

and the geographic focus of the research. Measuring populism presents significant challenges, which center on the lack of a universally accepted definition or classification of populism. Reaching a consensus, which currently does not exist, on how to define populism is necessary for effective and consistent empirical research. When measuring populism on the party level, it is important to avoid oversimplifying political parties into a basic spectrum, as this is a common tendency. This approach disregards the intricacies of individual policies and ignores the evolution of party stances over time. To avoid this pitfall, this thesis employs a measurement method based on *Stöckl and Rode*, which is more nuanced than a binary classification, but still has limitations in relying solely on manifesto data. Recent research indicates that manifesto data may not be entirely reliable in forecasting the emergence of new political parties, particularly those that are extreme, small, non-governmental, or frequently changing their positions—characteristics commonly associated with populist parties.[303]

In addition to the populism measure, the second limitation of the quantitative study focuses on the ICC derived from diverse empirical studies. Additional tests could have enhanced the reliability of equity cost estimates, such as incorporating methods proposed by *Hail and Leuz*.[304] Their methodology places a strong emphasis on utilizing accuracy-weighted average cost of equity estimates in regression models. This approach assigns greater importance to observations with higher forecast accuracy, in turn enhancing the robustness of the findings.[305] Furthermore, exploring alternative model specifications, particularly regarding different growth rate scenarios,[306] could have provided an extra perspective to verify the cost of equity estimates used in this thesis.

However, the ICC was calculated using four established models that inherently account for diverse economic scenarios. By averaging the estimates from these models, this approach mitigates potential biases and improves the reliability of the equity cost estimates. Given that these models are well-established and widely accepted in similar studies,[307] additional checks, while beneficial, were considered supplementary rather than essential. This method still enhances robustness by ensuring that various economic conditions and growth rate scenarios are considered, providing a reliable and comprehensive estimation framework.

---

[303] See Ecker et al. 2022, p. 530. See also Section 2.3.2.2 for a critical analysis of populism measurement on party level and with manifesto data.

[304] See Hail and Leuz 2006, pp. 15 f.

[305] See Rjiba et al. 2021, p. 16.

[306] See Hail and Leuz 2006, p. 512.

[307] See for example Rjiba et al. 2021; Xu 2020.

Besides potential concerns about the key variables used in quantitative research, disentangling the complex relationship between political influence and financial market reaction is challenging due to potential concerns about reverse causality. Although current theoretical and empirical research provides valuable insights, it does not definitively determine the direction of influence.[308] Therefore, it is essential to recognize that financial markets also have political consequences observable in various ways, such as examining the policy implications following financial crises.[309]

Another limitation of the study is its reliance on a sample that mainly comprises OECD countries, while largely excluding nations in Latin America due to data availability issues. This exclusion is particularly critical when considering the quantitative study's second hypothesis, which examines the influence of the ideology underlying populism. Excluding regions such as Latin America, where left-wing populism has historically prevailed, might explain why the hypothesis on the ideological influence of populism did not exhibit the hypothesized effect and raises concerns about the generalizability of the findings. During the scientific interviews, examples from countries such as Argentina and Brazil, which were not analyzed quantitatively, were frequently referenced, underscoring their importance in this discourse. These limitations emphasize the need for a cautious interpretation of the findings on a global scale and their integration.

3.4.3.1.2 Qualitative Constraints

The validity of the qualitative findings may be impacted by several limitations which require acknowledgment and clarification. Despite the quality assurance measures employed throughout the research process (see Subchapter 3.4.2), there are potential areas in need of attention, particularly with regard to the sample, the data analysis, and the generalizability of the derived framework.

The first limitation of the study is due to its contextual scope. It only includes interviews with a small number of professionals from a limited subset of financial market participants, primarily located and specialized in Western democracies. As a result, caution must be exercised in interpreting the findings due to this limited sample. Further analysis of the financial impact of populism is needed, perhaps involving experts who specialize in political risk analysis in other non-financial contexts.

The data analysis process faced several limitations, notably the fact that it was conducted by a single researcher responsible for the entire coding process. While

[308] See Heigermoser and Maier 2020, p. 17.

[309] See Ferrara and Sattler 2016, p. 16.

this process was employed with diligence, a more robust alternative could have involved multiple researchers participating collaboratively in the process. This collaborative approach, centering on consensus about codes and their meanings, would have facilitated data review, discussion among researchers, and the development of a shared understanding, ultimately reducing the potential bias inherent in coding by a single researcher.[310] Nevertheless, it is important to acknowledge that *Gioia et al.* argue that such an intercoder approach is not always seen as an essential step. In their view, the process of organizing the data itself can make the analysis robust and dependable. Therefore, the authors contend that the choice to utilize an intercoder process is reliant on the specific context and can fluctuate depending on the research objectives and the nature of the data.[311]

Some researchers adopting a constructivist grounded theory approach even view intercoder reliability as non-essential, arguing instead for testing the robustness and usefulness of codes through comparative analysis to establish credibility. Therefore, the decision not to use intercoder reliability in this study aligns with the perspective that credibility can be effectively established through the strength of analytic concepts and supporting evidence, rather than solely through multiple coders.[312] Instead, the study employed rigorous strategies suggested in the literature, such as thorough documentation of methods, transparent reporting of results, and the inclusion of illustrative quotes to substantiate themes. These strategies ensure a robust analytical process, as detailed in Subsection 3.4.2.3.2.

Further research limitations became apparent during the interview analysis, especially when examining the examples provided by respondents. While these examples added depth to the responses, they also uncovered discrepancies in how participants differentiate between left-wing and right-wing populism. A closer examination of these examples highlighted additional difficulties in reconciling the qualitative insights with the quantitative findings. Notably, the quantitative analysis did not capture certain examples provided by respondents, such as references to specific politicians or countries. This difference suggests a possible misalignment between the structured approach of the quantitative data and the interviewees' finer perceptions.

Additionally, the research framework also has limitations, the main one being its potential insufficiency in comprehensively capturing nuanced interactions. Although the visual representations of the relationship between populism, financial markets, and investor reactions provide a comprehensive overview, they may

---

[310] See Gioia et al. 2013, p. 22.

[311] See Gioia et al. 2013, p. 22.

[312] See Charmaz and Bryant 2011, 291–309.

inadvertently oversimplify or ignore certain complexities, such as when examining the connections between themes within the same dimension. As an example, when analyzing the "Conceptual Challenges" dimension, it is noteworthy that the themes of "Populism Understandings" and "Definitional Variations" are closely related and not as mutually exclusive as the framework might suggest. Similar concerns arise when exploring interdimensional connections that link different themes or concepts across dimensions not included in the research framework.

Another limitation of the research framework is the restricted representation of interconnections, which may not fully capture the inherent cyclical relationships and feedback loops. Two examples illustrate this. Firstly, the framework outlines how the dimension of "Contextual Dynamics", encompassing country-specific factors, interacts with the dimension of "Multifaceted Impacts". In doing so, it highlights the role of national dynamics in shaping the impact of populism in the political, social and economic spheres. Nonetheless, it fails to fully consider the reciprocal nature of these influences. Specifically, how they may loop back to shape the original circumstances that triggered populism's emergence. For example, if populism contributes to economic downturns, this may in turn reinforce the very economic challenges that gave rise to populism in the first place.

Secondly, akin to the issues of reverse causality in the quantitative study, the model's depiction of market reactions to populism recognizes the dynamics and investor reactions stemming from economic consequences. However, it does not effectively illustrate the feedback loop in which these market reactions subsequently affect the economy. Nevertheless, adverse market sentiment fueled by populism can lead to economic challenges. For example, if investors, cautious about the unpredictability associated with populism, withdraw their investments, it can lead the economy towards economic decline. As a result, these market-induced economic shifts could further strengthen the circumstances that initially gave rise to populism. Thus, it must be acknowledged that the qualitative study provides valuable insights into the influence of populism on financial markets and investment decisions but does not present a completed model, which is not, however, the aim of such qualitative research.[313] Instead, the framework derived from this study, though insightful, is not without limitations, having been developed within the unique context of this thesis research and remaining open to further refinement.

[313] See Durand 2016, p. 97; Gioia et al. 2013, p. 22.

3.4.3.2 Avenues of Future Research

The existing body of research at the nexus of finance and populism, including this thesis, points to several unexplored areas that require further investigation. The aim of this section is to provide a structured overview that can guide future research efforts at this intersection. This section presents several of these areas, following the structure provided by the five dimensions of the framework.

3.4.3.2.1 Conceptual Refinement

The conceptual landscape surrounding populism demands nuanced exploration and refinement, especially in its definition and measurement. The existing ambiguity of defining populism persists both in this thesis and in the broader literature. Populism's ability to adjust to different eras and geographies causes distinct interpretations. This variability highlights the need for a flexible model that reflects the evolving character of populism whilst preserving uniform essential features. While the ideational approach serves as a suitable starting point for empirical analysis (see Subsection 2.3.1.1.3), aiming for a multidimensional model may offer a more comprehensive understanding of populism (see Subsection 2.3.1.2.1).

Populism's inherent complexity becomes evident when attempting to categorize it into different varieties. Within the traditional classification of the left and right spectrum, it is crucial to analyze intriguing new questions, such as the reasons for the centrist shifts of some populist parties while others become more extreme. Simultaneously, this classification within traditional political labels such as "left" and "right" might not fully capture its elusive nature, challenging the effectiveness of current categorization methods. Therefore, it is imperative to focus on other classifications, for example, authoritarian populism.

A major challenge stemming from populism's multifaceted nature is its quantification. To address this issue, a constructive approach involves critically examining existing methodologies to identify potential shortcomings and biases. Advanced techniques beyond basic binary classifications can provide a deeper comprehension of populism. Refining the understanding and metrics of populism benefits from taking into account recent trends in related fields, such as the literature on political risk, which emphasizes less the national sphere and more differentiated levels. For example, taking a subnational perspective can provide valuable insights, which is primarily because regions within a single country can exhibit significant variations in culture, institutions, and economic status.[314] Several scholars advocate for this granular approach, emphasizing that comprehensive insights necessitate examining subnational dynamics.[315]

Furthermore, a distinct area of literature focuses on micro-level political analysis of individual firms. For instance, *Hassan et al.* developed a method to assess firm-level political risk by analyzing corporate earnings conference calls.[316] Adopting innovative subnational and micro-level methods holds promise for studying populism and refining definitions. Although data constraints may limit immediate integration, they suggest a future where populism research can be more robust, granular, and reflective of its multiple aspects, rather than being confined to general national studies.

3.4.3.2.2 Contextual Enhancements

Another key area for future research, closely tied to conceptual challenges, involves the contextual dynamics of populism. The research framework has shown that populism's effects and expressions are influenced by geographical location and historical period, highlighting a gap in the understanding of the specific contexts where populism manifests.

The escalation of populism since the mid-2000s, notably after the global financial crisis, has introduced a new layer of political uncertainty that spans emerging markets, established democracies, and traditionally authoritarian regimes.[317] This development underscores the importance of a more differentiated analysis of populism tailored to the distinct historical contexts of various countries. Such an analysis is essential to discern whether certain historical conditions amplify or mitigate populist movements. For example, an examination of Portugal—a country that has experienced relatively minimal populist growth compared to others—could offer valuable insights into the factors that curb or facilitate populist tendencies.[318]

The link between national political architecture and populism is another important aspect that requires in-depth study. The framework demonstrates that countries possess unique institutional structures that either enhance or hinder populist tendencies. Therefore, a more in-depth investigation into these structural factors is necessary. Analyzing different systems, including presidential,

[314] See Hutzschenreuter et al. 2020, pp. 1 ff.

[315] See for example Meyer and Nguyen 2005; Röell et al. 2022; Shapiro et al. 2018.

[316] See Hassan et al. 2019, p. 2135. See also Subsection 2.2.2.2.3.

[317] See Hartwell and Devinney 2024a, p. 305.

[318] See Guriev and Papaioannou 2022, p. 820.

parliamentary, centralized, or federal options, could provide insights into which structures are less susceptible to populist movements.

Further exploration is necessary to understand the political channels used by populists. *Devinney and Hartwell* propose a methodology that looks beyond traditional institutional leadership to uncover underlying drivers, which has the potential to identify previously overlooked channels through which populism permeates the lower echelons of institutions. However, the transition to such an analysis depends on the availability of detailed data on specific political or administrative figures within these institutions. The challenge is the scarcity of public records on these actors, especially when compared to the more accessible records of larger, well-established government bodies. Nevertheless, advanced textual analysis techniques offer a promising way to dissect the nuances of populism. These methods allow for a more detailed analysis of political institutions and conflicts, providing insights into the dynamics of populism that were previously hard to access.[319]

3.4.3.2.3 Impact Reevaluations

To gain a better understanding of the multifaceted impacts of populism, future research should further investigate its effects on political institutions, its appeal as a societal response, and its economic consequences. Previous research highlights the need to understand why mainstream parties often do not support charismatic leaders capable of countering populism. Additionally, it is recognized that populists effectively leverage social media and the Internet for communication, raising the question of why traditional parties have not adopted similar strategies. This inquiry suggests a potential mismatch between mainstream politicians' outreach efforts and the Internet's suitability for populist messaging. To explore these issues, an interdisciplinary approach involving data science, cognitive psychology, and economics could be essential.[320]

Another area of research that could benefit from further analysis is the political impact of the erosion of institutional independence resulting from the rise of populism in politics. Additionally, an interesting topic to explore is how populism resonates as a response to public discontent. By exploring its appeal in different global contexts and understanding its function as a mechanism to prevent extreme authoritarian tendencies, its more beneficial aspects can be revealed.

Similarly, when assessing the economic impact of populist regimes, the qualitative study found that most experts associate populism with negative economic

---

[319] See Devinney and Hartwell 2020, pp. 46 f.

[320] See Guriev and Papaioannou 2022, p. 820.

outcomes. This viewpoint aligns with wider research on the negative economic effects of populism.[321] However, there are notable exceptions that suggest that populism can have positive economic effects when it enables the government to exercise policy autonomy and engage in experimental economic policies during exceptional times.[322] Therefore, additional research could investigate potential advantageous economic trends associated with populism in certain scenarios.

3.4.3.2.4 Market Response Reconsiderations

The link between populism and financial markets necessitates thorough further analysis, particularly due to the potential disturbances that populism can bring to established market mechanisms. Understanding the varying responses of financial markets to populism is paramount, as it not only provides insight into current market dynamics, but also anticipates potential shifts as populist movements evolve.

Closely related to the quantitative study of this thesis, the impact of populism on firms' financing decisions could be further explored. It would be interesting to investigate whether heightened populism during certain periods discourages firms from issuing equity. This inquiry aligns with *Xu's* study examining the effects of EPU on financing decisions made by firms.[323] Adapting this methodology, an empirical test could be designed to determine whether there is an inverse relationship between the rise of populism and the likelihood of equity issuance.

Another pivotal avenue of research is to further investigate how distinctive financial markets react to the victory of populist parties in elections. As stated by the interviewed experts, while initial market reactions may be reactive, markets show a pattern of adjustment over time. This raises questions about the mechanisms by which financial markets adapt to populist influences. Instances such as closely contested elections introduce heightened market uncertainty and could be a point for further investigation.[324] Similarly, elections where results diverge significantly from polls offer another market surprise scenario that may provide more comprehensive perspectives on how markets respond to unforeseen populist shifts.[325]

Another area of future research could benefit from a systematic review that compares the campaign promises of populist leaders with their actual policy

[321] See for example Funke et al. 2023a.

[322] See for example Rodrik 2018a.

[323] See Xu 2020, pp. 1–15.

[324] See Redl 2020, p. 1.

[325] See Heigermoser and Maier 2020, p. 3.

implementation. This analysis would critically assess the discrepancy between stated intentions and enacted measures, examining the outcomes of promises that remained unfulfilled by populist administrations.

Further research is essential to comprehend the broader effects of populism on financial markets, in particular to shed light on the complex mechanisms through which populism affects a broader variety of financial markets. This thesis offers preliminary insights, indicating a potential impact of populism on sovereign credit risks, notably reflected in CDS spreads (see Section 3.2.3.4). These findings resonate with *Pan et al.'s* observation that political uncertainties contribute to higher CDS spreads,[326] suggesting that populism exacerbates such effects. Future investigations should delve into how populist policies, rhetoric, and economic choices influence investor perceptions and, in turn, could modify sovereign credit risk. This inquiry seeks to shed light on the complex, broader mechanisms through which populism affects financial markets.

Furthermore, financial markets encompass various entities with unique strategies and risk profiles. Uncovering how different firms or sectors interpret and respond to populism is essential. Businesses that have close affiliations with governmental policies or operations, either through political ties or state contracts, may endure a distinct set of challenges in populist environments. The challenges can range from amplified uncertainties to possible disruptions to operations. On the contrary, companies that are not deeply involved in government affairs may find opportunities amidst the challenges posed by populist governments.

3.4.3.2.5 Investors Reactions Reassessment

As the interviews conducted for this thesis have shown, the financial landscape is becoming increasingly complex and challenging in the era of rising populism. Therefore, a more sophisticated and adaptive approach to risk assessment, long-term investing, and understanding the interplay between populism and other global risks is required.

Future research should concentrate on enhancing risk assessment for investors to address risks associated with populism. With the rise of populist movements challenging conventional political paradigms, it may be necessary to reevaluate the definition and evaluation of political risk. Traditionally reliant on economic indicators and financial models to quantify political risk, the qualitative aspects of populism—marked by rhetoric, sentiment, and cultural shifts—present a unique challenge. In practice, this may require incorporating new indicators or metrics that are specifically designed to monitor the impact of populism on financial

[326] See Pan et al. 2024, p. 144.

markets. To explore these dynamics, it is necessary to consider the chronological evolution of risk tools across key populist events, combining qualitative political insights with quantitative metrics (see Section 2.2.2.2). One crucial point is that populism does not operate in isolation, as its rise coincides with several other global challenges, such as climate change, technological disruption, and geopolitical tensions. The complex relationship between populist choices and these global challenges can further complicate analysis. Therefore, to adequately assess risks, a more holistic approach is required due to the interrelated nature of contemporary challenges.

Given the growing influence of populism, it is important to understand its impact on the financial landscape, particularly on investor behavior. Drawing parallels from related studies on political risk can provide insight for future research. Specifically, *Drobetz et al.* take a step in this direction by investigating the impact of EPU on the relationship between business investment and the cost of capital. The authors find that firms tend to deviate from their usual investment behavior during periods of heightened economic uncertainty. This tendency is especially noticeable in sectors that depend on government subsidies. Given the inherent unpredictability in both economic policy uncertainty and populism, it is reasonable to analyze the effects of populism using the framework used within an EPU context.[327] The need for this research is underscored by the potential for populism to reshape business responses to conventional economic metrics, while potentially diluting the effectiveness of traditional policy mechanisms in such settings.

[327] See Drobetz et al. 2018, p. 28.

4 Conclusion

In recent years, populism has emerged as a significant challenge for modern societies, highlighted by extensive academic discourse, media analysis, and attention from leading political risk assessors. Populism's unique pose to the political and economic landscape stem from its multidimensional nature, encompassing strategic, stylistic, and ideological elements. As populism gains momentum, its influence inevitably extends beyond the political sphere into the economic sphere, including financial markets.

Financial markets are sensitive to political fluctuations as they reflect broader political and economic conditions. Changes in leadership, policy shifts, and global political events can trigger significant uncertainty and affect market dynamics. Understanding not only the political implications of populist parties, but also how they resonate in financial markets, is critical given their pervasive influence. This is crucial for investors and financial market participants as they try to navigate the growing web of political risks linked to the emergence of populism, which also opens up new research opportunities.

In response to this development, this thesis examines the relationship between populism and its effects on investor expectations and political risk assessments in financial markets, prompted by the research question: "*What are the effects of populism on investor expectations and political risk assessments in financial markets?*" The objective of this research endeavor is to assess how populism, known for its direct appeal to the public against the established elite, affects investor sentiment and modifies traditional political risk frameworks in financial contexts. To conduct this research, a mixed methods explanatory sequential design approach was applied, beginning with a quantitative investigation followed by a qualitative analysis to unravel the complex dynamics of the topic by enriching the quantitative findings with qualitative insights.

C. Schütz, *Populism and Financial Markets*, Studies in Finance and Accounting, https://doi.org/10.1007/978-3-658-46858-3_4

The quantitative phase of the thesis identifies how investors exhibit heightened sensitivity to populism in response to its unpredictability and potential to impede structural growth and create a less business-friendly environment. This part reveals the critical role of populism as a political factor shaping investors' return expectations in a comprehensive international dataset covering 25 countries from 1995 to 2021. The study found that populism notably alters investors' return requirements, demanding higher returns to compensate for the increased uncertainty it introduces, thereby affecting the pricing of financial assets. The research analyzes the Implied Cost of Equity Capital (ICC), a forward-looking, market-based measure that captures investors' return expectations, and demonstrates how these serve as a conduit for the uncertainty generated by populism. The findings, robust across different model variations, not only illustrate that increasing populism is associated with an increased ICC, but also highlight its distinct effect on financial markets, separating it from general political uncertainty and underscoring its potential to affect sovereign creditworthiness. Additionally, the research suggests that the impact of populism on return expectations is complex and may differ by ideological orientation.

Building on these quantitative insights, the qualitative investigation subsequently delves deeper into the specific mechanisms through which populism, identified as a relevant political risk factor, significantly affects investor behavior and reshapes market dynamics. Specifically, 22 financial experts from various sectors were interviewed in a semi-structured format to provide a balanced perspective on the assessment of populism as a potential political risk factor. This diversity of views provides a well-rounded perspective on how political risks are evaluated, managed, and considered within the financial industry. The *Gioia* Methodology facilitated a systematic examination of interviews, resulting in a comprehensive theoretical framework. This framework enables an in-depth exploration of personal experiences and expert opinions and accommodates the investigation of emergent themes associated with the volatile nature and multifaceted consequences of populism.

The multidimensional research framework developed captures the interplay between populism, financial markets, and investor behavior through five interrelated dimensions. It begins by exploring the definition and understanding of populism; examines the contexts that foster populism; details its broad impact on politics, society, and the economy; and focuses on financial market responses to populism, including market adjustments, sector-specific impacts, and ideological effects. Finally, it examines changes in investor behavior, such as risk management and investment strategy modifications.

Based on this framework and the findings of the quantitative study, the thesis provides substantial theoretical and practical contributions. From a theoretical angle, the thesis identifies a populism risk premium that illustrates how rising populism is associated to changes in market behavior and economic distortions, with investors adjusting their risk assessments in response to populist trends. The research goes beyond previous quantitative studies by applying detailed firm-level analysis to a large international dataset, providing a nuanced understanding of the impact of populism across time and countries. Additionally, the qualitative study illustrates the systemic and persistent influences of populism on investor behavior and the cost of equity, providing a holistic framework that links political dynamics with financial market reactions.

The research findings offer practical advice for investors, financial managers, and policymakers on addressing the challenges posed by populism, recommending the adaptation of risk assessment models and strategic adjustments in corporate and investment approaches to mitigate its effects. It emphasizes the importance of incorporating populism into financial modeling and policy development to effectively navigate the financial implications of populism. Therefore, the thesis contributes to a deeper practical understanding of the broader impact of populism on financial markets and provides valuable insights for addressing the challenges and opportunities of the populist trend in global financial settings.

This research offers not only insights into the current dynamics at the intersection of finance and populism, but also identifies several avenues for future study that are essential for deepening the understanding of this complex interplay. Future research should focus on refining the conceptual understanding of populism, exploring its contextual dynamics and diverse manifestations, assessing its multifaceted impacts on political, social, and economic realms, reconsidering financial market responses to populist movements, and reassessing investor reactions in an era of intensified populism. To address these issues effectively, a nuanced, granular, and interdisciplinary approach is needed to capture the complex and multifaceted relationship, contributing to valuable insights into the populist financial risk landscape.

As the year progresses and the "super election year" of 2024 unfolds, the research findings suggest that financial markets are facing increased uncertainty due to populism. The identified link between populism and market dynamics indicates that investors and policymakers should remain attentive. Markets are expected to remain sensitive to populist election outcomes, highlighting the need for advanced risk management strategies that can accommodate potential shifts in policy and regulatory environment. This situation highlights the significance of ongoing monitoring and adaptable strategies to alleviate the unexpected impacts of populism on the global financial landscape. In light of the transformative political events underway, and given that populism has historically occurred in waves, it remains to be seen whether this period will mark a peak in populism's influence or the beginning of a sustained wave, underscoring the need for continued diligence and adaptability in financial response strategies.

References

Abdullah Kamal, Siti S. L. B. (2019): Research Paradigm and The Philosophical Foundations of A Qualitative Study. In *PEOPLE: International Journal of Social Sciences* 4 (3), pp. 1386–1394. https://doi.org/10.20319/pijss.2019.43.13861394.

Abou-Chadi, Tarik; Krause, Werner (2020): The Causal Effect of Radical Right Success on Mainstream Parties' Policy Positions: A Regression Discontinuity Approach. In *British Journal of Political Science* 50 (3), pp. 829–847. https://doi.org/10.1017/S0007123418000029.

Acemoglu, Daron; Egorov, Georgy; Sonin, Konstantin (2013): A Political Theory of Populism. In *The Quarterly Journal of Economics* 128 (2), pp. 771–805. https://doi.org/10.1093/qje/qjs077.

Adams, John; Khan, Hafiz T. A.; Raeside, Robert (2014): Research methods for business and social science students. Second edition. Los Angeles: SAGE.

Adler, Michael; Dumas, Bernard (1983): International Portfolio Choice and Corporation Finance: A Synthesis. In *The Journal of Finance* 38 (3), pp. 925–984. https://doi.org/10.1111/j.1540-6261.1983.tb02511.x.

Agmon, Tamir (1985): Political economy and risk in world financial markets. Lexington, Massachusetts: Lexington Books.

Agmon, Tamir; Findlay, M. C. (1982): Domestic political risk and stock valuation. In *Financial Analysts Journal* 38 (6), pp. 74–77. https://doi.org/10.2469/faj.v38.n6.74.

Ahir, Hites; Bloom, Nicholas; Furceri, Davide (2022): The World Uncertainty Index. Cambridge, Massachusetts.

Akbari, Amir; Ng, Lilian (2020): International Market Integration: A Survey. In *Asia-Pacific Journal of Financial Studies* 49 (2), pp. 161–185. https://doi.org/10.1111/ajfs.12297.

Akbari, Amir; Ng, Lilian; Solnik, Bruno H. (2020): Emerging Markets Are Catching Up: Economic or Financial Integration? In *The Journal of Financial and Quantitative Analysis* 55 (7), pp. 2270–2303. https://doi.org/10.1017/S0022109019000681.

Akbari, Amir; Ng, Lilian; Solnik, Bruno H. (2021): Drivers of economic and financial integration: A machine learning approach. In *Journal of Empirical Finance* 61, pp. 82–102. https://doi.org/10.1016/j.jempfin.2020.12.005.

Akkerman, Agnes; Mudde, Cas; Zaslove, Andrej (2014): How Populist Are the People? Measuring Populist Attitudes in Voters. In *Comparative Political Studies* 47 (9), pp. 1324–1353. https://doi.org/10.1177/0010414013512600.

C. Schütz, *Populism and Financial Markets*, Studies in Finance and Accounting, https://doi.org/10.1007/978-3-658-46858-3

Al Khattab, Adel A. R.; Awwad, Abdulkareem; Anchor, John; Davies, Eleanor (2011): The use of political risk assessment techniques in Jordanian multinational corporations. In *Journal of Risk Research* 14 (1), pp. 97–109. https://doi.org/10.1080/13669877.2010.505346.

Al-Esia, Zena; Crane, Andrew; Iatridis, Kostas (2024): Political CSR and Populism: Toward an Information-Based Theory of Political CSR. In *Business & Society* 63 (2), pp. 373–408. https://doi.org/10.1177/00076503231168078.

Allison, Paul (2009): Fixed Effects Regression Models. Thousand Oaks, California: SAGE Publications.

Alon, Ilan; Herbert, Theodore T. (2009): A stranger in a strange land: Micro political risk and the multinational firm. In *Business Horizons* 52 (2), pp. 127–137. https://doi.org/10.1016/j.bushor.2008.09.004.

Alon, Ilan; Martin, Matthew A. (1998): A Normative Model of Macro Political Risk Assessment. In *Multinational Business Review* 6 (2), pp. 10–19.

Al-Thaqeb, Saud A.; Algharabali, Barrak G. (2019): Economic policy uncertainty: A literature review. In *The Journal of Economic Asymmetries* 20, e00133. https://doi.org/10.1016/j.jeca.2019.e00133.

Andreadis, Ioannis; Ruth-Lovell, Saskia P. (2019): Elite surveys. In Hawkins, Kirk A.; Carlin, Ryan E.; Littvay, Levente; Rovira Kaltwasser, Cristóbal (Eds.): The ideational approach to populism. Concept, theory, and analysis. London, New York: Routledge (Extremism and democracy, 42), pp. 112–128.

Anguera, Maria T.; Blanco-Villaseñor, Angel; Losada, José L.; Sánchez-Algarra, Pedro; Onwuegbuzie, Anthony J. (2018): Revisiting the difference between mixed methods and multimethods: Is it all in the name? In *Quality & quantity* 52 (6), pp. 2757–2770. https://doi.org/10.1007/s11135-018-0700-2.

Anshuman, Ravi; Martin, John; Titman, Sheridan (2011): Accounting for Sovereign Risk When Investing in Emerging Markets. In *Journal of Applied Corporate Finance* 23 (2), pp. 41–49. https://doi.org/10.1111/j.1745-6622.2011.00325.x.

Ardalan, Kavous (2019): Equity Home Bias: A Review Essay. In *Journal of Economic Surveys* 33 (3), pp. 949–967. https://doi.org/10.1111/joes.12302.

Arditi, Benjamin (2010): Review Essay: Populism is Hegemony is Politics? On Ernesto Laclau's on Populist Reason. In *Constellations* 17 (3), pp. 488–497. https://doi.org/10.1111/j.1467-8675.2010.00587.x.

Arouri, Mohamed E. H.; Nguyen, Duc K.; Pukthuanthong, Kuntara (2012): An international CAPM for partially integrated markets: Theory and empirical evidence. In *Journal of Banking & Finance* 36 (9), pp. 2473–2493. https://doi.org/10.1016/j.jbankfin.2012.05.004.

Arshanapalli, Bala; Doukas, John (1993): International stock market linkages: Evidence from the pre- and post-October 1987 period. In *Journal of Banking & Finance* 17 (1), pp. 193–208. https://doi.org/10.1016/0378-4266(93)90088-U.

Art, David (2022): The Myth of Global Populism. In *Perspectives on Politics* 20 (3), pp. 999–1011. https://doi.org/10.1017/S1537592720003552.

Asgharian, Hossein; Nossman, Marcus (2011): Risk contagion among international stock markets. In *Journal of International Money and Finance* 30 (1), pp. 22–38. https://doi.org/10.1016/j.jimonfin.2010.06.006.

Aslanidis, Paris (2016): Is Populism an Ideology? A Refutation and a New Perspective. In *Political Studies* 64, pp. 88–104. https://doi.org/10.1111/1467-9248.12224.

Attig, Najah; Cleary, Sean; El Ghoul, Sadok; Guedhami, Omrane (2013): Institutional Investment Horizons and the Cost of Equity Capital. In *Financial Management* 42 (2), pp. 441–477. https://doi.org/10.1111/j.1755-053X.2012.01221.x.

Autor, David H.; Dorn, David; Hanson, Gordon H. (2013): The China Syndrome: Local Labor Market Effects of Import Competition in the United States. In *American Economic Review* 103 (6), pp. 2121–2168. https://doi.org/10.1257/aer.103.6.2121.

Autor, David H.; Katz, Lawrence F.; Kearney, Melissa S. (2006): The Polarization of the U.S. Labor Market. In *American Economic Review* 96 (2), pp. 189–194. https://doi.org/10.1257/000282806777212620.

Axelrod, Robert (1967): The Structure of Public Opinion on Policy Issues. In *Public Opinion Quarterly* 31 (1), pp. 51–60. https://doi.org/10.1086/267481.

Azmi, Zul; Nasution, Abdillah; Wardayani; Muda, Iskandar; Supriyanto, Supriyanto; Rizal, Syamsul; Hidayat, Rahmat (2019): Grounded Theory in Accounting Research—Conference: Proceedings of The 2nd International Conference On Advance And Scientific Innovation, ICASI 2019, 18 July, Banda Aceh, Indonesia. https://doi.org/10.4108/eai.18-7-2019.2288566.

Baas, Derek (2010): Approaches and challenges to political risk assessment: The view from Export Development Canada. In *Risk Management* 12 (2), pp. 135–162. https://doi.org/10.1057/rm.2009.19.

Baker, Scott R.; Bloom, Nicholas; Davis, Steven J. (2016): Measuring Economic Policy Uncertainty. In *The Quarterly Journal of Economics* 131 (4), pp. 1593–1636. https://doi.org/10.1093/qje/qjw024.

Bakker, Ryan; De Vries, Catherine; Edwards, Erica; Hooghe, Liesbet; Jolly, Seth; Marks, Gary et al. (2015): Measuring party positions in Europe. In *Party Politics* 21 (1), pp. 143–152. https://doi.org/10.1177/1354068812462931.

Bale, Tim; Van Kessel, Stijn; Taggart, Paul (2011): Thrown around with abandon? Popular understandings of populism as conveyed by the print media: A UK case study. In *Acta Politica* 46 (2), pp. 111–131. https://doi.org/10.1057/ap.2011.3.

Bali, Turan G.; Cakici, Nusret (2010): World market risk, country-specific risk and expected returns in international stock markets. In *Journal of Banking & Finance* 34 (6), pp. 1152–1165. https://doi.org/10.1016/j.jbankfin.2009.11.012.

Bartha, Attila; Boda, Zsolt; Szikra, Dorottya (2020): When Populist Leaders Govern: Conceptualising Populism in Policy Making. In *Politics and Governance* 8 (3), pp. 71–81. https://doi.org/10.17645/pag.v8i3.2922.

Baur, Dirk G.; Lucey, Brian M. (2010): Is Gold a Hedge or a Safe Haven? An Analysis of Stocks, Bonds and Gold. In *Financial Review* 45 (2), pp. 217–229. https://doi.org/10.1111/j.1540-6288.2010.00244.x.

Beitin, Ben K. (2012): Interview and Sampling: How Many and Whom. In Gubrium, Jaber F.; Holstein, James A.; Marvasti, Amir; McKinney, Karyn (Eds.): The SAGE Handbook of Interview Research: The Complexity of the Craft. Thousand Oaks, California: SAGE Publications, pp. 243–254.

Bekaert, Geert (1995): Market Integration and Investment Barriers in Emerging Equity Markets. In *The World Bank Economic Review* 9 (1), pp. 75–107. https://doi.org/10.1093/wber/9.1.75.

Bekaert, Geert; Harvey, Campbell R.; Lundblad, Christian T.; Siegel, Stephan (2011): What Segments Equity Markets? In *Review of Financial Studies* 24 (12), pp. 3841–3890. https://doi.org/10.1093/rfs/hhr082.

Bekaert, Geert; Harvey, Campbell R.; Lundblad, Christian T.; Siegel, Stephan (2014): Political risk spreads. In *Journal of International Business Studies* 45 (4), pp. 471–493. https://doi.org/10.1057/jibs.2014.4.

Bekaert, Geert; Harvey, Campbell R.; Lundblad, Christian T.; Siegel, Stephan (2016): Political risk and international valuation. In *Journal of Corporate Finance* 37, pp. 1–23. https://doi.org/10.1016/j.jcorpfin.2015.12.007.

Bekaert, Geert; Hodrick, Robert J. (2018): International financial management. Third edition. Cambridge, New York, New York, Melbourne, Australia, New Delhi, Singapore: Cambridge University Press.

Bekaert, Geert; Hoerova, Marie (2014): The VIX, the variance premium and stock market volatility. In *Journal of Econometrics* 183 (2), pp. 181–192. https://doi.org/10.1016/j.jeconom.2014.05.008.

Belghitar, Yacine; Clark, Ephraim (2011): Capital Budgeting with Political/Country Risk. In Baker, H. K.; English, Philip (Eds.): Capital Budgeting Valuation. Financial analysis for today's investment projects. Hoboken, New Jersey: Wiley, pp. 241–259.

Belkhir, Mohamed; Boubakri, Narjess; Grira, Jocelyn (2017): Political risk and the cost of capital in the MENA region. In *Emerging Markets Review* 33, pp. 155–172. https://doi.org/10.1016/j.ememar.2017.08.002.

Benczes, István (2022): Taking back control over the economy: From economic populism to the economic consequences of populism. In *European Policy Analysis* 8 (1), pp. 109–123. https://doi.org/10.1002/epa2.1134.

Benischke, Mirko H.; Guldiken, Orhun; Doh, Jonathan P.; Martin, Geoffrey; Zhang, Yanze (2022): Towards a behavioral theory of MNC response to political risk and uncertainty: The role of CEO wealth at risk. In *Journal of World Business* 57 (1), Article 101265. https://doi.org/10.1016/j.jwb.2021.101265.

Ben-Nasr, Hamdi; Boubakri, Narjess; Cosset, Jean-Claude (2012): The Political Determinants of the Cost of Equity: Evidence from Newly Privatized Firms. In *Journal of Accounting Research* 50 (3), pp. 605–646. https://doi.org/10.1111/j.1475-679X.2011.00435.x.

Benoit, Kenneth R.; Laver, Michael (2006): Party policy in modern democracies. London: Routledge (Routledge research in comparative politics, 19).

Berman, Sheri (2021): The Causes of Populism in the West. In *Annual Review of Political Science* 24 (1), pp. 71–88. https://doi.org/10.1146/annurev-polisci-041719-102503.

Bielstein, Patrick (2018): International asset allocation using the market implied cost of capital. In *Financial Markets and Portfolio Management* 32 (1), pp. 17–51. https://doi.org/10.1007/s11408-017-0302-3.

Bierman, Harold; Smidt, Seymour (2007): The capital budgeting decision. Economic analysis of investment projects. Ninth edition. New York, London: Routledge Taylor and Francis Group.

Black, Fischer (1974): International capital market equilibrium with investment barriers. In *Journal of Financial Economics* 1 (4), pp. 337–352. https://doi.org/10.1016/0304-405X(74)90013-0.

Bonikowski, Bart; Halikiopoulou, Daphne; Kaufmann, Eric; Rooduijn, Matthijs (2019): Populism and nationalism in a comparative perspective: a scholarly exchange. In *Nations and Nationalism* 25 (1), pp. 58–81. https://doi.org/10.1111/nana.12480.

Born, Benjamin; Müller, Gernot J.; Schularick, Moritz; Sedláček, Petr (2019): The Costs of Economic Nationalism: Evidence from the Brexit Experiment. In *The Economic Journal* 129 (623), pp. 2722–2744. https://doi.org/10.1093/ej/uez020.

Botosan, Christine A.; Plumlee, Marlene A. (2005): Assessing Alternative Proxies for the Expected Risk Premium. In *The Accounting Review* 80 (1), pp. 21–53. https://doi.org/10.2308/accr.2005.80.1.21.

Botosan, Christine A.; Plumlee, Marlene A.; Wen, He (2011): The Relation between Expected Returns, Realized Returns, and Firm Risk Characteristics. In *Contemporary Accounting Research* 28 (4), pp. 1085–1122. https://doi.org/10.1111/j.1911-3846.2011.01096.x.

Boubakri, Narjess; El Ghoul, Sadok; Saffar, Walid (2014): Political rights and equity pricing. In *Journal of Corporate Finance* 27, pp. 326–344. https://doi.org/10.1016/j.jcorpfin.2014.05.009.

Bouchet, Michel H. (2003): Country risk assessment. A guide to global investment strategy. Hoboken, New Jersey: J. Wiley.

Boulianne, Shelley; Koc-Michalska, Karolina; Bimber, Bruce (2020): Right-wing populism, social media and echo chambers in Western democracies. In *New Media & Society* 22 (4), pp. 683–699. https://doi.org/10.1177/1461444819893983.

Bouoiyour, Jamal; Selmi, Refk; Wohar, Mark E. (2019): Safe havens in the face of Presidential election uncertainty: A comparison between Bitcoin, oil and precious metals. In *Applied Economics* 51 (57), pp. 6076–6088. https://doi.org/10.1080/00036846.2019.1645289.

Brennan, Michael J. (1970): Taxes, Market Valuation And Corporate Financial Policy. In *National Tax Journal* 23 (4), pp. 417–427. https://doi.org/10.1086/NTJ41792223.

Brinkmann, Svend (2018): The Interview. In Denzin, Norman K.; Lincoln, Yvonna S. (Eds.): The Sage handbook of qualitative research. Fifth edition. Los Angeles, California: SAGE.

Brogaard, Jonathan; Detzel, Andrew L. (2012): The Asset Pricing Implications of Government Economic Policy Uncertainty. In *Management Science* 61 (1), pp. 3–18. https://doi.org/10.2139/ssrn.2075375.

Bronk, Richard; Jacoby, Wade (2020): The Epistemics of Populism and the Politics of Uncertainty. In *SSRN Electronic Journal*. https://doi.org/10.2139/ssrn.3539587.

Brubaker, Rogers (2017): Why populism? In *Theory and Society* 46 (5), pp. 357–385. https://doi.org/10.1007/s11186-017-9301-7.

Brüggen, Alexander (2011): Capital Rationing for Capital Budgeting. In Baker, H. K.; English, Philip (Eds.): Capital Budgeting Valuation. Financial analysis for today's investment projects. Hoboken, New Jersey: Wiley, pp. 95–111.

Bryman, Alan (2006): Integrating quantitative and qualitative research: how is it done? In *Qualitative Research* 6 (1), pp. 97–113. https://doi.org/10.1177/1468794106058877.

Bunn, Derek. W.; Mustafaoglu, Mike M. (1978): Forecasting Political Risk. In *Management Science* 24 (15), pp. 1557–1567.

Butler, Kirt C. (2016): Multinational Finance. Evaluating the opportunities, costs, and risks of multinational operations. Sixth edition. Hoboken, New Jersey, USA: Wiley (Wiley Finance).

Çakmakli, Cem; Demiralp, Selva; Güneş, Gökhan Ş. (2023): Do Financial Markets Respond to Populist Rhetoric? In *Oxford Bulletin of Economics and Statistics*, Article 12591. https://doi.org/10.1111/obes.12591.

Caldara, Dario; Iacoviello, Matteo (2022): Measuring Geopolitical Risk. In *American Economic Review* 112 (4), pp. 1194–1225. https://doi.org/10.1257/aer.20191823.

Cambridge University Press (2017): 'Populism' revealed as 2017 Word of the Year by Cambridge University Press. Available online at https://www.cam.ac.uk/news/populism-revealed-as-2017-word-of-the-year-by-cambridge-university-press, checked on 2/4/2024.

Cameron, Roslyn (2011): Mixed methods research: the five Ps framework. In *Electronic Journal of Business Research Methods* 9 (2).

Campbell, Cynthia J.; Cowan, Arnold R.; Salotti, Valentina (2010): Multi-country event-study methods. In *Journal of Banking & Finance* 34 (12), pp. 3078–3090. https://doi.org/10.1016/j.jbankfin.2010.07.016.

Campbell, John L.; Dhaliwal, Dan; Schwartz, William C. (2012): Financing Constraints and the Cost of Capital: Evidence from the Funding of Corporate Pension Plans. In *Review of Financial Studies* 25 (3), pp. 868–912. https://doi.org/10.1093/rfs/hhr119.

Caño, Antonio; Ordaz, Pablo (2017): Pope Francis: "The danger is that in times of crisis we look for a savior". EL PAÍS. Available online at https://english.elpais.com/elpais/2017/01/21/inenglish/1485026427_223988.html#, checked on 1/4/2024.

Canovan, Margaret (1999): Trust the People! Populism and the Two Faces of Democracy. In *Political Studies* 47 (1), pp. 2–16. https://doi.org/10.1111/1467-9248.00184.

Cao, Chunfang; Li, Xiaoyang; Liu, Guilin (2019): Political Uncertainty and Cross-Border Acquisitions. In *Review of Finance* 23 (2), pp. 439–470. https://doi.org/10.1093/rof/rfx055.

Carhart, Mark M. (1997): On Persistence in Mutual Fund Performance. In *The Journal of Finance* 52 (1), pp. 57–82. https://doi.org/10.1111/j.1540-6261.1997.tb03808.x.

Castanho Silva, Bruno; Jungkunz, Sebastian; Helbling, Marc; Littvay, Levente (2020): An Empirical Comparison of Seven Populist Attitudes Scales. In *Political Research Quarterly* 73 (2), pp. 409–424. https://doi.org/10.1177/1065912919833176.

Castles, Francis G.; Mair, Peter (1984): Left–Right Political Scales: Some 'Expert' Judgments. In *European Journal of Political Research* 12 (1), pp. 73–88. https://doi.org/10.1111/j.1475-6765.1984.tb00080.x.

Cavusgil, S. T.; Deligonul, Seyda; Ghauri, Pervez N.; Bamiatzi, Vassiliki; Park, Byung I.; Mellahi, Kamel (2020): Risk in international business and its mitigation. In *Journal of World Business* 55 (2), Article 101078. https://doi.org/10.1016/j.jwb.2020.101078.

Celico, Andrea; Rode, Martin; Rodriguez Carreño, Ignacio (2022): Everybody is Populist to Some Extent: Measuring Parties' Populist Rhetoric with Machine Learning Tools. In *SSRN Electronic Journal*. https://doi.org/10.2139/ssrn.4004405.

Celik, Saban (2012): Theoretical and Empirical Review of Asset Pricing Models: A Structural Synthesis. In *International Journal of Economics and Financial Issues* 2 (2), pp. 141–178.

Chan, Yue-Cheong; Saffar, Walid; Wei, K.C. J. (2021): How economic policy uncertainty affects the cost of raising equity capital: Evidence from seasoned equity offerings. In *Journal of Financial Stability* 53, Article 100841. https://doi.org/10.1016/j.jfs.2020.100841.

Chapel Hill Expert Surveys (2022): Codebook. Chapel Hill Expert Survey-Trend File-Version 1.3. Available online at https://doi.org/10.1016/j.electstud.2021.102420, updated on 2/7/2024.

Charmaz, Kathy; Belgrave, Linda L. (2012): Qualitative Interviewing and Grounded Theory Analysis. In Gubrium, Jaber F.; Holstein, James A.; Marvasti, Amir; McKinney, Karyn (Eds.): The SAGE Handbook of Interview Research: The Complexity of the Craft. Thousand Oaks, California: SAGE Publications, pp. 347–366.

Charmaz, Kathy; Bryant, Antony (2011): Grounded theory and credibility. In Silverman, David (Ed.): Qualitative research. Third edition. Los Angeles, London, New Delhi, Singapore, Washington DC, Melbourne: SAGE, pp. 291–309.

Chen, Kevin C.; Chen, Zhihong; Wei, K.C. J. (2009): Legal protection of investors, corporate governance, and the cost of equity capital. In *Journal of Corporate Finance* 15 (3), pp. 273–289. https://doi.org/10.1016/j.jcorpfin.2009.01.001.

Chen, Zhiwu; Knez, Peter J. (1995): Measurement of Market Integration and Arbitrage. In *Review of Financial Studies* 8 (2), pp. 287–325. https://doi.org/10.1093/rfs/8.2.287.

Chiah, Mardy; Chai, Daniel; Zhong, Angel; Li, Song (2016): A Better Model? An Empirical Investigation of the Fama–French Five-factor Model in Australia. In *International Review of Finance* 16 (4), pp. 595–638. https://doi.org/10.1111/irfi.12099.

Christou, Christina; Cunado, Juncal; Gupta, Rangan; Hassapis, Christis (2017): Economic policy uncertainty and stock market returns in PacificRim countries: Evidence based on a Bayesian panel VAR model. In *Journal of Multinational Financial Management* 40, pp. 92–102. https://doi.org/10.1016/j.mulfin.2017.03.001.

Clark, Ephraim (1997): Valuing political risk. In *Journal of International Money and Finance* 16 (3), pp. 477–490. https://doi.org/10.1016/S0261-5606(97)00008-9.

Claus, James; Thomas, Jacob (2001): Equity Premia as Low as Three Percent? Evidence from Analysts' Earnings Forecasts for Domestic and International Stock Markets. In *The Journal of Finance* 56 (5), pp. 1629–1666. https://doi.org/10.1111/0022-1082.00384.

Çolak, Gönül; Durnev, Art; Qian, Yiming (2017): Political Uncertainty and IPO Activity: Evidence from U.S. Gubernatorial Elections. In *The Journal of Financial and Quantitative Analysis* 52 (6), pp. 2523–2564. https://doi.org/10.1017/S0022109017000862.

Cole, Wade M.; Schofer, Evan (2023): Destroying Democracy for the People: The Economic, Social, and Political Consequences of Populist Rule, 1990 to 2017. In *Social Problems* (spac060). https://doi.org/10.1093/socpro/spac060.

Conlon, Catherine; Timonen, Virpi; Elliott-O'Dare, Catherine; O'Keeffe, Sorcha; Foley, Geraldine (2020): Confused About Theoretical Sampling? Engaging Theoretical Sampling in Diverse Grounded Theory Studies. In *Qualitative health research* 30 (6), pp. 947–959. https://doi.org/10.1177/1049732319899139.

Connolly, Robert; Stivers, Chris; Sun, Licheng (2005): Stock Market Uncertainty and the Stock-Bond Return Relation. In *The Journal of Financial and Quantitative Analysis* 40 (1), pp. 161–194. https://doi.org/10.1017/S0022109000001782.

Corbin, Juliet; Strauss, Anselm L. (2008): Basics of Qualitative Research: Techniques and Procedures for Developing Grounded Theory. Third edition. Thousand Oaks, California: SAGE Publications.

Cosset, Jean-Claude; Suret, Jean-Marc (1995): Political Risk and the Benefits of International Portfolio Diversification. In *Journal of International Business Studies* 26 (2), pp. 301–318. https://doi.org/10.1057/palgrave.jibs.8490175.

Creswell, John W. (1999): Mixed-Method Research: Introduction and Application. In Cizek, Gregory J. (Ed.): Handbook of educational policy. San Diego, California: Academic Press (Educational psychology series).

Creswell, John W. (2016): Revisiting Mixed Methods and Advancing Scientific Practices. In Hesse-Biber, Sharlene N.; Johnson, R. B.; Creswell, John W. (Eds.): The Oxford Handbook of Multimethod and Mixed Methods Research Inquiry: Oxford University Press.

Creswell, John W. (2018): Qualitative inquiry and research design. Choosing among five approaches. Fourth edition. Thousand Oaks, California: SAGE Publications.

Creswell, John W.; Plano Clark, Vicki L. (2007): Designing and conducting mixed methods research. Thousand Oaks, California: SAGE.

Creswell, John W.; Plano Clark, Vicki L. (2018): Designing and conducting mixed methods research. Third edition. Los Angeles, London, New Delhi, Singapore, Washington DC, Melbourne: SAGE.

Dai, Lili; Zhang, Bohui (2019): Political Uncertainty and Finance: A Survey. In *Asia-Pacific Journal of Financial Studies* 48 (3), pp. 307–333. https://doi.org/10.1111/ajfs.12257.

D'Amico, Guglielmo; De Blasis, Riccardo (2020): A Review of the Dividend Discount Model: From Deterministic to Stochastic Models. In Barbu, Vlad S.; Vergne, Nicolas (Eds.): Statistical Topics and Stochastic Models for Dependent Data with Applications: Wiley, pp. 47–67.

Damodaran, Aswath (1999): Estimating Equity Risk Premiums. In *Finance Working Papers* FIN-99–021. Available online at http://archive.nyu.edu/handle/2451/26918.

Damodaran, Aswath (2003): Measuring Company Exposure to Country Risk: Theory and Practice. In *SSRN Electronic Journal*. https://doi.org/10.2139/ssrn.889388.

Damodaran, Aswath (2022): Country Risk: Determinants, Measures and Implications—The 2022 Edition. In *SSRN Electronic Journal*. https://doi.org/10.2139/ssrn.4161010.

Das, Panchanan (2019): Econometrics in Theory and Practice. Singapore: Springer Singapore.

Daske, Holger; Van Halteren, Jörn; Maug, Ernst G. (2010): Evaluating Methods to Estimate the Implied Cost of Equity Capital: A Simulation Study. In *SSRN Electronic Journal*. https://doi.org/10.2139/ssrn.1465294.

Dayananda, Don; Irons, Richard; Harrison, Steve; Herbohn, John; Rowland, Patrick (2010): Capital budgeting: an overview. In Dayananda, Don; Irons, Richard; Harrison, Steve; Herbohn, John; Rowland, Patrick (Eds.): Capital Budgeting: Cambridge University Press, pp. 1–11.

De Cleen, Benjamin (2023): The populist political logic and the analysis of the discursive construction of 'the people' and 'the elite'. In Reif, Monika; Polzenhagen, Frank (Eds.): Cultural Linguistics and Critical Discourse Studies, vol. 83. Amsterdam: John Benjamins Publishing Company (103), pp. 19–42.

De Cleen, Benjamin; Moffitt, Benjamin; Panayotu, Panos; Stavrakakis, Yannis (2020): The Potentials and Difficulties of Transnational Populism: The Case of the Democracy in Europe Movement 2025. In *Political Studies* 68 (1), pp. 146–166. https://doi.org/10.1177/0032321719847576.

De La Torre, Carlos (2019a): Global populism: histories, trajectotires, problems and challenges. In De La Torre, Carlos (Ed.): Routledge handbook of global populism. London, New York: Routledge Taylor and Francis Group, pp. 1–29.

De La Torre, Carlos (Ed.) (2019b): Routledge handbook of global populism. Routledge. London, New York: Routledge Taylor and Francis Group.

De Lara, Felipe B. (2019): Populist waves in Latin America. Continuities, twists, and ruptures. In De La Torre, Carlos (Ed.): Routledge handbook of global populism. London, New York: Routledge Taylor and Francis Group, pp. 435–451.

De Mortanges, Charles P.; Allers, Vivian (1996): Political risk assessment: Theory and the experience of Dutch firms. In *International Business Review* 5 (3), pp. 303–318. https://doi.org/10.1016/0969-5931(96)00012-1.

Del Negro, Marco; Brooks, Robin (2005): A Latent Factor Model with Global, Country, and Industry Shocks for International Stock Returns. In *IMF Working Papers* 05 (52), pp. 1–34. https://doi.org/10.5089/9781451860719.001.

Demata, Massimiliano; Conoscenti, Michelangelo; Stavrakakis, Yannis (2020): Riding the Populist Wave. Metaphors of Populism and Anti-Populism in the Daily Mail and The Guardian. Iperstoria, No 15 (2020): Populism and Its Languages, pp. 8–35. https://doi.org/10.13136/2281-4582/2020.i15.686.

Denzin, Norman K.; Lincoln, Yvonna S. (Eds.) (2018): The Sage handbook of qualitative research. Fifth edition. Los Angeles, California: SAGE.

Desta, Asayehgn (1985): Assessing Political Risk In Less Developed Countries. In *Journal of Business Strategy* 5 (4), pp. 40–53. https://doi.org/10.1108/eb039086.

Devinney, Timothy M.; Hartwell, Christopher A. (2020): Varieties of populism. In *Global Strategy Journal* 10 (1), pp. 32–66. https://doi.org/10.1002/gsj.1373.

Devinney, Timothy M.; Hartwell, Christopher A. (2021): Managing Around Populism. In Verbeke, Alain; Van Tulder, Rob; Rose, Elizabeth L.; Wei, Yingqi (Eds.): The Multiple Dimensions of Institutional Complexity in International Business Research: Emerald Publishing Limited (Progress in International Business Research), pp. 95–105.

Dewasiri, N. J.; Weerakoon, Yatiwelle K. B.; Azeez, Athambawa A. (2018): Mixed Methods in Finance Research. In *International Journal of Qualitative Methods* 17 (1), 1–13. https://doi.org/10.1177/1609406918801730.

Dhaliwal, Dan; Li, Oliver Z.; Tsang, Albert; Yang, Yong G. (2014): Corporate social responsibility disclosure and the cost of equity capital: The roles of stakeholder orientation and financial transparency. In *Journal of Accounting and Public Policy* 33 (4), pp. 328–355. https://doi.org/10.1016/j.jaccpubpol.2014.04.006.

Di Cocco, Jessica; Monechi, Bernardo (2022): How Populist are Parties? Measuring Degrees of Populism in Party Manifestos Using Supervised Machine Learning. In *Political Analysis* 30 (3), pp. 311–327. https://doi.org/10.1017/pan.2021.29.

Diamond, Douglas W.; Verrecchia, Robert E. (1991): Disclosure, Liquidity, and the Cost of Capital. In *The Journal of Finance* 46 (4), pp. 1325–1359. https://doi.org/10.1111/j.1540-6261.1991.tb04620.x.

Döring, Holger (2016): Mapping established democracies: Integrated data on parties, elections and cabinets. In *Electoral Studies* 44, pp. 535–543. https://doi.org/10.1016/j.electstud.2016.07.002.

Döring, Holger; Huber, Constantin; Manow, Philip (2022): Parliaments and governments database (ParlGov): Information on parties, elections and cabinets in estab-lished democracies. Available online at https://parlgov.org/data/parlgov-development_csv-utf-8/, updated on 2/10/2024.

Dornbusch, Rudiger; Edwards, Sebastian (1990): Macroeconomic populism. In *Journal of Development Economics* 32 (2), pp. 247–277. https://doi.org/10.1016/0304-3878(90)90038-D.

Dos Santos, Marcelo B. C.; Klotzle, Marcelo C.; Pinto, Antonio C. F. (2021): The impact of political risk on the currencies of emerging markets. In *Research in Inter-national Business and Finance* 56, Article 101375. https://doi.org/10.1016/j.ribaf.2020.101375.

Doussard, Marc (2023): Building distributive populism: basic income and political alternatives to ethno-nationalism. In *Cambridge Journal of Regions, Economy and Society*, Article rsad040. https://doi.org/10.1093/cjres/rsad040.

Drobetz, Wolfgang; El Ghoul, Sadok; Guedhami, Omrane; Janzen, Malte (2018): Policy uncertainty, investment, and the cost of capital. In *Journal of Financial Stability* 39, pp. 28–45. https://doi.org/10.1016/j.jfs.2018.08.005.

Durand, Muriel (2016): Employing critical incident technique as one way to display the hidden aspects of post-merger integration. In *International Business Review* 25 (1), pp. 87–102. https://doi.org/10.1016/j.ibusrev.2015.05.003.

Easton, Peter D. (2004): PE Ratios, PEG Ratios, and Estimating the Implied Expected Rate of Return on Equity Capital. In *The Accounting Review* 79 (1), pp. 73–95. https://doi.org/10.2308/accr.2004.79.1.73.

Easton, Peter D.; Sommers, Gregory A. (2007): Effect of Analysts' Optimism on Estimates of the Expected Rate of Return Implied by Earnings Forecasts. In *Journal of Accounting Research* 45 (5), pp. 983–1015. https://doi.org/10.1111/j.1475-679X.2007.00257.x.

Echterling, Fabian; Eierle, Brigitte; Ketterer, Simeon (2015): A review of the literature on methods of computing the implied cost of capital. In *International Review of Financial Analysis* 42, pp. 235–252. https://doi.org/10.1016/j.irfa.2015.08.001.

Ecker, Alejandro; Jenny, Marcelo; Müller, Wolfgang C.; Praprotnik, Katrin (2022): How and why party position estimates from manifestos, expert, and party elite surveys diverge: A comparative analysis of the 'left-right' and the 'European integration' dimensions. In *Party Politics* 28 (3), pp. 528–540. https://doi.org/10.1177/1354068821990.

Eiteman, David K.; Stonehill, Arthur I.; Moffett, Michael H. (2013): Multinational business finance. Thirteenth global edition. Boston, Munich: Pearson.

El Ghoul, Sadok; Guedhami, Omrane; Kim, Yongtae; Yoon, Hyo J. (2021): Policy Uncertainty and Accounting Quality. In *The Accounting Review* 96 (4), pp. 233–260. https://doi.org/10.2308/TAR-2018-0057.

El Ghoul, Sadok; Guedhami, Omrane; Kwok, Chuck C.; Mishra, Dev R. (2011): Does corporate social responsibility affect the cost of capital? In *Journal of Banking & Finance* 35 (9), pp. 2388–2406. https://doi.org/10.1016/j.jbankfin.2011.02.007.

Elliott, Douglas J. (2017): Financial Institutions In An Age Of Populism. Oliver Wyman. Available online at https://www.oliverwyman.com/our-expertise/insights/2017/mar/financial-institutions-in-an-age-of-populism.html, checked on 1/4/2024.

Elton, Edwin J. (1999): Presidential Address: Expected Return, Realized Return, and Asset Pricing Tests. In *The Journal of Finance* 54 (4), pp. 1199–1220. https://doi.org/10.1111/0022-1082.00144.

Elton, Edwin J.; Gruber, Martin J.; Brown, Stephen J.; Goetzmann, William N. (2014): Modern portfolio theory and investment analysis. Ninth edition. Hoboken, New Jersey: Wiley.

Engesser, Sven; Ernst, Nicole; Esser, Frank; Büchel, Florin (2017): Populism and social media: how politicians spread a fragmented ideology. In *Information, Communication & Society* 20 (8), pp. 1109–1126. https://doi.org/10.1080/1369118X.2016.1207697.

Erb, Claude B.; Harvey, Campbell R.; Viskanta, Tadas E. (1996): Expected Returns and Volatility in 135 Countries. In *The Journal of Portfolio Management* 22 (3), pp. 46–58. https://doi.org/10.3905/jpm.1996.409554.

Errunza, Vihang; Losq, Etienne (1985): International Asset Pricing under Mild Segmentation: Theory and Test. In *The Journal of Finance* 40 (1), pp. 105–124. https://doi.org/10.1111/j.1540-6261.1985.tb04939.x.

Esterer, Florian; Schröder, David (2014): Implied cost of capital investment strategies: evidence from international stock markets. In *Annals of Finance* 10 (2), pp. 171–195. https://doi.org/10.1007/s10436-013-0236-3.

Fabozzi, Frank J.; Jones, Frank J. (2019): Foundations of global financial markets and Institutions. With assistance of Francesco A. Fabozzi, Steven V. Mann. Fifth edition. London, England, Cambridge, Massachusetts: The MIT Press.

Faccio, Mara (2006): Politically Connected Firms. In *American Economic Review* 96 (1), pp. 369–386. https://doi.org/10.1257/000282806776157704.

Fama, Eugene F. (1970): Efficient Capital Markets: A Review of Theory and Empirical Work. In *The Journal of Finance* 25 (2), pp. 383–417. https://doi.org/10.2307/2325486.

Fama, Eugene F.; French, Kenneth R. (1993): Common risk factors in the returns on stocks and bonds. In *Journal of Financial Economics* 33 (1), pp. 3–56. https://doi.org/10.1016/0304-405X(93)90023-5.

Fama, Eugene F.; French, Kenneth R. (1997): Industry costs of equity. In *Journal of Financial Economics* 43 (2), pp. 153–193. https://doi.org/10.1016/S0304-405X(96)00896-3.

Fama, Eugene F.; French, Kenneth R. (2015): A five-factor asset pricing model. In *Journal of Financial Economics* 116 (1), pp. 1–22. https://doi.org/10.1016/j.jfineco.2014.10.010.

Feilzer, Martina Y. (2010): Doing Mixed Methods Research Pragmatically: Implications for the Rediscovery of Pragmatism as a Research Paradigm. In *Journal of Mixed Methods Research* 4 (1), pp. 6–16. https://doi.org/10.1177/1558689809349691.

Fernández-García, Belén (2021): The Triumph of (Underlying) Ideology Over Populism in Western Europe. In *Frontiers in Political Science* 3, Article 667320, pp. 1–15. https://doi.org/10.3389/fpos.2021.667320.

Ferrara, Federico M.; Sattler, Thomas (2016): The Political Economy of Financial Markets. In Pappas, Takis S. (Ed.): Oxford Research Encyclopedia of Politics: Oxford University Press.

Fitzpatrick, Mark (1983): The Definition and Assessment of Political Risk in International Business: A Review of the Literature. In *The Academy of Management Review* 8 (2), pp. 249–254. https://doi.org/10.2307/257752.

Flick, Uwe (2018a): Doing grounded theory. Second edition. Los Angeles, London, New Dehli, Singapore, Washington DC, Melbourne: SAGE.

Flick, Uwe (2018b): Managing Quality in Qualitative Research. London: SAGE Publications.

Flick, Uwe (Ed.) (2022): The SAGE Handbook of Qualitative Research Design. London: SAGE Publications.

Foley, Geraldine; Timonen, Virpi; Conlon, Catherine; O'Dare, Catherine E. (2021): Interviewing as a Vehicle for Theoretical Sampling in Grounded Theory. In *Inter-national Journal of Qualitative Methods* 20. https://doi.org/10.1177/1609406920980957.

French, Kenneth R.; Poterba, James: Investor Diversification and International Equity Markets. Cambridge, Massachusetts.

Frey, Carl B.; Berger, Thor; Chen, Chinchih (2018): Political machinery: did robots swing the 2016 US presidential election? In *Oxford Review of Economic Policy* 34 (3), pp. 418–442. https://doi.org/10.1093/oxrep/gry007.

Fuentes, Juan F. (2020): Populism. In *Contributions to the History of Concepts* 15 (1), pp. 47–68. https://doi.org/10.3167/choc.2020.150103.

Funke, Manuel; Schularick, Moritz; Trebesch, Christoph (2016): Going to extremes: Politics after financial crises, 1870–2014. In *European Economic Review* 88, pp. 227–260. https://doi.org/10.1016/j.euroecorev.2016.03.006.

Funke, Manuel; Schularick, Moritz; Trebesch, Christoph (2020): Populist Leaders and the Economy. In *CEPR Discussion Paper 15405*, pp. 1–203.

Funke, Manuel; Schularick, Moritz; Trebesch, Christoph (2023a): Populist Leaders and the Economy. In *American Economic Review* 113 (12), pp. 3249–3288. https://doi.org/10.1257/aer.20202045.

Funke, Manuel; Schularick, Moritz; Trebesch, Christoph (2023b): Populist Leaders and the Economy—Online Appendix. Available online at https://assets.aeaweb.org/asset-server/files/19727.pdf, checked on 2/10/2024.

Gala, Vito D.; Pagliardi, Giovanni; Zenios, Stavros A. (2023): Global political risk and international stock returns. In *Journal of Empirical Finance* 72, pp. 78–102. https://doi.org/10.1016/j.jempfin.2023.03.004.

Garzón-Jiménez, Renato; Zorio-Grima, Ana (2020): Corporate Social Responsibility and Cost of Equity: Literature Review and Suggestions for Future Research. In *Journal of Business Accounting and Finance Perspectives* 2 (3), pp. 1–19. https://doi.org/10.35995/jbafp2030015.

Gebhardt, William R.; Lee, Charles M.; Swaminathan, Bhaskaran (2001): Toward an Implied Cost of Capital. In *Journal of Accounting Research* 39 (1), pp. 135–176. https://doi.org/10.1111/1475-679X.00007.

Gehman, Joel; Glaser, Vern L.; Eisenhardt, Kathleen M.; Gioia, Denny; Langley, Ann; Corley, Kevin G. (2018): Finding Theory–Method Fit: A Comparison of Three Qualitative Approaches to Theory Building. In *Journal of Management Inquiry* 27 (3), pp. 284–300. https://doi.org/10.1177/1056492617706029.

Georgarakos, Dimitris; Pasini, Giacomo (2011): Trust, Sociability, and Stock Market Participation. In *Review of Finance* 15 (4), pp. 693–725. https://doi.org/10.1093/rof/rfr028.

Gerbaudo, Paolo (2018): Social media and populism: an elective affinity? In *Media, Culture & Society* 40 (5), pp. 745–753. https://doi.org/10.1177/0163443718772192.

Giambona, Erasmo; Graham, John R.; Harvey, Campbell R. (2017): The management of political risk. In *Journal of International Business Studies* 48 (4), pp. 523–533. https://doi.org/10.1057/s41267-016-0058-4.

Giddings, Lynne S. (2006): Mixed-methods research. In *Journal of Research in Nursing* 11 (3), pp. 195–203. https://doi.org/10.1177/1744987106064635.

Gidron, Noam; Bonikowski, Bart (2013): Varieties of Populism: Literature Review and Research Agenda. In *SSRN Electronic Journal*, pp. 1–39. https://doi.org/10.2139/ssrn.2459387.

Gioia, Dennis A.; Chittipeddi, Kumar (1991): Sensemaking and sensegiving in strategic change initiation. In *Strategic Management Journal* 12 (6), pp. 433–448. https://doi.org/10.1002/smj.4250120604.

Gioia, Dennis A.; Corley, Kevin G.; Hamilton, Aimee L. (2013): Seeking Qualitative Rigor in Inductive Research. In *Organizational Research Methods* 16 (1), pp. 15–31. https://doi.org/10.1177/1094428112452151.

Gioia, Dennis A.; Thomas, James B. (1996): Identity, Image, and Issue Interpretation: Sensemaking During Strategic Change in Academia. In *Administrative Science Quarterly* 41 (3), pp. 370–403. https://doi.org/10.2307/2393936.

Gioia, Dennis A.; Thomas, James B.; Clark, Shawn M.; Chittipeddi, Kumar (1994): Symbolism and Strategic Change in Academia: The Dynamics of Sensemaking and Influence. In *Organization Science* 5 (3), pp. 363–383. https://doi.org/10.1287/orsc.5.3.363.

Gioia, Denny (2021): A Systematic Methodology for Doing Qualitative Research. In *The Journal of Applied Behavioral Science* 57 (1), pp. 20–29. https://doi.org/10.1177/0021886320982715.

Gioia, Denny; Corley, Kevin; Eisenhardt, Kathleen M.; Feldman, Martha; Langley, Ann; Lê, Jane et al. (2022): A Curated Debate: On Using "Templates" in Qualitative Research. In *Journal of Management Inquiry* 31 (3), pp. 231–252. https://doi.org/10.1177/10564926221098955.

Glaser, Barney G. (1978): Theoretical sensitivity. Advances in the methodology of grounded theory. Fourth edition. Mill Valley, California: Sociology Press.

Glaser, Barney G.; Strauss, Anselm L. (1967): The discovery of grounded theory. Strategies for qualitative research. New York, New York: Aldine.

Glaser, Barney G.; Strauss, Anselm L. (2012): The discovery of grounded theory. Aldine Transaction. (Original work published 1967).

Globerman, Steven; Shapiro, Daniel M. (1999): The Impact of Government Policies on Foreign Direct Investment: The Canadian Experience. In *Journal of International Business Studies* 30 (3), pp. 513–532. https://doi.org/10.1057/palgrave.jibs.8490081.

Gode, Dan; Mohanram, Partha (2003): Inferring the Cost of Capital Using the Ohlson–Juettner Model. In *Review of Accounting Studies* 8 (4), pp. 399–431. https://doi.org/10.1023/A:1027378728141.

Godfrey-Smith, Peter (2021): Theory and reality. An introduction to the philosophy of science. Second edition. Chicago, London: The University of Chicago Press.

Goetzmann, William; Li, Lingfeng; Rouwenhorst, K. G. (2005): Long-Term Global Market Correlations. In *The Journal of Business* 78 (1), pp. 1–38. https://doi.org/10.1086/426518.

Goodwin, Matthew (2019): Extreme Politics: The Four Waves of National Populism in the West. In Needham, Duncan; Weitzdörfer, Julius (Eds.): Extremes: Cambridge University Press, pp. 104–123.

Gordon, Joseph R.; Gordon, Myron J. (1997): The Finite Horizon Expected Return Model. In *Financial Analysts Journal* 53 (3), pp. 52–61. https://doi.org/10.2469/faj.v53.n3.2084.

Graham, Benjamin A. T.; Johnston, Noel P.; Kingsley, Allison F. (2018): Even Constrained Governments Take. In *Journal of Conflict Resolution* 62 (8), pp. 1784–1813. https://doi.org/10.1177/0022002717701181.

Grauer, Frederick L.; Litzenberger, Robert H.; Stehle, Richard E. (1976): Sharing rules and equilibrium in an international capital market under uncertainty. In *Journal of Financial Economics* 3 (3), pp. 233–256. https://doi.org/10.1016/0304-405X(76)90005-2.

Greene, Jennifer C.; Caracelli, Valerie J.; Graham, Wendy F. (1989): Toward a Conceptual Framework for Mixed-Method Evaluation Designs. In *Educational Evaluation and Policy Analysis* 11 (3), pp. 255–274. https://doi.org/10.3102/01623737011003255.

Greene, William (2019): Econometric analysis. Eighth global edition. Harlow, England, London, New York, New York: Pearson (Pearson series in economics).

Groves, Robert M.; Fowler, Floyd J.; Couper, Mick; Lepkowski, James M.; Singer, Eleanor; Tourangeau, Roger (2009): Survey methodology. Second edition. Hoboken, New Jersey: Wiley (Wiley series in survey methodology).

Grzymala-Busse, Anna (2019): Conclusion: The Global Forces of Populism. In *Polity* 51 (4), pp. 718–723. https://doi.org/10.1086/705322.

Guba, Egon G.; Lincoln, Yvonna S. (1989): Fourth generation evaluation. Newbury Park, California: SAGE Publications.

Guba, Egon G.; Lincoln, Yvonna S. (1994): Competing paradigms in qualitative research. In Denzin, Norman K.; Lincoln, Yvonna S. (Eds.): Handbook of qualitative research. Thousand Oaks, California: SAGE Publications, pp. 105–117.

Gubrium, Jaber F.; Holstein, James A. (Eds.) (2001): Handbook of interview research. Context and method. Thousand Oaks, California: SAGE.

Guest, Greg; Namey, Emily; Chen, Mario (2020): A simple method to assess and report thematic saturation in qualitative research. In *PloS one* 15 (5). https://doi.org/10.1371/journal.pone.0232076.

Guetterman, Timothy C.; Babchuk, Wayne A.; Howell Smith, Michelle C.; Stevens, Jared (2019): Contemporary Approaches to Mixed Methods–Grounded Theory Research: A Field-Based Analysis. In *Journal of Mixed Methods Research* 13 (2), pp. 179–195. https://doi.org/10.1177/1558689817710877.

Guiso, Luigi; Herrera, Helios; Morelli, Massimo; Sonno, Tommaso (2017): Demand and Supply of Populism. In *Innocenzo Gasparini Institute for Economic Research* (Working Paper 610).

Gungoraydinoglu, Ali; Çolak, Gönül; Öztekin, Özde (2017): Political environment, financial intermediation costs, and financing patterns. In *Journal of Corporate Finance* 44, pp. 167–192. https://doi.org/10.1016/j.jcorpfin.2017.03.007.

Guriev, Sergei; Papaioannou, Elias (2022): The Political Economy of Populism. In *Journal of Economic Literature* 60 (3), pp. 753–832. https://doi.org/10.1257/jel.20201595.

Hail, Luzi; Leuz, Christian (2006): International Differences in the Cost of Equity Capital: Do Legal Institutions and Securities Regulation Matter? In *Journal of Accounting Research* 44 (3), pp. 485–531. https://doi.org/10.1111/j.1475-679X.2006.00209.x.

Hall, John H.; Westerman, Wim (2011): Basic Risk Adjustment Techniques in Capital Budgeting. In Baker, H. K.; English, Philip (Eds.): Capital Budgeting Valuation. Financial analysis for today's investment projects. Hoboken, New Jersey: Wiley, pp. 217–241.

Hartwell, Christopher A. (2018): The impact of institutional volatility on financial volatility in transition economies. In *Journal of Comparative Economics* 46 (2), pp. 598–615. https://doi.org/10.1016/j.jce.2017.11.002.

Hartwell, Christopher A. (2022): Populism and financial markets. In *Finance Research Letters* 46, Article 102479, pp. 1–10. https://doi.org/10.1016/j.frl.2021.102479.

Hartwell, Christopher A.; Devinney, Timothy M. (2021): Populism, political risk, and pandemics: The challenges of political leadership for business in a post-COVID world. In *Journal of World Business* 56 (4), Article 101225, pp. 1–17. https://doi.org/10.1016/j.jwb.2021.101225.

Hartwell, Christopher A.; Devinney, Timothy M. (2024a): A Responsibility to Whom? Populism and Its Effects on Corporate Social Responsibility. In *Business & Society* 63 (2), pp. 300–340. https://doi.org/10.1177/00076503231163536.

Hartwell, Christopher A.; Devinney, Timothy M. (2024b): The demands of populism on business and the creation of "corporate political obligations". In *International Business Review* 33 (2), Article 102075. https://doi.org/10.1016/j.ibusrev.2022.102075.

Hashmi, M. A.; Guvenli, Turgut (1992): Importance of political risk assessment function in U.S. multinational corporations. In *Global Finance Journal* 3 (2), pp. 137–144. https://doi.org/10.1016/1044-0283(92)90009-A.

Hassan, Tarek A.; Hollander, Stephan; Van Lent, Laurence; Tahoun, Ahmed (2019): Firm-Level Political Risk: Measurement and Effects. In *The Quarterly Journal of Economics* 134 (4), pp. 2135–2202. https://doi.org/10.1093/qje/qjz021.

Hausman, Jerry A. (1978): Specification Tests in Econometrics. In *Econometrica* 46 (6), pp. 1251–1271. https://doi.org/10.2307/1913827.

Hawkins, Kirk A. (2009): Is Chávez Populist? In *Comparative Political Studies* 42 (8), pp. 1040–1067. https://doi.org/10.1177/0010414009331721.

Hawkins, Kirk A.; Castanho Silva, Bruno (2019): Textual analysis: big data approaches. In Hawkins, Kirk A.; Carlin, Ryan E.; Littvay, Levente; Rovira Kaltwasser, Cristóbal (Eds.): The ideational approach to populism. Concept, theory, and analysis. London, New York: Routledge (Extremism and democracy, 42), pp. 27–49.

Hawkins, Kirk A.; Rovira Kaltwasser, Cristóbal (2017): The Ideational Approach to Populism. In *Latin American Research Review* 52 (4), pp. 513–528. https://doi.org/10.25222/larr.85.

Hawkins, Kirk A.; Rovira Kaltwasser, Cristóbal (2019): Introduction: the ideational approach. In Hawkins, Kirk A.; Carlin, Ryan E.; Littvay, Levente; Rovira Kaltwasser, Cristóbal (Eds.): The ideational approach to populism. Concept, theory, and analysis. London, New York: Routledge (Extremism and democracy, 42), pp. 1–24.

Heigermoser, Robert (2020): Uncertainty about Future Economic Policy and Expected Stock Returns—International Evidence. In *SSRN Electronic Journal*. https://doi.org/10.2139/ssrn.3563556.

Heigermoser, Robert; Maier, Marcel (2020): Politics and Finance—Disagreement in National Parliaments and Firms' Cost of Equity Capital. In *SSRN Electronic Journal*. https://doi.org/10.2139/ssrn.3563542.

Heinisch, Reinhard C.; Werner, Annika (2019): Who Do Populist Radical Right Parties Stand for? Representative Claims, Claim Acceptance and Descriptive Representation in the Austrian FPÖ and German AfD. In *Representation* 55 (4), pp. 475–492. https://doi.org/10.1080/00344893.2019.1635196.

Heinö, Andreas J. (2017): Timbro authoritarian populism index 2017. Timbro. Available online at https://timbro.se/app/uploads/2018/01/populism-index-2017.pdf, checked on 2/12/2024.

Henisz, Witold J. (2000): The Institutional Environment for Economic Growth. In *Economics & Politics* 12 (1), pp. 1–31. https://doi.org/10.1111/1468-0343.00066.

Hennink, Monique M.; Kaiser, Bonnie N.; Marconi, Vincent C. (2017): Code Saturation Versus Meaning Saturation: How Many Interviews Are Enough? In *Qualitative health research* 27 (4), pp. 591–608. https://doi.org/10.1177/1049732316665344.

Hesse-Biber, Sharlene N. (2015): Mixed Methods Research: The "Thing-ness" Problem. In *Qualitative health research* 25 (6), pp. 775–788. https://doi.org/10.1177/104973231 55805.

Hesse-Biber, Sharlene N. (2022): Mixed Methods Research Designs in Qualitatively Driven Research. In Flick, Uwe (Ed.): The SAGE Handbook of Qualitative Research Design. London: SAGE Publications.

Hill, Claire A. (2003): How Investors React to Political Risk. In *SSRN Electronic Journal*. https://doi.org/10.2139/ssrn.333021.

Hirose, Mariko; Creswell, John W. (2023): Applying Core Quality Criteria of Mixed Methods Research to an Empirical Study. In *Journal of Mixed Methods Research* 17 (1), pp. 12–28. https://doi.org/10.1177/15586898221086346.

Ho, Kung-Cheng; Lee, Shih-Cheng; Lin, Chien-Ting; Yu, Min-Teh (2017): A Comparative Analysis of Accounting-Based Valuation Models. In *Journal of Accounting, Auditing & Finance* 32 (4), pp. 561–575. https://doi.org/10.1177/0148558X15623043.

Holton, Glyn A. (2004): Defining Risk. In *Financial Analysts Journal* 60 (6), pp. 19–25. https://doi.org/10.2469/faj.v60.n6.2669.

Hooghe, Liesbet; Bakker, Ryan; Brigevich, Anna; De Vries, Catherine; Edwards, Erica; Marks, Gary et al. (2010): Reliability and validity of the 2002 and 2006 Chapel Hill expert surveys on party positioning. In *European Journal of Political Research* 49 (5), pp. 687–703. https://doi.org/10.1111/j.1475-6765.2009.01912.x.

Hopf, Christel (2004): Qualitative Interviews: An Overview. In Flick, Uwe; Kardoff, Ernst von; Steinke, Ines (Eds.): A companion to qualitative research. Los Angeles, California: SAGE, pp. 203–209.

Hou, Kewei; Van Dijk, Mathijs A.; Zhang, Yinglei (2012): The implied cost of capital: A new approach. In *Journal of Accounting and Economics* 53 (3), pp. 504–526. https://doi.org/10.1016/j.jacceco.2011.12.001.

Houston, Joel F.; Lin, Chen; Xie, Wensi (2015): Shareholder Protection and the Cost of Capital. In *SSRN Electronic Journal*. https://doi.org/10.2139/ssrn.2661292.

Howell, Llewellyn D. (2014): Evaluating Political Risk Forecasting Models: What Works? In *Thunderbird International Business Review* 56 (4), pp. 305–316. https://doi.org/10.1002/tie.21635.

Huang, Tao; Wu, Fei; Yu, Jin; Zhang, Bohui (2015): Political risk and dividend policy: Evidence from international political crises. In *Journal of International Business Studies* 46 (5), pp. 574–595. https://doi.org/10.1057/jibs.2015.2.

Huber, Robert A.; Schimpf, Christian H. (2017): On the Distinct Effects of Left-Wing and Right-Wing Populism on Democratic Quality. In *Politics and Governance* 5 (4), pp. 146–165. https://doi.org/10.17645/pag.v5i4.919.

Hunger, Sophia; Paxton, Fred (2022): What's in a buzzword? A systematic review of the state of populism research in political science. In *Political Science Research and Methods* 10 (3), pp. 617–633. https://doi.org/10.1017/psrm.2021.44.

Husted, Lucas; Rogers, John; Sun, Bo (2020): Monetary policy uncertainty. In *Journal of Monetary Economics* 115, pp. 20–36. https://doi.org/10.1016/j.jmoneco.2019.07.009.

Hutzschenreuter, Thomas; Matt, Tanja; Kleindienst, Ingo (2020): Going subnational: A literature review and research agenda. In *Journal of World Business* 55 (4), Article 101076, pp. 1–14. https://doi.org/10.1016/j.jwb.2020.101076.

Ince, Ozgur S.; Porter, R. B. (2006): Individual Equity Return Data from Thomson Datastream: Handle with Care! In *Journal of Financial Research* 29 (4), pp. 463–479. https://doi.org/10.1111/j.1475-6803.2006.00189.x.

Inglehart, Ronald F.; Norris, Pippa (2016): Trump, Brexit, and the Rise of Populism: Economic Have-Nots and Cultural Backlash. In *Cambridge University Press*. https://doi.org/10.2139/ssrn.2818659.

Ivankova, Nataliya V.; Creswell, John W.; Stick, Sheldon L. (2006): Using Mixed-Methods Sequential Explanatory Design: From Theory to Practice. In *Field Methods* 18 (1), pp. 3–20. https://doi.org/10.1177/1525822X05282260.

Jagers, Jan; Walgrave, Stefaan (2007): Populism as political communication style: An empirical study of political parties' discourse in Belgium. In *European Journal of Political Research* 46 (3), pp. 319–345. https://doi.org/10.1111/j.1475-6765.2006.00690.x.

Jarvis, Darryl; Griffiths, Martin (2007): Learning to Fly: The Evolution of Political Risk Analysis. In *Global Society* 21 (1), pp. 5–21. https://doi.org/10.1080/13600820601116435.

Jenkins, David (2023): Understanding and evaluating populist strategy. In *Philosophy & Social Criticism*. https://doi.org/10.1177/01914537231155171.

Jenner, Brandy M.; Myers, Kit C. (2019): Intimacy, rapport, and exceptional disclosure: a comparison of in-person and mediated interview contexts. In *International Journal of Social Research Methodology* 22 (2), pp. 165–177. https://doi.org/10.1080/13645579.

Jens, Candace E. (2017): Political uncertainty and investment: Causal evidence from U.S. gubernatorial elections. In *Journal of Financial Economics* 124 (3), pp. 563–579. https://doi.org/10.1016/j.jfineco.2016.01.034.

Jiang, Xiaoquan; Lee, Bon-Soo (2005): An Empirical Test of the Accounting-Based Residual Income Model and the Traditional Dividend Discount Model. In *The Journal of Business* 78 (4), pp. 1465–1504. https://doi.org/10.1086/430866.

John, Anna; Lawton, Thomas C. (2018): International Political Risk Management: Perspectives, Approaches and Emerging Agendas. In *International Journal of Manage-ment Reviews* 20 (4), pp. 847–879. https://doi.org/10.1111/ijmr.12166.

Johnson, R. B.; Onwuegbuzie, Anthony J. (2004): Mixed Methods Research: A Research Paradigm Whose Time Has Come. In *Educational Researcher* 33 (7), pp. 14–26. https://doi.org/10.3102/0013189X033007014.

Johnson, R. B.; Onwuegbuzie, Anthony J.; Turner, Lisa A. (2007): Toward a Definition of Mixed Methods Research. In *Journal of Mixed Methods Research* 1 (2), pp. 112–133. https://doi.org/10.1177/1558689806298224.

Jolly, Seth; Bakker, Ryan; Hooghe, Liesbet; Marks, Gary; Polk, Jonathan; Rovny, Jan et al. (2022): Chapel Hill Expert Survey trend file, 1999–2019. In *Electoral Studies* 75, Article 102420. https://doi.org/10.1016/j.electstud.2021.102420.

Judis, John B. (2016): The populist explosion. How the great recession transformed American and European politics. New York: Columbia Global Reports.

Julio, Brandon; Yook, Youngsuk (2012): Political Uncertainty and Corporate Investment Cycles. In *The Journal of Finance* 67 (1), pp. 45–83. https://doi.org/10.1111/j.1540-6261.2011.01707.x.

Julio, Brandon; Yook, Youngsuk (2016): Policy uncertainty, irreversibility, and cross-border flows of capital. In *Journal of International Economics* 103, pp. 13–26. https://doi.org/10.1016/j.jinteco.2016.08.004.

Juon, Andreas; Bochsler, Daniel (2020): Hurricane or fresh breeze? Disentangling the populist effect on the quality of democracy. In *European Political Science Review* 12 (3), pp. 391–408. https://doi.org/10.1017/S1755773920000259.

Kaczynski, Dan; Salmona, Michelle; Smith, Tom (2014): Qualitative research in finance. In *Australian Journal of Management* 39 (1), pp. 127–135. https://doi.org/10.1177/0312896212469611.

Kaiser, Karen (2012): Protecting Confidentiality. In Gubrium, Jaber F.; Holstein, James A.; Marvasti, Amir; McKinney, Karyn (Eds.): The SAGE Handbook of Interview Research: The Complexity of the Craft. Thousand Oaks, California: SAGE Publications, pp. 457–462.

Katsambekis, Giorgos (2022): Constructing 'the people' of populism: a critique of the ideational approach from a discursive perspective. In *Journal of Political Ideologies* 27 (1), pp. 53–74. https://doi.org/10.1080/13569317.2020.1844372.

Kaviani, Mahsa S.; Kryzanowski, Lawrence; Maleki, Hosein; Savor, Pavel (2020): Policy uncertainty and corporate credit spreads. In *Journal of Financial Economics* 138 (3), pp. 838–865. https://doi.org/10.1016/j.jfineco.2020.07.001.

Kefford, Glenn; Moffitt, Benjamin; Werner, Annika (2022): Populist Attitudes: Bringing Together Ideational and Communicative Approaches. In *Political Studies* 70 (4), pp. 1006–1027. https://doi.org/10.1177/0032321721997741.

Khan, Shahid N. (2014): Qualitative Research Method: Grounded Theory. In *International Journal of Business and Management* 9 (11), pp. 224–233. https://doi.org/10.5539/ijbm.v9n11p224.

Kirby, Chris (2019): Estimating the Cost-of-Equity Capital Using Empirical Asset Pricing Models. In *International Review of Finance* 19 (1), pp. 105–154. https://doi.org/10.1111/irfi.12179.

Kirikkaleli, Dervis; Torun, Melike; Sowah, James K. (2021): The Effect of Domestic Risks and Arab Spring on Economic Risk in Northern African Countries: Findings From the First- and Second-Generation Panel Approaches. In *The Review of Black Political Economy* 48 (3), pp. 328–348. https://doi.org/10.1177/0034644620946420.

Kivunja, Charles; Kuyini, Ahmed B. (2017): Understanding and Applying Research Paradigms in Educational Contexts. In *International Journal of Higher Education* 6 (5), pp. 26–42. https://doi.org/10.5430/ijhe.v6n5p26.

Knight, Frank H. (1921): Risk, uncertainty and profit. Boston, Massachusetts: Houghton Mifflin.

Kobrin, Stephen J. (1979): Political Risk: A Review and Reconsideration. In *Journal of International Business Studies* 10 (1), pp. 67–80. https://doi.org/10.1057/palgrave.jibs.

Kotabe, Masaaki; Kothari, Tanvi (2016): Emerging market multinational companies' evolutionary paths to building a competitive advantage from emerging markets to developed countries. In *Journal of World Business* 51 (5), pp. 729–743. https://doi.org/10.1016/j.jwb.2016.07.010.

Koutmos, Gregory; Booth, G. G. (1995): Asymmetric volatility transmission in international stock markets. In *Journal of International Money and Finance* 14 (6), pp. 747–762. https://doi.org/10.1016/0261-5606(95)00031-3.

Kraemer, Christian; Sim, Tom (2024): Deutsche Bank CEO warns rise of far right in Germany risks investment. Reuters. Available online at https://www.reuters.com/markets/europe/deutsche-bank-ceo-warns-rise-far-right-germany-risks-investment-2024-01-29/, checked on 1/4/2024.

Kriesi, Hanspeter; Grande, Edgar; Lachat, Romain; Dolezal, Martin; Bornschier, Simon; Frey, Timotheos (2012): West European Politics in the Age of Globalization: Cambridge University Press.

Kryzanowski, Lawrence; Rahman, Abdul H. (2009): Degrees-of-freedom problem and implied cost of equity capital. In *Finance Research Letters* 6 (3), pp. 171–178. https://doi.org/10.1016/j.frl.2009.03.002.

La Porta, Rafael; Lopez-De-Silanes, Florencio; Shleifer, Andrei; Vishny, Robert W. (1997): Trust in Large Organizations. In *The American economic review* 87 (2), pp. 333–338.

Laclau, Ernesto (2005): On populist reason. London: Verso Books.

Langley, Ann (1999): Strategies for Theorizing from Process Data. In *The Academy of Management Review* 24 (4), pp. 691–710. https://doi.org/10.2307/259349.

Larocque, Stephannie A.; Lyle, Matthew R. (2017): Implied Cost of Equity Capital Estimates as Predictors of Accounting Returns and Stock Returns. In *Journal of Financial Reporting* 2 (1), pp. 69–93. https://doi.org/10.2308/jfir-51874.

Laver, Michael (2014): Measuring Policy Positions in Political Space. In *Annual Review of Political Science* 17 (1), pp. 207–223. https://doi.org/10.1146/annurev-polisci-061413-041905.

Laver, Michael; Hunt, William B. (1992): Policy and party competition. New York: Routledge.

Lee, Charles M.; So, Eric C.; Wang, Charles C. Y. (2011): Evaluating Implied Cost of Capital Estimates. In *SSRN Electronic Journal*. https://doi.org/10.2139/ssrn.1653940.

Lee, Cheng-Few (1991): Markowitz, Miller, and Sharpe: The First Nobel Laureates in Finance. In *Review of Quantitative Finance and Accounting* 1 (2), pp. 209–228. https://doi.org/10.1007/BF02409673.

Lee, Junyong; Lee, Kyounghun; Oh, Frederick D. (2023): International portfolio diversification and the home bias puzzle. In *Research in International Business and Finance* 64, Article 101807, pp. 1–24. https://doi.org/10.1016/j.ribaf.2022.101807.

Lehkonen, Heikki (2015): Stock Market Integration and the Global Financial Crisis. In *Review of Finance* 19 (5), pp. 2039–2094. https://doi.org/10.1093/rof/rfu039.

Lehmann, Pola; Franzmann, Simon; Burst, Tobias; Matthieß, Theres; Regel, Sven; Riethmüller, Felicia et al. (2023): Manifesto Project Dataset. https://doi.org/10.25522/manifesto.mpds.2023a.

Lei, Lijun; Luo, Yan (2023): Political/Policy Uncertainty, Corporate Disclosure, and Information Asymmetry. In *Accounting Perspectives* 22 (1), pp. 87–110. https://doi.org/10.1111/1911-3838.12317.

Levers, Merry-Jo D. (2013): Philosophical Paradigms, Grounded Theory, and Perspectives on Emergence. In *SAGE Open* 3 (4). https://doi.org/10.1177/2158244013517243.

Levi, Maurice D. (2006): International finance. Fourth edition. London, New York, New York: Routledge Taylor and Francis Group. Available online at http://www.loc.gov/catdir/enhancements/fy0650/2004015325-d.html.

Li, Kevin K.; Mohanram, Partha (2014): Evaluating cross-sectional forecasting models for implied cost of capital. In *Review of Accounting Studies* 19 (3), pp. 1152–1185. https://doi.org/10.1007/s11142-014-9282-y.

Li, Tongxia; Lu, Chun; Si, Ieong C.; Zhao, Zucheng (2022): Employment protection and the cost of equity capital: Evidence from wrongful discharge laws. In *Finance Research Letters* 47, Article 102765, pp. 1–10. https://doi.org/10.1016/j.frl.2022.102765.

Li, Xiao-Ming (2017): New evidence on economic policy uncertainty and equity premium. In *Pacific-Basin Finance Journal* 46, pp. 41–56. https://doi.org/10.1016/j.pacfin.2017.

Li, Xiaorong; Luo, Jingbo; Chan, Kam C. (2018): Political uncertainty and the cost of equity capital. In *Finance Research Letters* 26, pp. 215–222. https://doi.org/10.1016/j.frl.2018.01.009.

Li, Yan; Ng, David T.-C.; Swaminathan, Bhaskaran (2012): Predicting Market Returns Using Aggregate Implied Cost of Capital. In *SSRN Electronic Journal*. https://doi.org/10.2139/ssrn.1787285.

Ligita, Titan; Harvey, Nichole; Wicking, Kristin; Nurjannah, Intansari; Francis, Karen (2020): A practical example of using theoretical sampling throughout a grounded theory study. In *Qualitative Research Journal* 20 (1), pp. 116–126. https://doi.org/10.1108/QRJ-07-2019-0059.

Lincoln, Yvonna S.; Guba, Egon G. (1985): Naturalistic inquiry. Newbury Park, California: SAGE.

Lintner, John (1965): Security Prices, Risk, and Maximal Gains From Diversification. In *The Journal of Finance* 20 (4), pp. 587–615. https://doi.org/10.2307/2977249.

Liu, Laura X.; Shu, Haibing; Wei, K.C. J. (2017): The impacts of political uncertainty on asset prices: Evidence from the Bo scandal in China. In *Journal of Financial Economics* 125 (2), pp. 286–310. https://doi.org/10.1016/j.jfineco.2017.05.011.

Longin, François; Solnik, Bruno H. (2001): Extreme Correlation of International Equity Markets. In *The Journal of Finance* 56 (2), pp. 649–676. https://doi.org/10.1111/0022-1082.00340.

López-Duarte, Cristina; Vidal-Suárez, Marta M. (2010): External uncertainty and entry mode choice: Cultural distance, political risk and language diversity. In *International Business Review* 19 (6), pp. 575–588. https://doi.org/10.1016/j.ibusrev.2010.03.007.

Magnani, Giovanna; Gioia, Denny (2023): Using the Gioia Methodology in international business and entrepreneurship research. In *International Business Review* 32 (2), Article 102097, pp. 1–22. https://doi.org/10.1016/j.ibusrev.2022.102097.

Maiti, Moinak (2020): A Critical Review On Evolution Of Risk Factors And Factor Models. In *Journal of Economic Surveys* 34 (1), pp. 175–184. https://doi.org/10.1111/joes.12344.

Mangram, Myles E. (2013): A Simplified Perspective of the Markowitz Portfolio Theory. In *Global Journal of Business Research* 7 (1), pp. 59–70.

March, Luke (2017): Left and right populism compared: The British case. In *The British Journal of Politics and International Relations* 19 (2), pp. 282–303. https://doi.org/10.1177/1369148117701753.

March, Luke (2019): Textual analysis: the UK party system. In Hawkins, Kirk A.; Carlin, Ryan E.; Littvay, Levente; Rovira Kaltwasser, Cristóbal (Eds.): The ideational approach to populism. Concept, theory, and analysis. London, New York: Routledge (Extremism and democracy, 42), pp. 49–67.

March, Luke; Mudde, Cas (2005): What's Left of the Radical Left? The European Radical Left After 1989: Decline and Mutation. In *Comparative European Politics* 3 (1), pp. 23–49. https://doi.org/10.1057/palgrave.cep.6110052.

Margalit, Yotam (2019): Economic Insecurity and the Causes of Populism, Reconsidered. In *Journal of Economic Perspectives* 33 (4), pp. 152–170. https://doi.org/10.1257/jep.33.4.152.

Markowitz, Harry (1952): Portfolio Selection. In *The Journal of Finance* 7 (1), pp. 77–91. https://doi.org/10.2307/2975974.

Mayring, Philipp (2022): Qualitative content analysis. A step-by-step guide. Los Angeles, London, New Delhi, Singapore, Washington DC, Melbourne: SAGE.

McGregor, Sue L.; Murnane, Jennifer A. (2010): Paradigm, methodology and method: intellectual integrity in consumer scholarship. In *International Journal of Consumer Studies* 34 (4), pp. 419–427. https://doi.org/10.1111/j.1470-6431.2010.00883.x.

Meijers, Maurits J.; Zaslove, Andrej (2020): Populism and Political Parties Expert Survey 2018 (POPPA). https://doi.org/10.7910/DVN/8NEL7B.

Meijers, Maurits J.; Zaslove, Andrej (2021): Measuring Populism in Political Parties: Appraisal of a New Approach. In *Comparative Political Studies* 54 (2), pp. 372–407. https://doi.org/10.1177/0010414020938081.

Meldrum, Duncan H. (2000): Country risk and foreign direct investment. In *Business economics* 35 (1), pp. 33–40.

Merton, Robert C. (1973): An Intertemporal Capital Asset Pricing Model. In *Econometrica* 41 (5), pp. 867–887. https://doi.org/10.2307/1913811.

Meschi, Pierre-Xavier (2005): Environmental uncertainty and survival of international joint ventures: the case of political and economic risk in emerging countries. In *European Management Review* 2 (2), pp. 143–152. https://doi.org/10.1057/palgrave.emr.1500037.

Meyer, Klaus E.; Estrin, Saul; Bhaumik, Sumon K.; Peng, Mike W. (2009): Institutions, resources, and entry strategies in emerging economies. In *Strategic Management Journal* 30 (1), pp. 61–80. https://doi.org/10.1002/smj.720.

Meyer, Klaus E.; Nguyen, Hung V. (2005): Foreign Investment Strategies and Sub-national Institutions in Emerging Markets: Evidence from Vietnam. In *Journal of Management Studies* 42 (1), pp. 63–93. https://doi.org/10.1111/j.1467-6486.2005.00489.x.

Mian, Atif; Sufi, Amir; Trebbi, Francesco (2014): Resolving Debt Overhang: Political Constraints in the Aftermath of Financial Crises. In *American Economic Journal: Macroeconomics* 6 (2), pp. 1–28. https://doi.org/10.1257/mac.6.2.1.

Mikhaylov, Slava; Laver, Michael; Benoit, Kenneth R. (2012): Coder Reliability and Misclassification in the Human Coding of Party Manifestos. In *Political Analysis* 20 (1), pp. 78–91. https://doi.org/10.1093/pan/mpr047.

Miller, Kent D. (1992): A Framework for Integrated Risk Management in International Business. In *Journal of International Business Studies* 23 (2), pp. 311–331. https://doi.org/10.1057/palgrave.jibs.8490270.

Mishra, Dev R. (2023): Firm-level political risk and implied cost of equity capital. In *International Review of Finance* 23 (3), pp. 615–644. https://doi.org/10.1111/irfi.12411.

Mishra, Dev R.; O'Brien, Thomas J. (2019): Fama-French, CAPM, and implied cost of equity. In *Journal of Economics and Business* 101, pp. 73–85. https://doi.org/10.1016/j.jeconbus.2018.08.002.

Moffitt, Benjamin (2016): The Global Rise of Populism. Performance, Political Style and Representation. In *Stanford University Press*. https://doi.org/10.11126/stanford/9780804796132.001.0001.

Morse, Janice M.; Niehaus, Linda (2009): Mixed method design. Principles and procedures. Walnut Creek, California: Left Coast Press (Developing qualitative inquiry, 4).

Mossin, Jan (1966): Equilibrium in a Capital Asset Market. In *Econometrica* 34 (4), pp. 768–783. https://doi.org/10.2307/1910098.

Mounk, Yascha (2018): The Undemocratic Dilemma. In *Journal of Democracy* 29 (2), pp. 98–112. https://doi.org/10.1353/jod.2018.0030.

Mudde, Cas (2004): The Populist Zeitgeist. In *Government and Opposition* 39 (4), pp. 541–563. https://doi.org/10.1111/j.1477-7053.2004.00135.x.

Mudde, Cas (2009): Populist Radical Right Parties in Europe. In *Cambridge University Press*. https://doi.org/10.1017/CBO9780511492037.

Mudde, Cas (2016): Europe's Populist Surge: A Long Time in the Making. In *Foreign Affairs* 95 (6), pp. 25–30.

Mudde, Cas (2017): Populism: An Ideational Approach. In Rovira Kaltwasser, Cristóbal; Taggart, Paul; Espejo, Paulina O.; Ostiguy, Pierre (Eds.): The Oxford handbook of populism. Oxford: Oxford University Press, pp. 27–47.

Mudde, Cas; Rovira Kaltwasser, Cristóbal (2012): Populism in Europe and the Americas. In *Cambridge University Press*. https://doi.org/10.1017/CBO9781139152365.

Mudde, Cas; Rovira Kaltwasser, Cristóbal (2013): Exclusionary vs. Inclusionary Populism: Comparing Contemporary Europe and Latin America. In *Government and Opposition* 48 (2), pp. 147–174. https://doi.org/10.1017/gov.2012.11.

Mudde, Cas; Rovira Kaltwasser, Cristóbal (2014): Populism and Political Leadership. In Rhodes, R. A. W.; ' T Hart, Paul (Eds.): The Oxford Handbook of Political Leadership. First edition. Oxford: Oxford University Press (Oxford handbooks in politics & international relations).

Mueller, Lukas; Bartel, Merlin; Schiereck, Dirk (2023): Europe's gone "right"—A comparative study of stock market reactions to populist success in Sweden and Italy. In *Finance Research Letters* 55, Article 103829, pp. 1–9. https://doi.org/10.1016/j.frl.2023.103829.

Müller, Jan-Werner (2017): What is populism? London, United Kingdom: University of Pennsylvania Press.

Mwita, Kelvin (2022): Factors to consider when choosing data collection methods. In *International Journal of Research in Business and Social Science* 11 (5), pp. 532–538. https://doi.org/10.20525/ijrbs.v11i5.1842.

Netjes, Catherine E.; Binnema, Harmen A. (2007): The salience of the European integration issue: Three data sources compared. In *Electoral Studies* 26 (1), pp. 39–49. https://doi.org/10.1016/j.electstud.2006.04.007.

Neuendorf, Kimberly A. (2017): The Content Analysis Guidebook. Thousand Oaks, California: SAGE Publications.

Norris, Pippa (2020a): Global Party Survey—Methods. Global Party Survey. Available online at https://www.globalpartysurvey.org/methods, updated on 1/30/2020, checked on 2/6/2024.

Norris, Pippa (2020b): Global Party Survey Questionnaire. Harvard Dataverse, updated on 2020, checked on 2/14/2024.

Norris, Pippa (2020c): Measuring populism worldwide. In *Party Politics* 26 (6), pp. 697–717. https://doi.org/10.1177/1354068820927686.

Norris, Pippa; Inglehart, Ronald F. (2019): Cultural Backlash. Trump, Brexit and Authoritarian-Populism: Cambridge University Press.

Oetzel, Jennifer (2005): Smaller may be beautiful but is it more risky? Assessing and managing political and economic risk in Costa Rica. In *International Business Review* 14 (6), pp. 765–790. https://doi.org/10.1016/j.ibusrev.2005.09.002.

O'Hanlon, John; Peasnell, Ken (2002): Residual Income and Value-Creation: The Missing Link. In *Review of Accounting Studies* 7 (2/3), pp. 229–245. https://doi.org/10.1023/A:1020230203952.

Ohlson, James A. (1995): Earnings, Book Values, and Dividends in Equity Valuation. In *Contemporary Accounting Research* 11 (2), pp. 661–687. https://doi.org/10.1111/j.1911-3846.1995.tb00461.x.

Ohlson, James A.; Juettner-Nauroth, Beate E. (2005): Expected EPS and EPS Growth as Determinants of Value. In *Review of Accounting Studies* 10 (2–3), pp. 349–365. https://doi.org/10.1007/s11142-005-1535-3.

Okesina, Musiliu (2020): A Critical Review of the Relationship between Paradigm, Methodology, Design and Method in Research. In *IOSR Journal of Research & Method in Education* 10 (3), pp. 57–68. https://doi.org/10.9790/7388-1003015768.

Oliver, J. E.; Wood, Thomas J. (2014): Conspiracy Theories and the Paranoid Style(s) of Mass Opinion. In *American Journal of Political Science* 58 (4), pp. 952–966. https://doi.org/10.1111/ajps.12084.

Onwuegbuzie, Anthony J. (2012): Introduction. In *International Journal of Multiple Research Approaches* 6 (3), pp. 192–219. https://doi.org/10.5172/mra.2012.6.3.192.

OpenAI (2022): Introducing Whisper. Available online at https://openai.com/research/whisper, checked on 2/14/2024.

Ostiguy, Pierre; Panizza, Francisco; Moffitt, Benjamin (2020a): Introduction. In Ostiguy, Pierre; Panizza, Francisco; Moffitt, Benjamin (Eds.): Populism in Global Perspective. A performative and discursive approach. New York, London: Routledge (Conceptualising comparative politics, 13), pp. 1–18.

Ostiguy, Pierre; Panizza, Francisco; Moffitt, Benjamin (2020b): Reflections on the Lessons Learned. In Ostiguy, Pierre; Panizza, Francisco; Moffitt, Benjamin (Eds.): Populism in Global Perspective. A performative and discursive approach. New York, London: Routledge (Conceptualising comparative politics, 13), pp. 255–275.

Osuna, José J. O. (2021): From chasing populists to deconstructing populism: A new multidimensional approach to understanding and comparing populism. In *European Journal of Political Research* 60 (4), pp. 829–853. https://doi.org/10.1111/1475-6765.12428.

Osuna, José J. O.; Rama, José (2022): Recalibrating populism measurement tools: Methodological inconsistencies and challenges to our understanding of the relationship between the supply- and demand-side of populism. In *Frontiers in sociology* 7, Article 970043. https://doi.org/10.3389/fsoc.2022.970043.

Oswald, Michael (Ed.) (2022): The Palgrave Handbook of Populism. Cham: Springer International Publishing.

Otjes, Simon; Louwerse, Tom (2015): Populists in Parliament: Comparing Left-Wing and Right-Wing Populism in the Netherlands. In *Political Studies* 63 (1), pp. 60–79. https://doi.org/10.1111/1467-9248.12089.

Palinkas, Lawrence A.; Horwitz, Sarah M.; Green, Carla A.; Wisdom, Jennifer P.; Duan, Naihua; Hoagwood, Kimberly (2015): Purposeful Sampling for Qualitative Data Collection and Analysis in Mixed Method Implementation Research. In *Administration and policy in mental health* 42 (5), pp. 533–544. https://doi.org/10.1007/s10488-013-0528-y.

Pan, Wei-Fong; Wang, Xinjie; Xiao, Yaqing; Xu, Weike; Zhang, Jinfan (2024): The effect of economic and political uncertainty on sovereign CDS spreads. In *Inter-national Review of Economics & Finance* 89, pp. 143–155. https://doi.org/10.1016/j.iref.2023.07.110.

Pappas, Takis S. (2016): Modern Populism: Research Advances, Conceptual and Methodological Pitfalls, and the Minimal Definition. In Pappas, Takis S. (Ed.): Oxford Research Encyclopedia of Politics: Oxford University Press.

Pástor, Ľuboš; Sinha, Meenakshi; Swaminathan, Bhaskaran (2008): Estimating the Intertemporal Risk–Return Tradeoff Using the Implied Cost of Capital. In *The Journal of Finance* 63 (6), pp. 2859–2897. https://doi.org/10.1111/j.1540-6261.2008.01415.x.

Pástor, Ľuboš; Veronesi, Pietro (2012): Uncertainty about Government Policy and Stock Prices. In *The Journal of Finance* 67 (4), pp. 1219–1264. https://doi.org/10.1111/j.1540-6261.2012.01746.x.

Pástor, Ľuboš; Veronesi, Pietro (2013): Political uncertainty and risk premia. In *Journal of Financial Economics* 110 (3), pp. 520–545. https://doi.org/10.1016/j.jfineco.2013.08.007.

Pauwels, Teun (2017): Measuring Populism: A Review Of Current Approaches. In Heinisch, Reinhard C.; Holtz-Bacha, Christina; Mazzoleni, Oscar (Eds.): Political Populism: Nomos Verlagsgesellschaft, pp. 123–136.

Peng, Mike W.; Wang, Denis Y. L.; Jiang, Yi (2008): An institution-based view of international business strategy: a focus on emerging economies. In *Journal of International Business Studies* 39 (5), pp. 920–936. https://doi.org/10.1057/palgrave.jibs.8400377.

Penman, Stephen H. (2005): Discussion of "On Accounting-Based Valuation Formulae" and "Expected EPS and EPS Growth has Determinants of Value". In *Review of Accounting Studies* 10 (2–3), pp. 367–378. https://doi.org/10.1007/s11142-005-1536-2.

Penman, Stephen H.; Sougiannis, Theodore (1998): A Comparison of Dividend, Cash Flow, and Earnings Approaches to Equity Valuation. In *Contemporary Accounting Research* 15 (3), pp. 343–383. https://doi.org/10.1111/j.1911-3846.1998.tb00564.x.

Persson, Torsten; Tabellini, Guido (2006): Democracy and Development: The Devil in the Details. In *American Economic Review* 96 (2), pp. 319–324. https://doi.org/10.1257/000282806777212396.

Peters, B. G.; Pierre, Jon (2020): A typology of populism: understanding the different forms of populism and their implications. In *Democratization* 27 (6), pp. 928–946. https://doi.org/10.1080/13510347.2020.1751615.

Petrović, Nikola; Raos, Višeslav; Fila, Filip (2023): Centrist and Radical Right Populists in Central and Eastern Europe: Divergent Visions of History and the EU. In *Journal of Contemporary European Studies* 31 (2), pp. 268–290. https://doi.org/10.1080/14782804.2022.2051000.

Pierru, Axel; Babusiaux, Denis (2011): Financing Mix and Project Valuation: Alternative Methods and Possible Adjustments. In Baker, H. K.; English, Philip (Eds.): Capital Budgeting Valuation. Financial analysis for today's investment projects. Hoboken, New Jersey: Wiley, pp. 381–402.

Pilbeam, Keith (2018): Finance & financial markets. Fourth edition. London: Palgrave Macmillan Education.

Polk, Jonathan; Rovny, Jan (2017): Anti-Elite/Establishment Rhetoric and Party Positioning on European Integration. In *Chinese Political Science Review* 2 (3), pp. 356–371. https://doi.org/10.1007/s41111-017-0068-9.

Pop-Eleches, Grigore (2010): Throwing out the Bums: Protest Voting and Unorthodox Parties after Communism. In *World Politics* 62 (2), pp. 221–260. https://doi.org/10.1017/S0043887110000043.

Pukthuanthong, Kuntara; Roll, Richard (2009): Global market integration: An alternative measure and its application. In *Journal of Financial Economics* 94 (2), pp. 214–232. https://doi.org/10.1016/j.jfineco.2008.12.004.

Radelet, Steven; Sachs, Jeffrey D. (1998): The Onset of the East Asian Financial Crisis. In *National Bureau of Economic Research* Working Paper No. w6680.

Redl, Chris (2020): Uncertainty matters: Evidence from close elections. In *Journal of International Economics* 124, Article 103296, pp. 1–16. https://doi.org/10.1016/j.jinteco.2020.103296.

Reinhart, Carmen M.; Rogoff, Kenneth S. (2004): Serial Default and the "Paradox" of Rich-to-Poor Capital Flows. In *American Economic Review* 94 (2), pp. 53–58. https://doi.org/10.1257/0002828041302370.

Rjiba, Hatem; Saadi, Samir; Boubaker, Sabri; Ding, Xiaoya (2021): Annual report readability and the cost of equity capital. In *Journal of Corporate Finance* 67, Article 101902, pp. 1–25. https://doi.org/10.1016/j.jcorpfin.2021.101902.

Roberts, Kenneth M. (1995): Neoliberalism and the Transformation of Populism in Latin America: The Peruvian Case. In *World Politics* 48 (1), pp. 82–116. https://doi.org/10.1353/wp.1995.0004.

Roberts, Kenneth M. (2017): Populism and Political Parties. In Rovira Kaltwasser, Cristóbal; Taggart, Paul; Espejo, Paulina O.; Ostiguy, Pierre (Eds.): The Oxford handbook of populism. Oxford: Oxford University Press, pp. 287–304.

Robock, Stefan H. (1971): Political risk-identification and assessment. In *Columbia Journal of world business* 6 (4), pp. 6–20.

Rodrik, Dani (2018a): Is Populism Necessarily Bad Economics? In *AEA Papers and Proceedings* 108, pp. 196–199. https://doi.org/10.1257/pandp.20181122.

Rodrik, Dani (2018b): Populism and the economics of globalization. In *Journal of International Business Policy* 1 (1–2), pp. 12–33. https://doi.org/10.1057/s42214-018-0001-4.

Rodrik, Dani; Wacziarg, Romain (2005): Do Democratic Transitions Produce Bad Economic Outcomes? In *American Economic Review* 95 (2), pp. 50–55. https://doi.org/10.1257/000282805774670059.

Röell, Christiaan; Osabutey, Ellis; Rodgers, Peter; Arndt, Felix; Khan, Zaheer; Tarba, Shlomo (2022): Managing socio-political risk at the subnational level: Lessons from MNE subsidiaries in Indonesia. In *Journal of World Business* 57 (3), Article 101312. https://doi.org/10.1016/j.jwb.2022.101312.

Rooduijn, Matthijs (2019): State of the field: How to study populism and adjacent topics? A plea for both more and less focus. In *European Journal of Political Research* 58 (1), pp. 362–372. https://doi.org/10.1111/1475-6765.12314.

Rooduijn, Matthijs; Pauwels, Teun (2011): Measuring Populism: Comparing Two Methods of Content Analysis. In *West European Politics* 34 (6), pp. 1272–1283. https://doi.org/10.1080/01402382.2011.616665.

Rooduijn, Matthijs; Pirro, Andrea L.; Halikiopoulou, Daphne; Froio, Caterina; Van Kessel, Stijn; Lange, Sarah L. de et al. (2023): The PopuList: A Database of Populist, Far-Left, and Far-Right Parties Using Expert-Informed Qualitative Comparative Classification. In *British Journal of Political Science*, pp. 1–10. https://doi.org/10.1017/S0007123423000431.

Root, Franklin R. (1968): The expropriation experience of American companies. In *Business Horizons* 11 (2), pp. 69–74. https://doi.org/10.1016/0007-6813(68)90088-8.

Ross, Andrew (1996): Science wars. Durham, North Carolina, London: Duke University Press.

Ross, Stephen A. (1976): The arbitrage theory of capital asset pricing. In *Journal of Economic Theory* 13 (3), pp. 341–360. https://doi.org/10.1016/0022-0531(76)90046-6.

Roulston, Kathryn; Choi, Myungweon (2018): Qualitative Interviews. In Flick, Uwe (Ed.): The SAGE Handbook of Qualitative Data Collection. London: SAGE Publications, pp. 233–249.

Roulston, Kathryn; Halpin, Sean N. (2022): Designing Qualitative Research Using Interview Data. In Flick, Uwe (Ed.): The SAGE Handbook of Qualitative Research Design. London: SAGE Publications.

Rovira Kaltwasser, Cristóbal (2012): The ambivalence of populism: threat and corrective for democracy. In *Democratization* 19 (2), pp. 184–208. https://doi.org/10.1080/13510347.2011.572619.

Rovira Kaltwasser, Cristóbal; Taggart, Paul; Espejo, Paulina O.; Ostiguy, Pierre (2017a): Populism: A Socio-Cultural Approach. In Rovira Kaltwasser, Cristóbal; Taggart, Paul; Espejo, Paulina O.; Ostiguy, Pierre (Eds.): The Oxford handbook of populism, vol. 1. Oxford: Oxford University Press, pp. 73–98.

Rovira Kaltwasser, Cristóbal; Taggart, Paul; Espejo, Paulina Ochoa; Ostiguy, Pierre (Eds.) (2017b): The Oxford handbook of populism. Oxford: Oxford University Press.

Rovira Kaltwasser, Cristóbal; Van Hauwaert, Steven M. (2020): The populist citizen: Empirical evidence from Europe and Latin America. In *European Political Science Review* 12 (1), pp. 1–18. https://doi.org/10.1017/S1755773919000262.

Roy, Ashok; Roy, Patricia G. (1993): Despite past debacles, predicting sovereign risk still presents problems. In *Commercial Lending Review* 9, pp. 92–95.

Rubin, Herbert J.; Rubin, Irene S. (2012): Qualitative interviewing. The art of hearing data. Third edition. Los Angeles: SAGE.

Rueda, Daniel (2021): Is Populism a Political Strategy? A Critique of an Enduring Approach. In *Political Studies* 69 (2), pp. 167–184. https://doi.org/10.1177/0032321720962355.

Sabal, Jaime (2004): The Discount Rate in Emerging Markets: A Guide. In *Journal of Applied Corporate Finance* 16 (2–3), pp. 155–166. https://doi.org/10.1111/j.1745-6622.2004.tb00547.x.

Sachs, Jeffrey D. (1989): Social Conflict and Populist Policies in Latin America. In *National Bureau of Economic Research* (Working Paper 2897). https://doi.org/10.3386/w2897.

Salmons, Janet (2014): Qualitative Online Interviews: Strategies, Design, and Skills. London: SAGE Publications.

Sandbergh, Jörgen (1997): Are Phenomenographic Results Reliable? In *Higher Education Research & Development* 16 (2), pp. 203–212. https://doi.org/10.1080/0729436970160207.

Sartori, Giovanni (1970): Concept Misformation in Comparative Politics. In *American Political Science Review* 64 (4), pp. 1033–1053. https://doi.org/10.2307/1958356.

Saunders, Benjamin; Sim, Julius; Kingstone, Tom; Baker, Shula; Waterfield, Jackie; Bartlam, Bernadette et al. (2018): Saturation in qualitative research: exploring its conceptualization and operationalization. In *Quality & quantity* 52 (4), pp. 1893–1907. https://doi.org/10.1007/s11135-017-0574-8.

Schoonenboom, Judith (2022): Developing the Meta-Inference in Mixed Methods Research through Successive Integration of Claims. In Hitchcock, John H.; Onwuegbuzie, Anthony J. (Eds.): The Routledge Handbook for Advancing Integration in Mixed Methods Research. London: Routledge, pp. 55–70.

Schroeder, Susan K. (2008): The Underpinnings Of Country Risk Assessment. In *Journal of Economic Surveys* 22 (3), pp. 498–535. https://doi.org/10.1111/j.1467-6419.2007.00541.x.

Schulz, Anne; Müller, Philipp; Schemer, Christian; Wirz, Dominique S.; Wettstein, Martin; Wirth, Werner (2018): Measuring Populist Attitudes on Three Dimensions. In *International Journal of Public Opinion Research* 30 (2), pp. 316–326. https://doi.org/10.1093/ijpor/edw037.

Schumacher, Gijs; Van Kersbergen, Kees (2016): Do mainstream parties adapt to the welfare chauvinism of populist parties? In *Party Politics* 22 (3), pp. 300–312. https://doi.org/10.1177/1354068814549345.

Schütz, Claudio; Pape, Ulrich (2024): Are investors afraid of populism? In *Finance Research Letters* 61, p. 105049. https://doi.org/10.1016/j.frl.2024.105049.

Scotland, James (2012): Exploring the Philosophical Underpinnings of Research: Relating Ontology and Epistemology to the Methodology and Methods of the Scientific, Interpretive, and Critical Research Paradigms. In *Electoral Studies* 5 (9). https://doi.org/10.5539/elt.v5n9p9.

Seitz, Sally (2016): Pixilated partnerships, overcoming obstacles in qualitative interviews via Skype: a research note. In *Qualitative Research* 16 (2), pp. 229–235. https://doi.org/10.1177/1468794115577011.

Sengul, Kurt (2019): Populism, democracy, political style and post-truth: issues for communication research. In *Communication Research and Practice* 5 (1), pp. 88–101. https://doi.org/10.1080/22041451.2019.1561399.

Shafir, Michael (2008): From Historical to "Dialectical" Populism: The Case of Post-Communist Romania. In *Canadian Slavonic Papers* 50 (3–4), pp. 425–470. https://doi.org/10.1080/00085006.2008.11092591.

Shapiro, Daniel M.; Hobdari, Bersant; Oh, Chang H. (2018): Natural resources, multinational enterprises and sustainable development. In *Journal of World Business* 53 (1), pp. 1–14. https://doi.org/10.1016/j.jwb.2017.09.005.

Sharpe, William F. (1964): Capital Asset Prices: A Theory Of Market Equilibrium Under Conditions Of Risk. In *The Journal of Finance* 19 (3), pp. 425–442. https://doi.org/10.1111/j.1540-6261.1964.tb02865.x.

Shih, Yi-Cheng; Chen, Sheng-Syan; Lee, Cheng-Few; Chen, Po-Jung (2014): The evolution of capital asset pricing models. In *Review of Quantitative Finance and Accounting* 42 (3), pp. 415–448. https://doi.org/10.1007/s11156-013-0348-x.

Shleifer, Andrei; Vishny, Robert W. (1994): Politicians and Firms. In *The Quarterly Journal of Economics* 109 (4), pp. 995–1025. https://doi.org/10.2307/2118354.

Sieber, Joan E.; Tolich, Martin B. (2013): Planning ethically responsible research. Thousand Oaks, California: SAGE Applied social research methods series (31).

Sim, Julius; Saunders, Benjamin; Waterfield, Jackie; Kingstone, Tom (2018): Can sample size in qualitative research be determined a priori? In *International Journal of Social Research Methodology* 21 (5), pp. 619–634. https://doi.org/10.1080/13645579.2018.1454643.

Simon, Jeffrey D. S. (1982): Political risk assessment-past trends and future-prospects. In *Columbia Journal of world business* 17 (3), pp. 62–71.

Singh, Tanya (2022): Populism and its Economic Impact: What Does the Evidence Say? In *International Journal of Social Science and Human Research* 05 (05). https://doi.org/10.47191/ijsshr/v5-i5-16.

Solnik, Bruno H. (1974): The International Pricing of Risk: An Empirical Investigation of the World Capital Market Structure. In *The Journal of Finance* 29 (2), pp. 365–378. https://doi.org/10.2307/2978806.

Solodkov, Vasily; Tsyganova, Yana (2017): Country Risk: Case Study on Crises Examples and Lessons Learnt. In Pompella, Maurizio; Scordis, Nicos A. (Eds.): The Palgrave Handbook of Unconventional Risk Transfer. Cham: Springer International Publishing, pp. 299–325.

Staller, Karen M.; Chen, Yun (2022): Choosing a research design for qualitative research–a ferris wheel of approaches. In Flick, Uwe (Ed.): The SAGE Handbook of Qualitative Research Design. London: SAGE Publications.

Standage, Tom (2023): Tom Standage's ten trends to watch in 2024. A letter from the editor of The World Ahead. The Economist. Available online at https://www.economist.com/the-world-ahead/2023/11/06/tom-standages-ten-trends-to-watch-in-2024, checked on 2/2/2024.

Stavrakakis, Yannis; Andreadis, Ioannis; Katsambekis, Giorgos (2017): A new populism index at work: identifying populist candidates and parties in the contemporary Greek context. In *European Politics and Society* 18 (4), pp. 446–464. https://doi.org/10.1080/23745118.2016.1261434.

Stavrakakis, Yannis; Katsambekis, Giorgos (2014): Left-wing populism in the European periphery: the case of SYRIZA. In *Journal of Political Ideologies* 19 (2), pp. 119–142. https://doi.org/10.1080/13569317.2014.909266.

Stevens, Charles E.; Xie, En; Peng, Mike W. (2016): Toward a legitimacy-based view of political risk: The case of Google and Yahoo in China. In *Strategic Management Journal* 37 (5), pp. 945–963. https://doi.org/10.1002/smj.2369.

Stiglitz, Joseph E. (1993): The Role of the State in Financial Markets. In *The World Bank Economic Review* 7 (suppl 1), pp. 19–52. https://doi.org/10.1093/wber/7.suppl_1.19.

Stöckl, Sebastian; Rode, Martin (2021): The Price of Populism: Financial Market Outcomes of Populist Electoral Success. In *Journal of Economic Behavior and Orga-nization* 189, pp. 51–83. https://doi.org/10.1016/j.jebo.2021.06.037.

Stulz, René M. (1981): A model of international asset pricing. In *Journal of Financial Economics* 9 (4), pp. 383–406. https://doi.org/10.1016/0304-405X(81)90005-2.
Sun, Xiaolei; Feng, Qianqian; Li, Jianping (2021): Understanding country risk assessment: a historical review. In *Applied Economics* 53 (37), pp. 4329–4341. https://doi.org/10.1080/00036846.2021.1899120.
Taggart, Paul (2004): Populism and representative politics in contemporary Europe. In *Journal of Political Ideologies* 9 (3), pp. 269–288. https://doi.org/10.1080/1356931042000263528.
Ţăranu, Andrei (2012): Populism as the 'Democratic Malaise'. In *European Journal of Science and Theology* 8, Supplement 1, pp. 131–141.
Tarragoni, Federico (2024): Populism, an ideology without history? A new genetic approach. In *Journal of Political Ideologies* 29 (1), pp. 42–63. https://doi.org/10.1080/13569317.2021.1979130.
Učeň, Peter; Gyárfášová, Oľga; Krivý, Vladimír (2005): Centrist Populism in Slovakia from the Perspective of Voters and Supporters. In *Slovak Foreign Policy Affairs* 6 (1), pp. 28–46. Available online at https://www.jstor.org/stable/44952261.
Urbinati, Nadia (2019): Political Theory of Populism. In *Annual Review of Political Science* 22 (1), pp. 111–127. https://doi.org/10.1146/annurev-polisci-050317-070753.
Van der Brug, Wouter; Van Spanje, Joost (2009): Immigration, Europe and the 'new' cultural dimension. In *European Journal of Political Research* 48 (3), pp. 309–334. https://doi.org/10.1111/j.1475-6765.2009.00841.x.
Van Hauwaert, Steven M.; Schimpf, Christian H.; Azevedo, Flavio (2019): Public opinion surveys: evaluating existing measures. In Hawkins, Kirk A.; Carlin, Ryan E.; Littvay, Levente; Rovira Kaltwasser, Cristóbal (Eds.): The ideational approach to populism. Concept, theory, and analysis. London, New York: Routledge (Extremism and democracy, 42), pp. 128–150.
Van Hauwaert, Steven M.; Schimpf, Christian H.; Azevedo, Flavio (2020): The measurement of populist attitudes: Testing cross-national scales using item response theory. In *Politics* 40 (1), pp. 3–21. https://doi.org/10.1177/0263395719859306.
Vijayakumar, Jayaraman; Rasheed, Abdul A.; Tondkar, Rasoul H. (2009): Foreign Direct Investment and Evaluation of Country Risk: an Empirical Investigation. In *Multinational Business Review* 17 (3), pp. 181–204. https://doi.org/10.1108/1525383X200900023.
Vu, Huong; Alsakka, Rasha; Ap Gwilym, Owain (2017): What drives differences of opinion in sovereign ratings? The roles of information disclosure and political risk. In *International Journal of Finance & Economics* 22 (3), pp. 216–233. https://doi.org/10.1002/ijfe.1579.
Wajner, Daniel F. (2022a): Global Populism. In Oswald, Michael (Ed.): The Palgrave Handbook of Populism. Cham: Springer International Publishing, pp. 351–367.
Wajner, Daniel F. (2022b): The populist way out: Why contemporary populist leaders seek transnational legitimation. In *The British Journal of Politics and International Relations* 24 (3), pp. 416–436. https://doi.org/10.1177/13691481211069345.
Wajner, Daniel F.; Wehner, Leslie (2023): Embracing or Rebuffing "the International"? Populist Foreign Policy and the Fourth Wave of Populism in Latin America. In *Global Studies Quarterly* 3 (2). https://doi.org/10.1093/isagsq/ksad026.

Warren, Carol A. (2001): Qualitative Interviewing. In Gubrium, Jaber F.; Holstein, James A. (Eds.): Handbook of interview research. Context and method. Thousand Oaks, California: SAGE, pp. 83–101.

Weiss, Robert S. (1995): Learning from strangers. The art and method of qualitative interview studies. New York: Free Press.

Welch, Catherine; Piekkari, Rebecca (2017): How should we (not) judge the 'quality' of qualitative research? A re-assessment of current evaluative criteria in International Business. In *Journal of World Business* 52 (5), pp. 714–725. https://doi.org/10.1016/j.jwb.2017.05.007.

Werner, Steve; Brouthers, Lance E.; Brouthers, Keith D. (1996): International Risk and Perceived Environmental Uncertainty: The Dimensionality and Internal Consistency of Miller's Measure. In *Journal of International Business Studies* 27 (3), pp. 571–587. https://doi.org/10.1057/palgrave.jibs.8490144.

Westerman, Wim; Hall, John H. (2011): Analyzing Foreign Investments. In Baker, H. K.; English, Philip (Eds.): Capital Budgeting Valuation. Financial analysis for today's investment projects. Hoboken, New Jersey: Wiley, pp. 111–131.

Weyland, Kurt (1999): Neoliberal Populism in Latin America and Eastern Europe. In *Comparative Politics* 31 (4), pp. 379–401. https://doi.org/10.2307/422236.

Weyland, Kurt (2001): Clarifying a Contested Concept: Populism in the Study of Latin American Politics. In *Comparative Politics* 34 (1), pp. 1–22. https://doi.org/10.2307/422412.

Weyland, Kurt (2013): Latin America's Authoritarian Drift: The Threat from the Populist Left. In *Journal of Democracy* 24 (3), pp. 18–32. https://doi.org/10.1353/jod.2013.0045.

Weyland, Kurt (2017): Populism: A Political-Strategic Approach. In Rovira Kaltwasser, Cristóbal; Taggart, Paul; Espejo, Paulina O.; Ostiguy, Pierre (Eds.): The Oxford handbook of populism, vol. 1. Oxford: Oxford University Press, pp. 48–72.

Wiesehomeier, Nina (2019): Expert surveys. In Hawkins, Kirk A.; Carlin, Ryan E.; Littvay, Levente; Rovira Kaltwasser, Cristóbal (Eds.): The ideational approach to populism. Concept, theory, and analysis. London, New York: Routledge (Extremism and democracy, 42), pp. 90–112.

Wiesehomeier, Nina; Singer, Matthew; Ruth-Lovell, Saskia P. (2019): Conditions & Codebook. With assistance of Nina Wiesehomeier, updated on 2019, checked on 2/14/2024.

Wojczewski, Thorsten (2023): The Populist Challenge to International Relations: Concept-Stretching, Methodological Nationalism and the Omission of Popular Sover-eignty. In Wojczewski, Thorsten (Ed.): The Inter- and Transnational Politics of Populism. Cham: Springer International Publishing, pp. 25–71.

World Bank (2023): World Development Indicators. Available online at https://databank.worldbank.org/source/world-development-indicators, checked on 2/12/2024.

Xu, Zhaoxia (2020): Economic policy uncertainty, cost of capital, and corporate innovation. In *Journal of Banking & Finance* 111, Article 105698, pp. 1–15. https://doi.org/10.1016/j.jbankfin.2019.105698.

Yi, Yingting; Luo, Jiangshui; Wübbenhorst, Michael (2020): Research on political instability, uncertainty and risk during 1953–2019: a scientometric review. In *Scientometrics* 123 (2), pp. 1051–1076. https://doi.org/10.1007/s11192-020-03416-6.

Zulianello, Mattia; Larsen, Erik G. (2021): Populist parties in European Parliament elections: A new dataset on left, right and valence populism from 1979 to 2019. In *Electoral Studies* 71, Article 102312. https://doi.org/10.1016/j.electstud.2021.102312.

The manufacturer's authorised representative in the EU is Springer Nature Customer Service Centre GmbH, Europaplatz 3, 69115 Heidelberg, Germany. If you have any concerns regarding our products, please contact ProductSafety@springernature.com

Printed and bound by CPI Group (UK) Ltd, Croydon, CR0 4YY
30/09/2026
02225601-0004